UNIVERSITY OF CAMBRIDGE
ORIENTAL PUBLICATIONS

No. 3

THE JAPANESE FAMILY STOREHOUSE

OR THE MILLIONAIRES' GOSPEL MODERNISED

University of Cambridge Oriental Publications
published for the Faculty of Oriental Studies

1. *Averroes' Commentary on Plato's Republic*, edited and translated by E. I. J. ROSENTHAL
2. *Fitzgerald's 'Salaman and Absal'*, edited by A. J. ARBERRY

Also published for the Faculty
Archaeological Studies in Szechwan, by T.-K. CHÊNG

10.—

IHARA SAIKAKU

THE JAPANESE FAMILY STOREHOUSE

OR THE MILLIONAIRES' GOSPEL MODERNISED

NIPPON EITAI-GURA

OR

DAIFUKU SHIN CHŌJA KYŌ

(1688)

TRANSLATED FROM THE JAPANESE
WITH INTRODUCTION AND COMMENTARY
BY

G. W. SARGENT
M.A., Ph.D. (Cantab.)

With the original illustrations and decorations

CAMBRIDGE
AT THE UNIVERSITY PRESS
1959

PUBLISHED BY
THE SYNDICS OF THE CAMBRIDGE UNIVERSITY PRESS

Bentley House, 200 Euston Road, London, N.W. 1
American Branch: 32 East 57th Street, New York 22, N.Y.

Printed in Great Britain at the University Press, Cambridge
(*Brooke Crutchley, University Printer*)

To

MARGARET

CONTENTS

Book III

Book IV

Book V

Book VI

COMMENTARY ON THE TRANSLATION

APPENDICES

MAPS

(*following page* 281)

PREFACE

My aim in producing this study and translation of Saikaku's *Nippon Eitai-gura* has been to give a reasonably accurate impression of a single work of Japanese literature, presenting it in the context of the society and literature of its age. The whole volume—and not merely that section in which a modern English approximation is given for the seventeenth-century Japanese text—is an essay in translation, seeking to provide the information necessary if western readers are to arrive at a just appreciation of the merits (or, if they wish, the defects) of *Nippon Eitai-gura*. In the introduction I have concentrated upon literary analysis, and have attempted, by viewing *Nippon Eitai-gura* in the context of types of antecedent literature with which the reader of 1688 would have recognised its stylistic or ideological affinities, to suggest something of the significance which it had for its contemporaries. This approach has seemed necessary in view of the current tendency in Japan to lay stress, to the confusion of its original merits as a work of art, on certain secondary virtues which the book now possesses for the student of social, economic or literary history. My commentary, too, touches upon points of style and literary structure, but its main purpose is to clarify the numerous references in the text to persons, places, institutions and customs of the day. I hope that I have thus given the reader a better chance to appreciate the sense of actuality which the work had for its contemporaries. The commentary should also be of interest to those who will read *Nippon Eitai-gura* mainly for the insight which it affords into the cultural history of seventeenth-century Japan.

In the translation and commentary, in particular, I am deeply indebted to the half-dozen fully annotated Japanese editions of *Nippon Eitai-gura*, often incorporating a modern-language paraphrase, which have appeared in the last thirty years. My initial researches were rendered possible by a generous grant from the Treasury Committee for Studentships in Foreign Languages and Cultures, for which I wish to express my gratitude. My thanks are due also to the many friends who have given me encouragement and practical assistance during the seven years in which this book has been in preparation—to Professor K. Noma of Kyōto University, Professor T. Kamei of Hitotsubashi University, Professor D. L. Keene of Columbia University, various students and members of the staff at Kōchi University, and many others to whom I must apologise for failing to mention by name. The greater part of the work on the index and maps, together with the tedious labour of typing and correcting the manuscript of a writer incapable of consistency, was undertaken by my wife, to whom, in unsatisfactory return for this and much more, the book is dedicated. Mr E. B. Ceadel, Lecturer in Japanese at Cambridge University, who first suggested that I should attempt to publish these researches through the medium of the University of Cambridge Oriental Publications, has very kindly undertaken a multitude of labours in connection with the work's final revision, and I must acknowledge that without his assistance its publication would hardly have been possible.

As regards the illustrations, I am indebted to the editors of *Iwanami Bunko*, Tōkyō, for permission to use the reproductions contained in their 1956 edition of *Nippon Eitai-gura*, to the Shinyōsha Company of Kyōto for the manufacture of the blocks, and to Dr Bunshō Jugaku of Kōnan University for his kind mediation in both these matters.

The expenses of publication have been covered by a grant from the Publications Committee of the Oriental Faculty, Cambridge, and I must also acknowledge with thanks the assistance which I have received both from the committee and from my mother towards the cost of inserting the illustrations.

G. W. S.

KŌNAN UNIVERSITY, JAPAN
April 1957

INTRODUCTION

I. SAIKAKU THE HAIKAI POET

IHARA SAIKAKU (1642–93), generally considered the most distinguished of the popular fiction writers of the Tokugawa period, turned to the composition of novels and short stories comparatively late in life. For the greater part of his literary career he was associated exclusively with movements in *haikai* verse, and by the time his first novel appeared he was already notorious as an *avant-garde* poet, the leader of a group whose aim was to adapt the traditional forms and imagery of Japanese verse to the needs of the new city society of the seventeenth century. Saikaku's verse, however, is no longer read. After the diversion of his talents to prose his school of *haikai* was quickly superseded by new movements basing themselves on the fundamentally more conservative outlook of Matsuo Bashō (1644–94), and Bashō's influence upon poetic taste in Japan has been so overwhelming that Saikaku's *haikai* now appears to be the negation of all that is accepted as the essence of Japanese poetic feeling. Its wealth of allusions to temporary phenomena of the times has also rendered it largely incomprehensible to the non-specialist reader. But, whatever the intrinsic value of Saikaku's verse, the influence of his training in *haikai* upon both the style and the structure of his prose works is undeniable, and from that viewpoint alone the verse deserves study. Before giving an outline of Saikaku's career it will be necessary briefly to explain the nature and history of the verse-form in which he wrote.

Haikai is properly an abbreviation of *renga no haikai*.[1] That is to say, it was an offshoot, more popular and less dignified (*haikai* means 'a joke'), of the linked verse (*renga*) which had reached its zenith in the fifteenth century.[2] Linked verse, in its turn, had been a development of the classical Japanese *tanka*. Whereas the *tanka* had consisted of no more than two brief word-groups,[3] the first of seven-

[1] For a brief but comprehensive explanation of the development and techniques of *haikai* linked verse see *Haikai Meisaku Shū* (Ehara Taizō, 1935), pp. 549–96 (*Hyōshaku Edo Bungaku Sōsho*, VII).

[2] An English translation of excerpts from a fifteenth-century *renga*, with commentary, appears in *Japanese Literature* (Keene, 1953), pp. 34–7, and in *Anthology of Japanese Literature* (Keene, 1955), 'Three Poets at Minase'.

[3] I prefer to regard a *tanka* as a two-line poem, and a *hokku* (or *haiku*) as a single rhythmic line. To mark each caesura precisely, presenting a *tanka* as a five-line poem and a *hokku* as a three-line poem, seems to be unnecessarily pedantic.

teen syllables, and the last of fourteen, and had been composed by one person, linked verse was a chain of these word-groups—17, 14, 17, 14—and no two links together were the work of the same poet. There was no limit to the number of persons who could collaborate in a poem of this nature, nor to the number of links which could be composed. The connection between the two word-groups of a *tanka* had been logical, the last group complementing the sense of the first, but the connection between any two successive lines in a linked verse composition was by a parallel association of ideas, the sense of the second not necessarily complementing the sense of the whole of the first, but merely developing one word or idea in it. At first sight it seems a tremendously free form, and in its early days it was possibly intended to be so, but in time an extremely elaborate set of rules grew up governing the permissible mood and grammatical structure of lines in a given position, the permissible subjects and vocabulary, and the permissible associations with given words. *Haikai* was a more light-hearted form of this linked verse, with broadly parallel rules but a more homely choice of vocabulary and an element of humour. Like its parent, it was essentially a communal activity, and could not therefore dispense altogether with the elaborate system of rules. Each participant needed to understand not only his rights but his obligations. The more strictly codified the rules, the more smoothly the game proceeded.

The *haikai* movement started tentatively in the troubled eras of the sixteenth century, and was given great impetus later, after the establishment of political security by the Tokugawa shogunate in 1600, by the rapid emergence of an energetic urban population in centres of trade and industry. These *chōnin* (lit. 'men of the city-blocks'), as they were called, wielded no direct political power, but they soon found themselves exercising an influence on the nation's economy out of all proportion to their numbers. During the seventeenth century their prosperity steadily increased, and at the same time there developed within their class a spirit of optimism and self-confidence in marked contrast with the melancholy fatalism which had characterised much Japanese thought in the preceding centuries of civil war. The arts, of course, might be expected to play a very minor role in the lives of people so busily occupied in making money, and at first that was to an extent true. There was no traditional culture with which they could feel wholly in sympathy. For centuries the arbiters of taste had been courtiers, priests, or warriors, and the literary forms they had evolved—the *tanka* and *renga* in verse, the Noh in drama, the leisurely *monogatari* and military romances in narrative prose, or the reflective *zuihitsu* essays—had all taken shape to suit the demands and reflect the experience of a society whose demands and experience were very different from those of the seventeenth-century townsmen. By the end of the sixteenth century there had already emerged the elements of a popular drama, but it was not to this that the townsmen instinctively turned for their means of literary expression. They turned instead to *haikai* verse, which was in its infancy as an independent form, and therefore malleable, but had behind it a little of the prestige and ready-made technique of *renga*. The leaders in the early *haikai* movement, who were not themselves townsmen but men with the traditional outlook and culture of the military class, seem to have regarded *haikai* as partly a gentle amusement and partly a means of introducing the less educated to the technique of pure *renga*. There was no lack of trained teachers in the early years of the seventeenth century—many of them ex-*samurai* who had lost, or willingly abandoned, their military careers in the upheavals which accompanied the establishment of the Tokugawa autocracy—and the middle class of the cities proved apt pupils. The first movement of importance, the *Teimon* school, was headed by Matsunaga Teitoku (1571–1654), under whom the tendency towards a greater freedom from the traditional subjects and imagery of Japanese verse made considerable advances. It is the second movement, however, headed by Nishiyama Sōin (1605–82) and known as the *Danrin* school,[1] which is held by modern literary historians to have effected a true emancipation of *haikai* from its forbears, and to have produced the first literature of townsmen, written by townsmen in terms of their own experience. It was as a leading exponent of the *Danrin* style of *haikai* that Saikaku first achieved distinction.

Surprisingly little is known of Saikaku's life, but it is possible to construct a fairly reliable skeleton biography from a study of the chronology of his own works, which survive almost in their entirety, and from

[1] *Danrin*, a word often written with the characters meaning 'Talk-Forest', was a Buddhist term for 'a pulpit'. *Haikai Danrin* ('The *Haikai* Pulpit') was the name given by a group of Edo *haikai* poets to their meeting-place, where, in 1674, they invited the visiting Ōsaka *haikai* master Nishiyama Sōin to join them in a performance of linked verse. Sōin, one of whose soubriquets was Baiō (The Plum Master) contributed the following opening verse:

> *Sareba koko ni Danrin no ki ari, ume no hana.*
> Here are the trees of the Talk-Forest, their blossoms are plum.

The complete poem was published as *Danrin Toppyaku In* (1675), and from that time Nishiyama Sōin's school was popularly known as the *Danrin* school.

incidental references in the works of contemporaries.[1] Saikaku was born in Ōsaka in 1642. His real name was Hirayama Tōgo (Saikaku was the pen-name he adopted later in life, and Ihara is possibly his mother's surname). His parents seem to have been rich, and he inherited control of the family business, whatever it may have been, fairly early in life. His association with *haikai* began when he was only fourteen years old, and by the age of twenty he had become sufficiently proficient in the art to be awarded the rank of *tenja*, or 'judge' of *haikai* compositions. At this time he was presumably a member of the orthodox *Teimon* school, which was then fashionable, and his earliest known compositions are three *hokku* (single opening verses for *haikai* sessions) contributed to a collection of that school's *haikai* in 1666.[2] Saikaku was then twenty-four, and was writing under the pen-name of Ihara Kakuei. He continued to contribute to various collections of *haikai* in the next six or seven years, and at some time during this period he came under the influence of Nishiyama Sōin, who was later to found the *Danrin* school. His first major publication, *Ikutama Manku* (1673), which appeared when he was thirty-two, was a selection of three hundred verses from the ten thousand composed by himself and some one hundred and fifty colleagues in a twelve-day *haikai* session held at the Ikutama shrine in Ōsaka. It appears from the preface that these poets represented an 'advanced' group whose unorthodox methods had caused their exclusion from a similar *haikai* session held a little earlier. They had been stigmatised as disciples of a 'Dutch Manner' (*Oranda-ryū*)—a phrase which suggested to the Japanese things exotic and bizarre, like the Dutch traders who were to be seen at Nagasaki. Only ten of the three hundred verses in the book were Saikaku's, but the fact that he contributed the introduction, that the wood-block printing was done from his hand, and that he was given the honour of composing the *hokku* of the final chain, which was capped by a verse from Nishiyama Sōin, is sufficient to show that he was a prominent member of the group. In the same year Saikaku—or Kakuei, as he was then still known—was granted permission by his master Sōin to make use of the character *Sai*

[1] Most of the scanty information we have on Saikaku's personal history is derived from a single source, a brief passage in *Kenmon Dansō*, VI. This work was written in 1738 by the scholar Itō Baiu, and the passage in question is a report of anecdotes which his brother heard about Saikaku in Kyōto, possibly in the year 1730. Some of the information is obviously incorrect, but the rest is now generally accepted. The most recent and detailed study of the chronology of Saikaku's works and the existing biographical material is *Saikaku Nenpu Kōshō* (Noma Kōshin, 1952). It is on the latter work that I have based the present brief outline of Saikaku's career.

[2] *Enkin Shū* (Nishimura Chōai-shi, 1666).

(the *Nishi* of Nishiyama Sōin) in his pen-name, and henceforth he signs himself Saikaku or Ihara Saikaku.

The rather late source which informs us that Saikaku was a rich Ōsaka townsman also states that his wife died young, leaving him with an only daughter, who was blind, and that soon after this Saikaku retired from business, entrusting all practical matters to his clerks. He did not, however, retire from the world and become a priest—we are told—but took instead to travelling alone about Japan, remaining away from home for one half of each year. How much of this is the literal truth we do not know, though we can infer from Saikaku's own works that he was widely travelled, and from the sheer volume of his productions that he could not have devoted much time to the prosecution of any business outside that of writing. We also know, from a work published by Saikaku in 1675, that his wife died in that year at the age of twenty-four, leaving him with three very young children, and can guess from the apparent sincerity of his verses that he was deeply affected by his loss. The work is *Haikai Dokugin Ichinichi Senku*, a collection of one thousand *haikai* verses composed by Saikaku alone in a single day, in commemoration of his wife's death. What happened to his three children after this is not clear. Possibly only one, the 'blind daughter' mentioned in our other source, lived beyond infancy.

Apart from its intrinsic merit and its value as the source of our one intimate glimpse into Saikaku's life, *Haikai Dokugin Ichinichi Senku* is also of interest as the first known example of Saikaku's use of *haikai* as a medium for solo composition. The *haikai* form was developed for group composition, but—like chess—it was a game which could be played by one man scrupulously observing the rules. Considered as an intellectual contest, of course, there was an element of cheating in a solo performance, since the player could dictate his own subject-matter throughout and make frequent use of ready-made verses. The element of spontaneity was to a certain extent safeguarded by the custom of having the opening nine verses in each hundred composed by a disinterested second party, but inevitably solo *haikai* could be composed at a far greater rate than the orthodox group *haikai*. As an art-form it offered greater freedom of expression for the poet and greater freedom in the choice of subject-matter, though it meant that the elaborate rules—which had grown from the necessity of organising the smooth running of a group performance—became a mere handicap with no justification beyond tradition. It was, perhaps, natural that Saikaku should have turned to solo *haikai* for the composition of verses in his wife's memory, for other poets could hardly share his private grief on such an occasion. From a historical point of view too, Saikaku, as a representative of the new, assertive, self-confident middle-class of the cities, might have been expected in time to seek a more individual means of expression than was offered by group *haikai*. He was not alone in this tendency, for many of his fellow poets of the advanced 'Dutch Manner' shared his social background and outlook, if not his ability, and *Danrin haikai* was now developing into a form truly representative of townsman culture. Saikaku was also—and this was partly a personal trait, and partly a result of the vulgar (by traditional standards) outlook of his class—attracted by the possibility of rapid composition offered by solo *haikai*, and the resulting opportunities for startling exhibitions of virtuosity. But, whatever the reasons, henceforth he devoted more and more of his energies to solo performances.

His next publication of solo *haikai* was *Saikaku Haikai Ōkukazu* (1677), containing one thousand six hundred verses composed by himself in a day and a night, in the presence of independent witnesses, at the Ikutama Honkaku temple in Ōsaka. Saikaku tells us elsewhere[1] that he asked his master, Nishiyama Sōin, to append detailed criticisms to this work for publication, but that Sōin declined on the plea that it was too long. Saikaku appears at this time to have been recognised as the most promising of all Sōin's followers, but it is possible that Sōin looked with a certain amount of distaste upon his tendency to use *haikai* as a medium for the exhibition of personal virtuosity, and there is evidence of a growing coolness in the professional relations between Saikaku and the acknowledged leader of the *Danrin* school from this time onwards. *Yakazu haikai* ('arrow-counting *haikai*'), as this new phenomenon was termed,[2] was in itself a natural development from the principles of speed and freer associations of ideas which Sōin encouraged, but it seemed to place the emphasis too heavily on volume rather than quality.

In the next three years (1677–80) while Saikaku was busily engaged in the normal round of *haikai* activities, and increasing his reputation as an exponent of the 'Dutch Manner', his record of one thousand

[1] *Sendai Ōyakazu* (Ōyodo Sanzenpū, 1679), epilogue.

[2] The expression arose from *tōshiya*, a type of archery contest in which the participants shot as many arrows as they could over a given distance within a fixed time. In 1662 a *samurai* of Owari shot 6600 arrows the length of the Sanjūsangen Hall in Kyōto. His record was beaten a few years later, and in 1669 he recaptured it with a shoot of 8000 arrows between dusk and noon. The all-time record was set by a *samurai* of Kii in 1686, with a total of 13,000 arrows shot, of which 8033 reached the required distance.

six hundred verses was twice broken. In 1677 a priest of Nara[1] claimed to have bettered the figure by two hundred verses, but Saikaku declined to recognise his performance as official, on the grounds that there were no reliable witnesses. In 1679, however, a poet of Sendai composed three thousand verses in a twenty-four hour session,[2] and when this was published Saikaku contributed an epilogue to the work in praise of the performance. In this Saikaku refers to himself as the originator of the current style of 'free *haikai*'—a claim which did less than justice to his master Sōin, and which may well have aggravated the differences between the two. In the following year Saikaku recovered his lost record by composing four thousand verses in twenty-four hours at the Ōsaka Ikutama shrine, published later (1681) under the title *Saikaku Ōyakazu*. The topics which Saikaku treated in his two solo *haikai* compositions, *Ōkukazu* and *Ōyakazu*, were far removed indeed from those of the traditional *renga* or even the *haikai* of a generation before his own—they arose largely from the life of the great cities. Birds and flowers and autumn moons were still in evidence, but were obliged to compete for attention with brothel quarters, *daimyō's* concubines, *kabuki* actors, the price of rice, lawsuits, house-rents, pawnshops, bankruptcies and all the other prosaic phenomena of the city society in which the new poets lived. They were the same topics which Saikaku was soon to cover more extensively in his prose works, and he may well have sensed at this stage that *haikai* verse was too restrictive a medium for his talents.

Even after the publication of his first novel, *Kōshoku Ichidai Otoko*, in 1682, Saikaku never completely severed his connection with *haikai*. Indeed, it was two years after this date that he performed the most celebrated feat of his *haikai* career, the composition in a day and a night of twenty-three thousand five hundred verses, thus improving upon his previous record almost sixfold, and effectively bringing to an end all efforts to rival him in the field of 'arrow-counting *haikai*'.[3] For a period of five years after 1685, during which he published more than a dozen novels or volumes of short stories, he appears to have produced no verse at all; but from 1690 until his death in 1693 he showed a revived interest, and contributed a considerable number of *hokku* to various collections, besides attempting some longer productions in collaboration

[1] A priest of a temple at Tafu-*no-mine*, Yamato province. These verses were published in 1678 as *Ōyakazu Sen Happyaku In*.

[2] *Sendai Ōyakazu*.

[3] From this time Saikaku adopts the soubriquet *Niman-ō* (Twenty-Thousand Master). No copy of the verses survives, and the authenticity of Saikaku's claim has been questioned. There is nevertheless ample corroboratory evidence. For this see *Saikaku no Haireki* (Ehara Taizō, 1933).

with others and entering spiritedly into a controversy which had arisen over his qualifications as a *haikai* judge.[1] The output is insignificant in quantity compared with that of his most active period ten years earlier, and it is noticeable that he concentrates upon brief seventeen-syllable *hokku* rather than sustained efforts of linked verse. There is also a marked change in tone—a quietness and restraint which is remarkable in the erstwhile leader of the 'Dutch Manner'. This is perhaps due in some measure to the influence of the new school of Bashō,[2] which was displacing *Danrin* as the most popular form of *haikai*, but it is more fruitful to view it as a natural development arising from within. There was no longer any necessity for Saikaku to attempt to use *haikai* for a purpose to which it was not suited. He had achieved that purpose in prose, and now that the fever had left him he was able to come to reasonable terms with the form with which he had battled in vain, and to recognise more clearly wherein lay its limitations and its strength.

The *Danrin* school of *haikai*, centred in Ōsaka, soon lost its position of eminence after the death of its founder Nishiyama Sōin in 1682, and after the diversion of Saikaku's talents to prose at about the same time. In Edo, however, a branch of the school continued to flourish for many years, and in 1792, one hundred years after his death, Saikaku was officially recognised by the members of the Edo branch as the second in the line of the leaders of the *Danrin* school.

Considering that Saikaku's greatest achievements are in prose it may seem that a disproportionate amount of space has been devoted to outlining his career as a poet. But the influence of his training in *haikai* upon his prose style, and upon the whole structure of his novels and short stories, can hardly be overstated. He continued in his prose to think in short staccato verse-like phrases, claiming all the grammatical licence of a *haikai* poet, and to employ the special techniques of *haikai*—the substitution of association of ideas for logical progression, the mixing of modern and traditional imagery, and the introduction of 'pivot phrases' to effect rapid transitions from topic to topic—all of which had become second nature to him in the course of his more than twenty years' active preoccupation with the *haikai* form. In the subject-matter of his stories he was to retread more carefully the same ground which he had rapidly covered in solo *haikai*. Perhaps the most important

[1] The criticism of Saikaku and other *tenja* was contained in a work entitled *Monomi-guruma* (The Excursion Coach), published in 1690. Saikaku made his reply the following year in *Haikai Ishi-guruma* (The Stone Wagon).

[2] The emergence of *Shōfū*, or the Bashō style of *haikai*, is generally dated from the publication of *Fuyu no Hi* (1684).

influence of all, however, is that upon his conception of how to construct a story—a matter which will be discussed below.

2. SAIKAKU THE NOVELIST

It will be convenient first to give a chronological table[1] of Saikaku's novels and story collections, together with brief synopses of their contents:

1682 *Kōshoku Ichidai Otoko*, with illustrations by Saikaku[2]

A novel in fifty-four loosely connected chapters, recounting the amorous adventures of Yonosuke, a townsman of prodigious vitality. Each chapter is devoted to one year of his life, from seven till the age of sixty, when he finally sails from Japan in search of 'The Island of Women'. The episodes take place largely in the brothel quarters of the cities and towns of Japan.

1684 *Shoen Ōkagami*,[3] with illustrations by Saikaku

A sequel to the above, in forty-eight chapters, containing further descriptions of life in the brothel quarters. The stories are related by a brothel go-between, and concern the experiences of a variety of her customers, including Yonosuke's illegitimate son.

1685 *Saikaku Shokoku-banashi*, with illustrations by Saikaku

Thirty-five strange or humorous stories set in various parts of Japan. Some were possibly collected by Saikaku on his travels, others are adaptations of Chinese stories.

1685 *Wankyū Isse no Monogatari*, with illustrations by an unknown artist

A short novel in thirteen chapters, relating the amorous adventures and downfall of Wankyū, based on the life of a recently deceased citizen of Ōsaka. Many of Wankyū's adventures are with boy-prostitutes.

1686 *Kōshoku Gonin Onna*, with illustrations by Yoshida Hanbei

Five novelettes, each based on a love-affair of recent notoriety. Here, in contrast with Saikaku's other works on erotic themes, the women involved are not professionals but the young daughters or wives of merchants.

[1] The table lists only those works which are accepted in *Saikaku Nenpu Kōshō* as certainly, or almost certainly, of Saikaku authorship. The identifications of the illustrators follows the same work, or *Teihon Saikaku Zenshū* (Ehara Taizō, Teruoka Yasutaka, Noma Kōshin, 1949–55). The abstracts of subject-matter are largely based on *Edo Bungaku Jiten* (Teruoka Yasutaka, 1940). For further details on the illustrations see pp. 4–5.

[2] The illustrations for the first Edo edition (1684) of *Kōshoku Ichidai Otoko* followed the design of the Saikaku originals, but were the work of Hishikawa Moronobu (prob. 1618–94), the artist who is regarded as the founder of the *ukiyo-e* style.

[3] Also known as *Kōshoku Nidai Otoko*.

1686 *Kōshoku Ichidai Onna*, with illustrations by Yoshida Hanbei

The memoirs of an old woman who has been connected all her life with the trade of prostitution. Starting her career as a *daimyō*'s private concubine, she next becomes a professional courtesan of the highest grade, and thereafter gradually sinks through all the manifold lower grades of licensed and unlicensed prostitution. In her old age she finds enlightenment in Buddhism.

1686 *Honchō Nijū Fukō*, with illustrations by Yoshida Hanbei

Twenty stories of unethical behaviour and appropriate punishment. Most of the stories concern townsmen, but *samurai* themes are also treated. The contents are intended to be more amusing than edifying.

1687 *Nanshoku Ōkagami*, with illustrations by Yoshida Hanbei

Forty stories on the theme of sodomy. The first half deals with the practice among *samurai* in Edo, the second half with boy-actors of the *kabuki* theatre, mostly in the Ōsaka area.

1687 *Futokoro-suzuri*, with illustrations by Yoshida Hanbei

Twenty-five strange stories from all parts of Japan, on a mixture of townsmen and *samurai* themes. There is a greater emphasis on anecdote than is usual in Saikaku's work.

1687 *Budō Denrai Ki*, with illustrations by Yoshida Hanbei

Thirty-two stories of violent *samurai* vendettas, ancient and contemporary. The stories are related without any trace of the conventional attitude of admiration or sympathy for either party.

1688 *Nippon Eitai-gura*, with illustrations by Yoshida Hanbei

Thirty stories on the rise to wealth of members of the merchant class, the examples being drawn from a wide variety of regions in Japan. Some of the stories are based on fact, some on tradition, some are possibly fictional.

1688 *Buke Giri Monogatari*, with illustrations by Yoshida Hanbei

Twenty-six stories of *samurai* loyalty in ancient and modern times.

1688 *Irozato Mitokoro-zetai*, with illustrations by an unknown artist

A short novel in fifteen loosely connected episodes, recounting the experiences of a rich patron of the brothels who exhausts his strength in dissipation and is finally terrified to death by ghosts of the prostitutes whom he has cast aside.

1688 *Shin Kashō Ki*, with illustrations by Yoshida Hanbei

Twenty-six stories mostly concerned with examples of *samurai* loyalty. Some are taken from contemporary events, some are adaptations of Chinese or Japanese traditions.

1688 *Kōshoku Seisui Ki*, with illustrations by Yoshida Hanbei

Twenty-five stories of rich patrons of the brothel quarters.

1689 *Honchō Ōin Hiji*, with illustrations by Yoshida Hanbei

Forty-four stories of judgements delivered in courts of law, the material mostly borrowed or adapted from various popular works of the period.

1689 *Hitome Tamaboko*, with illustrations by an unknown artist

An illustrated guide-book to Japan (mainly Honshū and Kyūshū), probably based on notes made during the author's own travels. There are brief factual comments on places of note, and numerous appropriate quotations from old poems.

1691 *Wankyū Nise no Monogatari*, with illustrations by an unknown artist

A short novel in fourteen chapters relating the experiences in hell of a man who had grown tired of sodomy. He has numerous painful experiences in a hell peopled by boy-devils, but achieves Buddhist enlightenment and returns miraculously to life, resolved to be a more sympathetic customer for boy-prostitutes in future.

1692 *Seken Munesanyō*, with illustrations by Makieshi Genzaburō

Twenty stories on the collection of debts and the avoidance of debt-collectors. All are concerned with townsmen, and the action of each story takes place on the last day of the year—the final reckoning day for tradesmen.

POSTHUMOUS PUBLICATIONS

1693 *Saikaku Okimiyage*, with illustrations by Makieshi Genzaburō

Fifteen stories of erstwhile rich patrons of the brothels who have fallen on evil days.

1694 *Saikaku Oritome*, with illustrations by Makieshi Genzaburō

Twenty-three stories on the general theme of townsmen and money-making.

1695 *Saikaku Zoku Tsurezure*, with illustrations by Makieshi Genzaburō

Eighteen miscellaneous stories, many on the theme of ruin through drink.

1696 *Yorozu no Fumi-hōgu*, with illustrations by Makieshi Genzaburō

Twenty stories in the form of letters from townsmen, *samurai*, or courtesans.

1699 *Saikaku Nagori no Tomo*, with illustrations by an unknown amateur

Twenty-seven stories concerning *haikai* poets with whom Saikaku had been associated.

From amongst this large output the works which are generally accepted in Japan as Saikaku's masterpieces are *Kōshoku Ichidai Otoko* (1682), *Kōshoku Gonin Onna* (1686), *Kōshoku Ichidai Onna* (1686), *Nippon Eitai-gura* (1688), and *Seken Munesanyō* (1692).[1]

It will be noted that a number of the works produced in the first four years of this period (1682–6) have some claim to be classified as 'novels' —that is to say, they have a framework of continuous narrative, are in some way centred about the experiences of a single fictional personage, and have their action set firmly in a context of contemporary life, realistically depicted. But, if we except *Kōshoku Gonin Onna* (where it may have been part of Saikaku's scheme to imitate the technique and approach of the theatre), the narrative framework is slight, and there is little development of character. Mostly, in fact, these 'novels' consist of a series of fortuitously linked semi-independent chapters, and even inside the chapters themselves any movement of events is likely to be of secondary importance to the depiction of contemporary manners. It is therefore not surprising to find that in the subsequent five or six years this tentative novel-form is largely abandoned, and Saikaku turns instead to writing collections of related short stories in which the stories are linked to one another not by identity of principal character, nor by their place in the development of a plot, but solely by a broad community of theme. In view of Saikaku's tendency to focus his attention upon social manners rather than the fortunes or psychology of any individual, this was in reality a much stronger link. The present work, *Nippon Eitai-gura* (*The Japanese Family Storehouse*), is constructed upon this principle, and may be taken as representative of the type to which the majority of Saikaku's prose works belong.

The reader who judges Saikaku from the brief account of his subject-materials given in the above table might be excused for imagining that he was primarily a dealer in pornography and sensation. That is, indeed, the verdict delivered by at least one western historian of Japanese literature,[2] and it is still a popular supposition in Japan. There

[1] The works which find least favour might be listed as: *Wankyū Isse no Monogatari* (1685); *Budō Denrai Ki* (1687); *Irozato Mitokoro-zetai* (1688); *Shin Kashō Ki* (1688); *Hitome Tamaboko* (1689); *Wankyū Nise no Monogatari* (1691); *Saikaku Zoku Tsurezure* (posth. 1695); *Saikaku Nagori no Tomo* (posth. 1699).

[2] Aston, W. G., *A History of Japanese Literature* (1899): 'Saikaku was a man of no learning. ...His books, most of which have very little story, are mainly descriptions of the manners and customs of the great lupanars....The very titles of some of them are too gross for quotation. The immoral tendency of his works was denounced even in his own day by a hostile critic under the suggestive title *Saikaku no Jigoku-meguri* (Saikaku in Hell), and led to their suppression by the government....Saikaku has written one decent work, *Saikaku Nagori no Tomo*....For various reasons it is impossible to give a really characteristic specimen

is a marked preponderance of stories concerned with brothel quarters or with homosexual relationships—themes which are now common enough in literature, but which are still largely associated with disciples of the muddier forms of 'realism', with authors concerned to redress social injustices, or with writers of cheap magazine fiction. Saikaku falls conveniently into none of these classifications. He is pursuing no cult of 'realism', nor does he write as a reformer, and, if his purpose is primarily entertainment, his themes were not selected in the first place for their pornographic value. The experiences of brothel customers, or of the courtesans themselves, constituted the obvious literary material for a townsman writer of the age drawing inspiration from the contemporary manners of his class. Saikaku treated other aspects of townsman life in what later historians term his *chōnin-mono* ('townsman books')—such works as *Nippon Eitai-gura* and *Seken Munesanyō*—but if he had written nothing except his *kōshoku-mono* ('erotic books') it would still be unfair to accuse him of concentrating upon the abnormalities of his society. No one could, or wished to, deny the existence of the large and splendid licensed brothel quarters in the cities of Japan—the Shimabara quarter in Kyōto, Shin-*machi* in Ōsaka, Shin-Yoshiwara in Edo, Maruyama in Nagasaki—or of the myriads of smaller quarters, licensed and unlicensed, plying an open trade throughout the length

of Saikaku's writings. The following is a story from *Fudokoro no Suzuri*, a work which is less objectionable than most of his productions...' (pp. 268–9). This brief passage, in a book which has remained the standard English work on Japanese literature for more than fifty years, must have been responsible for many of the misconceptions on Saikaku now current in the West. Aston may be excused on the grounds that he is reproducing a view of Saikaku which was fairly widely held in Japan at the end of the nineteenth century, and that he could hardly have had much understanding of Saikaku's difficult texts in an age before the Japanese themselves had seriously turned to their elucidation. Saikaku's lack of a conventional *samurai* education in Chinese learning has no more bearing upon the literary value of his work than Shakespeare's failure to go to a university. The word *Kōshoku*, 'pleasure in love', in some of his titles (presumably the word to which Aston objects) has respectable ancestry in Confucius and Mencius, and, as widely used in the titles of popular literature of the seventeenth and eighteenth centuries, has no more significance than to indicate that the general theme is to be 'love', not necessarily treated from a pornographic viewpoint. 'Saikaku in Hell' (*Saikaku no Jigoku-meguri* is presumably a mistake for *Saikaku Meido Monogatari*, 1697) is not an attack upon Saikaku's morals but a satire upon the degenerate technique of contemporary *haikai* poets. There is no evidence to show that any of Saikaku's works were banned in his own lifetime, and the attempted suppression of '*kōshoku-bon*' thirty years after his death seems to have been aimed specifically at the flood of illustrated pornography, often secretly printed, which had begun to emerge before Saikaku wrote his first novel, and not indiscriminately at any work which bore the word *kōshoku* in its title. Saikaku, if at fault at all in official eyes, was certainly not the principal offender. (For a recent assessment of the persistent legend that Saikaku's works were banned by the Tokugawa government see *Saikaku Kenkyū Nōto* (Teruoka Yasutaka, 1953), pp. 107–18.) There are, of course, traces of pornographic intent and of Rabelaisian vulgarity in Saikaku's many works on erotic themes, but these are elements of importance only for those whose main interest lies in finding them.

and breadth of Japan. Why they existed is another question: it is enough, in seeking the reason for Saikaku's apparent obsession with them, to realise that they did, and that they played an important part in the lives of Saikaku and his contemporaries. They were centres of fashion and of the new bourgeois culture. A great deal of popular literature (and, of course, of popular art), throughout the two hundred and fifty years of the Edo period, draws its inspiration from them. The painted and gorgeously attired *tayū*—courtesans of the highest grade—represented the popular ideal of womanly grace and beauty, and those who could afford to associate with them were openly envied by a large proportion of their fellow townsmen. There was a reverse side to the picture, of course. The less fortunate prostitutes (the great majority) led wretched lives with no future, and large numbers of townsmen ruined themselves and their families by extravagant spending in the fashionable brothel quarters. Saikaku's works do not overlook or minimise these aspects. Nor do they emphasise them. They are written in a lively but unemotional style, with scant trace of the tendency to sentimentalise which is observable, for instance, in the contemporary drama when it treats of similar themes. In a literature which has exploited sentiment to such a degree as that of Japan, in fact, Saikaku is a strange phenomenon.

A word should be added on male-prostitution, which features largely in certain of Saikaku's works. The practice of sodomy spread in *samurai* circles in Japan in the long years of war during the fourteenth and fifteenth centuries, and it was also traditionally associated with the celibate Buddhist priesthood. By its association with these two classes it achieved a certain prestige, and was even regarded as a superior form of relationship. Debates on the relative merits of the 'two ways of love' were made the central theme of several popular works of literature,[1] and in dealing at length with this practice Saikaku was breaking no new ground, nor was he shocking his contemporaries.

Saikaku is regarded as the founder of a bourgeois literature which accurately depicted the scene, and reflected the spirit, of the new society of which he was a member. He is the first of the townsmen who wrote of his world from the standpoint of a townsman, in sympathy with the attitudes and ideals of his class. In *haikai* he had already been in the vanguard of a movement with those tendencies. When he transferred

[1] E.g. *Denpu Monogatari* (*c.* 1624–44); *Yodare-kake* (1665); *Keisei Kintan Ki* (Ejima Kiseki, 1711). A considerable group of Muromachi novels—e.g. *Saga Monogatari* (*c.* 1460?)—contained romantic accounts of homosexual love-affairs.

his attentions to novels and stories in 1682, and published *Kōshoku Ichidai Otoko*, he added the finishing touch to a parallel movement in prose which had been developing since the opening of the century. The developments in prose, however, had been more hampered by tradition than those in verse, since there had been no semi-emancipated form ready for development comparable with the *haikai* form, and Saikaku's application to prose of the techniques and outlook he had evolved in the *Danrin* school represented a considerable advance. But Saikaku did not only give. If his style was unique, his subject-matter and the form in which he presented it owed much to his predecessors. In literary history *Kōshoku Ichidai Otoko* is classified as the first of the *ukiyo-zōshi*,[1] but no such clear break with past forms or spirit seems to have been felt by contemporaries. Saikaku's pupil Hōjō Dansui, writing after Saikaku's death, does not find it necessary to make any differentiation in terminology between his master's collections of stories and the miscellaneous works of popular prose which had appeared in the eighty years before *Kōshoku Ichidai Otoko*. All were simply *kana-zōshi*.

The term *kana-zōshi* covers a great variety of educational or purely entertaining prose works which, although written largely by men of *samurai* stock, with a background of the traditional culture of the preceding ages, were intended for the consumption of the newly arisen townsman class of the great cities, particularly of Kyōto and Ōsaka. Whereas the medium for 'serious' works—treatises on government, ethics, religion, or medicine—was Chinese, these popular productions, which were sometimes concerned with the same topics on a more elementary level, were written straightforwardly in Japanese. Broadly speaking they fall into three categories: entertainments, practical guides, and Buddhist or Confucianist tracts. The entertainments included war tales, romantic and melancholy novelettes on the loves of court ladies and *samurai* (often ending in suicide for one party and the priesthood or a nunnery for the other), collections of strange stories, drawn from local Japanese traditions or translated or adapted from Chinese sources, and humorous parodies of classical literature. The tracts on religion or ethics were sometimes in the form of a debate between Buddhist

[1] The term *ukiyo-zōshi*, as now used, refers not so much to a specific form of literature as to a group of popular prose works, varying considerably in style and approach, composed in a specific period and region. The period is that from 1682 (the date of publication of *Kōshoku Ichidai Otoko*) to the middle of the eighteenth century, and the region is the *kamigata*—that is, mainly Kyōto and Ōsaka. *Ukiyo* has the sense of 'contemporary life', as in *ukiyo-e*. The classification does not begin to emerge until after the first decade of the eighteenth century, and Hōjō Dansui, writing in the preface to *Saikaku Oritome* (posth. 1694), refers to all Saikaku's works as *kana-zōshi*.

priests and Confucian scholars, sometimes collections of short sermons relating common sayings to Buddhist or Confucian concepts, or collections of short stories illustrating divine justice. The practical guides consisted of stories written in the form of letters (as models of the art of letter-writing), travel guides, and guides to the brothel quarters.[1] It is in these last two groups, the *kana-zōshi* of a direct or indirect instructional nature, that are to be found the seeds of most of the popular prose literature of the succeeding two centuries. The *ukiyo-zōshi* of Saikaku and his contemporaries are first in the line of descent. It might seem that only the first group of *kana-zōshi*, the 'entertainments' in short-story or novel form, could have much value in themselves as literature, but strangely enough this was the group which exercised the least influence on subsequent developments. The reason lay in their conservatism: their models were the life and literature of a former age. The works which had the closest connection with the experience of townsmen were the guide-books, with their descriptions of travel in contemporary Japan and of the newly established brothel quarters. Their purpose was practical. The travel books offered information on inns, prices, distances, local customs, local products, beauty-spots and famous shrines or temples. The brothel guides set out the prices of the various grades of courtesans, their addresses, plans of the quarters, hints on fashions and etiquette, and evaluations of the charms of the leading courtesans of the day.[2] However, since there was yet no literature for literature's sake which treated these themes, the practical guide-books gradually trespassed on to that vacant ground, enlivening their factual information with humorous or romantic observations, an elegance of style, and—in the case of travel books—the beginnings of a plot. It is noticeable that with the appearance of *ukiyo-zōshi* and later forms of Tokugawa literature dealing with contemporary travel or the life of the brothel quarters the guide-books became once more severely practical. Saikaku himself had covered some of the same ground, particularly the

[1] For examples of works in these various classifications see *Edo Bungaku Jiten*, intro. For more detailed treatment of individual *kana-zōshi* see *Retsudentai Shōsetsu Shi* (Mizutani Futō, 1929). The most prolific of all *kana-zōshi* writers was Asai Ryōi (*c.* 1610–91). Three others, Jorai Shi (*c.* 1580–1650), Suzuki Shōzō (1579–1655), and Yamaoka Genrin (1631–72), also deserve mention for the quantity and quality of their work.

[2] Representative of the travel guides (*meisho ki*) are *Chikusai* (Karasumaru Mitsuhiro, *c.* 1620) and *Tōkai-dō Meisho Ki* (Asai Ryōi, *c.* 1658–61). Representative of the brothel guides (*yūjo hyōban ki*) are *Naniwa Monogatari* (author unknown, 1655—Shimabara quarter); *Yoshiwara Kagami* (author unknown, 1661—Shin Yoshiwara quarter); *Okashi-otoko* (author unknown, 1662—Shin-machi quarter). The most comprehensive, *Shikidō Ōkagami* (Hatakeyama Kizan, 1678—the three principal quarters), is, perhaps, a work of disinterested scholarship rather than a *yūjo hyōban ki*.

topic of the quarters, in his *haikai*, and it cannot be said that his selection of subject-matter for the prose works was dictated by *kana-zōshi* precedents, but his factual approach and his accurate and detailed delineation of scene, dress, and customs are possibly deeply influenced by the informative nature of *kana-zōshi* guides. The multitude of minor characters in Saikaku's *ukiyo-zōshi*, however casually introduced and quickly forgotten, are seldom 'a certain courtesan', 'a certain merchant', or 'a certain actor'. The names of the personages are given, perhaps together with the street in which they live, the theatre company to which they belong, or the brothel proprietor for whom they work, and even if the events with which they are associated are semi-fictional, the names are those of actual contemporaries. These intimate bonds with the life which they knew added immensely to the appeal of such literature for the contemporary public, though they unfortunately constitute one of its greatest difficulties for the modern reader.

When we have given due credit to the achievements of the *kana-zōshi* writers, however, and have acknowledged that Saikaku did not create popular Tokugawa prose literature from a vacuum, the gulf between Saikaku and his predecessors remains. It is not only a difference of style, though that in itself is tremendous. The similarities in subject-matter between Saikaku and the guide-books, or the occasional similarities in tone between Saikaku and the purveyors of enlightenment, do not reflect an identity of outlook. Saikaku derives his attitude towards the function of literature primarily from his long association with the *Danrin* school of *haikai*, a movement which had few tendentious undertones. It is difficult to teach ethics or convey any form of useful, practical information within the conventions of linked verse, even if the subject-matter is largely the manners of contemporary society. In prose, as in verse, Saikaku is first and foremost a skilled entertainer.

3. HAIKAI PRINCIPLES IN 'NIPPON EITAI-GURA'

Nippon Eitai-gura (*The Japanese Family Storehouse*),[1] subtitled *Daifuku Shin Chōja Kyō* (*The Millionaires' Gospel Modernised*) and published in the first

[1] A more literal translation might be 'The Japanese Eternal Storehouse' or 'The Japanese Storehouse for Posterity'. These make conveniently vague titles in English, but the expression *Eitai-gura* would not have been vague to members of Saikaku's society. It meant a merchant's private storehouse, stocked high with goods which would serve that merchant's family for generation after generation into the dim future—an image of endless *family* prosperity. Neither 'eternity' nor 'posterity' have sufficiently strong family connotations for English readers, and I have therefore fallen back on the above translation, which for all its failure to imply the future, at least brings out the social unit implied. As regards the pronunciation of

year of Genroku (1688),[1] is a collection of thirty short stories illustrating, mostly through examples drawn from the careers of celebrated merchants of the preceding half-century, the methods which tradesmen might profitably adopt in their pursuit of wealth, the code of conduct which they should observe, and the pitfalls which they should avoid. The great majority—possibly all—of the merchants who feature in the work actually existed,[2] though the names are sometimes slightly altered and the author makes liberal use of his imagination in presenting his versions of their careers. The stories are set in a variety of the cities and smaller towns of Japan, with Kyōto, Ōsaka and nearby towns predominating—partly, no doubt, because Saikaku himself was a native of Ōsaka, but also because it was that region, rather than the *shōgun*'s capital in Edo, which was the commercial and cultural hub of Japan in the seventeenth century. In some ways the book was a continuation of the traditional 'tales from all the provinces' pattern which Saikaku had already followed in *Saikaku Shokoku-banashi* (1685) and *Futokoro-suzuri* (1687), but in its subject-matter—the tradesman's pursuit of wealth—it broke entirely new ground for this type of literature, and its success was responsible in later years for the appearance of a number of works on a similar theme,[3] many of which paid *Nippon Eitai-gura* the compliment of unconcealed imitation. These later works not only borrowed whole episodes but reproduced, and usually accentuated, the didactic note which is rather surprisingly prominent in *Nippon Eitai-gura*. Saikaku's didactic approach in this book, however, results to a large extent from his attempt to reproduce something of the form and flavour of *Chōja Kyō* (1627),[4] an established classic on the art of getting rich,

the title in Japanese, it is worth mentioning (since there is often confusion on this point among the Japanese themselves) that the phonetic side-script in the 1688 editions clearly indicates that the first two characters are to be read *Nippon*, not *Nihon*.

[1] There appear to have been three editions issued in the first month of this year, varying only in the colophon. For a consideration of their order of publication see *Saikaku Nenpu Kōshō*, pp. 195–7. Saikaku's name appears in none of them, but, leaving aside the evidence of the style, the work is attributed to Saikaku by Hōjō Dansui, Saikaku's pupil, in the preface to *Saikaku Oritome*, and by Itō Baiu in *Kenmon Dansō* (1738), VI. Hōjō Dansui states that *Nippon Eitai-gura* was intended to be the first part of a trilogy on merchant themes, but there is no indication within *Nippon Eitai-gura* itself that this was the case.

[2] For discussions on the various characters' identities the reader is referred to the Commentary to each story.

[3] These works, together with Saikaku's *Nippon Eitai-gura*, *Seken Munesanyō* and *Saikaku Oritome*, form a group known as *chōnin-mono*. They include *Risshin Daifuku-chō* (Yuiraku-ken, 1703), *Shison Daikoku-bashira* (Getsujin-dō, 1709), *Tedai Sode Soroban* (Hachimonji Jishō, 1713), *Nippon Shin Eitai-gura* (Hōjō Dansui, 1713), and *Seken Tedai Katagi* (Ejima Kiseki, 1730).

[4] A complete translation of *Chōja Kyō* (*The Millionaires' Gospel*) is given in Appendix 2 and its relationship with *Nippon Eitai-gura* is more fully discussed in the next section.

and a work which occupied a unique position in the affections of seventeenth-century townsmen. This is not to say that *Nippon Eitai-gura* is merely a literary pastiche. The advice which it conveys is manifestly sincere, if not always strikingly original, and there can be little doubt that the author is genuinely concerned over questions of business morality. But *Nippon Eitai-gura* is not a practical guide-book for ambitious merchants, nor a set of sugared sermons on townsman ethics. Judged as either it must be accounted inconsistent and a failure. It is a collection of brief entertainments on a given theme, in Saikaku's usual manner. It so happened that the theme on this occasion—the merchant's way to success—was inseparable, both by its nature and by literary tradition, from the didactic approach.

As has been said, the book is a collection of thirty short stories. The phrase 'short stories', however, is possibly misleading, since many lack the unity of plot and the sense of subordination to a single climax which are most commonly associated with that form. Rather less than one-half of the stories in *Nippon Eitai-gura* could be said to concentrate, to the exclusion of extraneous matter, upon the careers of single personages or families. The unity of the collection of anecdotes which make up *The Foremost Lodger in the Land* (II, 1), each illustrating some facet of the merchant Fuji-ichi's notorious parsimony, for example, needs no comment. Equally obvious is the unity of the story of the draper Chūsuke (III, 5) whose incompetence costs him his inherited fortune, but whose daughter's charms ultimately restore the family to undeserved prosperity; or that of *A Dose of What the Doctor Never Orders* (III, 1), in which the hero, by mixing ingenuity with the ingredients of a nostrum called 'The Millionaire Pill', works his way up from carving chopsticks to selling forests of timber. There are several others which have the same comparatively simple structure, in which there is either one connected narrative or a number of closely related anecdotes, but even in this group there are occasionally disturbing elements which the reader may feel to be not entirely germane to the point of the story, and better omitted, or at least considerably abbreviated. There is, for instance, the amount of space devoted in *A Feather in Daikoku's Cap* (II, 3) to the life histories of the three beggars, incorporating a lengthy catalogue of the artistic accomplishments of one of their number. The function of the episode in the framework of the plot is first to dampen the hero's hopes of making good in Edo, and then to suggest to him a possible plan, and to that extent its insertion is justifiable—but such an effect could have been achieved with far greater economy of words. As it is, the passage seems a distracting interlude, entertaining in itself but dimming the reader's recollection, rather than sharpening his awareness, of the principal character's predicament. In *A Genius as a Foster-child* (VI, 2), to take another example, the episode of the boy from Ise has the makings of a very satisfactory short story, and both the anecdote on salesmanship and the description of Edo extravagance at the Feast of Ebisu, which precede it, could be regarded as a legitimate and lively introduction; but the impression is given that Saikaku lacks the artist's sense of where to stop. When the boy from Ise has made his astounding fortune and retired, apparently at the early age of twenty-eight, to devote himself to dutiful attendance upon his less gifted foster-parents, we are ready to applaud and leave the theatre, but Saikaku has two more anecdotes ready for us, like unsolicited encores.

But these stories and many others like them, in spite of the occasional suspicion of irrelevance or long-windedness, are all comparatively easy to regard as satisfactory units—compared, that is to say, with a further group, which we shall now consider, in which the items included in a single story seem to bear little relation to each other and to be arranged in a bemusingly haphazard order, without sense of beginning, middle, or end. It may not be true to say that these latter stories are more typical of Saikaku than the others, but a consideration of them does at least afford us clearer insight into Saikaku's individual approach to the construction of a short story, and enables us also to read with a more intelligent appreciation those others which approximate more closely to our preconceived idea of what they should be. The reader of *The Man who built the Cenotaph of Debts on Mount Kōya* (III, 4), which opens with an exhortation to avoid dangerous fishfoods and promiscuity in the interests of a long life, and concludes with the story of a model bankrupt, might well feel that the whole was no more than a collection of bits and pieces, which the author had failed to work into his other stories. The logic behind the movement of thought in *Steady Trade Winds for the Good Ship Jinzū* (I, 3), or *Making a Clock in Slow Motion* (V, I), is equally difficult to follow. These are obviously not stories conceived on the pattern of an accumulation of interest culminating in a climax, or of a central episode with appropriate introduction and conclusion. If that had been the aim, it is difficult to imagine that a professional writer, however careless, could have failed so abysmally.

It may be useful to attempt an analysis of one or two of these stories, indicating (with greater clarity than Saikaku does, since he was writing for a public who knew what to expect from him) the connecting links between each passage:

III, 4. *The Man who Built the Cenotaph of Debts on Mount Kōya*

(1) A short sermon, in reported speech, on the theme that abstinence from dangerous luxuries brings long life. (2) An anecdote of a miser in Ōsaka whose undoubted abstinence did not result in longevity, and who was fated, by events in a previous existence, to be stingy all his life. (3) A discussion of the part which fate, or luck, plays in this world: honest and intelligent people may work hard and remain poor all their lives, whilst dishonest people—people like fraudulent bankrupts, for example—may live in idle luxury. (4) An anecdote of spendthrift creditors in a bankruptcy case. (5) Brief comment on the increasing scale of bankruptcies, particularly in Ōsaka. (6) An anecdote of an honest, genuine bankrupt of Ōsaka.

There is no indication, until past half-way, that the subject of bankruptcy is to be raised. It then occurs, almost incidentally, as part of a discussion of undeservedly rich people, and from that point it becomes the main thread. The first section has only relevance to the second, the second relevance to the first in its opening, but relevance to only the third in its concluding part, and the third has relevance to the conclusion of the second at first and then, imperceptibly, less relevance. We wonder where the constant movement is leading us, and then, finally, we come to rest in the topic of bankruptcy. We still drift a little, but we remain in the waters of bankruptcy till Saikaku sees fit to stop. The technique is that of *haikai* linked verse, in which a number of poets cap each other's brief verses, forging a chain in which each link is associated by some idea with the preceding and the succeeding, but has only the vaguest connection with the verse two links above or below. In this case, of course, it is solo *haikai*, the virtuoso technique which Saikaku developed as his speciality towards the climax of his *haikai* career. The most important verse in a *haikai* chain was the first, the *hokku*, and it is noticeable in *Nippon Eitai-gura* that Saikaku generally contrives to start each story with a striking phrase—sometimes a proverb, a parody of a classical poem, or an echo of a popular song. The verses which follow the *hokku* are all of equal importance. The reader of *haikai* does not worry because he cannot understand the significance of the poem as a whole—there is none—nor where it is leading him—it is leading him nowhere. He savours each seventeen- or fourteen-syllable verse for its own sake, noting the image evoked and the skill with which the transition of topic is effected. In Saikaku's short stories the reader should similarly restrain his impatience to be shown 'the point of it all', and be prepared to appreciate each semi-independent passage as it is presented. A Japanese reader would appreciate the smaller turns of phrase, too, and the dextrous conjuring with the traditional verbal conceits of poetry or poetic prose—though this is admittedly difficult for the reader who must rely on an English translation. And when does a *haikai* linked verse end? It ends when the chain has run on to a satisfactorily round number of links, or when the participants are mentally or physically exhausted. There is no logical conclusion. This may help to explain why, in the example of the boy from Ise quoted above, Saikaku produces two more related anecdotes when we feel that he has already reached the logical climax. His approach is influenced by *haikai* training, and though he is perfectly aware of the more normal techniques of story-telling, of the usefulness, for instance, of suspense and an effective climax—as is evidenced in the small anecdotes themselves, and in the group of stories where that basic design is dominant—he does not cleave automatically to those techniques in the construction of a complete short story. His instinct is primarily that of a *haikai* poet, not that of a dramatist.

The mental adjustments required in the modern western reader for a full appreciation of Saikaku's short stories, it should be emphasised, are not great. The stories contain a great deal which raises an immediate response, and the difficulties are largely confined to the question of the overall pattern. Granted this modicum of sympathetic adjustment, Saikaku should not be now, any more than he was in his own age and society, caviare to the general. He was a popular writer, in all senses of the phrase, and the *haikai* conventions behind his prose works were not complex. They were widely understood in the by no means highly cultured townsman public at which he aimed. It may be thought that, if each element in a story is to be read for its own sake as much as, if not occasionally more than, for its part in a general movement towards an appointed end, the pace is inevitably slackened. But, in effect, the reverse is the case. The essence of the *Danrin* school of *haikai* in which Saikaku was trained was speed and lightness of touch, and this tendency was intensified, almost to absurdity, in the 'arrow-counting' solo *haikai* in which Saikaku achieved personal notoriety.

> *Karu-kuchi ni makasete, nake yo! Hototogisu.*
>
> Sing, summer warbler! Let the notes flow lightly, at their will.

—so Saikaku exhorts himself in the opening verse of a solo *haikai* chain.[1]

[1] *Ōsaka Dokugin Shū* (1675). These hundred verses were composed in the passenger boat going down the Yodo river from Fushimi to Ōsaka.

His prose is equally rapid, with the syntax abbreviated to the bare essentials.

We shall now consider in detail one further example of the group of stories in which the *haikai* element is prominent:

I, 3. *Steady Trade Winds for the Good Ship Jinzū*

(1) A short passage on the vast differences in rice-revenue between great and little feudal lords. (2) An example of a great shipowner and merchant of Ōsaka, a transporter of rice. (3) A passage on the bold enterprise of merchants who speculate in the 'futures' of rice in the Kitahama rice-exchange in Ōsaka. (4) A description of the busy scene on the docks and in the river at Kitahama, ending with a brief catalogue of retired merchants who have made their fortunes in this district. (5) An assertion, backed by tracing the typical career of an apprentice, that in Ōsaka even the humblest of country people may rise to wealth if they seize their opportunities and avoid the pitfalls. Training is more important than birth. (6) A reservation, illustrated by the story of two apprentices, that there is an element of luck. Those who happen to be apprenticed to insignificant merchants or craftsmen are fated to remain insignificant themselves. (7) An anecdote of a woman employed to sweep up spilt rice in Kitahama who made a surprising profit by secretly hoarding and selling the rice she collected. (8) The story of her son, who increased the family fortune by hard work and ingenuity, and who, in spite of his humble background, became a man of social distinction and power.

This is a far more obviously unified piece than *The Man who Built the Cenotaph of Debts on Mount Kōya*, analysed before. It is possible to regard the whole of the first two-thirds as a varied introduction with a unity of theme and place—the opportunities for advancement in Ōsaka, particularly in the Kitahama rice trade—to the final episode of the Kitahama rice-sweeper and her son's success. But the elements do not quite harmonise with that view, and one has no strong sense, as one reads from section to section, that all this is moving in one direction, converging on a preconceived climax. It is significant, too, that Saikaku's title does not refer to the final episode, but to the comparatively unremarkable second section. The first three sections are firmly linked by the topic of rice—the commodity in which the feudal lords' revenues are assessed, which the shipowner transports, and in which the Kitahama merchants deal. All the rice exchanged in the mart at Ōsaka, of course, originated in the fiefs, and the opening of the story points by implication both to this fact and to the process of transportation. The thought is not logically progressive, however: each brief section is permitted to develop in a way which has no direct bearing on what is to follow, and the transitions, when effected, are brought about abruptly and almost casually, sometimes by mechanical means. The change from the topic of revenues to that of the shipowner is effected by the introduction of a pregnant phrase, 'the world is broad', which was commonly associated with the vastness of the ocean, and the change from the shipowner to the merchants of Kitahama follows an incidental remark that the former dealt in rice at the port of Ōsaka. A common pivot-phrase (*yo wo wataru*) leads us from the third to the fourth section, from the merchants' methods of 'crossing life' to the bridge of Naniwa which 'crosses' the river at Kitahama, and this paves the way for a vivid description of the busy Kitahama wharves as viewed from the bridge. The descriptive passage concludes with a list of successful rice merchants whose granaries are located on the island across the river, and this, coupled with an incidental reference to the large numbers of servants and other dependants whom they support, leads on to the more general topic, no longer closely connected with the rice trade, of the usual processes by which Ōsaka people rise in the world, with particular reference to the apprentice system. These central sections, which give a not very encouraging picture of the prospects of the average apprentice, and which emphasise also the element of sheer luck, good or bad, may strike the reader as a confusing digression: but here too, by *haikai* standards, the links with what has preceded and what follows are fairly firm. The locality is still Ōsaka (and, towards the end, the Kitahama district again), and the theme remains the making of fortunes under Ōsaka conditions. A transition is also made from the earlier concentration on Ōsaka's prosperity and its established merchant princes to a consideration of those who have yet to share in this prosperity. The eventual return to the locality of Kitahama and the shift to a more humble context leads naturally to the final sections, set once more against a background of the Kitahama rice-exchange, which illustrate a steady rise from poverty to wealth in two generations. It should be noted, however, that Saikaku does not show us the rise of a diligent or ingenious apprentice, which we might have expected to follow from his extensive remarks on that theme, but the rise of a man and woman denied that initial advantage. If the moral to be drawn is 'Since even a man like that can make a fortune in Kitahama, how much easier for someone given the start of apprenticeship!', Saikaku nowhere explicitly says so, nor does he even hint at the possibility. The episode is to be taken simply as one further link in the chain, related, but not a logical culmination. A *haikai* short story is less closely knit, less compelling to the reader, than one constructed on dramatic principles. It is basically a succession of related digressions; but the fact that its principles admit the introduction of a broader variety of material is not entirely to its disadvantage as a literary form.

The above analyses are not, of course, intended to provide a complete explanation of the theory underlying Saikaku's conception of a short story, but merely to throw some light on one important aspect of his art. The charges of structural weakness and digressive tendencies levelled against his work—even in Japan—seem to be based upon the too ready assumption that this deviation from the norm, Saikaku's most characteristic contribution to the art of the short story, arose entirely through negligence. It is obvious enough, of course, to anyone who reads his stories, that Saikaku was also heir to a more conventional tradition of story-telling, and that any other principles there may be are often subordinate to a straightforward narrative design. But the *haikai* principles, if not always dominant, are always there, and no balanced assessment of Saikaku can ignore their presence.

In addition to these general principles mention must be made of two further elements which contribute towards the special flavour of a Saikaku story. These are, first, a strong sense of locality, and, secondly, the Saikaku style. Traditional ideas associated with place-names, whether rooted in local topography and history or arising merely from the chance meaning which certain names possess (e.g. Ausaka = meeting-hill; Wake = brothel fee), have always, together with associations derived from the four seasons, played an important part among the conventions of Japanese poetry and poetic prose. A linked-verse poet, in particular, was required to have a mind well stocked with these associations: the mention of a place-name should immediately have suggested some related idea which might serve as the basis of his own contribution to the developing chain. There is abundant evidence of the presence of this habit of thought in the stories of *Nippon Eitai-gura*. When Saikaku introduces a story set in the northern provinces with a passing reference to snow-measuring rods, when in the context of Sakata he modifies a common proverbial expression to include a reference to dried salmon, when he commences his description of a draper's shop in Suruga province with metaphors from Mount Fuji, when he refers to the legend of Mano's millions in the context of Bungo province, and when he finds it almost impossible to mention Yodo without somehow introducing the water-wheel of Yodo castle, he is drawing upon a stock of conventional regional associations which was the common property of his society, and is transferring to prose a technique which he and hundreds of his fellow *haikai* practitioners had exploited in verse for many years. Not all the associations utilised in *haikai* or in a Saikaku story are of a regional origin, of course, but Saikaku's professional interest in this particular branch of the technique seems to have been deepened by his experiences as a traveller, and to have developed into a genuine, personally felt awareness of local differences, particularly of the contrasts in mood between the great cities. In *Nippon Eitai-gura* this sense is strong, and not only is it brought to our notice in the lists of contents, where the location of each story is carefully indicated, but it is an important element in the structure of many of the stories.[1] Whilst human individuals in the book tend to emerge as little more than personifications of merchantly virtues or vices—Thrift, Ingenuity, Enterprise, Industry, Low Cunning, Extravagance, or Incompetence—there are several extensive character-sketches of cities, touching not only upon the surface scene but upon the contrasting philosophies of life which underlay the behaviour of each city's merchant community. An example where this becomes a dominating force in a story's structure is *Extortionate Prices for Ise Lobsters* (IV, 5). The practical advice here is conveyed through the example and precept of a certain Hinokuchiya, an economically-minded citizen of Sakai, but the whole story is set in a framework of contrasts between Sakai on the one hand and Edo and Ōsaka on the other, with the result that Sakai itself has as much right as Hinokuchiya to be considered the story's protagonist. Elsewhere in the book Saikaku vividly evokes the moods of Kyōto and of lesser trading centres such as Nagasaki, Ōtsu, Tsuruga, Fushimi and Ise. *Nippon Eitai-gura*, in fact, includes within its wide scheme a parade of the merchant towns and communities of Japan no less than of outstanding individual merchants.

A little has already been said, in tracing the *haikai* influence upon his work, of Saikaku's distinctive style. It derives its rhythmic quality, its compression, its special verse techniques, and its amalgam of elegant and colloquial vocabulary from the *Danrin* source. The style is one of the elements which render Saikaku a difficult writer for the modern

[1] It is significant that, in what appears to be an unauthorised edition of *Nippon Eitai-gura*, published later in 1688, the stories are completely rearranged in groups based on geographical identity. *Kōchū Nippon Eitai-gura*, I (Shuzui Kenji, 1937) gives full details of this 'pirate' edition, including the numerous variant readings. Shuzui implies, however, that this was an 'Edo edition', whereas it is now known to have been published in Ōsaka (see *Saikaku Nenpu Kōshō*, pp. 202–5).

Japanese,[1] though there is no basis for any assumption that his contemporaries found him abstruse. The punctuation is eccentric, and Saikaku's economy of words and haste in composition often result in grammatical solecisms (e.g. 'in former ages this is the first time'—*zendai kore ga hajime nari*) which would be the delight of any compiler of books on 'How Not to Write Japanese'. It seems unlikely that Saikaku ever revised his works before sending them to the printer. But, in spite of occasional grammatical lapses and a strange diversity of imagery and vocabulary, whereby proverbialisms and the special jargons of brothels and counting-houses mingle with delicate allusions to ancient Japanese poetry and even with quotations from the Chinese classics, it is a practised and consistent style, by no means artless or slipshod. In this type of light literature style is undoubtedly a matter of considerable importance, and the reader should therefore be warned that the present translation makes no claim to have successfully transposed this intangible into English. The punctuation in the translation is conventional; dependent clauses have been introduced where Saikaku has only a succession of brief phrases whose logical relationship has to be inferred from the context; the continuous flow of the original has been interrupted, for clarity's sake, by division into paragraphs; speech has been clearly separated from narrative (there are no quotation-marks in Saikaku's text, and it is often particularly difficult to decide exactly where a character has started talking); and solecisms, should they be discovered, are accidental. The general stylistic aim has been to avoid clumsiness rather than to achieve brilliance. As far as possible, however, the sentences and periods have been made to flow at a reasonable pace, with some semblance of rhythm. This is undoubtedly a slower, less imaginative, more commonplace Saikaku than the original, but it has seemed more advisable to bring out the meaning clearly than to becloud it with stylistic experiments.

4. MODERNISED MILLIONAIRES

Nippon Eitai-gura's subtitle *The Millionaires' Gospel Modernised* contains a reference to *Chōja Kyō* (*The Millionaires' Gospel*),[2] a brief work of unknown authorship first published in 1627. In this section the relation-

[1] Another is the constant need for reference to notes to elucidate vocabulary or identify personalities, for Saikaku deals in the particularities of a society which is almost as remote to modern Japanese as to modern Englishmen.

[2] The subtitle *Daifuku Shin Chōja Kyō* carries, in addition to the sense of 'A New *Chōja Kyō*', a verbal play on *daifuku-chō*, the principal account-book of a business firm. There is also a reference to the common variant of *chōja*—*daifuku-chōja*.

ship between *Chōja Kyō* and *Nippon Eitai-gura* will be considered, and it is hoped that the discussion will also serve to illustrate certain of Saikaku's customary literary methods, and enable the reader to appreciate something more of *Nippon Eitai-gura*'s significance to its contemporary public than would otherwise be possible.

In length *Chōja Kyō* does not much exceed one of Saikaku's longer short stories. It is written almost entirely in simple phonetic script, in a terse epigrammatic style, and purports to set forth the views of three *chōja* (millionaires) on the problem of how to get rich. After each *chōja* has briefly outlined the methods and the psychological approach which he recommends on the basis of his own experience, there follows a considerable section devoted to lists of exhortations, collections of humorous cautionary verses, and groups of family names with didactic implications. The whole is concluded by a passage in which the god of poverty, after voicing objections to the basic assumption that wealth is desirable, is duly put in his place by the author's assertion that such an attitude is dictated by envy, and that money, whatever the god of poverty says, is all-powerful and supremely desirable.[1]

Chōja Kyō demonstrated surprising powers of survival, and remained a force in townsman society until well into the eighteenth century. Several editions and adaptations are extant, and the title occurs with frequency in the booksellers' catalogues of the period. In literature the work finds occasional reference in seventeenth-century *haikai* verse, underlies the conception of *Nippon Eitai-gura*, and is briefly parodied in a play by Chikamatsu in 1718. In 1680 we find it being presented to the thirteen-year-old daughter of a townsman on the occasion of her marriage, together with several other works calculated to fit the young girl for her new responsibilities.[2] Its popularity was due, no doubt, partly to the wholesome nature of the advice it contained, though there is evidence that not everyone treated it seriously,[3] and partly to its entertainment value. It would also appeal to townsmen by its uncompromising championship of a materialist philosophy which they regarded with affection as typical of the outlook of their class, even if they accepted it in practice with many reservations. Originally, however, some of its

[1] A complete translation of *Chōja Kyō* is given in Appendix 2.

[2] For these editions of *Chōja Kyō*, the *haikai* references, the entries in booksellers' catalogues, and the record of *Chōja Kyō*'s presentation to the daughter of the townsman Enomoto Yazaemon of Musashi province see *Chōja Kyō Kō*, published as an appendix to *Saikaku Shinkō* (Noma Kōshin, 1948). The parody of *Chōja Kyō* appears in *Hakata Kojorō Nami-makura* (Chikamatsu Monzaemon, 1718).

[3] The evidence is chiefly in *haikai* and in Chikamatsu's parody (for both, see p. xlvi, below).

point seems to have lain in its parody of a certain type of Buddhist literature in which the futility of worldly ideals, as exemplified by a *chōja's* pursuit of satisfaction in this life through wealth, had been contrasted with the nobler and more ultimately satisfactory ideals of Buddhism.[1] *Chōja Kyō* retains the outline of its Buddhist-inspired predecessors—the visit of a young boy to the *chōja*, the allegory of Mount *Chōja*, the broad principles of the *chōja's* recommendations, and much Buddhist phraseology—but reverses the traditional Buddhist moral which had been at the core of this type of literature. The role of introducing the conventional moral is assigned, with malicious intent, to the disreputable god of poverty. Whether this element of parody was appreciated in Saikaku's day is not certain, but—for whatever reasons—*Chōja Kyō* had plainly by that time become something of a minor townsman classic.

Saikaku is justly honoured as a writer who sought inspiration in the realities of his own age and society, but no one will deny that for the outward form and even certain incidental details of his works he sometimes made extensive use of his reading in ancient or contemporary literature. His first work of prose, *Kōshoku Ichidai Otoko* (1682), had been a modernisation of the revered eleventh-century classic *Genji Monogatari* (*The Tale of Genji*).[2] The leisurely, sentimental amours of Lady Murasaki's romantic hero, Prince Hikaru Genji, became the frankly sensual escapades of Saikaku's Yonosuke, the seventeenth-century man-

[1] No work of this nature, which can be proved conclusively to antedate *Chōja Kyō*, survives; but it is reasonably conjectured that a passage incorporated in a *kana-zōshi* of 1662 (*Iguchi Monogatari*, VI, 16; *Aru daifuku-chōja deshi ni oshiyuru koto*) is, if not the actual model for *Chōja Kyō*, based fairly closely upon that model (see *Chōja Kyō Kō*). The *Iguchi Monogatari* passage is clearly indebted to *Tsurezure-gusa* (*c*. 1330), 217 and 166, which may be regarded as the ultimate source of the particular tradition of *chōja* literature to which *Chōja Kyō* belongs. The correspondences in structure and phraseology between these three works are close. The *chōja* of *Tsurezure-gusa* is a miser who seeks worldly satisfaction by amassing, but not spending, money; and Yoshida Kenkō, the author, dismisses this philosophy as perverse and stupid. In *Iguchi Monogatari*, where the Buddhist influence is more evident, the philosophy is that a would-be *chōja* should devote the prime of his life to amassing wealth (the process is illustrated by the simile of the toilsome, dangerous ascent of Mount *Chōja*, a mountain in the shape of a calabash, a common symbol for good luck) and use the money for personal pleasure in his declining years. But the *chōja* who gives this advice himself admits that such a temporary paradise is a poor thing compared to the Nirvana which awaits those who follow the equally rigorous and ascetic way of the Buddha. It should be noted that, for all the worldliness of the contents, the title of the 1627 publication *Chōja Kyō* suggests a Buddhist sutra (e.g. *Chōja On-etsu Kyō*, *Chōja Shisei Kyō*, *Shumadai Chōja Kyō*, etc., but the resemblance goes no deeper than the title in any of these cases).

[2] For the relationship between *Genji Monogatari* (*c*. 1001–20) and *Kōshoku Ichidai Otoko* see 'Saikaku no Kōshoku Ichidai Otoko no Seiritsu' in *Edo Bungaku Kenkyū* (Yamaguchi Gō, 1933) and 'Saikaku to Koten Bungaku' (Shimazu Hisamoto) in *Kokugo to Kokubungaku* (1939–40).

about-town, and the scene was moved from ancient courts to modern brothel quarters. Both works are in fifty-four chapters, and in many of the incidents in *Kōshoku Ichidai Otoko* there are echoes of *Genji Monogatari* which the author trusted that his readers would recognise as such. The technique has similarities with that of literary 'pastiche', but in Saikaku's case the reminiscent flavour is less obvious, many of the references being as indirect and elusive as those of *haikai* linked verse. The technique, in fact, contributes no more than an incidental grace, and in no way detracts from the originality of the works in which it is employed, in that they continue to derive their inspiration in overwhelming proportion from contemporary realities.

The relationship of *Chōja Kyō* to *Nippon Eitai-gura* seems to be of this nature. The marked didactic tone of *Nippon Eitai-gura* and its broad structural scheme, whereby persons approximating to *chōja* are introduced to offer practical guidance by their word or example, constitute a literary reference to the tone and structure of the older work. *Nippon Eitai-gura*, like its celebrated forbear, is ostensibly a 'Guide to Wealth'. It starts from the same assumption that the achievement of wealth is a supremely desirable goal, disposing in its opening passage of Buddhist-inspired arguments to the contrary, much as *Chōja Kyō* had refuted the objections of the god of poverty. Its materialism, if part sincere, is also in part a conscious echo of the attitudes associated with its model:

> Money is the only family tree for a townsman. A man may be descended from the noblest of the Fujiwara, but if he dwells among shopkeepers and lives in poverty he is lower than a vagabond monkey-trainer. There is no alternative for a townsman: he must pray for wealth and aim to be a *chōja*. To be a *chōja* he must have the heart to climb a great mountain. (VI, 5.)

Saikaku here speaks specifically of the townsman society of his own age, but the phraseology—by its *haikai* association of *chōja* and 'mountain'[1]—is designed to recall the allegory of Mount *Chōja* in *Chōja Kyō*. The sentiment itself, too, is not basically different from *Chōja Kyō's* assertion that:

> If a man is without money he is not to be reckoned as a human being.

And its ancestry (in case it may be assumed that this outlook is purely a product of seventeenth-century conditions) may be traced even further back, to days when a townsman society was not dreamed of. The *chōja*

[1] Throughout this concluding story of *Nippon Eitai-gura* the word *chōja* occurs with markedly greater frequency than in the rest of the book. The point is not noted by any of the commentators, who also overlook the possibility of a *haikai* link between *chōja* and *yama no gotoku ni shite* in the passage quoted.

who makes an appearance in the fourteenth-century miscellany *Tsurezure-gusa* states that:

Men should set all else aside and concentrate solely on making money. If a man is poor he might as well not be alive. Only riches make a Man.[1]

If such underlying premises as these, and the basic didactic form, are the most important echoes from *Chōja Kyō*, there are nevertheless many others. There is, for instance, Saikaku's use of the archaic term *chōja*, which seems to have become by his day chiefly associated either with *Chōja Kyō* or with men of fabulous wealth in old romances. Its presence in a work on contemporary business men produces a humorous effect of incongruity. The style, too, though it remains the highly individual style which is found in all Saikaku's *ukiyo-zōshi*, has reminiscent qualities in its constant recourse to proverbialisms, or in its occasional casual introduction of brief apophthegms prefaced by the formula: 'a certain rich man said'.[2] Further traces of *Chōja Kyō* may be discerned in certain of the incidents in the stories, as in the visit of the young men to the house of the rich merchant Fuji-ichi 'to seek advice on how to become *chōja*' (II, I), or in the account of the marvellous increase by interest of the Mizuma temple money (I, I).[3]

Saikaku's book is a new 'Millionaires' Gospel', but it is not really the advice which is brought up to date. Saikaku recommends the old-established merchantly virtues for which, in the minds of his contemporaries, the name *Chōja Kyō* stood, and his only modernisation is an emphasis on the need for originality and enterprise to complement those virtues. In both *Chōja Kyō* and *Nippon Eitai-gura* the road to wealth is a rigorous course of economy, abstinence, and unremitting toil. The goal of the ancient *chōja*, the use of money for personal pleasure in old age, is likewise part of the philosophy which Saikaku attributes to his model tradesmen. The classical progress to success is most clearly illustrated in the story entitled *A Dose of What the Doctor Never Orders* (III, I), the hero of which rises to fabulous wealth (from chopstick-carver to wholesale timber merchant) by observing certain recommendations

[1] *Tsurezure-gusa*, 217.

[2] One of these 'certain rich men' is named, and the name is significantly Kamadaya (I, 2). Another of the *Chōja Kyō* names, Nabaya, is casually introduced in V, 5. In VI, 4 a 'certain *chōja*' reproduces verbatim a phrase from *Chōja Kyō*: 'Sell what you begrudge, and refrain from buying what you fancy.'

[3] For a longer list of incidents possibly suggested by *Chōja Kyō* see *Nippon Eitai-gura Hyōshaku* (Satō Tsurukichi, 1930), intro. pp. 5–12. The story which makes most play with the technique of reminiscence, however, draws not upon *Chōja Kyō* but upon a *chōja* legend incorporated in a Muromachi novelette. (See Commentary III, 2, 6.)

given in the form of a prescription for a *Chōja* Pill, supplemented by a catalogue of 'noxious things' from which he must abstain. The same story gives us the classical use to which a *chōja's* wealth should be put: fortune made, the hero abandons the course of treatment and passes his declining days in luxury and self-indulgence.[1] Similarly, if we look at the advice proffered him, we find that—fanciful though it is—much of it is of a strictly traditional nature. The ingredients of the *Chōja* Pill are The Family Trade, Economy, Work after Hours, Sound Health, and Early Rising, and the noxious items include:

> Expensive foods and silken clothes for every-day wear.
> Perfume appreciation and poetry gatherings.
> The tea ceremony.
> Flower-viewing, boating excursions.
> Gambling parties and playing *go* or backgammon.
> Temple-going and preoccupation with the next world.
> Giving too generously to temple funds. (III, I.)

Even in such detailed prohibitions Saikaku is often reproducing stock elements from previous literature on how to get rich, or from the philosophy of the merchants of a bygone age. Many parallels may be found in *Chōja Kyō*, but here a few quotations will be given from doggerel cautionary verses which are incorporated in *Iguchi Monogatari* (1662) in a passage thought, in spite of its late date of publication, to contain material which antedates *Chōja Kyō*:[2]

> Forget not the calls of business in *sake* and gambling, in backgammon, *go*, or chess. (Verse 26.)

> Pride, envy, and self-pity; love-affairs, sight-seeing, and mornings in bed —all are forbidden. (Verse 20.)

> Pleasant though such pastimes be, learn no arts which are useless in trade. (Verse 83.)

[1] If not the attitude of the *chōja* of *Tsurezure-gusa*, it becomes the attitude of the *chōja* of the later *Iguchi Monogatari* and *Chōja Kyō*. See *Iguchi Monogatari*, VI, 16 where the *chōja* says: 'The man who dwells on the pinnacle of Mount *Chōja* wants for no single thing, be it gold, silver, rice, *zeni*, or precious silks of China and Japan....Every desire to adorn his person or house is satisfied....Cool in the summer, warm in the winter, free from annoyance, he lives in vast ease and comfort.' To which the Buddhist reply is given: 'In the case of the Way of a *Chōja*, if a man lives for a hundred years he must spend eighty of them enduring toil and hardship, and only for twenty years does he enjoy the pleasures of a *chōja*.' See also *Chōja Kyō*: 'Since youth comes not twice do not relax: even for the old there is pleasure from money.'

[2] *Iguchi Monogatari*, VI, 16, see n. 1, p. xli.

Look first to your means of livelihood: all else is neither here nor there. (Verse 40.)

These maxims of *Chōja Kyō* or the *Iguchi Monogatari* passage were not, of course, unrelated to life. They reflected the homely wisdom of merchants of their age, as is evidenced by the appearance of the same philosophy in a private document of 1610, 'The Seventeen Injunctions of Shimai Sōshitsu'.[1] The correspondences of the advice conveyed in *Nippon Eitai-gura* with that given by Shimai Sōshitsu are no less close than those noted above with works of literature. A few quotations from Shimai will suffice:

Rise early in the morning. As soon as day is over retire to bed. To use lamp oil for idle purposes is wasteful. (Article 14.)

On no account must you become an invalid. No matter how you feel at the time, apply herbal poultices and drink medicine with regularity. (Article 17.)

Dice, backgammon, and gambling games are forbidden throughout life. *Go*, chess, fencing, and recitations or dances from Noh plays are forbidden, at least until the age of forty....Excursions to pine-slopes, expeditions on the river, moon-viewing, blossom-viewing, and all kinds of sightseeing are naturally forbidden. (Article 3.)

As for artistic interests, eccentric tastes, the tea ceremony...ornamental swords and daggers, and smart clothes—in all these things a little is enough: a conspicuous display is absolutely forbidden....Until the age of forty cotton *kimono*, or clothes of an inconspicuous sort, are most suitable. (Article 4.)

It is forbidden to worry about the after-life until you have reached the age of fifty. Such thoughts are for old men only, or for members of the Jōdo or Zen sects. Above all conversion to Christianity is forbidden....Christianity is the greatest of afflictions for a man whose concern is the management of a household....Bear it well in mind that preoccupation with the next world is not permissible until you have reached the age of fifty. (Article 2.)

Shimai Sōshitsu was a brewer and financier of Hakata,[2] and these injunctions were recorded for the guidance of his son, who was to inherit control of the family business and fortune. It is a sober, practical document, in which there is no attempt to eulogise the *chōja* ideal (the word *chōja* is not mentioned) or the power of money. By and large it

[1] *Shimai Sōshitsu no Yuikun Jūshichi-ka-jō* (Shimai Sōshitsu, 1610). A translation of the greater part of this document is given in Appendix 3.

[2] Shimai Sōshitsu died in 1622 at the age of seventy-six. His trade appears to have been a combination of *sake*-brewing and the advancement of loans to overseas traders. For his career see *Tokugawa Shoki no Kaigai Bōeki-ka* (Kawashima Genjirō, 1916), pp. 426–51.

is the merchant philosophy of Shimai's generation which Saikaku is reproducing in *Nippon Eitai-gura*; but the work which represented that philosophy to Saikaku and his contemporaries was *Chōja Kyō*. Thrift was a cardinal virtue in that philosophy, as is amply illustrated in Shimai's document, but to later generations it began to seem more akin to stinginess. This is indicated by certain *haikai* verses of the mid-seventeenth century, in which *Chōja Kyō* and Stinginess are related-words (*engo*),[1] and—thirty years after the publication of *Nippon Eitai-gura*—by the brief parody of *Chōja Kyō* which appears in Chikamatsu's play *Hakata Kojorō Nami-makura*:

> Rise in the morning at four. Never lend without surety. It is a profit if you do not buy what you long for. It is a loss if you omit to work on nights when the moon is bright....Observe the proper methods for burning firewood, and never discard the charcoal embers. Nothing should ever be wasted: the soot around a pot is useful for painting false eyebrows; pieces of vegetable stalk make a fine medicine for the palsy; a dried-up well is a good place to store a ladder; even rats' tails can be made into sheaths for awls. Dry your umbrella well after use, and never lend it. Every time you lend a pestle, whetstone or medicine grinder—though the loss may not be visible to the eye—it is inevitably worn a little thinner when returned. If you observe these points carefully 'dust will pile up and become a mountain'. The golden sayings of the *chōja* are infallible.[2]

Saikaku, however, does not set out to produce an unsympathetic parody—any more than he had sought to parody *Genji Monogatari* in his *Kōshoku Ichidai Otoko*—but a modernisation. The essence of the *Chōja Kyō* message is presented against a more modern physical and economic background. Sufficient of the old is retained to render the model recognisable, but the new work is conceived in the spirit of a radically different category of literature. It has all the characteristics of Saikaku's *ukiyo-zōshi*—the up-to-date, sophisticated literary form which dealt with the present rather than the past, with people and manners rather than with ideas, and placed considerably more emphasis on entertainment than enlightenment. Once *Chōja Kyō* has provided the framework for *Nippon Eitai-gura*—the didactic form and the broad attitudes towards

[1] Cf. a *haikai* couplet of 1666, quoted in *Chōja Kyō Kō*:

> *Jitai kyō-shū wa shiwai ga kizu ja—*
> *Chōja Kyō tsui ni yaburete usenikeri.*

(Kyōto people are stingy with their money—it's their weakness. *Chōja* [*Kyō*] like that fade away to bankruptcy.)

[2] *Hakata Kojorō Nami-makura*, I.

the accumulation of wealth—its further influence is secondary, and Saikaku draws freely upon his own extensive stock of observations, following the methods and the outlook which he had adopted in previous works on other facets of contemporary townsman life. The modernisation arises naturally from this.[1] The merchants introduced are real personages who had made their fortunes in modern times. Kamadaya, Nabaya, and Izumiya of *Chōja Kyō* were shadowy figures of no apparent abode or trade, but Saikaku's merchants, like the characters in his other *ukiyo-zōshi*, are given the trappings of solid reality. They bear the names of actual contemporaries, they ply a variety of clearly defined trades, and they live in specified cities, towns, or villages. They move against a contemporary physical and cultural background which is equally carefully delineated, and, above all, they are members of a human society. It is a society of townsmen, and no reader of *Nippon Eitai-gura* is suffered to overlook that fact. The emphasis of townsmen upon the essential differences between themselves and the socially superior classes, the note of humility only faintly veiling the underlying self-satisfaction, was a new phenomenon, peculiar to Saikaku's age. The defiant materialism which characterises *Chōja Kyō* is sometimes loosely referred to as an early manifestation of the townsman spirit of the seventeenth century, but it should be borne in mind that the word 'townsman' is nowhere to be found in that document. The word is likewise conspicuously absent in the injunctions of Shimai Sōshitsu. *Chōja Kyō* was concerned with the philosophy of *chōja*, not *chōnin*, and Shimai does not appear to have identified himself with any group larger than the family. Class-consciousness amongst townsmen developed in pace with the growth of their cities and their economic power, and it was not until the fourth or fifth decades of the seventeenth century that the new city trading communities were sufficiently well entrenched to pause and contemplate with ironic pleasure the unique position which they had won for themselves, against all the social laws of Heaven, in feudal society. The new spirit first found literary expression in popular *haikai* movements, and later, more fully, in Saikaku's *ukiyo-zōshi*. All Saikaku's literature—not merely *Nippon Eitai-gura*—reflects the buoyant confidence of the townsmen of his time, and more particularly of the citizens of his native Ōsaka, the stronghold *par excellence* of the towns-

[1] Its most mechanical application is perhaps in the precise up-to-date definition, in terms of the new silver currency, of a *chōja* (I, I); but the definition is largely forgotten thereafter. The word *chōja*, in fact, is used sparingly: it is found chiefly in proverbial phrases, or where some allusion is intended either to *Chōja Kyō* or to millionaires of ancient times.

man's economic power. That Saikaku's 'modernisation' of *chōja* literature should include the infusion of this sense was inevitable.

This transposition of ideas which had been partly shaped by the demands of a Buddhist literary tradition into the context of a real human society inevitably resulted in a certain amount of confusion and contradiction. The *chōja* of the *Chōja Kyō* tradition were individuals seeking only to gratify personal desires. But contemporary Japanese merchants were members of family businesses, acknowledging responsibilities to their family units. Thus, side by side with an emphasis on the pleasures which money will bring the individual, we find in *Nippon Eitai-gura* a conflicting emphasis on the social responsibilities of the rich:

> To consider the welfare of those in one's charge, to share the family inheritance, to establish senior clerks in branches of the family business—this is the meaning of townsman success, the true way of a master. (IV, 1.)

Again, a *chōja* was a self-made man. Like a Buddha he was obliged to start from nothing.[1] Saikaku, in his own definition (I, 1), stresses that a *chōja* must make his fortune without assistance from inherited capital, and the examples which the stories in *Nippon Eitai-gura* provide are largely of people who achieved that feat. Consequently there are traces of a prejudice against the idea of inheriting capital:

> Inheriting your father's fortune, making money at gambling, dealing in fakes, marrying a rich widow...all these are ways of getting rich, but they are not good ways. (VI, 4.)

The aim of the normal business man, however, was the typically Japanese ideal of establishing a prosperous family line. He wished to bequeath a worthy inheritance to his successors, and he regarded it as by no means degrading or immoral to receive one from his father. Shimai's injunctions are the earliest known example of a common type of Tokugawa document, the private Merchant Household Code,[2] which owed its appearance in Japanese society to this widespread desire to ensure the future prosperity of a family business and the safe preservation of a family inheritance. There are many indications of the presence of this feeling in *Nippon Eitai-gura*, not least in the title itself, which

[1] The parallel between the Way of a *Chōja* and the Way of a Buddha, implicit in the opening passage of *Chōja Kyō*, is most clearly pointed in *Iguchi Monogatari*, VI, 16.

[2] Examples of these merchant codes (*kahō*), which became particularly numerous in the eighteenth century, may be found in *Kinsei Shōnin Ishiki no Kenkyū* (Miyamoto Matatsugu, 1941), pp. 173 *seq.* At least one of the merchants whom Saikaku introduces, Mitsui Hachirōemon (1655–1737), was responsible for draughting such a code—the *Sōjiku Yuisho* (1720) of the now celebrated Mitsui family.

indicates that the book is a storehouse of examples which will bring prosperity to 'endless succeeding generations in a family-line' (a phrase conveyed more briefly in Japanese by *eitai*). The title and the subtitle, in fact, indicate the duality of Saikaku's attitude in this work, which resulted from his chosen approach to the realities of his age through the conventions of *chōja* literature.

We cannot justly appreciate *Nippon Eitai-gura* without some knowledge of the literary tradition in which it consciously elects to stand. To interpret the work at its face value, as a simple attempt to provide enlightenment in an entertaining form, is to ignore the difference in outlook between Saikaku and his predecessors, the *kana-zōshi* moralists, and to do an injustice to the intelligence of the contemporary townsman reader. It is a sophisticated book for a sophisticated public—a public familiar with the allusive techniques of *haikai*, and by no means blindly materialist in its philosophy. *Nippon Eitai-gura*, by proclaiming its adherence to the form and attitude of a well-known, though slightly outworn, tradition of literature, is enabled to embrace within its broad scheme, without artistic contradiction, both honest advice, arising from the author's sympathetic observation of the condition of his class, and ironic parody of that type of advice. If it had been the first of the books on 'How to Become a Millionaire', such equivocation would have been inadmissible. In many ways, in fact, it is more helpful to view *Nippon Eitai-gura* as the culmination of *chōja* literature than as the pioneer of *chōnin-mono*. Both views are historically justified, but the latter, though doing greater justice to Saikaku's originality, has the disadvantage of underplaying those older elements which gave the work its basic form and flavour, and which were most readily appreciated by the contemporary reader.

Though each of the thirty stories is a satisfactory unit, the book is to be judged as a whole, for Saikaku was not so much a writer of short stories as a writer of collections of short stories. It was his practice to link the stories in any single publication to a common theme. The notion of gathering together unrelated stories purely on a basis of variety and contrast was alien to him. It might be thought that in *Nippon Eitai-gura* he had handicapped himself unnecessarily by selecting a theme—the rise of contemporary merchants to material wealth—which was too narrow in every sense, and that the repetition of this in thirty successive brief stories could only result in monotony. The effect is avoided partly by the introduction of a broad diversity of trades and localities, and the interpolation of occasional examples of failures, but above all by the freedom of structure and diffusion of emphasis which characterises the *haikai* form of short story. Beneath the apparent narrow dogmatism of the philosophy, too, there is that sophistication of approach which we have noted in this section. *Nippon Eitai-gura* is sometimes criticised as an inhuman work, and, indeed, we should not expect to find much human feeling in a work which is essentially a *tour de force* in praise of material success, with its attitudes often dictated by literary convention. Even when writing on more emotionally charged topics—on love suicides or *samurai* revenge and loyalty—the author was prone to maintain an air of detachment. But, if the chosen thesis in *Nippon Eitai-gura* is the glorification of success, failures are nevertheless not infrequently accorded a measure of sympathy. We should remember, moreover, that the concluding success story of the book concerns a family whose happiness is of a quieter and deeper nature than that achieved merely by the possession of great wealth. Other criteria than the purely material are recognised, and it is surely no accident that Saikaku concludes on this note. Ultimately, in spite of the example of its literary model, the ideal which *Nippon Eitai-gura* instinctively accepts as truly worth while is not striking individual success but the lasting prosperity and harmony of the family.

THE JAPANESE FAMILY STOREHOUSE

OR

THE MILLIONAIRES' GOSPEL

MODERNISED

COINS, RICE MEASURES AND SILVER WEIGHTS

INTRODUCED IN THE TRANSLATION

1. COINS (Gold, Silver, and Copper).* Under each heading the coins are given in ascending order of value.

Gold	Silver	Copper
Ichibu	*Mame-ita*	*Zeni*
Koban	*Chōgin*	
Bankin		

2. RICE MEASURES (Capacity)

10 *gō* = 1 *shō*
10 *shō* = 1 *to*
10 *to* = 1 *koku* (approx. 5 bushels)

3. WEIGHTS (for Silver, etc.)

10 *rin* = 1 *fun*
10 *fun* = 1 *monme*
1000 *monme* = 1 *kanme* (approx. $8\frac{1}{2}$ lb.)

* For further details on coinage, see Appendix 1.

NOTE ON THE ILLUSTRATIONS

THE illustrations to popular literature of the Tokugawa era, like each page of text itself, were reproduced by the wood-block process. For his first three *ukiyo-zōshi* Saikaku provided his own illustrations, but thereafter he generally employed the services of the professional *ukiyo-e* artists, Yoshida Hanbei and Makieshi Genzaburō. Little biographical material exists on these artists, and their dates are uncertain. Yoshida Hanbei lived in Kyōto. In *Kankatsu Heike Monogatari* (1710) there is a passage which gives some indication of the popularity of his work, and suggests that in his day he was ranked as the equal of his now more celebrated contemporary, Hishikawa Moronobu (*c.* 1618–94) of Edo: '...The same applies to the *ukiyo-e* wood-block masters. Yoshida Hanbei first studied the old-fashioned style of Shōgorō (Hinaya Ryūho Shōemon?—trans.), but when he started to produce pictures in a style of his own, it became the fashion for every book published in Kyōto or Ōsaka to have illustrations by Yoshida Hanbei, to the exclusion of all other artists. In Edo there was Hishikawa Moronobu, known as the first of the *Yamato-e* masters, and the productions of these two men monopolised the *kansai* and *kantō* respectively.' It seems probable that Yoshida Hanbei died in the last decade of the seventeenth century. Apart from the illustrations which he provided for the works of others, he wrote and illustrated two works of his own, which are now valuable sources of information on the customs and scenes of the brothel quarters of Saikaku's day. These are *Kōshoku Kinmō Zui* (1686) and *Kōshoku Kaiawase* (1687), and are his most celebrated works. Makieshi Genzaburō, who illustrated certain later *ukiyo-zōshi* by Saikaku, was probably a younger contemporary of Yoshida Hanbei. He is known to have provided the illustrations, and possibly the text, for *Jinrin Kinmō Zui* (1690), which is also a valuable source for students of Saikaku's society.

The illustrations to *Nippon Eitai-gura* carry no signature but are attributed, on stylistic grounds, to Yoshida Hanbei. In addition to the decorations which head the list of contents to each of the six books—a row of doorways displaying the shop-blinds of the merchants concerned in the stories—there are ten single-page illustrations, roughly 5 in. × 7 in. in dimension, and twenty-one double-page illustrations. There is, of course, no use of colour. The time-honoured Japanese convention is observed of viewing each scene from a point above, at an angle of forty-five degrees, and the upper or lower portion of the picture is frequently decorated with a formalised cloud. If the roof of a house is in such a position as to block our view of the principal subjects, it is removed, though the drifting clouds are retained. Season, locality, and the ages or occupations of the characters are frequently suggested by the use of well-known symbols—bamboo for New Year, a water-wheel for Yodo, a flat cap for the master of a household, the implements of the particular trade somewhere in view. Occasionally two separate incidents of a story are suggested in one illustration: the episodes of the Ise lobsters and the pit-digging in IV, 5, of the clock and the clerks' gossip in V, 1, of the lacquer and the water-wheel in VI, 4. The art, as may be judged, is not purely representational.

I. THE SHOP-BLINDS (*nōren*) HEADING EACH BOOK

It is not clear how many of these are fanciful, and how many represent the blinds actually displayed by the contemporary merchants concerned. Probably most are imagined by the artist.

II. ILLUSTRATIONS TO THE TEXT

A brief explanation of each illustration is given below.

Book I

p. 15. The interest on the borrowed thousand *zeni* arrives at Mizuma-*dera*. At the left a black-robed priest sits before the register of loans. Two pilgrims return with temple souvenirs across their shoulders.

p. 19. Ōgiya shows the letter to the courtesan's manageress (*yarite*) in the Shimabara quarter. In the background are, from left to right, a male attendant (*rokushaku*), an attendant courtesan (*hiki-bune*), a girl apprentice (*kaburo*), and the *tayū* Morokoshi.

p. 21. The Jinzū-*maru*, with seamen and merchants. Bales of rice are near the sail. The ship in the illustration is very much smaller than that described in the text, and is not intended to be a realistic representation.

p. 28. Mitsui Kurōemon's drapery store in Edo. A *samurai* customer sits on the platform at the shop-front, an attendant with clothes-box (*hasami-bako*) nearby. One clerk weighs coins on a *hakari-zao*, another makes entries in the great register (*daifuku-chō*), and another calculates on the abacus. A fourth displays rolls of cloth to a customer. Mitsui Kurōemon sits on the right, wearing a flat cap (*oki-zukin*) and formal dress of starched jacket and overskirts (*kataginu* and *hakama*). He carries at his waist two swords (a privilege granted only to *samurai* and special categories of merchants).

p. 32. The lottery for the widow's house. The widow is possibly seated second from the left, and those seated with her are either witnesses or specially honoured participants—a *Shintō* and a Buddhist priest to her left, an ascetic of the Jugen-dō sect (*yamabushi*) before her, and a two-sworded *samurai* seated at the front of the group. The girl on the extreme right of the left-hand picture, with a ribbon about her sleeves, is a maidservant—probably the one who wins. The five men at the right are the officials in charge of the lottery.

Book II

p. 37. The rice cakes (*mochi*) are delivered at Fuji-ichi's shop by female porters. A clerk in the shop-front tests the weight of the cakes on a large balance (*chigi*). In the interior Fuji-ichi makes entries in the ledger (*daifuku-chō*). To his left is the box in which the ledger is stored, marked *Daifuku-chō*, and before him is his ink-tablet chest (*kake-suzuri*). A clerk weighs coins on a *tenbin* balance, and another calculates on the abacus (*soroban*). On the extreme right is an apprentice from the cake-shop carrying the moneybag. Various vendors are selling articles connected with New Year—fern decorations, sea-bream (*tai*), and children's battledores (*hago-ita*). On the left, in the garden, are dancing beggars, with ferns on their heads.

p. 42. The thunderbolt god (*kaminari*) smashes Kibeiji's cooking pot (*nabe-gama*). Kibeiji, his wife, and his child are shown. The sign at the right reads 'Soy sauce' (*shōyu*).

p. 45. Shinroku is chased by his father from the bathroom. At top left is the tub in the bathroom, and at bottom left is a servant holding Shinroku's clothes. The old man and his wife wear flat caps. The illustration shows the master in the act of pursuing Shinroku with a stick, but the text implies that Shinroku hastily departed before his father discovered him.

p. 51. Tengu Gennai harpoons the monstrous whale. Gennai is in the boat top right. Each boat displays a windflower-crested flag. The man in the bow of the boat top left prepares to jump on the whale's back to cut a hole with his sword and attach the hawser.

p. 54. The scene in the kitchen and a reception room of the broker Abumiya. Boiled rice is being ladled from a vat above a large furnace into wooden pails. A servant is fanning a charcoal brazier, upon which fish are being broiled. The vat in the raised section of the kitchen possibly contains bean-paste soup (*miso-shiru*). A kitchen-maid, with cords holding back the sleeves of her *kimono*, stands before a set of dishes. In the reception room refreshments are being set before the visiting clients by service girls (*shaku*), their sashes bound in bows at their backs.

NOTE ON THE ILLUSTRATIONS

Book III

p. 61. Jinbei stands at the southern end of Nihon bridge in Edo. A *samurai* on horseback, preceded by attendant *samurai* and a standard-bearer, and accompanied by servants bearing clothes-boxes (*hasami-bako*), passes over the bridge. The man behind Jinbei is possibly a carpenter, carrying a wooden box.

p. 65. Sanya, seated on an imported rug and leaning on an elbow-rest, watches a 'Fan Battle'.

p. 69. A priest raises the curtain before the image of Kannon at Hase-*dera*. Kikuya no Zenzō is probably the worshipper in the foreground of the balcony. A feature of Hase-*dera* is the long flight of covered stone steps leading to the principal shrine, which stands on a high platform on the hillside. Pilgrims are climbing the steps. The pilgrims on the platform are viewing the image at Kikuya's expense.

p. 74. Strings of *zeni*, equivalent in value to Izuya's outstanding debts, are presented to the priests (in black robes) on Mount Kōya. The money is being piled in a Buddhist graveyard, to symbolise 'the cenotaph of debts'. In the background is a temple.

p. 77. The rich Edo merchant, returning on horseback from the Ise pilgrimage, sees Chūsuke's daughter selling baskets in Fuchū. Two-sworded *samurai* stare at her.

Book IV

p. 82. The poor dyer Kikyōya and his wife worship the god of poverty at New Year. Before the straw dummy is an offering tray and an incense-burner. The implements of a dyer are at bottom left. The roof-style, wooden shingles held down by rocks (*torifuki-yane*), indicates poverty. The significance of the cat chasing a rat is not clear, though rats in houses are held to be bringers of good luck.

p. 84. Kikyōya and his wife are seen as master and mistress of a prosperous household. In the background is a bag of *zeni* and a *tenbin* balance for weighing money. The other persons are presumably employees.

p. 88. Kanaya tearfully leaves the Maruyama brothel quarter with the priceless folding screen (*byōbu*). The *tayū* Kachō is in the centre. Behind her are an attendant courtesan (*hiki-bune*) and a girl apprentice (*kaburo*), the latter weeping.

p. 91. Fundōya, seated in a palanquin (*kago*), has scattered *zeni* to the beggars along the road between the Ise shrines. The two men squatting in the rear are palanquin bearers. One attendant carries a clothes-box (*hasami-bako*), whilst the others scatter the *zeni*. Three female beggars, gaudily dressed, have emerged from behind the net curtain of their wayside hut and are scrambling for the money. One holds a *samisen*, another a bean-paste sieve (*miso-koshi*).

p. 95. The dying tea dealer, clutching his money, rushes about the sick-room. On the floor are strings of *zeni*, packages of silver coins, and gold *koban*. The bedclothes are piled in the room behind, and a pillow is at the dealer's feet. The men-servants have grasped sticks, and a priest is sitting with the women-servants. At the right are jars and baskets of tea, and a weighing-rod. In the garden at the left is a storehouse (*niwa-gura*).

p. 100. Hinokuchiya bids his idle servant dig a pit. On both sides of the doorway are New Year pine and bamboo decorations (*kado-matsu*), and over the doorway is a *Shintō* symbol of New Year (*shime-kazari*). In the interior the mistress is receiving guests near a *hōrai* tray, which is laden with ferns, oranges, fish and prawns. The tray is set on an offering stand (*sanbō*).

Book V

p. 107. Chinese traders land their wares at Nagasaki. The traders have Chinese beards and moustaches, and hold Chinese-style fans, but their dress and hats seem more reminiscent of Portuguese or Dutch styles. At the left a Chinese trader is being interviewed by a representative of the military government of Nagasaki, who holds a Japanese folding fan, and wears formal dress of starched jacket and overskirts (*kataginu* and *hakama*). Behind him are spear-head standards. The Japanese near the trader is possibly an official interpreter. On the verandah are rolls of imported silk, and a clock (the object surmounted by a cross). The scene at the top right is possibly intended to suggest the episode in which the clerks tell each other stories about their employers.

p. 111. *Shaka Jirō* of Yodo hawks fish to a *ryōgaeya* in Kyōto. The fishmonger himself was later to become a wealthy *ryōgaeya*. The man sitting on the shop-front, smoking a long pipe (*kiseru*) and taking refreshments, is a customer of the *ryōgaeya*, changing money. A clerk is weighing the customer's money on a *tenbin* balance.

p. 116. Kawabata no Kusuke's farm in Yamato. The master is smoking a *kiseru*. Rice is being sifted at the left. Bales of rice are in the background. At the right cotton is being ginned, and bales of ginned cotton are being weighed and loaded on horses for transport to the cotton brokers.

p. 121. The *rōnin* in their house on Higurashi's farm, near Edo. The two at the rear are fencing with wooden sticks. In the adjoining room a *rōnin* is teaching Higurashi's son how to construe the Chinese classics.

p. 125. Yorozuya's wife, returning to Mimasaka province from her pilgrimage to Ise, sees the fine fashions of Kyōto and Ōsaka. Yorozuya's wife, in travelling dress (dust-guard across her face, and straw hat) is at top right with her attendants. It is not clear whether the scene is Kyōto or Ōsaka. The dog attacking a cat would appear to be no more than an incidental decoration.

Book VI

p. 130. The young Toshigoshiya shows his father the betrothal presents. The son sits to the left of the pair of sea-bream, his mother to the right. At bottom left is a storehouse (*niwa-gura*). On the right are shown activities connected with the family trade. Customers are calling for bean-paste (*miso*). The small barrels are of soy sauce (*shōyu*). The signs over the doorway read 'Bean-paste for Sale', and 'Soy sauce for Sale'.

p. 133. The apprentice boy from Ise at the feast of Ebisu. The master is top centre, in formal dress (*kataginu* and *hakama*), wearing a sword (*waki-zashi*). The mistress is on his right. The apprentice boy sits directly in front, facing them. In the foreground are two clerks, and between them and the mistress is a maid-servant with a pot of tea. In the alcove (*tokonoma*) is hanging a picture of Ebisu. The god has a fishing-rod in one hand, a large sea-bream under his arm, and an *eboshi* cap on his head. Before the picture are *sake* and sea-bream on offering stands (*sanbō*).

p. 138. Bales of imported silks are carried into Kogatanaya's storehouse in Sakai, to be kept until prices rise. The waves indicate that the goods have come from overseas, and the rows of pine trees possibly suggest the long years of prosperity to come. A clerk notes the purchase in a ledger, an ink-tablet chest by his side (*kake-suzuri*).

p. 140. The lump of lacquer in the river Yodo. In the background are the Yodo water-wheel and Yodo castle. The former suggests the episode of Yōzaemon's private water-wheel.

p. 145. The three couples at New Year, celebrating the grandfather's eighty-eighth anniversary. New Year pine and bamboo decorations are by the doorway, and at the extreme left, beyond the verandah, is a branch of flowering plum. Pine, bamboo and plum are symbols of long life. The three couples are seated in order of seniority from the right of the illustration. A maid-servant sits by a teapot. Before the grandfather and grandmother are offering stands (*sanbō*) bearing rice cake, a lobster, and a *Shintō* symbol (*nusa*). At the left, on the platform for visitors, are two lengths of bamboo across a rice-measure (*masu*) and a handsaw.

BOOK I

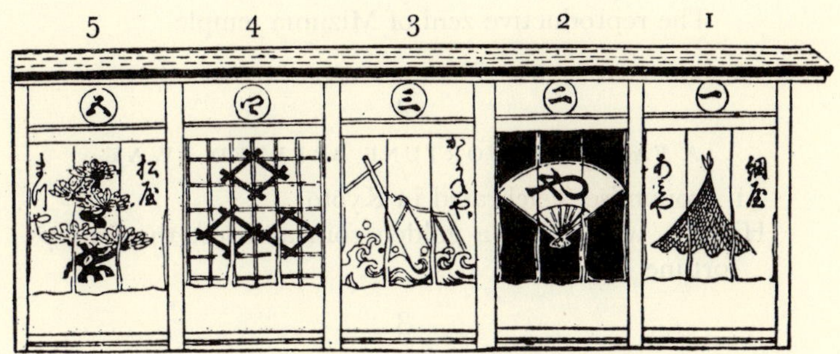

BOOK I

I. *Riding to success on a lucky horse*

HEAVEN says nothing, and the whole earth grows rich beneath its silent rule.[1] Men, too, are touched by heaven's virtue; yet, in their greater part, they are creatures of deceit. They are born, it seems, with an emptiness of soul, and must take their qualities wholly from things without.[2] To be born thus empty into this modern age, this mixture of good and ill, and yet to steer through life on an honest course[3] to the splendours of success—this is a feat reserved for paragons of our kind, a task beyond the nature of the normal man.

But the first consideration for all, throughout life, is the earning of a living. And in this matter, each one of us must bow before the shrine of the Heavenly Goddess of Thrift (not Shintō priests alone, but samurai, farmers, traders, artisans, and even Buddhist bonzes), and we must husband gold and silver as the deity enjoins. Though mothers and fathers give us life, it is money alone which preserves it.[4]

But the life of man, at the longest estimate, is a day which knows no morrow. To some it seems a day cut short at eventide. Heaven and earth, the poets say, are but a wayside inn for Time, a traveller, on journey through the ages, and our fleeting lives are phantoms in Time's dreams.[5] People will tell us that when we die, and vanish in a moment's wisp of smoke, all our gold is less than dross and buys us nothing in the world beyond. It is true enough, and yet—is not what we leave behind of service to our sons and our posterity? And while we live (to take a shorter view) how many of life's desirable things is it not within the power of gold to grant us? In all the world there are five,[6] perhaps: no more than that. Has any treasure which we see on prints of treasure ships[7] more potency? Those invisible-making hats and capes,[8] for instance, worn by devils on an island no one has ever seen—they would leak as much as any in a cloud-burst. So lay aside your dreams of things beyond man's reach, turn your minds to what lies close at hand, and work with a will at the trades you have chosen. Since luck and profit come only to those who persevere, let none of you squander a moment in sloth between dawn and dusk.

Above all you must make humanity and justice the basis of your conduct, and worship the gods and the Buddhas. This is the custom of Japan.

It was the day of the Horse, the first in the second moon.[9] Through the spring haze shrouding the hills men and women, rich and poor, were making their way on pilgrimage to the shrine of Kannon at Mizuma temple in Izumi province.[10] None went in search of enlightenment. The road they trod together was the road of greed. Passing along endless mossy by-ways, and over weary new-swaled wastes of reed and mugwort, and coming in time to this desolate village, still bare of any form of blossom, they made their vows to the temple's Buddha—but their prayers were mere requests for wealth, varying only in the quantity each considered his due. Even for Kannon the thought of replying to them all, one by one, was too much. Instead, a general pronouncement was made, in a miraculous voice issuing from behind the sacred alcove's curtain.

'Nowadays, in this vale of sorrow,' it said, 'there is no such thing as easy money, and it is obvious enough, without your asking me, what each must do. You country people have your allotted means and skills. The men must dig the fields; the women must weave at the loom; and each must work at his task from dawn to dusk. To every one of you I say the same.'

But (such is human stupidity) even this inspired advice failed to sink into the pilgrims' ears.

Nothing on earth is more terrifying than the interest which grows from debts. It was the custom at this temple for the pilgrims to borrow small sums of lucky zeni.[11] If they took one, the following year they returned two; if a hundred, they repaid two hundred; and since these coins were Kannon's everyone took care to use them for no idle purpose, and to return them in due time to the temple. Amongst the pilgrims on this occasion, most of whom were borrowing the usual sums of three, five, or perhaps as much as ten zeni, was a certain powerfully built, plainly dressed[12] young man of twenty-three or four.[13] The top-knot at the back of his head was too far forward for the fashion; his kimono was of a long out-dated cut, with sleeves too short and skirts too tight; the layers underneath, like the kimono itself, were of stout pongee dyed in patternless deep blue, and the collar band was reinforced with the same material; he wore a cloak of striped Ueda pongee[14] lined with cotton; the dagger at his waist was short, and muffled in a dust-protector.[15] The impression he gave was evidently of no importance to him, and now he had hitched the bottoms of his skirts to his loin-

The interest arrives at Mizuma temple

cloth, and was to all appearances already on his way home, carrying the rough-made basket of local potatoes, strung from a wild camellia branch, which was the usual souvenir for pilgrims to this temple. He turned aside, however, and approached the platform before the shrine.

'One thousand zeni, please,' he said.

The priest on duty gave him what he asked, a whole thousand zeni on a string, and even forgot to enquire his name and address. When he had gone no one had any idea where to find him again.

'In all the years since the foundation of our temple,' said the priests, when they gathered together to discuss the matter, 'there has been no other case of our loaning a thousand zeni, and of all our borrowers this man is the first to ask for so much. It seems hardly likely that he will ever repay it, and henceforth we must make it a temple rule not to lend such large sums.'

The man's home was Edo in Musashi province, and there, by the wharves at the end of Koami-chō,[16] he ran a shipping agency.[17] From now on his household's fortunes steadily improved, and in his delight at this he placed the temple money in a small ink-tablet chest,[18] and on the lid he wrote the words 'The Good Ship Luck'. Once, when certain fishermen were about to set out in their boats, he told them where this money came from, and lent them a hundred zeni each. After that the rumour spread all along the coast that good fortune befell any who borrowed the money, and the number of borrowers steadily increased. Returned with interest on each occasion, and immediately re-loaned, the sum grew larger every year. The merchant meanwhile carefully calculated the interest due to the temple, at the rate of one hundred per cent. per annum, and in the thirteenth year, by which time the original one thousand zeni had swollen to a debt of eight million one hundred and ninety-two thousand, he sent the whole sum along the Tōkai-dō[19] on specially hired pack-horses.[20] When it was unloaded in heaps at the temple, the priests at first could only clap their hands in dumb amazement; but later they called a conference, and all agreed that the matter should be made a source of edification for future generations. They hired hosts of carpenters from Kyōto, and in commemoration of this truly wondrous profit from their zeni they raised a fine pagoda. The merchant, to mark his success, set lamps to burn with never-dying flames within his money storehouse.[21] His name was Amiya,[22] and he was famed throughout Musashi province.

Those who inherit nothing from their fathers and whose fortunes, won by sheer ability, exceed five hundred kanme of silver,[23] are known as Men of Substance. If their fortunes mount above a thousand kanme, we call them Millionaires.[24] By interest alone such money grows to tens on tens of thousands, and its voices swell in silvery songs to sing its lord's posterity ten thousand years of luck.[25]

2. *A fan-shop fortune breezed away*

THE things which best suit private houses, it has been said, are plum, cherry, pine, and maple[1]—but what of gold, silver, rice, and zeni? A garden landscape is a charming sight, but more charming still is a row of garden store-sheds; and more fascinating than the changing colours of the seasons are the changing prices of the goods within those sheds. These are the joys we shall find in the Paradise of Kikenjō![2]

Such, at least, was the settled conviction of a certain merchant who lived, not so long ago, in Kyōto. Not once in his life did he stray eastwards across Shijō bridge,[3] nor venture off Ōmiya street to the quarter west of Tanba-guchi.[4] He kept his money safe from temple priests and avoided the acquaintance of unemployed samurai.[5] In the event of a slight cold, or some stomach-worm trouble, he used only medicines concocted by himself. All day long he worked industriously at his proper calling, and when evening came he never set off for town, but amused himself at home by repeating Noh excerpts remembered from his youth—and even in this, in deference to the neighbours, he kept his voice low and provided entertainment for none but himself. Nor did he burn lamp oil to follow a text, but sang only the songs he knew by heart. By these habits he avoided all possible sources of expense. Not once in his whole career did he wear out the thong of a sandal, nor tear a sleeve by catching it on the head of a nail, and as a result of this constant attention to the smallest of details he collected in a single lifetime the great sum of two thousand kanme. When he reached the auspicious age of eighty-eight he became the envy of his neighbourhood, and people begged bamboo grain-levels [6] from him that they might share his luck. However, life has its limit, and that very year, when the rains of the tenth moon were falling, clouds of sickness suddenly gathered about the old man and he passed quietly away. Since he left only one son behind him, this young man became the sole legatee of his father's whole fortune, and at the tender age of twenty-one, by accident of birth, became a millionaire. The son was even more devoted to the principle of economy than his father. At the so-called 'distribution of mementoes of the deceased' he bestowed upon his numerous relations not so much as a single chopstick. The seven days of mourning completed, on the eighth day he threw open the shutters at the shop-front, and turned his whole mind to the business of earning a living. For fear of creating an expensive appetite he would even remember not to hurry when enquiring about friends after a fire, and he remained completely absorbed in economies of this nature for that year and well into the next.

One day he suddenly realised that it was exactly a year since his father had died, and, as an act of commemoration, he visited the family temple. On his way back memories of the old days kept returning. Tears fell, and even as he wiped them away with his sleeve, he recalled that this homespun check cloth was his father's.

'He told me he chose it because it would never wear out', he reflected. 'When you think of it, he ought never to have died when he did. If he had only lived another twenty-two years it would have lasted him a full century, [7] and to die so young was a waste of good cloth.'

As he continued homewards, with parsimonious reflections gradually gaining the upper hand even in such matters as this, he reached the vicinity of Murasakino. [8] At the foot of the bamboo fence around the

Imperial Herbal Gardens a sealed letter was lying, and the apprenticed maid-servant who accompanied him, carrying the empty basket which had contained the rice offering to the temple, picked the letter up and handed it to him. It was addressed, he noted, to 'Hanakawa-sama', and on the reverse was written 'From Nisan'.[9] The flap was still pasted down, and in addition to a seal which had been carefully impressed, over all was inscribed in bold strokes of the brush the prayer 'Go Dairiki Bosatsu'.[10]

'Hanakawa must be some court noble,' he thought, 'though it's not a name I've ever heard before.'

Later, on reaching home, he asked a friend's opinion.

'It seems to be for some prostitute[11] in Shimabara', the man said, glancing at the address and immediately tossing the letter aside.

However, thinking that at least there was a scrap of Sugiwara paper[12] to be gained, and nothing to be lost, he waited until the man was gone, and then broke the seal and looked inside. To his astonishment a one-bu piece[13] dropped out. First he tested it on a touchstone; next he weighed it—and noted with delight that according to the scale on the arm of the balance it was precisely one monme two fun. Quieting the palpitations within his breast he congratulated himself on this unexpected stroke of luck, and warned his servants not to mention the matter to a soul. Then he read the letter; but there was very little of romance and passion in it—from start to finish it was set out methodically, point by point:

> Your request has come at an awkward time of the year, but you are dearer to me than my own life, so I have borrowed something on the security of my next spring's salary[14] and am sending it to you. Two monme of this is payment for your services at various times. The whole of the remainder is a gift. Use it to repay some of the debts which have accumulated over the years. Every one must plan according to his means—a rich patron from Kyūshū gave Madam Nokaze of the Ōzakaya[15] three hundred one-bu pieces for her Chrysanthemum festival expenses,[16] but this single coin of mine carries with it no less solicitude. If I had more do you think I should begrudge it to you?

It was a pathetic note, and as he read his compassion mounted. Whatever he did, he could hardly pocket the money. It would be a dreadful thing to do in the face of such constancy as this letter showed. He would have liked to return it to the man, but he did not know his address; so he decided to go to Shimabara—he knew where that was—enquire for Hanakawa and hand the letter to her.

Smoothing back his stray side-locks a little he started out from the house. It was only a one-bu piece that he was returning, but the more he thought about it, the more he begrudged it, and he changed his mind six or seven times. However, at length he arrived before the gateway of the pleasure quarter. Unable to bring himself to enter immediately, he dawdled awhile outside until he saw a man emerge, coming from a reception house[17] to fetch saké. He approached him diffidently.

'Excuse me,' he said, 'do you suppose there would be any objection if I passed through this gate without previous notice?'

The man was too surprised to reply, and merely motioned him on with a jerk of the chin. There was no further excuse for delay. He removed his braided hat[18] and clutched it in his hand. Bowing apologetically all the way he passed before the row of tea houses inside the entrance[19] and finally reached the streets of the courtesans. There he chanced to meet the present Madam Morokoshi of Ichimonjiya,[20] who was walking in public procession with her attendants.

Ōgiya meets Madam Morokoshi

'Pardon me,' he ventured, 'but could you possibly direct me to a lady by the name of Hanakawa?'

'I am not acquainted with her', said the great courtesan briefly, and referred him with a glance to her manageress.

'You must ask somewhere over there', said the manageress, pointing to a row of doorways hung with blue curtains.[21]

Standing in the rear was a male attendant, showing obvious signs of impatience.

'And when you're with the strumpet, we'll all go and watch you!' he shouted.

'Really!' exclaimed the young man. 'If that was the sort of thing I had in mind I should hardly have troubled these ladies for their kind assistance.'

He moved away to the rear, and, after a further round of enquiries, eventually found the place he was seeking. But when he asked after the lady in question he was brusquely informed that Hanakawa was a prostitute of the fourth grade, price two monme, that she had been indisposed these last two or three days, and was not receiving visitors. Without delivering the package he prepared to return home. But even as he did so, disreputable instincts—which had never previously entered into his calculations—began to assert themselves.

'After all, it's not really my own money,' he argued to himself, 'and it will be something to remember all my life. Provided I limit myself to this piece of gold, and just this one day of amusement, it will be all right—and it should provide some good stories for my old age, too.'

His mind was resolved. The expensive Reception House street, of course, was out of the question, so he called at the tea houses. There, climbing to the first floor of a place owned by a certain Fujiya Hikoemon, [22] he hired a girl on the day-shift, at nine monme, [23] and fuddled his head with more saké than he had ever drunk before.

From this arose further visits: first he practised the rudiments; later he commenced the interchange of amatory correspondence; finally, after a graded ascent, he started to hire even courtesans of the premier rank. It was at this time that the Kyōto brothel entertainers known as 'The Four Heavenly Kings' [24] were active, and under the encouragement and guidance of these—Gansai, Kagura, Ōmu, and Ranshu—he became marvellously accomplished in this mode of life. Subsequently new fashions for the well-dressed pleasure-seeker were modelled on whatever he wore. He earned the nickname of 'The Love Breeze of the Fan Shop', and he blew gales of silver through the brothel quarter. Man is unpredictable. In four or five years he had wafted away two thousand kanme: the fires in his household were dying out, but he soon had no wind left to blow them into life again. He had only an old fan, a memento of his business name, [25] and with this in his hand he scraped a daily living as an Utai beggar, [26] singing his own fate in the words 'Life has its peak, but soon its decline'. Whenever a certain Kamadaya, [27] a man of steady wealth, saw or heard him, he sighed to think of that wasted money, so difficult to make these days, and he told this story to his children.

The Jinzū Maru with seamen and merchants

3. *Steady trade winds for the good ship Jinzū*[1]

VIRTUOUS indeed must have been the lives of the daimyō in former existences! Seeing them now, sublimely satisfied in every desire, they seem like Latter Day Buddhas. No other title can adequately describe them. Be that as it may, there are distinctions even in the revenues of daimyō. Start from the year of the Buddha's death,[2] calculating through the centuries to the present day, and deduct annually from a certain lord's one million two hundred koku[3] of rice the five hundred koku of a lesser lord, and you will still have a remainder. A world in which even the differences between major and minor lords are so immense is truly broad.[4]

In Izumi province there is a certain Karakaneya,[5] master of 'The House of Bronze', who has lately made a fortune in gold and silver. He has built himself a great ocean-going merchant ship, which he calls the Jinzū Maru,[6] and in this ship—which carries, without danger from overloading, cargoes of rice up to three thousand and seven hundred koku—he voyages where he chooses along our northern coasts,[7] and then makes back to the port of Ōsaka, where, by dealing in the rice market, he has brought his household steadily to great prosperity. And all has been due solely to his own good management.

Ōsaka is the foremost trading centre of Japan, and in the Kitahama rice-exchange [8] five thousand kanme in promissory notes change hands within the quarter-hour. While the rice lies heaped in mountains in the granaries, speculators scan the heavens for signs of a storm this evening or rain tomorrow morning, [9] and ponder the quarter whence the clouds are drifting. All night they calculate the risks, and on the morrow boldly buy or sell. A possible rise of one fun per ten koku, or a fall of two fun, are the stakes in their competition. They form a solid fraternity in which every member knows the face of every other, and, though it be a matter of a thousand or ten thousand koku, once two parties have clapped hands over a deal neither retracts an inch from his promise. In the general run of business deals—even if formal notes are produced bearing a surety's seal, and a contract is recorded that the money will be returned 'without fail, no matter at what time, in accordance with your convenience'—promises are deferred and irksome lawsuits follow; but here contracts whose surety is as uncertain as the clouds of a fickle sky are never broken. Within the agreed time, regardless of gain or loss, sales or purchases are honoured. The great merchants of Ōsaka, the foremost in Japan, are great in spirit, too; and such are their methods of business.

The bridge of Naniwa [10] spans their world, [11] and from here, looking westwards, a Hundred Views unfold themselves. The whiteness of earthen walls beneath the closely-ranged rooftops of a thousand brokers' agencies is a theft from an early morning snow-scape. The tapering stacks of rice-bales are no other than mountains—mountains which move as carters haul them to the warehouses—and their rumbling on the broad highway is like some subterranean explosion of mortars. Lighters and other small craft [12] glide in endless procession over the river waves, looking not unlike willow leaves scattered on autumn streams. The lithe and powerful porters on the wharves, brandishing their pointed shafts [13] in eager rivalry, call to mind Chinese scenes of tigers lurking in a bamboo forest. Great ledgers flutter their pages in clouds, and counting-frames rain hails of beads. Night and day the tap of mallets on metal scales drowns the hour-chimes of the Kitahama Bell, [14] and a breeze of prosperity flowing through the shops blows back the awnings in their doorways. There is a whole host of merchant houses here, and amongst them, to take only those on Naka-no-shima, [15] are such as Oka, Hizenya, Kiya, Fukaeya, Higoya, Shioya, Ōtsukaya,

Kuwanaya, Kōnoikeya, Kamiya, Bizenya, Uwajimaya, Tsukaguchiya, and Yodoya, the masters of which, after long and successful careers in this district, have now ceased to trouble themselves over petty business matters,[16] and live in great state, with vast numbers of people dependent on them for their livelihoods.

In Ōsaka even persons who started life with very little, and who formerly lived in the country-side round about, have risen to be addressed as 'Master', to wear flat caps, to carry hammer-headed walking sticks, and to go about in style accompanied by shoe-change boys. Generally they are all sons of nearby farming people from Yamato, Kawachi, Settsu, and Izumi provinces.[17] The eldest son is kept at home, but the younger ones are sent out to serve as apprentices. At first, with noses unwiped and country smells still clinging to their hands and feet, they are employed to run small errands for bean-curd or lemon flavouring. In a few years, after they have been presented with two or three sets of clothes,[18] they are allowed to select a crest for themselves, and they start to worry about the way their hair is cut. As their appearance becomes more grown-up, they are employed as attendants, and are summoned to accompany their master to Noh plays or on boating excursions. There—if they do not 'write numbers on the flowing stream'[19]—at least, while minding the children, they practise writing characters on trays of sand, and additions and subtractions on the abacus. As soon as they have come of age and adopted the 'sumimae'[20] haircut, they start to carry the moneybags on debt-collecting rounds, and so, in due course, they reach the status of clerk. Thereupon, perhaps, learning quickly to do as they see others do, they speculate in secret with the firm's credit, quietly pocketing all private profits and arranging for the master's books to bear all private losses; and before the all-important time arrives for such young men to be set up in independent businesses, they have brought trouble on master and guarantor alike. If there is no hope of reclaiming the money they have spent, the matter is finally settled out of court by arbitration—but the future holds for them nothing but a life of hawking in the streets.[21] The numbers of such young men are beyond counting. But others, of better character and wit, have even become millionaires! For, as a rule, a well-to-do person in Ōsaka is not the heir to generations of wealth. He is more often some humble clerk—a 'Kichizō' or 'Sansuke' —who has a quick rise in the world and comes into money. Gradually, as opportunities offer, he acquires the elements of Chinese and Japanese verse composition, kickball, archery, the koto, the flute, the drums, incense blending, and the tea ceremony,[22] and by associating with the best people he even loses his old vulgarities of speech. In life it is training rather than birth which counts, and it is not unknown for the unwanted offspring of noble families to be obliged to earn their livings by hawking home-made paper flowers.

So it is that for an apprentice the most decisive stroke of fortune lies in the type of master by whom he is trained. Compared with this even the prosperity of the neighbourhood in which he works is of little significance. There was a petty joiner who lived somewhere in Kasho-machi in Kitahama, and even he had two small apprentice boys. He regularly supplied ten-kanme money-chests to bankers like Atarashiya and Tennōjiya,[23] and knew the measurements by heart, but he had never seen that amount of money himself; and when his apprentices reached manhood and he set them up in their own businesses, they too, just like their master, manufactured nothing much better than saucepan lids and tinder-boxes. They had never learned how to do anything else. Yet if they had only been apprenticed to one of the larger businesses in the same neighbourhood they would presumably have grown into proportionately greater tradesmen. When you see cases like theirs, you can only feel pity.

There are probably as many ways of making a living as there are straw brooms.[24] In this same district of Kitahama there was an old woman who earned a meagre daily living as a sweeper,[25] clearing up the grains spilt from the porters' testing-shafts when the rice cargoes from the western provinces were brought ashore. Her features were unattractive, and although she had been widowed from the age of twenty-three no one was willing to become her second husband, and she passed her years in sadness, with an only child as her one consolation for the future. One year, some time ago, as the result of a general revision of the rates of taxation in all the provinces[26] and a simultaneous bumper harvest, rice was shipped to this market in great volume, the unloading of each ship taking more than a day and a night, and the rented warehouses became so packed that it was a problem where to store it all. A great deal of the rice was spilt in the process of moving it to new places, and this the old woman swept on to her rubbish heap. Each day, after taking enough for the morning and evening meals, she had a pile of fourteen or fifteen shō[27] left over. This was enough to make her wish for more, and by exercising economy in the course of that year she quickly increased her store to seven and a half koku. This she secretly sold. The following year she again collected a store of rice, and each year her hoard of money grew, so that in a little over twenty years she had put by a nest-egg of twelve and a half kanme. Nor was her son suffered to remain idle. From the age of nine she made him collect the discarded lids of rice-bales, weave them into zeni-strings,[28] and sell them to the money-changers and the brokers. In this small way he made surprising profits. Having thus started to earn his way by his own efforts, he later loaned koban to reliable people at the usual daily rates of interest, and smaller sums to others at 'no security' rates. Next he had the idea of setting up a zeni-shop[29] in a quiet part of Imabashi.[30] Kept busy from morn till night by calls from farming people, he changed their petty silver into zeni and, as his capital grew, their chōgin into komagane, and koban into mame-ita.[31] Not for a moment was he away from the scales. Day by day his profits mounted, and within ten years he had become the leading figure in the trade of his federation, lending money in all directions but a debtor to no one. Things reached the point where even clerks coming from the larger money-exchanges to buy zeni bowed low before him and sought his favours. In the koban market, too, no sooner had he bought than prices would suddenly rise, and whenever he sold they straightway sank. Naturally people closely studied his methods in these matters, and lowering their hands in obeisance all acknowledged him as their master. Though there were some who, having looked up his pedigree, proudly declared that it was degrading to make a living by imitating such a common fellow, even these, when business was bad and they were short of cash, came to him with requests for loans. Such is the power of money! Later, when he became a daimyō's agent[32] and made a speciality of business with the various great mansions, no one mentioned his past any more. He married into a distinguished merchant's family and built a mansion with many storehouses attached. As for the broom, small reed brush, and cheap round fan, which his mother had used in sweeping up the rice—though it is said that to keep such things is to invite poverty—he preserved each one as a family treasure, displaying them all in the north-west corner of his house.

Though a man may travel through all the provinces, the place where (even in these days) he should try working for a fortune is Kitahama in Ōsaka. Here, they say, money flows by the wharves and walks in the streets.

4. *Ancient on-account and modern cash-down*

ANCIENT simplicity is gone. With the growth of pretence the people of today are satisfied with nothing but finery, with nothing but what is beyond their station or purse. You have only to look at the way our citizens' wives and daughters dress. They can hardly go further. To forget one's proper place is to invite the wrath of heaven.[1] Even the august nobility[2] are satisfied with clothes of nothing more splendid than Kyōto habutae[3] silk, and in the military class the formal black dress of five crests[4] is considered ill-suited to none, from minor retainers to the greatest daimyō. But of recent years, ever since some ingenious Kyōto creatures started the fashion, every variety of splendid material has been used for men's and women's clothes, and the drapers' sample-books have blossomed in a riot of colour. What with delicate Ukiyo stencil-patterns,[5] multi-coloured 'Imperial' designs, and dappled motifs in wash-graded tints, man must now seek in other worlds for an exotic effect, for every device on earth has been exhausted. Paying for his wife's wardrobe, or his daughter's wedding trousseau, has lightened the pocket of many a merchant, and blighted his hopes in business. A courtesan's daily parade of splendour is made in the cause of earning a living. Amateur beauties—when they are not blossom-viewing in spring, maple-viewing in autumn, or being married—can manage well enough without dressing in layers of conspicuous silks.

Not long ago, in a tailor's shop set back a little from Muromachi street,[6] and displaying on its curtains the crest of a fragrant citron, there was a craftsman who tailored stylish clothes with even more than the usual Kyōto dexterity. Such piles of silk materials and cotton wadding were deposited with him that he enjoyed a constant prospect of the 'Mount of Clothes'[7] without stirring a step from his shop. Though it was always a rush to remove the tacking stitches and apply the smoothing iron in time, each year on the first day of the fourth moon, in readiness for the season's 'Change of Clothes'[8]—even as the impatient cuckoo sounded its first notes in the skies above Mount Machikane[9]—he had ready in his shop a fresh array of splendidly coloured summer kimono. Amongst them one might have seen garments of three distinct layers—scarlet crêpe enclosed within translucent walls of delicate white silk—and garments with sleeves and neck-pieces stiffened with padding. Such things had been unheard of in former days. One step further and we might have been wearing imported

Chinese silks as working clothes. The recent Clothing Edicts [10] were truly for the good of every one of us, in every province in the land; and, on second thoughts, we are grateful. A merchant wearing fine silks is an ugly sight. Homespun is not only more suited to his station, but he looks smarter in it.

With samurai, of course, for whom an imposing appearance is essential in the course of duty, it is not desirable that even the most servantless among them should dress like an ordinary person. In Edo, where peace reigns changeless as the pine, on foundations as firm as the ageless rocks of Tokiwa bridge, [11] drapers' establishments were recently opened in Hon-chō to cater for the great lords. They were branches of Kyōto firms, and proudly advertised their crests in all the 'Guides to Trade'. Managers and clerks, in single-minded devotion to duty, applied their united efforts to the task of securing orders from the various great mansions which favoured them with patronage. Never relaxing for a moment from matters of business, they displayed eloquence and finesse, judgement and ingenuity. Expert in accountancy, and never deceived by a dubious coin, they would gouge the eyes from a living bull for profit. To pass beneath the Tiger gate in the darkness of the night, to prowl a thousand miles [12] in search of custom—such things they accepted as no more than necessary duties; and early next day, while the stars were still shining overhead, they would be hard at work in the shops, checking weights on the rods of their scales. From dawn till dusk they courted the favour of customers—but things were no longer as they used to be. The broad and fertile plain of Musashi [13] was still there, but every inch of the ground had been exploited, and there were no easy pickings left. Formerly, on the occasion of a lord's wedding or a distribution of presents, it had been possible for the contractor—with the friendly co-operation of the lord's chamberlain—to do a little trade on satisfactory terms, but nowadays, with tenders invited from all sides, the expectation of profit was meagre, and the incidental expenses more than balanced it. [14] The true condition of these businesses was a sad story, and orders were supplied to the great households for prestige only. Not only that, but the greater part of the sales were on credit, and accounts remained unsettled year after year. Such money would have been more profitably invested even with a Kyōto banker. The shops were in constant difficulty over the shortage of ready cash to negotiate new bills of exchange, and as a result and also because it was unthinkable suddenly to close down businesses which had only just been opened, they were obliged to limit themselves to small-scale transactions only.

But, do what they might, the accounts balanced no better, and before long the main shops in Kyōto were closed and only the Edo branches remained, with their losses running into hundreds and thousands of kanme. Each firm began devising methods of cutting expenses while the position was still retrievable.[15] But other ways of trade existed, had they known.

In Suruga-chō—a name which brings back memories of the gleam of old koban[16]—a man called Mitsui Kurōemon,[17] risking what capital he had in hand, erected a deep and lofty building of eighteen yards frontage and eighty yards depth,[18] and opened a new shop. His policy was to sell everything for cash, without the inflated charges customary in credit sales. There were more than forty skilled clerks in his service, constantly under the master's watchful eye, and to each he assigned full charge of one type of cloth: one for gold brocades, one for Hino and Gunnai silks,[19] one for habutae, one for damask, one for scarlets, one for hempen overskirts,[20] one for woollen goods, and so on. Having divided the shop into departments in this manner, he willingly supplied anything which his customers asked for, however trifling—a scrap of velvet an inch square, a piece of imported damask suitable for the cover of an eyebrow tweezer, enough scarlet satin to make a spear-head flag, or a single detachable cuff of ryūmon silk.[21] Whenever a samurai required a formal waistcoat[22] for an immediate audience with his lord, or someone was in urgent need of a gown for a dress occasion, Kurōemon asked the messenger to wait, marshalled a score or so of the tailors on his staff, manufactured the garment on the spot, and delivered it immediately to the customer. By such means the business flourished, and the average daily sales were said to amount to one hundred and fifty ryō. The shop was a marvel of convenience to all. To look at, the master was no different from other men—he had the usual eyes, nose, hands, and feet—but in

Mitsui Kurōemon's drapery store

his aptitude for his trade a difference lay. He was the model of a great merchant.

Neatly folded in the alphabetically arranged drawers [23] of his shop were all the materials of Japan and countries overseas, a varied selection of antique silks, Lady Chūjō's homespun mosquito net, [24] Hitomaro's Akashi crêpe, Amida's bib, a strip of Asahina's 'flying-crane' kimono, the mattress which Daruma Taishi used for meditation, Rin Wasei's bonnet, and Sanjō Kokaji's sword sheaths. Absolutely nothing was missing. A firm with such well-filled stock books is indeed fortunate!

5. *A lucky draw from the world of greed*

TAKE care! Kingdoms are destroyed by bandits, houses by rats, and widows by suitors. [1] Marriages are not matters for haste. Nowadays a marriage-broker is no longer a friendly mediator, but a business-woman who makes a profit in proportion to the bride's dowry. If the sum is fifty kanme, she claims a commission of five. To pay out a tenth of a dowry like this as extras, before sending your daughter to her suitor's house, may well break the back of your finances. Marrying off your daughter is a piece of business you may expect to do only once in a lifetime, and, bearing in mind that none of the losses are recoverable later, you should approach the matter with extreme caution.

A glance at the world about will quickly reveal that a rich man who is modest in the display of his wealth is a rare phenomenon, and that those who cut a fine figure on a slender income are more in the fashion of these degenerate times. As soon as their sons arrive at a marriageable age, parents turn their minds to house repairs and interior decorations which they have never been able to afford before, buy new stocks of household equipment, hire extra men-servants and maids, and seek to give an impression of splendid prosperity. All their hopes are centred on a bride's dowry, which it is their secret and disreputable purpose to use as capital in business deals. To give the right impression they travel everywhere in palanquins, and all their family and distant relatives join in the extravagant display, determined to be outdone by no one. Their useless expenditure mounts and mounts, till even the wherewithal to patch a hole in the roof is gone, and the house falls about them in ruins. The parents of eligible daughters, for their part, are no better. For them, only families far above their own station are good enough;

and, in addition to considerations of wealth, they make enquiries for a son-in-law who is an artistic genius, and strikingly handsome into the bargain. But an adept at Noh drums is an adept at dice; [2] a young clerk of fashion will never get out of the habit of visiting brothels; and a man who wins acclaim for his elegant manners at parties is likely to spend your fortune on theatre boys. [3] When you think of it, if you seek a son-in-law who is handsome, sharp in business, a social success, a model of filial piety, untouched by scandal, and a blessing to mankind, where will you find such a creature? Besides, too many good qualities can be embarrassing. Even people of exalted station have their shortcomings, and with lesser beings it is doubly so. Five faults in ten should be overlooked: a man may be short and bald, but if he has a gift for sales talk and has not diminished the fortune his father left him, he is a suitable prospect for marriage. 'That's the young man who married Mr So-and-So's daughter, of Such-and-Such a business!' people will exclaim, as, on one of the five festival days, [4] some fashionable fellow passes bravely by, his overskirts and starched jacket [5] impeccably arranged, a small gold-wrought dagger next his crested silken kimono, a procession of boys and clerks bearing luggage-boxes in his wake. Remarks of this kind gladden the hearts of mothers-in-law. But once this same man has reduced himself to bankruptcy, and all his costumes and daggers have passed into other hands, he is less to look at than an ill-favoured creature who has habitually worn a pongee kimono with plain blue crests, or overskirts of cotton. As regards brides too—those of the aristocracy being a case apart—in commoners' houses a girl who can stretch a wad of silk-wool is better than one who strums the koto; and a girl who stokes the furnace, when the fire is burning low, is better than a mistress in the art of burning incense. Brides look their best when behaving in a manner most suited to their station.

The hills of Nara! There at least, in a world of sham and deceit, is the constancy of the autumn rains, falling in their season. [6] Amid the hills, in Kasuga village, there lived a rich merchant named Matsuya So-and-So, [7] who ran a broker's agency for the sales of the Nara bleaching industry. In the old days his firm was more prosperous than the present Akitaya or Kureya, [8] and, just as the double cherry in its moment of glory spreads wide its blossom here in the old capital of Nara, so Matsuya passed the spring of life in splendour. But while he spent the days and nights in revelry, merrily feasting on sliced raw shark [9] washed down with cups of local bitter saké, his business fell steadily into decline. At the age of fifty—just when a man reaches the time of wisdom[10]—he suddenly died, undermined by endless dissipation. To his wife and children he left a great many debts, and this was his only legacy. Not until a man dies can we truly know his circumstances.

His widow was now thirty-eight years old, but, being a woman of slight build, exceptionally smooth-skinned and fair in complexion, she passed at a casual glance for twenty-seven or eight. She would still have made an attractive and stylish wife, and with such looks might well have forgotten her duties to the departed and married again. However, her children were still young, and they remained her chief concern. That no one should mistake her intentions she cut short her hair, abandoned white face-powder, and left her painted lips to fade. Kimono of manly patterns, and even narrow masculine sashes, were her favoured garb. But though a woman may surpass a man in intelligence, she cannot wield a mattock; nor is the changing of the decaying supports of a house a task for delicate hands, however skilled. Soon rain seeped through the eaves and damp growths spread along the walls. To see a wilderness like this growing within one's own home is more depressing than listening all day to the melancholy cries of deer. All natural feeling apart, she sadly missed her husband, and she realised now that it was hard for a woman to support a living by herself.

Nowadays, if a widow does not remarry, it generally means that her husband has left her a considerable fortune in money and real estate, and that her relations—acting as her advisers in their own interest—have forced her, though she may be still no more than a girl, to crop short her hair, adopt a life of pious seclusion for which she has no mind, and observe with regularity the annual commemoration of her husband's death. Inevitably she earns a bad name, and takes some long-trusted family clerk as a paramour. How often have we seen this happen! Rather than this, it is better for her to marry into some other family at once; and there is no reason why people should mock her for it.

In such a world Matsuya's widow was an example to all. Though she tried various ways of earning a living, none came up to her hopes. She could think of no method of repaying her husband's debts. As she fell deeper and deeper into distress, she racked her brains for a plan. She offered to hand over her house to her creditors, but they all felt sorry for her and not one of them would accept it. As for selling the house, she would get less than three kanme for it—and her debts were five kanme. So, begging the co-operation of the people in her ward,

The lottery for the widow's house

the widow decided to dispose of the house by a sweepstake.[11] She charged each participant four monme, and the person whose token was drawn from the box was to receive the house. With a prize like that for only four monme, there was such a mad rush to buy tokens and put them in the box that before long there were three thousand inside. Twelve kanme! Five paid off the debts, and seven remained. With this as a start the widow once more became rich. A hired servant girl won the sweepstake, and for four monme acquired a house of her own.

BOOK II

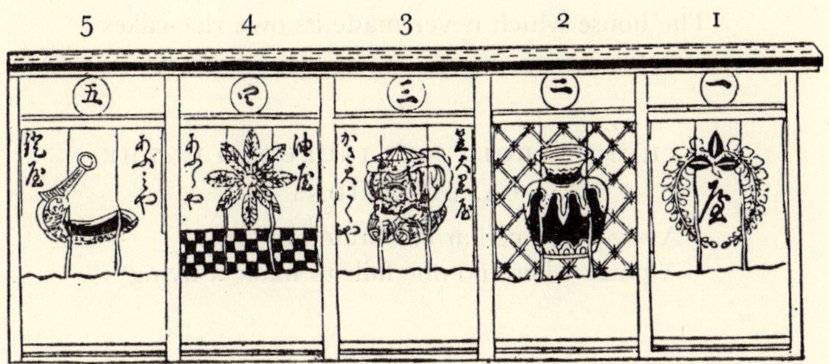

1

THE FOREMOST LODGER IN THE LAND

A man of resource celebrated in Kyōto
The house which never made its own rice-cakes

2

A THUNDERBOLT NOT INCLUDED IN THE CALCULATIONS

A soy-sauce pedlar celebrated in Ōtsu
A place where no one fails to make a living

3

A FEATHER IN DAIKOKU'S CAP

A storehouse-holder celebrated in Edo
Black Powder of Dog to revive fading hopes of success

4

THE DEMON WITH A WINDFLOWER CREST

The Whale-Ebisu shrine celebrated in Taiji
The home of the Yokote-bushi

5

BY LAND AND SEA TO THE ABUMIYA

The efficiency of a celebrated broker of Sakata
Opening a trunk before closing the year

BOOK II

1. *The foremost lodger in the land*

'This is to certify that the person named Fuji-ichi, [1] tenant in a house belonging to Hishiya Chōzaemon of Muromachi, is to my certain knowledge the possessor of one thousand kanme in silver....'

Such would be the style of his testimonial when Fuji-ichi sought new lodgings. He was unique, he claimed, among the wealthy of this world, for although he was worth a thousand kanme he lived in a rented house no more than four yards wide. In this way he had become the talk of Kyōto, but having one day accepted a house in Karasuma street [2] as surety for a loan of thirty-eight kanme, in the course of time, as the interest mounted, the surety became forfeit, and for the first time Fuji-ichi became a property owner. He was much vexed at this. Up to now he had achieved distinction as 'the rich man in lodgings', but now that he had a house of his own he was nobody—his money in itself was mere dust by comparison with what lay in the strong-rooms of the foremost merchants of Kyōto.

Fuji-ichi was a clever man, and his substantial fortune was amassed in his own lifetime. But first and foremost he was a man who knew his own mind, and this was the basis of his success. In addition to carrying on his regular business, he kept a separate ledger, bound from odd scraps of paper, in which, as he sat all day in his shop, pen in hand, he entered a variety of chance information. As the clerks from the money-exchanges passed by he noted down the market ratio of copper and gold; [3] he enquired about the current quotations of the rice-brokers; he sought information from druggists' and haberdashers' assistants on the state of the market at Nagasaki; [4] for the latest news on the prices of ginned cotton, salt, and saké, he noted the various days on which the Kyōto dealers received dispatches from the Edo branch shops. Every day a thousand things were entered in his book, and people came to Fuji-ichi if ever in doubt. He became an invaluable asset to the citizens of Kyōto.

His dress consisted invariably of a thin undervest beneath a cotton kimono, the latter stuffed if necessary with three times the usual amount of padding. [5] He never put on more than one layer of outer garments.

It was he who first started the wearing of detachable cuffs [6] on the sleeves—a device which was both fashionable and economical. His socks were of deerskin and his clogs were fitted with thick leather soles, but, even so, he was careful not to walk too quickly along the hard main roads. Throughout life his only silk garments were of pongee, dyed plain dark blue—there was one, it is true, which he had dyed a persistently undisguisable seaweed brown, but this was a youthful error of judgement, and he was to regret it for the next twenty years. For his ceremonial dress he had no settled crests, being content with a three-barred circle or a small conventional whirl, and even during the summer airing time he was careful to keep these from direct contact with the mats. His overskirts were of hemp, and his starched jacket of an even tougher variety of the same cloth, so that they remained correctly creased no matter how many times he wore them.

When there was a funeral procession which his whole ward was obliged to join, he followed it perforce to the cemetery on Toribe hill, [7] but coming back he hung behind the others and, on the path across the moor at Rokuhara, he and his apprentices pulled up sour Senburi herbs by the roots.

'Dried in the shade,' he explained, 'they make excellent stomach medicine.'

He never passed by anything which might be of use. Even if he stumbled he used the opportunity to pick up stones for fire-lighters, and tucked them in his sleeve. The head of a household, if he is to keep the smoke rising steadily from his kitchen, must pay attention to a thousand things like this.

Fuji-ichi was not a miser by nature. It was merely his ambition to serve as a model for others in the management of everyday affairs. Even in the days before he made his money he never had the New Year rice-cakes [8] prepared in his own lodgings. He considered that to hire a man for pounding the rice, and to bother over the various utensils, was too much trouble at such a busy time of the year; so he placed an order with the rice-cake dealer in front of the Great Buddha. [9] However, with his intuitive grasp of good business, he insisted on paying by weight—so much per kanme. Early one morning, two days before New Year, a woman from the cake-maker arrived before Fuji-ichi's shop, hurrying about her rounds, and setting down her load shouted for someone to receive the order. The newly pounded cakes, invitingly arrayed, were as fresh and warm as spring itself. The master, pretending not to hear, continued his calculations on the abacus, and the

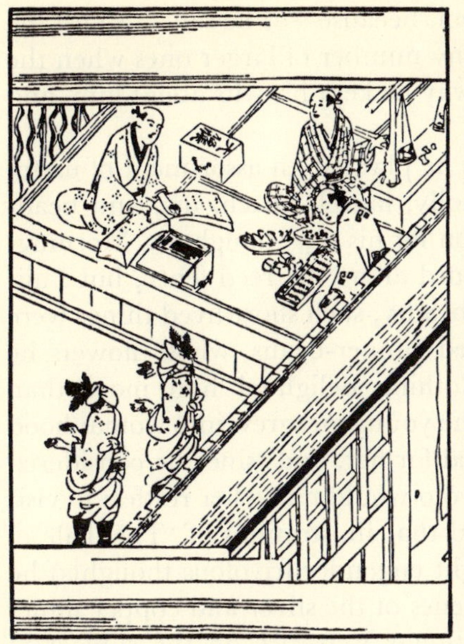

The rice-cakes are delivered at Fuji-ichi's shop

woman, who begrudged every moment at this busy time of the year, shouted again and again. At length a young clerk, anxious to demonstrate his businesslike approach, checked the weight of the cakes on the large scales with a show of great precision, and sent the woman away.

About two hours later Fuji-ichi said: 'Has anyone taken in the cakes which arrived just now?'

'The woman gave them to me and left long ago', said the clerk.

'Useless fellow!' cried Fuji-ichi. 'I expect people in my service to have more sense! Don't you realise that you took them in before they had cooled off?'

He weighed them again, and to everyone's astonishment their weight had decreased. Not one of the cakes had been eaten, and the clerk stood gazing at them in open-mouthed amazement.

It was the early summer of the following year. The local people from the neighbourhood of the Tōji [10] had gathered the first crop of egg-plants in wicker baskets and brought them to town for sale. 'Eat young egg-plants and live seventy-five days longer' goes the saying, and they are very popular. The price was fixed at two zeni for one egg-plant, or three zeni for two, which meant that everybody bought two. But

Fuji-ichi bought only one, at two zeni, because—as he said—'With the one zeni now in pocket I can buy any number of larger ones when the crop is fully grown.' That was the way he kept his wits about him, and he seldom made a mistake.

In an empty space in his grounds he planted an assortment of useful trees and flowers such as willow, holly, laurel, peach, iris, and bead-beans.[11] This he did as an education for his only daughter. Morning-glory started to grow of its own accord along the reed fence, but Fuji-ichi said that, if it was a question of beauty, such short-lived things were a loss, and in their place he planted runner-beans, whose flowers he thought an equally fine sight. Nothing delighted him more than watching over his daughter. When the young girl grew into womanhood he had a marriage screen constructed for her, and (since he considered that one decorated with views of Kyōto would make her restless to visit the places she had not yet seen, and that illustrations of 'The Tale of Genji' or 'The Tales of Ise'[12] might engender frivolous thoughts) he had the screen painted with busy scenes of the silver and copper mines at Tada.[13] He composed Instructional Verses[14] on the subject of economy and made his daughter recite them aloud. Instead of sending her to a girls' temple school, he taught her how to write himself, and by the time he had reached the end of his syllabus he had made her the most finished and accomplished girl in Kyōto.[15] Imitating her father in his thrifty ways, after the age of eight she spilt no more ink on her sleeves, played no longer with dolls at the Doll festival,[16] nor joined in the dancing at Bon. Every day she combed her own hair and bound it in a simple bun. She never sought others' help in her private affairs. She mastered the art of stretching silk padding and learned to fit it perfectly to the length and breadth of each garment. Since young girls can do all this if properly disciplined, it is a mistake to leave them to do as they please.

Once, on the evening of the seventh day of the New Year, some neighbours asked leave to send their sons to Fuji-ichi's house to seek advice on how to become millionaires. Lighting the lamp in the sitting room, Fuji-ichi set his daughter to wait, bidding her let him know when she heard a noise at the private door from the street. The young girl, doing as she was told with charming grace, first carefully lowered the wick in the lamp. Then, when she heard the voices of the visitors, she raised the wick again and retired to the scullery. By the time the three guests had seated themselves the grinding of an earthenware mortar could be heard from the kitchen, and the sound fell with pleasant promise on their ears. They speculated on what was in store for them.

'Pickled whale-skin soup?' hazarded the first.

'No. As this is our first visit of the year, it ought to be rice-dumpling gruel',[17] said the second.

The third listened carefully for some time, and at last confidently announced that it was noodle soup. Visitors always go through this amusing performance. Fuji-ichi then entered and talked to the three of them on the requisites for success.

'Why is it that today is called the Day of the Seven Herbs?'[18] one asked him.

'That was the beginning of economy in the age of the gods: it was to teach us the ingredients of a cheap stew.'

'Why do we leave a salted bream hanging before the god of the kitchen range until the sixth moon?'[19] asked another.

'That is so that when you look at it at meal times you may get the feeling of having eaten fish without actually doing so.'

Finally he was asked the reason for using thick chopsticks at New Year.

'That is so that when they become soiled they can be scraped white again, and in this way one pair will last the whole year. They also signify the two divine pillars of the state, Izanagi and Izanami.'

'As a general rule,' concluded Fuji-ichi, 'give the closest attention to even the smallest details. Well now, you have kindly talked with me from early evening, and it is high time that refreshments were served. But not to provide refreshments is one way of becoming a millionaire. The noise of the mortar which you heard when you first arrived was the pounding of starch for the covers of the account-book.'[20]

2. *A thunderbolt not included in the calculations*

PINT-SIZED pots, even if dipped beneath the rippling waves of Lake Biwa, will hold no more than a pint.[1]... In the town of Ōtsu,[2] there lived a soy-sauce pedlar named Kibeiji. Ōtsu, which is not only a shipping port for the northern provinces but a stage on the Tōkai-dō, is a picture of prosperity and bustle, as relay horses and palanquins are changed, freight carts rumble along the streets, and porters labour beneath their loads. Even a shopkeeper who specialised in snake-meat rice-rolls, miniatures carved from devils' horns,[3] or similar rarities, would have no difficulty here in finding customers. In Brokers' block[4] where the houses are now built like millionaires' mansions, with a magnificence unknown in the old days, the soft strumming of samisens is heard from upstairs rooms, where girls from the Shibaya-machi[5] quarter are summoned to provide entertainment for the brokers' clients at all hours of the day and night. Nor is there ever a moment's pause in the tapping of mallets on the scales. There are certainly places in Ōtsu where money exists, and, where it does, it is used as freely as if it were pebbles.

'There is nothing so unfairly balanced as people's incomes', Kibeiji would grumble, as he eased his buckets from his shoulders and mused awhile on life's inconsistencies. 'Wherever I go on my rounds there are the world's usual differences of joy and sorrow, wealth and poverty, but they are never as I would expect them to be. I see clever people in clothes of plain paper, and stupid people wrapping themselves in fine silks. Making money seems to have no connection with good management. Still, for myself, if ever I stop working, not a single zeni drops from heaven, nor jumps up at me out of the earth. Even being strictly honest has never got me anywhere, but the only thing to do, after all, is to carry on conscientiously with the sort of job for which I'm fitted.'

Having said this, he would feel more happy in his unrewarding daily labours.

In the Sekidera district of Ōtsu there was a man called Moriyama Genkō. There was nothing extraordinary about him. He was a physician, both skilled and long-experienced in his profession, but—though epidemics might rage as furiously as the gales on Mount Hiei—his medicines would never sell. Voices at the gateway no longer announced the arrival of patients; whilst inside his house even the picture of Shinnō, the patron of doctors, shivered with loneliness on his hanging scroll, and thousands of medicine packets and their inscriptions lay buried beneath the dust. Winter or summer Genkō's physician's gown was the same unlined garment of habutae silk, the prescription for his own clothes never varying from 'the mixture as before'. A doctor's lot is similar to that of a courtesan, in that neither may visit houses to which they have not been invited, nor can they remain too long in their own lodgings without giving a bad impression. So every day, at the time for the morning rounds, Genkō set out from his home and went to look at the paintings of horses at Yonomiya shrine,[6] or climbed to the platform of the High Kannon temple[7] to admire the Eight Views of

Ōmi province. But even these, if admired all day, lose their attraction. There is nothing more distressing than to have no means of support and an abundance of leisure. People laughed at Genkō as a 'Painted Horse Doctor', and his plight was a sad one. However, some friends came to the rescue by organising a chess club [8] in his lodgings, and he took three monme from each player for each game as a charge for refreshments. The fact that he now barely avoided starvation seemed, in his eyes, a matter for positive congratulation. There were people like that in Ōtsu.

Then there was the case of Sakamotoya Nibei, a man living in the district called Mumaya-machi. [9] Formerly he had been a prosperous merchant, but he ran quickly through large sums of money, and when he had only his house and store-sheds left he sold even these—for twenty-eight kanme—and set out into the world with the proceeds. After tryin gtwenty-four or -five different types of trade, and having, in the process, emptied his pockets of every penny he possessed, he at last had no idea what to do next. Even his once glossy side-locks had worn thin, and since his general appearance was now so ludicrous, and he had shown himself such a nincompoop in practical affairs, the only advice his relations would give him was to seek a post as caretaker for the god of poverty's shrine; and after that they refused to see him any more. However, his mother had ten kanme which she had set aside for her retirement, and as Nibei was her only son she felt sorry for him. She only wished that she could give him the money outright and trust him to use it as a means of support in life. But if she handed it to Nibei it would probably not last a year. Instead she lent it to her elder sister's husband, and every month she gave Nibei the eighty monme interest. She made the condition that he must support his household of five on this, and this alone. First there was himself, with his wife and child; next there was his younger brother [10] Nisaburo, a cripple; and lastly there was the old nurse who had fed Nibei at her breast, and who was no longer able to fend for herself. Knowing no port to which to run for shelter, all had been obliged to throw a line to Nibei's ship, and now, even if he sailed into better weather, there was not one of them whom he could cut loose and send off alone. At any rate, he found it no easy task to support five people on the eighty monme interest from ten kanme. The money was collected on the first of each month: the rent of five monme was put aside, the necessary stocks of clean hulled rice, bean-paste, salt, and firewood were purchased, and after that it was pickled vegetables with every meal. They could afford absolutely nothing more. When bream were at their cheapest in the third moon, or even when mushrooms sold at two fun a pound, they could only feast their eyes in the shops. If they were thirsty they drank spiced warm water. In the middle of the living-room a solitary oil lamp was lit, and promptly at bedtime it was extinguished—let the rats romp as they might. They made no special festival clothes for Bon or New Year, but disciplined themselves to a calendar of unrelieved economy. For recreation they twisted paper chains. Discomfort was their lot from dawn till dusk. Yet there were some—with better heads for business—who supported families of seven or eight on less than a hundred monme, and passed the annual reckoning day with ample to spare.

The thunderbolt smashes Kibeiji's cooking pot

There were also sharp people like the widow in Matsumoto village.[11] She dressed her only daughter in a loose-sleeved fawn kimono and traveller's reed hat, and sent her out to beg 'alms for a runaway pilgrim to Ise',[12] mimicking some distant provincial accent which she had practised for the occasion. It was like hawking the Ise goddess herself, but the two of them had earned their living now for some twelve or thirteen years by the constant repetition of this same deceit. Then there was the Ike-no-kawa needle maker.[13] People had always thought his means were as slender as his needles, but one day it was learnt that he wished to marry his daughter into a Kyōto family, and the old woman who acted as marriage broker rushed here, there, and everywhere with the tale that he was prepared to give a dowry of two thousand chōgin![14] And she added, confidentially, that if pushed he might raise it to a hundred kanme.

'The whys and wherefores of people's money are things you can never begin to understand', Kibeiji would say. 'Even here in Ōtsu they are all jumbled up.'

Wherever he called on his rounds, selling soy sauce, he kept his eyes and ears open, and on returning to his lodgings he would tell all that he had observed.

Kibeiji's wife was an extremely efficient woman: she kept her children neatly clothed; she never borrowed from others; she started laying in next year's stocks from the beginning of the twelfth moon; and—since her idea of happiness was to keep herself ever free of visits from men with bills at New Year—she settled all her accounts in good time. But when she totted up her store of coins year after year, though there might sometimes be a remainder of seven monme five or eight fun, sometimes seven monme six fun, or sometimes eight monme eight or nine fun, never had she passed the turn of a year with so much as ten monme in hand. The pattern of the household's finances was as unvaried as if stamped from a wood-block.[15] One year, on the night of the twenty-ninth of the twelfth moon, even as she was praying to a block-print of the god of luck for larger profits next year, CRASH!—down from the overcast skies hurtled a winter thunderbolt, and her one and only cooking pot lay smashed in smithereens. There was no point in crying over it, and as she needed a pot immediately she bought another. But at the end of this year she found herself short by the price of the pot, and as she had bought a total of nine monme's worth of goods on credit at a score of shops, at last she heard the shouts of debt collectors at her door. There is always something to upset the most careful of human calculations.

'Until that thunderbolt fell,' said Kibeiji disconsolately, 'I was really doing rather well. But now....'

3. *A feather in Daikoku's cap*

One for his bales of rice,
Two for his two-floor mansion,
Three for his store-sheds, three floors high....[1]

So ran the Daikoku dancers' song and if you looked for someone to fit it, in Kyōto there was the wealthy merchant called Daikokuya. When Gojō bridge was being changed from wood to stone,[2] he had purchased the third plank from the western end, and had caused it to be carved into a likeness of the god Daikoku, praying that by spending his life, as this plank had done, in useful service beneath the feet of customers, he might attain to great wealth. In faith there is profit,[3] and his household steadily grew more prosperous. He called himself Daikokuya Shinbei, [4] and the name was known to all.

He had three sons, all safely reared to manhood and all gifted with intelligence. The old man, delighted at such good fortune, was passing his declining years in great satisfaction, getting ready for retirement, when the eldest son, Shinroku, suddenly started to spend recklessly, visiting the brothel quarters again and again with no account of expense. After half a year the clerks discovered that one hundred and seventy kanme of the money recorded in their cash-books had disappeared. When it became clear, however, that Shinroku could never repay the money, they worked secretly together on his behalf and, by falsifying the prices of goods being held in stock, managed to get him safely through the next reckoning day in the seventh moon. [5] But, for all their earnest pleas that he should live less extravagantly in future, he took no notice, and at the last reckoning for the year the cash was short again—by two hundred and thirty kanme. A fox with his tail exposed, Shinroku could play his tricks no more, and he fled for refuge to a friend who lived by the Fox shrine at Fushimi. [6] His father, a strait-laced old man, was furious, and no amount of pleading softened his temper. Summoning the neighbourhood group to attend his house in formal dress, he publicly disowned his son [7] and abandoned him to his own devices. When a father dissociates himself in this way from his own son it is for no trifling misdemeanour. Shinroku was now in sorry straits: it was impossible to linger long in the vicinity, even in his present refuge, but if he was to leave and make for Edo he must have money, and at the moment he had not even the price of a pair of sandals for the journey.

'Was there ever a more unhappy case than mine?' he moaned. But self-pity did nothing to mend his fortune.

It was on the evening of the twenty-eighth of the twelfth moon, soon after Shinroku had entered the bath-tub in his lodgings, that someone shouted the dread alarm of his father's approach. Terrified, Shinroku leapt from the tub, hastily draped a padded kimono about his dripping body, and fled into the street. He held his sash in one hand, but had somehow forgotten to retrieve his underwear—and now that Shinroku was eager at last to gird his loins for the walk to Edo, the absence of his loin-cloth was truly unfortunate. It was not until the twenty-ninth that he finally set out. The skies were overcast, and, as he passed Fuji-no-mori, [8] the snow which had long threatened began to fall and settle on the pines. Shinroku was hatless, and icy drops oozed past his collar.

By sundown, his spirits still further depressed by the boom of temple bells, he was gazing with longing at the steaming tea-urns in the cosy rest-houses of Ōkamedani and Kanshuji. A sip of tea, he felt, was the very thing to ward off this bitter cold. Having no money, however, he bided his time until he noticed a house before which the palanquins from Fushimi or Ōtsu were drawing up with particular frequency. It was jammed tight with customers, and there in the general confusion he quenched his thirst free of charge, and moreover took the opportunity, as he left, to appropriate a straw cape which someone had momentarily laid aside. After this initiation into the art of thieving he proceeded along the road towards the village of Ono. There, beneath the branches of a desolate, leafless persimmon tree, he came across a group of children bewailing some misfortune.

Shinroku is chased by his father

'What a shame!' he heard one say. 'Poor old Benkei's dead!'

Stretched on the ground before them was a huge black dog, the size of a carter's ox. Shinroku went up to the children and persuaded them to let him have the carcass. Wrapping it in the straw cape he had stolen, he carried it with him as far as the foot of Otowa hill, and there accosted some labourers who were digging in the fields.

'This dog', said Shinroku, 'should make a wonderful cure for nervous indigestion. For more than three years I've fed him on every variety of drug, and now I intend to burn him into black medicinal ash.' [9]

'Well, that's something we should all profit from!' exclaimed the labourers, and fetching brushwood and withered bamboo-grass from round about, they produced their tinder wallets and started a fire.

Shinroku gave a little of the ash to each of them, flung the remainder across his shoulders in the cape, and set off again. Crying 'Burnt Wolf Powder!', mimicking the curious local dialect, he proceeded to hawk his wares along the road. Passing the Ōsaka barrier gate, where 'people come and people go, both those you know and those you know not', [10] he persuaded all and sundry to stop and buy. Even pedlars of needles and hawkers of writing-brushes, who had long experience themselves in swindling travellers, were taken in by him, and between Oiwake and Hatchō he sold five hundred and eighty zeni's worth of ash.

What a pity, he told himself, never to have realised till now what a born genius he was! If he had used his wits like this in Kyōto no wearisome walk to Edo would ever have been necessary. Laughing at the thought, and at the same time on the verge of tears, he pressed on across the long bridge at Seta, and steeled himself to think only of what lay eastwards. He passed New Year's Day at a lodging house in Kusatsu, [11] where, even as he refreshed himself on the local Uba cakes, he caught a glimpse of Mirror mount and wept again for Kyōto and the old familiar mirror-cakes of home. But soon, like those first blossoms on Cherry hill, buds of hope were stirring in his breast, and then, as he sensed the fragrance and the colour of his full-flowering youth, he knew that he was ready and able to work, and he laughed at the weak-kneed, ancient god of poverty struggling to keep pace with him there behind. At Oiso even the age-old shrine was young with the spirit of spring, its trees white with sacred festoons, and the moon above, so sad in autumn, shone bright with promise for the future. Doubts lay demolished, like the old barrier-gates he passed at Fuwa, and day in, day out, he trudged onwards. Taking the Mino road to Owari, and hawking his powder around every town and village on the Tōkai-dō, at last, on the sixty-second day after leaving Kyōto, he arrived at Shinagawa. [12]

Now that he had not only supported himself all this way but had made an overall profit of two thousand three hundred zeni, he sank the unsold remains of the Black Powder in the waves by the shore and hurried on towards Edo. But it grew dark, and as he had nowhere in Edo to stay he passed the night before the gate of the Tōkai-ji temple at Shinagawa. [13] Beneath its shelter a number of outcasts [14] were lying, stretched out under their straw capes. It was spring, but the wind from the sea was strong, and the roar of the waves kept him from closing his eyes until midnight. The others were recounting their life stories, and, lying awake, he listened to them. Though all were beggars now, it seemed that none was so by inheritance. [15] One was from the village of Tatsuta in Yamato, [16] and had formerly been a brewer of saké in a small way, supporting a family of six or seven in tolerable comfort. However, when the money he had been steadily putting by amounted to one hundred koban, he decided that getting rich by running a local business was a slow process, and—disregarding all that his relations and friends said to dissuade him—he abandoned his shop and came down to Edo. Following his own foolhardy impulses, he rented a shop from a fishmonger in Gofuku-chō,[17] and started business alongside all the high-class saké stores. However, he could not compete with the products of Kōnoike, Itami, and Ikeda, nor with the cedar-matured saké of the long-established, powerful Nara breweries,[18] and when the capital with which he had started his shop had dwindled to nothing, he took the straw matting from a sixteen-gallon tub of saké to serve as a coat and took to the roads as a beggar.

'I thought I should go back to Tatsuta in scarlet embroidered silks,[19] but now I'd go back if I had even so much as a new cotton kimono', he wailed. 'It just shows that you should never abandon a business you're used to.'

But words were useless. Though the time of wisdom had come, it was already too late.

Another was from Sakai[20] in Izumi province. Being past master of a thousand arts, he had come to Edo in high hopes, swollen with conceit. In calligraphy he had been granted lessons by Hirano Chūan.[21] In tea he drank at the stream of Kanamori Sōwa. Chinese verse and prose composition he learned under Gensei of Fukakusa, and for linked verse and Haikai he was a pupil of Nishiyama Sōin. In Noh he mastered the dramatic style of Kobatake, and the drum technique of Shōda Yoemon. In the morning he listened to Itō Genkichi expounding the classics, in the evening he practised kickball under Lord Asukai, during the afternoon he joined in Gensai's chess classes, and at night he learned the fingering of the koto from Yatsuhashi Kengyō, or the blowing of the flute as a pupil of Sōsan. In Jōruri recital he learned the style of Uji Kadayū, and in dancing he was the equal of Yamatoya no Jinbei. In the art of love he was trained by the great Shimabara courtesan Takahashi, and in revels with boy actors he copied to perfection the mannerisms of Suzuki Heihachi. Under the guidance of the professional entertainers in both the Shimabara and the unlicensed quarters he had developed into a pleasure-seeker of exquisite refinement. If there was anything which man could do he sought out a specialist in it, and copied his technique, and he now proudly regarded himself as one qualified to succeed in any task to which he might turn his hand. But these years of rigorous training proved of little use in the immediate business of earning a living, and he soon repented that he had never used an abacus and had no knowledge of the scales. At a loss in samurai households, useless as a merchant's apprentice, his services were scorned by all. Reduced to his present plight, he had cause to reconsider his opinion of himself, and he cursed the parents who had taught him the arts, but had omitted any instruction in the elements of earning a living.

A third beggar was Edo born and bred, like his father before him. Though he had once owned a large mansion and grounds in Tōri-chō,[22] drawing a regular income of six hundred koban per annum from house rents, he had no conception of the meaning of the simple word 'economy', and before long he had sold everything except the walls and roof of his house. Left without means of support, he abandoned society and his home, and took to the life of a beggar—an outcast in practice, even if not registered as one with Kuruma Zenshichi's guild.[23]

Listening to each of these life stories, different though they were from each other Shinroku yet felt that all were very like his own, and his sympathy was aroused. He moved nearer to where the others were lying.

'I too am from Kyōto', he said, and added, concealing nothing of his disgrace, 'I have been disowned by my father and was going to Edo to try my luck—but listening to your stories has disheartened me.'

'Was there no way of excusing yourself?' the beggars exclaimed. 'Had you no aunt to intercede for you? You would have been far better advised never to have come to Edo.'

'That is past, and I cannot retrace my steps. It is advice for the future which I require. It surprises me that men so shrewd as each of you should be reduced to such distress. Surely, you could have made a living of some sorts, no matter what trade you chose.'

'Far from it. This may be the great castle-town of the Shōgun, but it is also the meeting-place for all the sharpest men in Japan, and they will not give you three zeni for nothing. In Edo you can get nowhere without capital.'

'But during all the time in which you have been looking about have no fresh ideas for trade occurred to you?'

'Well, you could pick up the empty shells which people scatter all over the town, burn them at Reigan-jima,[24] and sell the ashes as lime. Or, since people are hard pressed for time in this place, you could shred edible seaweed or shave dried bonito into "flower-strips" and sell them by the plateful. Or you could buy a roll of cotton and sell it piecemeal as hand towels. Apart from things like this there seems to be no way of starting trade on an almost empty pocket.'

Their words had given him the idea he wanted. At dawn he took his leave, and when he gave the three of them a parting gift of a hundred zeni each, their delight knew no bounds.

'Your luck has come!' they cried. 'You'll make a pile of money as high as Mount Fuji!'

After this he went to visit an acquaintance who had a cotton-goods shop in Tenma-chō,[25] and there he related the details of his present predicament and his plans. The shop-keeper was sympathetic.

'In a case like this honest work is the only answer', he said. 'Try your luck at trade for a bit.'

Taking heart, Shinroku purchased a roll of cotton, on which he had set his mind, and cut it up for sale as hand towels. On the twenty-fifth of the third moon, the festival day of the Tenjin shrine at Shitaya,[26] he started his new business. Seated at the base of the holy-water font by the entrance, he offered his towels for sale. The pilgrims, believing that this was another way of improving their luck,[27] bought them gladly, and at the end of the first day he had already made a profit. Every day thereafter he made more money, and within ten years he was rumoured to be worth five thousand koban. For shrewdness he was considered in a class of his own. People took Shinroku's advice on many matters, and he became a treasured asset in his locality. On his shop awnings he printed a picture of the god Daikoku wearing a reed hat, and his firm was known as the Hatted Daikokuya....

> 'Eight for the daimyō's agent,
> Nine for the nuggets of gold in his stock,
> Ten for a tale's happy ending.'[28]

And happy too was his lot in living in this tranquil age!

4. *The demon with a windflower crest*

As limitless as the seas are the accomplishments of the men of Japan. There is even an amusing story that the poet Po Chü-i[1] of China, a land where art comes before earning a living, took fright and fled from our country when he observed the natives' skill in versification. Chinese verse is strange and remote. Japanese songs like 'Yokote-bushi'[2] are more to our taste—and if you want to know where the 'Yokote-bushi' comes from, it is a song sung by the women and children of Taiji village,[3] a large harbour in Kii province. Taiji is a prosperous place, and its people render thanks at a shrine amid a grove of young pines—the shrine of Whale-Ebisu.[4] The gateway, some thirty feet high, is constructed from the skeletons of whales, and if your curiosity should be aroused by this unusual sight, and you should question a local inhabitant, he will tell you the story of 'Demon' Gennai,[5] a skilled harpoon-master in the whaling industry of this shore.[6]

Gennai enjoyed a reputation as a bringer of good luck, and every year in the old days, whenever fleets of whaling boats were fitted out, his services were in demand. Once a huge spout of water was seen rising near the coast, like a summer thunder-cloud, and when the whalers set off in pursuit their very first harpoon struck home. Once more, it was Gennai who had aimed it, as everyone knew when his windflower crest[7] was hoisted in each boat. Singing together in lusty songs which drowned the roar of the waves, taking their time from drum, gong, and flute, the fishermen tied the whale to a stout hawser wound around a winch, and hauled it to the shore. Thirty-three fathoms two feet six inches in length, it was a monstrous whale of the type called 'Semi',[8] whose equal had never been seen before. Prosperity came to seven villages at one stroke,[9] and endless billows of smoke rose from the furnaces. When the oil was extracted, a thousand barrels would not hold it; and, with not a scrap of flesh nor hide nor fin to be thrown away, this one whale was enough to make a man a millionaire. Its blubber and meat, sliced and heaped, presented a rare spectacle, bringing snow-capped Fuji and maple-covered Takao[10] to that mountainless shore. Even the bones, which were usually discarded, were solicited on this occasion by Gennai, who crushed them and produced yet more oil. The profits from this exceeded everyone's expectation and he became a rich man. It was a method which might have meant a great deal to the smaller fishermen, and it was strange that no one had thought of it till now. In recent years—thanks also to an invention of Gennai's—whale-nets[11] have been devised, so that once a whale is spotted it has little chance of escape, and these nets have now come into use on every coast. At first Gennai had dwelt in a thatched hut on the beach, but now he built for himself a long-roofed mansion of cedar wood, and in addition to employing more than two hundred fishermen he owned about eighty whaling boats. His luck never failed him, and at length the gold and silver sighed beneath its own weight in his strong-rooms, and no matter how much of it he spent it grew no less. When a man's fortune is as firmly rooted as this we say that he is 'as sound as a camphor tree'.[12]

Tengu Gennai harpoons the monstrous whale

In faith, they say, there is profit, [13] and Gennai was most scrupulous in his services to the Buddha and worship of the gods. He held the shrine at Nishi-no-miya [14] in particular esteem, and every year, at the Feast of Ebisu on the tenth of the first moon, he was the first to arrive there and pay his respects. One year, however, having lost all track of time while drinking to celebrate the annual binding of the account-books, [15] dawn had already broken before he finally got his twenty-oared cutter under way. He was anxiously wondering how this unusually late arrival would affect his future prospects when his trusted servant Fukudayū, who was this year's master of ceremonies, addressed the company as follows, with an air of mock gravity.

'For twenty years now', he said, 'the master has paid his respects to Ebisu in the morning. This year he will not arrive until after lighting-up time. It signifies, perhaps, that a shower of sparks as large as lanterns will overwhelm his household.' [16]

This unexpected sally put Gennai in an even uglier mood, and he placed his hand to his dagger. But he checked himself, reflecting that a hasty action now would only aggravate matters.

'The more lanterns the better,' he said, 'especially in the dark nights before spring, picking your way through a maze of bills.'

He stretched his limbs, controlled his temper, and forced a smile.

Soon the speedy boat touched on the beach at Hirota, [17] and Gennai proceeded to the shrine in a more restful state of mind. But the pine-fringed beach had a deserted air, and the lamp before the shrine was burning low. Observing that everyone he met was going home and he alone was coming, his apprehensions returned. Approaching the main shrine he requested a performance of ritual dance, [18] but the attendants, who were squatting in a circle and had already started to string together the day's takings, each tried to pass him on to someone else. Eventually no more than a solitary drum was tapped as the girl danced, and she too, after running through her performance in slipshod haste, finally contrived to jingle the bells over his head from a distance. God or no god, Gennai was rather angry, and after a cursory round of the lesser shrines he once more boarded his boat, where, without bothering to remove his carefully pressed overskirts, he immediately dropped off to sleep, lulled by the waves.

Behind him came Ebisu. Mindless of whether his hat stayed on or fell off [19]—such was his haste—he pulled back his sleeves, augustly securing them with a bright ribbon, and transferred himself at one leap from the point of a rock into the boat.

'Dear, dear!' he exclaimed, miraculously giving voice. 'Such a fine idea had struck me, but I forgot to mention it. While I was in the humour I intended to offer this splendid tip to each one of the fishermen; but people nowadays are in such a hurry—they say their say and are gone in a flash. I have no time to explain anything to them. But you have come after all the rest, and you are in luck.'

He bent close to the lobe of Gennai's ear, and whispered: 'There is a way of transporting sea-bream in floating tanks, alive and fresh, to any destination—at the Uojima [20] or any other season. When a fish is weakening, prick its stomach, the trick being to insert your sharpened bamboo about three inches from the tail. The fish revives and frisks about at once. First Aid for sea-bream is a novel idea, don't you think?'

At this point Gennai awoke from his dream.

'Amazing!' he thought. 'A most unusual method!'

When he tried out the god's suggestion, it was as predicted: not a fish was lost. Here again he made handsome profits, and ever after his ships bowled along on a tide of luck, with sails full-spread to seasonable trade winds.

5. *By land and sea to the Abumiya*

FOURTEEN feet of snow is not unknown. It is recorded every year on the snow-rods [1] in our northern provinces. From the start of the tenth moon until the festival of Buddha's death [2] in the following year, while mountain roads lie buried, impassable to man and beast alike, there is a natural period of fasting in the north. Pickling vats must be fully stocked with vegetable stalks, for even the cries of vendors of salted mackerel will be heard no more. A warm fire becomes the only source of pleasure; and, with visits next door or across the street no longer possible, there is little to do for half a year but brew endless pots of tea. If starvation is avoided, it is only because stocks of every kind are taken in and hoarded well in advance. But if goods for such remote coastal and mountain places were transported by land, their prices would be extortionate, and people would find it difficult to keep alive—wherefore the world may be truly thankful for the blessing of ships.

In the town of Sakata [3] was the house of the great broker, Abumiya. [4] In former times he had been no more than a small innkeeper, but his flair for business had brought about a steady improvement in his position, and nowadays, catering for customers from every province, he was the foremost purchasing agent [5] for rice crops in the north country. The name of Abumiya Sōzaemon was known to everyone. His grounds, sixty yards broad and a hundred and thirty deep, were packed close with reception buildings and storehouses. The catering departments were an astounding sight. There was a receiver and distributor of rice and bean-curd, a director of firewood, an overseer for fish, a chef, a supervisor of the crockery cupboards, a controller of cakes, a tobacco officer, a tea-room officer, and a bathroom officer. Again, there was even a special runner of errands. Amongst the accountants there was one for public business, one for private; one for issuing money, one for noting it in the books. With one function, no matter how trifling, apportioned to one man, everything was made to run smoothly. Day in and day out the master wore formal overskirts, and never once unbent his back in the presence of a client. His wife, smartly dressed in plain silks, was constantly at hand in her room. The two of them, smiling from morn till night—so unlike the home provinces brokers—did all they could to please, and their business was always their first consideration. The reception rooms were numberless, and a separate one was allotted to each client. In Kyōto the brokers have 'lotus-leaf girls', [6] but in

The kitchen and a reception room of the Abumiya

these parts they are called 'service girls',[7] and thirty-six or seven of them were employed at the Abumiya. For their dress, the layers underneath were silk, the outer garment cotton with vertical stripes, and the waistband—bound at the back—was generally a strip of Kyōto gold braid. These girls too had an overseer who instructed them, and who allotted each to one client to lay and pack away his bedding.

'Where ten men gather ten provinces meet.'[8] Here clients from Ōsaka or from Banshū Aboshi[9] exchanged gossip with men from Fushimi in Yamashiro, from Kyōto, Ōtsu, Sendai, and Edo. But no matter whence they came, their talk was uniformly clever, and not one was ill-equipped to watch his employer's interest. The old hands, of course, are content to fill their own pockets, and the younger ones enjoy themselves at the brothels and exceed their expense allowances—neither way being to the employer's benefit—but, after all, when you send a clerk on business to a distant province, a man of rigid morals is not your best choice. To think twice in every matter and follow the lead of others is no way to make money. The sort who will adventure boldly, albeit at his employer's expense, is all the quicker to conclude a favourable deal which will handsomely atone for previous failures, and cover his private debts as well.

Among the clients calling over the years at this agency many varieties of approach to business were observable. There was the sort who was no sooner down from his horse than he had lifted off the clothes trunk, [10] doffed his travelling gear, and changed into a formal crested suit of the latest dye discovered in Kyōto. Removing the dust-cover from his dagger, [11] he would pull on brand new socks and sandals, smooth back his side-locks, explore his gums with a toothpick, trim his personage till he judged himself ready for exhibition, and then announce that he was off to view the local sights—for which he would commandeer some usefully employed clerk as a guide. There had been many of these, but no examples of their getting very far in the world. Those destined to rise quickly from employed to employer turned their attentions to very different matters. As soon as they arrived they would approach an assistant in the front office and ply him with enquiries. Was he sure that market quotations had not changed since the letters they had received in the middle of last month? Local conditions varied so, and strangers could never predict the weather—would he mind looking at those clouds over that hill? Might a storm break before the two hundredth day, [12] did he think? How was this year's safflower crop? [13] And what about the green hemp?—not a question but was to the purpose. Such men were as hard to twist as the local dried salmon, [14] and in time they became merchants of greater account than their current masters back in the home provinces. There is a right and a wrong approach for everything.

The transactions of the Abumiya were as extensive as the plain of Musashi, and it was difficult to keep them under strict control. Brokers' establishments look like the homes of millionaires, [15] but wherever they are, they are built on shaky foundations. The income from the regulation commissions amounts to little, and the temptation is strong for a broker to speculate privately with the goods in his care. If the gamble fails, he calculates that he may usually saddle his client with the losses. When a broker concentrates on brokerage, of course, and takes proper care of his purchases and sales, he has little cause to worry. But the outsider's impression of a broker's finances is far from the truth. There are an amazing number of unsuspected sources of expense, and running the household on a more economical budget leads inevitably to diminished custom and the rapid decline of the firm. It is only once a year—in the first hour after dawn [16] on New Year's morning—that the balance of a year's losses and gains becomes clear. At any other time it is impossible to check the position. This was once the case at the

Abumiya too, but one year, when business was good, the master purchased in the twelfth moon the complete requisites of the catering department for the coming year. The department was thus concerned during that period with receipts alone, and a trap was cut in the lid of a large wooden trunk to catch the takings as they came in. The eleventh day of the twelfth moon came to be fixed as the day for opening the trunk and checking the accounts. A reliable broker's agency is a place where every guest may have a good night's sleep, even though his money is in the hands of the proprietor.

BOOK III

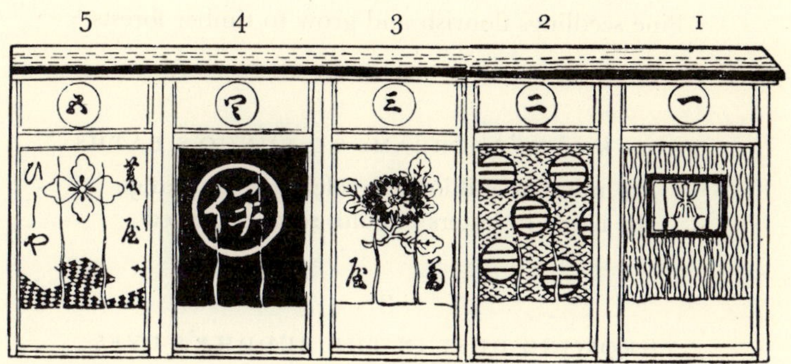

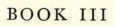

I

A DOSE OF WHAT THE DOCTOR NEVER ORDERS

A chopstick-carver celebrated in Edo
Pine seedlings flourish and grow to timber forests

2

FROM KYŌTO'S STREAMS TO BUNGO'S BATHS

An imitative millionaire celebrated in Bungo
His name in letters of gold, soon tarnished

3

THROWING DUST IN THE BUDDHA'S EYES

A disbeliever celebrated in Fushimi
Chrysanthemum blossoms from pawn-seeds

4

THE MAN WHO BUILT THE CENOTAPH OF DEBTS ON MOUNT KŌYA

A strait-lace celebrated in Ōsaka
The cat in the Almanac of Three Existences

5

A PAPER FORTUNE TORN TO SHREDS

The diamond crest celebrated in Suruga
A miss-hit on the Muken bell

1. *A dose of what the doctor never orders*

FOR each of the four hundred and four bodily ailments [1] celebrated physicians have produced infallible remedies, but the malady which brings the greatest distress to mankind—to even the wisest and cleverest of us—is the plague of poverty. [2]

'Is there a treatment to cure this?' a poor man asked a gentleman of great wealth.

'My dear fellow,' the rich man replied, 'if you have lived till now without knowing such things, you have wasted precious years. In matters of health the best time to take preventive measures is before you reach the wrong side of forty, [3] and you have left this consultation until rather late. However, I observe certain factors which may yet pull you through—your custom of wearing deerskin socks, for example, and bamboo clogs with thick leather soles. If that indicates your approach to life, we may even make a moderately rich man out of you. I have, it so happens, an excellent nostrum called "The Millionaire Pill", and I shall give you the prescription:

Early rising	5 parts
The family trade	20 parts
Work after hours	8 parts
Economy	10 parts
Sound health	7 parts

Grind the ingredients thoroughly, use common sense to get the proportions correct, mix carefully, swallow and inwardly digest twice daily—and there is no reason why you should not become a millionaire. However, during treatment it is imperative to abstain from certain noxious things: [4]

(1) Expensive foods, expensive women, silken suits for day-to-day wear.

(2) Private palanquins for wives; private lessons in music or poem-cards for eligible daughters.

(3) A professor of percussion for the sons of the house.

(4) Kickball, miniature archery, perfume appreciation, and poetry gatherings.

(5) A craze for the tea ceremony, and for remodelling the best rooms on tea principles.

(6) Flower-viewing, boating excursions, baths in the middle of the day.

(7) Evenings out with friends, gambling parties, playing Go or backgammon.

(8) Classes for townsmen in sword-drawing and duelling.

(9) Temple-going, and preoccupation with the next world.

(10) Getting involved in others' troubles, and standing surety.

(11) Lawsuits over reclaimed land, and meddling in new mining projects.

(12) Saké with supper, excessive pipe-smoking, unnecessary journeys to Kyōto.

(13) Backing Sumō contests for charity, and giving too generously to temple funds.

(14) Carving knick-knacks during business hours, and collecting fancy sword-accessories.

(15) Familiarity with Kabuki actors, and with brothel quarters.

(16) Borrowing money at a monthly rate of more than eight in the thousand monme.

All these things are more deadly than blister-fly drugs[5] or arsenic. I need hardly say, of course, that to taste any one of them is fatal—but the very idea of them must never enter your head.'

He bent close to his questioner's ear—a little ear, full of the promise of poverty—and the man listened enraptured, accepting every word as a drop of pure gold. He resolved to follow this wealthy person's advice, and to work unremittingly from morn till night.

But this was Edo, unfortunately, where the competition would be stiff in whatever trade he chose. He would do well to select some line of business which was a little out of the ordinary. With this in mind, seeking inspiration, he stood for one whole day, from early dawn, at the southern end of Nihon bridge.[6] Truly, this was the place where all the provinces of Japan rubbed shoulders. The bridge was a mountain which moved, and no crowds at the Gion festival in Kyōto, nor at Ōsaka's Tenma carnival,[7] were ever more tightly packed. Day after day brought new prosperity to Edo, and age after age the power of its lord and the breadth of its highways grew. But even this great road of Tōri-chō,[8] recently widened to twenty-four yards from side to side, was already too narrow. On the bridge itself, at any moment of the day he might have counted at least one horseman, one priest, and one

Jinbei at the bridge

halberdier. But no one dropped anything of value, and, screw his eyes though he might, he could not detect a single zeni. Reflecting on this, he came to appreciate the true value of the coin: it was not a thing to be lightly spent.

'The only way is to try my luck at a trade', he told himself. 'But if you start with empty hands these days—unless you're a wrestling instructor or a midwife—there's no hope of making money. I've never heard of a koban nor even a zeni sprouting from seedless soil. Can there be no way of making something out of nothing, I wonder?'

He was still looking about him and racking his brains when, back from the day's work at the various daimyō mansions, walking in their separate groups—now two hundred, now three hundred strong—came a procession of carpenters and roof-thatchers, chattering loudly and discordantly, side-locks falling over ears, heads comically dishevelled, kimonos dirty at the collar, waistbands tied outside their coats, sleeves frayed at the cuff. Some brandished two-yard measures as walking sticks. Most walked with hands in pockets and shoulders hunched. He needed no signboard to tell him their employment. Behind them they had apprentice boys to carry shavings and wood-ends, but if precious scraps of cypress were dropped and wasted, no one bothered. It must indeed be the castle-town of castle-towns, he thought, where even workmen are as liberal as daimyō. Keeping his eyes about him and picking up the dropped pieces one by one, he followed along from the Suruga-chō crossroads [9] to Sujikai bridge in Kanda, and in that distance collected as much as he could safely carry in one load across his shoulders. He sold the pieces just as they were, and made a clear profit of two hundred and fifty zeni. It irked him to think that he had overlooked till now opportunities which lay at his very feet, and every day thereafter, waiting impatiently for nightfall, he kept a look-out for the homeward-bound carpenters and picked up whatever they left in their wake. His catch was never less than five full loads. On days when it was too wet to do anything else he carved the wood scraps into chopsticks, and then sold them wholesale to the grocers' stores in Suda-chō and Setomono-chō. [10] He became famous along Kamakura bank as Chopstick Jinbei, [11] and gradually acquired a considerable fortune. Later, when the scraps in which he dealt had grown to trees, he bought a large mansion in Timber Merchants' block, [12] where he employed more than thirty clerks alone, and he bought up forest land no less extensive than the holdings of Kawamura, Kashiwagi, or Fushimiya. [13] Next—his ambition boundless as the ocean, his fortune's sails set square to the winds of trade—he stocked his timber yard with tall ships' masts, [14] and sold them all at prices merchants dream about. In a mere forty years he made a hundred thousand ryō. All this was the result of taking millionaire pills in his younger days.

Now that he was well past his seventieth year he judged that a little relaxation of the treatment would do no harm, and for the first time in his life he changed into a complete outfit of Hida homespun silk, and even cultivated a taste for the marine delicacies of Shiba. On his way back from regular morning worship at the Nishi Honganji temple in Tsukiji [15] he dropped in at theatres in Kobiki-chō, and in the evenings he played Go at home with groups of friends. While snow fell outside he held social gatherings to mark the opening of the winter's first tea-jars, [16] and as soon as the early daffodils were in bloom he set out tasteful flower arrangements in the impressionist manner. [17] Exactly when he had learnt all these refinements is not clear—but money makes everything possible.

There are people who draw no distinction between the beginning and the end, and who remain close-fisted all their lives; but Jinbei, who knew that even if he saved a Fuji-yama of silver his body was nevertheless destined to be smoke above Hashiba [18] and dust on Musashi plain, had wisely set aside a portion for his declining days, and with this he thoroughly enjoyed himself. When he reached eighty-eight[19] all who knew of his good fortune begged him to cut them lucky bamboo rice-levels and to choose names for their new-born children. At last, weary of the ways of men, craving no further earthly honours, he died as a saint might die, in a spiritual state conducive to the immediate attainment of Nirvana, and people felt all the more admiration and envy at the thought that he might fare no worse in the next world than in this.

The golden rule for men is to save in youth and spend in old age. It is impossible to take your money to heaven, and it is essential to have it on earth.

2. *From Kyoto's streams to Bungo's baths*

THE local doctors had pronounced the old man beyond hope. The end was near. Quickly, a parting drink was pressed to his lips—a clam-shell of fresh water against the seas of death[1]—but even a few drops choked him. Tugging at his arms and legs, his sons begged him to heed their last injunctions.

'Listen! Take the road straight to the Western Paradise—don't stop anywhere on the way! You won't forget, father, will you?'

The old man's eyes half opened again.

'Don't worry about me', he said. 'I have lived for sixty-three years, and by normal standards that leaves no deficit. I have closed my account, and am ready to have the entries crossed from life's books and transferred by Enma[2] to the books of Hades. I have no desire to stay. It is you I am anxious about: never forget, my sons, that your future livelihood depends upon the seeds you sow in youth....' Before he could say another word, he had gone.

Without further lamentation they turned to the laying out of the body. Really, a dead man's requirements were practically nil! Simply a shroud, it seemed, and six zeni for the road. The thought of the old man making his last journey under these conditions depressed them. It was a meagre allowance for forty-nine days' travel to the next world,[3] and would make even a ride on a hell-horse[4] out of the question.

The son who inherited the family fortune resided, as his father had done, in the town of Funai in Bungo province.[5] His name was Yorozuya Sanya,[6] and he was a celebrated figure in the locality. For three years, abiding strictly by the rules of mourning, he suffered not so much as a dislodged roof-tile to be replaced, and at each anniversary of his father's death he performed the proper rites with genuine emotion. He accumulated merit by the performance of charitable deeds, and he demonstrated the utmost filial consideration for his widowed mother. It was only natural that such perfection should meet its reward. In his father's dying words, as he remembered, the possible importance to his livelihood of certain 'seeds' had been mentioned, and since rape-seeds could be pressed for oil he had begun to think these might be the ones intended. He gave the matter continual thought, but could not decide whether it meant making a fortune by buying a stock of seeds on speculation, or simply growing them. A fortune, at any rate, he was determined to make, and night and day he revolved possible schemes in his mind. One day, travelling in rough open country far from any village, he passed by a broad stretch of overgrown land which had lain fallow since time immemorial, and the thought struck him that such a place left as a breeding ground for wolves was a loss to the national economy. Accordingly, some time later he secretly made the experiment of scattering rape-seeds there, and in due time blossoms appeared, and then more seeds. Seeing that the land, even untilled, could produce such results, he now applied for permission to reclaim it for cultivation.[7] He was granted tax exemption for ten years, and during that period—having uprooted weeds, levelled hillocks, erected scattered groups of dwelling houses, and hired labourers to till the ground with spade and hoe—he made a yearly profit and increased his stocks of money by no one knows how much. With the capital thus acquired he sought new markets in the home provinces, transporting his wares by sea, and greatly expanded the numbers of his assistants. Step by step he rose to the position of the leading millionaire of Kyūshū, and the very thought of want was banished from his presence.

Some time later, accompanied by his mother, he set off to see Kyōto in the spring. Though the attractions of cherry blossom may be said to differ little from place to place, there are marked variations in the attractiveness of the blossom viewers, and here in Kyōto, city of alluring women, it was not the blossoms bedecking hillsides and floating down streams which claimed Sanya's attention, but the blossoms walking the streets.[8] Cruel fate! For what past sins, he wondered, was he born in the backwoods? Memories of Bungo province quickly faded, and day after day he abandoned himself to the round of city pleasures. His time was limited, but before leaving he took into his service a bevy of comely concubines, twelve in number, and with these he travelled back

Sanya watches a 'Fan Battle'

to Bungo. Next he set about the remodelling of his home on Kyōto lines, a task which he executed with the greatest thoroughness. On the faces of the tiles lining the overhanging eaves he set his initials in gold relief;[9] close by each of his four walls he raised a three-storied stronghold for treasure; and immediately beyond the entrance-hall—the focal point for one hundred and twenty yards of corridor—he set aside a spacious waiting room,[10] lined with book-cases and hanging scrolls. Along the east and west of his garden he raised miniature mountain ranges, and to the south he sank a private inland sea, its shores lined with boulders to suggest the cliffs of Lake Hsi.[11] The stepping-stones studding its surface were semi-precious rocks, and the hanging bridges were of Chinese sandal-wood. In a nearby pavilion whirls of painted dragons in the Sesshū style[12] adorned the ceiling, and crystal lanterns in silver frames cast lights on ornamental bolt-heads of agate and beam-ends capped with pearl. The floor was spread with velvet-trimmed tatami mats padded with pure silk wool. Here, amid further perfections to which no pen can do justice, Sanya whiled away time gazing at the morning snow or relaxing in the cool of summer evenings. He invented a new game called 'The War of the Fans', a modification of the flower battles held at the court of Hsüan Tsung,[13] dividing the comely girls in his service into battalions on his left and right, and arming them with sticks surmounted by fans. Seated directly between them, all perspiration banished in gusts of gold-flashing air from either quarter, he smiled graciously on the ladies from whose direction the breezes blew the hardest. The battle over, he twisted the drooping fans [14] of the defeated from their sticks and cast them on to the pond, crowning his enjoyment with the poetic spectacle of fans adrift on the stream. Even old Mano, with all his millions, [15] never did anything so extravagant.

A man's affairs are his own, and others can never judge their rights and wrongs, but there remains the censure of heaven with which to reckon. Sanya's whole household lamented his behaviour, but Sanya went on as before. So long as the family's senior clerk was at hand to guard the cash-books, and to see that, if the stores of copper and silver could not be defended from the master's incursions, at least the sixty square yards reserved for stocks of gold should never be at his mercy, there was little danger of the household being seriously endangered. But there are no certainties in life, and in the early winter of his fifty-eighth year, from a mere chill taken on a frosty morning, the clerk departed this world. From then on, with the keys of every storehouse in his charge, the master gave full rein to his extravagant fancies. After investigating the properties of various waters available in his own province he became convinced that, after all, there was no water like Kyōto water, and he arranged for the falls at Otowa [16] in Kyōto to be tapped every day on his behalf. Barrel after barrel of it was shipped over the seas to far-away Bungo, to be boiled up daily for the brand-new bathrooms and wash-cubicles in Sanya's private residence. In ancient times there had been a 'Lord Burner-of-Salt' [17] who had transported salt water to his garden in the sixth ward of Kyōto to remind him of the salt-works along the Chika coast. Sanya, who filled his tubs with water from the capital, was nicknamed 'Lord Boiler-of-Bath', and the neighbours waiting expectantly for the last puff of smoke to fade above his kitchen chimneys [18] were not long disappointed. Late one winter, when a complete review of the accounts was undertaken, the total disbursals of more than five thousand kanme [19] were discovered to be one monme three fun in excess of the family capital. Thereafter the gap grew steadily wider, and, just as a two-mile dyke may be overwhelmed by the water which trickles at first through an ant-hole, [20] so Sanya's business finally collapsed. On Sanya himself, too, misfortunes accumulated, until his own life became forfeit, and all that had yet remained to him was confiscated by others.

3. *Throwing dust in the Buddha's eyes*

IT was in Fushimi,[1] long ago when Hideyoshi was lord of the castle,[2] and when daimyō from every quarter of Japan were congregated there, that the name 'Day-dreamer' was first bestowed on a mendicant prayer-chanter.[3] A gleaming Gate of Honour[4] fronted each of the great mansions at that time, and the gateway of the lord of Echizen[5] in particular presented a spectacle of indescribable magnificence. On its arches some now forgotten craftsmen had carved the stories of the Twenty-four Filial Sons and Daughters of distant China,[6] reproducing each figure with startling realism and beauty, and so contriving the traceries of coral inlaid with gems and precious metals that spring blossomed along rose-tinted branches, rainbow hues glowed quietly amid drifting clouds, dragons uncoiled before one's eyes, and fierce tigers crouched and sprang. The work is said to have consumed three years' revenues from the lord's five hundred and fifty thousand koku fief. By this gateway,[7] just as the rays of the morning sun were falling across it, there once chanced to pass a certain mendicant gong-beater, coming down from Kyōto on his begging rounds at the time of Bon. He stopped in amazement and stared. It seemed hardly possible that those dappled oxen, in the scene of Ta Shun at the plough, were carvings of coral—even the oxen hauling waggons back from Kyōto to Yodo or Toba[8] must surely pause here, he thought, mistaking these for friends of theirs, and seek their company for the rest of the journey; and, as for the scene of Lao Lai-tzu's dance, he could almost see the legs moving and hear the music, and the grasses and shrubs near the toy windmill in Lao Lai-tzu's hand seemed to be swaying to and fro in the breeze; then there was Kuo Chü unearthing the great golden stewing pot—too grand for boiling tea or cooking the dinner, of course, but if broken up into koban it would keep a man free of work for a lifetime. He could make use of a pot like that! Now it was this scene holding him and stirring his imagination, and now it was another entrancing him by its beauty; and when the light of day began rapidly to fail—early, it is true, but no earlier than one expects in autumn—he was taken completely by surprise. The time for collecting alms was over, and shouldering his empty bag he returned to Kyōto. The people who had noticed him, idling there from dawn to dusk, nicknamed him 'The Day-dreamer' and his descendants are famous by that name to this day.

The glory of those times was soon to vanish. The former mansions of daimyō became potato plots, and all around spread a desolate wilderness of peach trees. The forests had their moments of blossoming in the spring, but it seemed hardly possible that human life too could thrive in such a place. Even at mid-day one sensed that there should be bats flying or fire-flies gleaming. The main Kyōto highway, it is true, retained something of its old form, and there were houses here with shop-fronts facing the road, but in the regions behind people disappeared as their houses decayed, and in one block there might be no more than three families left to struggle for existence, raising pitiful wisps of smoke from their kitchens, passing summer nights without mosquito nets, and shivering through blanketless winters. Those of the old-established wicker basket makers and blow-pipe cutters [9] who remained here were now the leaders of Fushimi society. For the rest, they made hoops for shingle roofs, [10] carved pivots for folding fans, fashioned tweezers for poultice applications, or twisted rope for luggage binding—but life was longer, leaner, and less easily strung together than any rope, and for people living on such slender means the world was a comfortless place.

On the edge of the town lived Zenzō, proprietor of the Chrysanthemum pawnshop. [11] Though his establishment boasted not even the customary store-shed (a single wooden trunk on wheels serving in the dual capacity of money-chest and general locker) Zenzō himself lacked none of the qualifications of a pawnbroker, and with profits steadily swelling his original capital of barely two hundred monme he contrived to support his household of eight in tolerable comfort. Far worse off were those who pawned their possessions in his shop, and many were the pitiful scenes enacted there. As the rain pours down on a parting customer who has just deposited his only umbrella for six fun, another arrives to beg a hundred zeni on the family cooking pot, its interior still sticky with remnants of the morning's breakfast; a housewife enters, already scantily clothed against the autumn chill, and removes her soiled underslip in the shop as a deposit for a loan of three fun, leaving to brave mocking glances at her now translucent dress; a bent old woman of eighty, memories of a lifetime behind her, and a prospect of not so much as a year before her—but still obliged to fight for every day—borrows forty-eight zeni on a fish plate and a handless figure of the Buddha; or a girl of twelve and her urchin brother of six or seven struggle into the shop at either end of a massive ladder, and draw thirty zeni which they immediately spend at the side-counter on five gō of unhulled rice and a bundle of firewood. Glancing for even a few moments into the secrets of these harassed households is enough to make

The curtain before the image of Kannon

one weep. But the proprietor of a pawnshop can have no room for sympathy. Indeed, there is no more disagreeable trade.

For each deposit, even at this shop, a document of guarantee was demanded, and as closely scrutinised as at any pawnbroker's in Japan. Business was conducted strictly in accordance with the letter of the law.[12] In loans, they say, one guarantor is enough for a thousand kanme—but for Zenzō one guarantor was the *sine qua non* for the most trifling transactions. His profits were small but they mounted up, and in four or five years he had made a sum of more than two kanme. He was a mean-minded man, with no sympathy to spare for others, and since he had never once visited even Abbot Kōsen's temple,[13] which was practically on his doorstep, nor entered the Fushimi Gokō shrine[14] at a festival, nor ever troubled to offer a prayer to god or Buddha, people were not a little surprised when he suddenly manifested a reverence for the Kannon of the remote Hase temple[15] and departed there on a pilgrimage. It seemed miraculous that a man's nature should be so transformed, and the affair caused a sensation in the town.

For the privilege of raising the curtain before the sanctuary of Kannon at this temple there had been a fixed levy, since ancient times, of one gold bankin[16] for every seven days. Zenzō, whose worldly wealth amounted to two kanme of silver, paid to have the curtain raised for three such periods in succession. His name was on the lips of everyone in the temple, from the head priest down, and it was remarked that such zeal for salvation was unprecedented: never, in ancient or modern times, had one man paid for three weeks of curtain-raising. One day, however, on looking closely at the curtain, they noticed a rather dreadful thing: the relentless prodding and pushing it had received from the long rod had caused an unexpected amount of damage to about one half of the ten twelve-yard lengths of material, and the curtain was looking decidedly shabby.

'It is because I have had it raised and lowered so many times that the curtain has become worn like this,' said Zenzō, 'and I feel that I should hang up a new one, as a donation to the temple.'

His offer was accepted with delight, and a length of gold brocade was ordered from Kyōto to replace the worn cloth.

'If I could have the old curtain,' said Zenzō later, 'I should like to make a pilgrimage to the thirty-three shrines of Kannon in Kyōto, and offer up a section of it to each.'

The priests, to whom this seemed a trifling return for such services, made a present of the curtain, and Zenzō took every scrap of it back with him to Fushimi.

These Chinese embroideries (I need hardly say) were priceless articles imported in ancient times, woven in a variety of intricate designs—delicately coiling vines on a persimmon-coloured background, flowers and hares on hyacinth blue, and clouds and phoenixes on indigo. By cutting them all up into small luxury goods—pouches for tea canisters or mounts for hanging scrolls—Zenzō made an enormous sum of money, and brought prosperity to his household. The current rumour that he was worth five hundred kanme was not far wrong. His reverence for Kannon, of couse, was mere pretence, a trick to gain this end—and one must admit that he was a clever impostor.

In this one instance his plans had worked perfectly, but, lacking the background of a true man of wealth, Zenzō soon lost everything he had gained and found himself in circumstances even more miserable than when he had started. Later he set up a saké stall by Kyō bridge,[17] where the river boats start for Ōsaka, and badgered passengers to buy his drinks, but—whether he offered the smoothest trade wines or rough home brew, whether he wheedled or whether he pushed—people were reluctant to swallow anything more from him.[18]

4. *The man who built the cenotaph of debts on Mount Kōya*[1]

'EVERYTHING has its season, and no amount of weeping will stop flowers from fading or men from dying. Still, while we are alive care of health must be our first consideration. Why do people go on drinking dangerous swell-fish soup,[2] when rock-cod[3] tastes exactly the same and is perfectly harmless? And why, when their wives are on hand from the bridal night till old age—to be taken when required, like fish from a private pond—do people wilfully exhaust their strength in promiscuous living? These are not recoverable losses, but remain on the books for a lifetime. It is in things like this that people should observe moderation—and if you want to live a long life bear this in mind.'

Lectures of this sort are often given to clerks by strait-laced old employers, and long ago in Imabashi street[4] in Ōsaka there was a notorious skinflint, a man of great wealth, who lived his whole life in accordance with such precepts. He was a bachelor, and his economy-inspired daily diet was completely innocuous. Even he, however (perhaps from sheer boredom), departed this world in the prime of life. Since he had no heirs the whole of his remaining gold and silver was presented to a temple, and there, by paying for forty-eight masses for his departed soul, it performed the only useful service it had ever rendered him. But before long the money which had lain hidden year after year in his strong-room, innocent of the world, was circulating from hand to hand, helping Kuken-chō[5] brothel keepers to settle their monthly tradesmen's bills and Dōtonbori[6] theatre managers to pay their actors' salaries. The designs on the surface of the silver coins[7] were rubbed smooth with use, and people laughed to think that at least the man's money had worn itself out in the gay quarters. This miserly fellow, who died at the age of fifty-seven, was born in a tenth year of the Dragon, and it was also in a tenth year of the Dragon, on a Dragon day at the Dragon hour,[8] that he died. This amazing coincidence prompted a scholar of occult lore to consult 'The Almanac of Three Existences',[9] and after some research he discovered that the miser had formerly been the golden cat[10] presented to the priest Saigyō by lord Yoritomo, the Kamakura shōgun. Through chance contact with such an illustrious person it had at length been born into the human world, and although its body was of gold it could naturally not spend it. The fact that this gold had become a plaything for other people's children was also fated—for Saigyō had held the golden cat in his arms for only a few moments, and had then presented it to the boys of the village. Generations of people, reading this story in the old chronicles, had felt envious of these boys at the mere thought of that precious cat, and the late miser had been born from the crystallisation of all these greeds.

To make a fortune some assistance from fate is essential. Ability alone is insufficient. There are highly intelligent people plagued with poverty, and fools blessed with riches—a double injustice which even the treble-headed deity of luck [11] can do nothing to rectify. Or a man may follow the injunctions of Bishamon of Kurama, [12] driving himself as mercilessly as if he had a hundred legs to spare, like Bishamon's centipedes, and yet fail to become rich. There is nothing which can be done about this either, but such a man is sure at least of heaven's compassion and his neighbours' sympathy. And how do the others fare? Too idle to follow an honest trade, they yet have splendid mansions raised, make every meal a banquet of the finest wines and foods, stuff their wardrobes full with suits and fancy accessories, and mix with people far beyond their station. Their money, lavished on courtesans and actors, disappears as rapidly as a row of badly finished stitching, and if sewing-needles were koban a storehouse-full would never pay their bills. [13] But, so long as they can maintain appearances on other people's money, their credit never fails—and the more they borrow the less they intend to repay. Barefaced deceit of this nature makes a daylight robber, stretching out his hand to snatch your money, seem an honest tradesman by comparison. It is their intention, at some distant date, to declare themselves bankrupt, and since they are fully resolved on this as much as five or seven years in advance, they split their property forthwith and set up a younger brother as head of a collateral house, sufficiently independent to escape liability. If they live in Kyōto, they arrange to purchase a residence in Fushimi under someone else's name, and if they are Ōsaka people they get their relations in the country [14] to buy farm land for them. When the question of where to retreat has been satisfactorily settled, they surrender the empty shell of their property to the creditors, and curl up defiantly on a soft bed of dishonoured bills. If, through the intercession of the neighbourhood group, [15] they are offered the chance to rebuild their fortunes, settling the debts in yearly instalments, they seem strangely embarrassed and ungrateful. They leave the district for good, and—as far as the world can see—they have surrendered everything, even the ashes under the stove. By the next quarter-day, on the third of the third moon,[16] they are drinking their cups of festival wine with not a care in the world.

There was once a bankruptcy case[17] involving debts of eleven kanme in which there were eighty-six creditors. The remaining effects of the bankrupt were valued at only two kanme five hundred monme, and the creditors met together day after day to settle the matter of their shares. As no one stinted himself at these meetings the petty expense book grew black with entries of macaroni, noodles,[18] saké, relishes, and sweetmeats of every kind. For more than half a year they frittered away precious time, until all the money under debate had disappeared. At the final settlement each was obliged to contribute four fun five rin[19] from his own pocket, and—exchanging bows of abject apology and looking very foolish—they set off on their round of the ward to offer small tokens of gratitude to the local officials.

When, in Ōtsu long ago,[20] a man who owed a thousand kanme went bankrupt, people thought there could never be another case to equal it, but nowadays in Kyōto and Ōsaka bankruptcies of three thousand or two thousand five hundred kanme are not uncommon. Such things, of course, can hardly occur in small towns in remote provinces. It is only in a place like Ōsaka, the greatest port in Japan, that there are people to lend such sums, and people to borrow them. For the borrower too must be a merchant worthy of the name. Even if a man borrows only for the glory of the thing, it is said, a hundred kanme is the limit of one's credit.

Many years ago, in Enoko-jima in Ōsaka,[21] there was a respected merchant called Izuya who, through circumstances beyond his control, was obliged to go bankrupt. With his head bowed in genuine shame he expressed his regrets to his creditors and surrendered to them the whole of his property, which amounted to sixty-five per cent of his total debts. Resolved to honour his obligations in full and to repay the remaining thirty-five per cent at some future opportunity, when his luck should change, he left town and returned to his native place, the island of Ōshima in Izu province,[22] to seek assistance from his relatives. Working at a trade ceaselessly, day and night, he was inspired with such determination to recover his fortune that he managed to make a considerable sum of money. Once more he made the journey to Ōsaka, and there he paid up every penny of the debts which had remained unsettled since his bankruptcy. Seventeen years had elapsed from that time, and some of his creditors had disappeared to distant parts of the

Izuya's debts are paid

country. He offered their portions to the goddess at the great shrine of Ise.[23] Again, six or seven of the creditors had died, and for those who had no descendants to receive their money he erected a stone memorial in a temple on Mount Kōya,[24] before which he had prayers said for their souls. He called this the Cenotaph of Debts. One would search history in vain to find a parallel for such honesty.

5. *A paper fortune torn to shreds*

UNDER Chūsuke's management the family drapery business had gone steadily downhill.[1] Formerly the firm of Hishiya, readily distinguished by the bold diamond crest[2] on its shop blinds, had stood in Hon-chō in the town of Fuchū[3] alongside the foremost drapers' of Suruga province, and had not only competed successfully for local custom but had dispatched numbers of its clerks to the eastern and northern provinces, where they had established thriving branch shops. The staff increased yearly, and the domestic catering grew to such proportions that smoke as dense as the clouds above Fuji in eruption[4] rose ceaselessly from the great kitchen range, and Lake Biwa would have been needed to fill the water buckets. There were more red lacquered bowls than there are fallen maple leaves at Tatsuta, and the rows of gleaming white chopsticks looked like frost pillars [5] covering Musashi plain. Frost pillars are erect in the morning and melted by nightfall, and when the house of Hishiya melted away it may have seemed that this, too, was no more than the way of the world, the end of an appointed season. But the true cause lay elsewhere, in the master's carelessness. Chūsuke's father had started life with very little, but it was he who discovered the method of crêping Abegawa paper kimono [6] and colouring them with a variety of fine stencil patterns, and when his products had become established as the speciality of this district he sold them to merchants from all over Japan. At first he had no rivals in his field, and it is rumoured that in a little over thirty years he made one thousand kanme. His son Chūsuke was blessed with no such ability, and for more than ten years [7] after he inherited the business book-keeping and common sense alike were in abeyance. The beads on his abacus hung as motionless as dew drops on a branch of willow—except when rudely shaken by the vernal gales which blow on reckoning day. [8] Like ice beneath the sun's rays—to such poverty did he fall, in a decline for which few parallels exist—his fortune melted to water. Had he even thought to warm the water for a drink he would have found his firewood locker empty.

If making money is a slow process, losing it is quickly done. Now that Chūsuke had run through his whole fortune he realised the truth of this, but the knowledge was acquired too late. He was obliged to move to the outskirts of the town, to a house in front of the Sengen shrine, [9] and there, in hired rooms, he prepared to eke out the remainder of this fleeting life. People's sympathy had lasted only as long as his prosperity. Even his relatives and friends kept their distance now, and he could hardly complain if the rest of the world ignored him. The clerks who had helped to bring their master to these straits set up in business on their own, under a different name, and abandoned him to his own devices without so much as a letter of condolence. He received no skewered mackerel [10] at Bon, and no mirror-cakes at New Year. One day was as wretched as another, and even in the last moon, when everyone else was so busy, he had nothing to do.

Towards the end of one year his neighbours had gathered together and were playing at guessing each other's ages.

'You have the appearance of a fairly young man,' they said, when it came to Chūsuke's turn, 'and yet there is something old in your expression. And, of course, you have grown-up children. It's a rough guess, but we should not be far out if we put you at forty-eight or forty-nine.'

'Gentlemen, you are making a big mistake', said Chūsuke, apparently taking offence. 'At the moment I am thirty-nine.'

No one could understand this.

'Come, you can hardly expect us to believe that you are thirty-nine, or even forty. Tell us your real age, please.'

'The number of years I have lived is forty-seven', he admitted, in answer to persistent questions, 'But, all the same, my age is thirty-nine.'

'How can that be?'

'On New Year's Day,' he said, 'I celebrated the occasion with no zōni stews, nor even a clean suit of clothes. Nothing is further from my thoughts than pine decorations. I haven't even an almanack to look at, to tell me the lucky quarter has shifted east,[11] or the plums are in blossom in the south. And as the years in which I have thus failed to pass into the next now number eight, although I am forty-seven I am thirty-nine.'

They were still laughing over this when Chūsuke remarked, with evident confidence, that one day, when he had enough money to cover a journey to Nissaka in Tōtōmi province,[12] he would go there and become a rich man in no time. His companions promptly made a collection, and presented him with a string of one thousand two hundred zeni, which was no small mark of kindness from people living in such straitened circumstances. Delighted, Chūsuke rose from his place without further delay and set off on the journey.

'He must have rich relations there,' they thought, 'and is going to tell them of his troubles. Or perhaps he plans to demand payment for some old credit sales. But wherever he goes, at least he should get enough to pay for a real New Year.'

Full of curiosity they waited for his return. But Chūsuke's plan was very different from anything they had imagined. Crossing the river Ōi, with its ever-shifting channels,[13] he went on pilgrimage to the temple of Kannon which stands on a peak above the pass of Sayo-no-Naka-yama.[14] The after-life, however, could take care of itself: he had come to pray for better luck in this one. Asking where it was that, long ago, they had buried the Wishing Bell of Muken,[15] he stood over the spot and spoke his wish.

'In my own lifetime, just once, make me a millionaire. If my children

The rich merchant and Chūsuke's daughter

in their day become beggars, it is no matter. Help me now—that is all I ask.'

So passionately did he pray, and so violently did he strike the ground above the bell, that the reverberations must have penetrated to Hell itself. Nowadays even the prospect of becoming a snake in the next existence is no deterrent to money-lovers.[16] And how much less—if striking this bell could really bring riches—could they be halted by paltry threats of leech-hells![17]

Foolish Chūsuke, by coming here, spent his travelling money to no purpose. On this occasion he had luckily not much to lose. On returning to Suruga he explained what he had done, and everyone who heard the story laughed at him. It was obvious, they said, why such a simpleton was living in poverty.

In his neighbourhood there were a number of skilled craftsmen specialising in mulberry joinery and bamboo weaving. Chūsuke watched them at their work and taught himself how to make lacquered boxes for hair-oil and bamboo flower baskets. His daughter was now thirteen years old, and by entrusting his products to her, and sending her out on to the main thoroughfares of Fuchū to sell them, he managed to make just enough to support himself from day to day. The filial conduct of this child was widely commented upon throughout the province. What is more, she was a rare beauty, so perfectly formed that people would stop in their tracks to stare at her. One day a rich citizen of Edo, passing by on his way back from the Ise pilgrimage, was so impressed by his first glimpse of her that he went straight to her father and begged permission to make her his only son's bride. Chūsuke and his wife, together with the rest of their household, subsequently removed to Edo, and there—thanks to their luck in having such a beautiful daughter—they lived the rest of their lives in comfort.

Good looks, they say, are earned in previous existences. [18] When the people round about heard of Chūsuke's success they began to take the greatest care in bringing up their daughters, but for myself— though I know nothing about the courtesans in the Abegawa quarter [19]— I have noticed no improvement. All were evidently predestined to be plain. With Chūsuke's case in mind, one cannot help thinking that Ling Chao, the daughter of the Chinese hermit P'ang, [20] must have been an ill-favoured girl. If she had been a beauty she would surely not have been left selling baskets so long.

BOOK IV

1

A TRAY OF GOOD THINGS FOR A GOD

Kikyōya, a dyer celebrated in Kyōto
The dream of a talking straw doll

2

A SUBTERFUGE BEHIND A LITERARY SCREEN

An overseas trader celebrated in Hakata
A spider spins a web and shows the way

3

SHOWERS OF ZENI

Fundōya, celebrated in Edo
Every man to his natural trade

4

ALL THE GOODNESS GONE FROM TEA

A pedlar celebrated in Tsuruga market
A fiery finish for a skinflint

5

EXTORTIONATE PRICES FOR ISE LOBSTERS

Hinokuchiya, celebrated in Sakai
Watching Noh from the best seats

BOOK IV

I. *A tray of good things for a god*

AMONGST the large paintings[1] hanging before the Buddha of Kiyomizu temple in Kyōto is one inscribed with the name of a certain court draper.[2] There is a story that he presented this to the temple when his prayer for a fortune of one hundred kanme was granted. Those who knew his business then can hardly credit that his present prosperous establishment is the same place, and in Muromachi street[3] they never cease to marvel that so much money was made in one lifetime. Even now, of course—for greed is only human—we beg favours from Ebisu, Daikoku, Bishamon, and Benzai-ten,[4] tug at temple bell-ropes, and offer up prayers for enough capital to start a business, but the chances of satisfaction have grown slim. Worldly cunning is more effective in our generation.

There was a man called Kikyōya[5] who, with the assistance of his wife, ran a small dyer's shop in Kyōto. Though they set high store by their chosen employment, working without a moment's respite and racking their honest brains[6] for means of improving trade, each year they were obliged to admit that they were too busy to pound the rice in time for New Year's Day, and too short of money to buy any salted yellow-tails to hang on the kitchen hooks.[7] At Setsubun they placed 'treasure ship' charms beneath their pillows,[8] scattered beans all over the house and shouted 'Luck, come in!'[9]—but it made no difference: they remained as poor as ever. In desperation, they changed their tactics.

'The usual thing is for everyone to worship gods and Buddhas of luck,' said Kikyōya, 'but from now on we shall worship the god whom everyone else dislikes—Binbō-gami, the god of poverty.'[10]

He made a queer-looking dummy of wood and straw, draped its body in a scanty russet kimono, set a paper cap on its head, and fixed a battered old fan in one hand. He placed this grotesque figure in the centre of the season's decorations, and from New Year's Day to the Festival of Seven Herbs[11] he did everything possible to honour it and offer it suitable refreshments. On the night of the last day the god himself, trembling with pleasure, appeared in Kikyōya's dreams.

Kikyōya and his wife worship the god of poverty

'For years,' said the god, 'in the course of my routine visits to poor families, I have lain hidden and neglected in piles of debts in all kinds of wretched homes. If ever I heard my name mentioned it was used as an insulting word [12] to reprove naughty children. And even if I went to a rich man's house life was no less difficult: my liver was unsettled by the interminable tap-tap-tapping on the scales as he weighed his silver coins, and my stomach was turned by his fancy meals of vinegar-flavoured raw duck or cryptomeria casseroles. [13] Naturally I am the god assigned to rich men's wives, and I must go around with them everywhere. When I am in their bedrooms, with layers of mattresses beneath me, eiderdowns suspended from the ceiling above, [14] and my face smothered in cotton-wool pillows, [15] the feel of it makes me itch all over; and the perfumes they smoke into their lily-white nightdresses are suffocatingly thick. I loathe their flower-viewing and theatre-going trips: being shaken about in a palanquin, behind stuffy velvet-edged blinds, sends my head round in circles. And to come back at night to face glaring candles against gold-lacquered screens makes it even worse. The lights in poor men's houses, subdued by lanterns which have needed a change of paper for ten years, are much more soothing. Sights like that of a housewife rising at midnight to refill a spluttering lamp, and using her hair-oil as a makeshift, scenes of necessity—these are the things which give me pleasure. For years now I have stood by and watched, but no one has ever acknowledged my presence. I have been snubbed; and being treated like a poor relation has made me all the more perverse. Until you took note of me this spring I had been spending all my time dragging people deeper and deeper into debt. This is the first time in history that the god of poverty has been worshipped, and has taken his meals from a private tray. I am eternally obliged to you. I shall transfer the penury which this house has inherited to some spendthrift second-generation millionaire, and I shall bring you prosperity at once.

'Remember,' he said—and he repeated his words two, three, four, five times—'there are innumerable ways of earning a living. We all have our special talents—willows are good at greenness, but flowers are better at being red!'

Kikyōya awoke, and the divine vision of his dreams was gone, but he did not forget these last words. They were evidently auspicious, and he pondered their meaning for some time.

'Since I am a dyer by trade', he thought, 'the god's remark about redness must surely refer to redflower dyes.[16] But the Kobeniya firms[17] have large stocks of these already, more than enough to meet the demand. Not only that, but recently sugar-red dyes[18] have come on to the market, and in a place as discriminating as Kyōto it will be hardly possible for me to make profits from any second-rate imitation.'

Day and night he experimented with new processes, and at last, by applying vinegar to a first layer of sapan-dye[19] and re-steaming the whole, he produced a colour which was indistinguishable from genuine 'redflower'. Keeping his discovery a secret he dyed a quantity of cloth in this way and set off for Edo,[20] walking all the way with the cloth across his shoulders. He sold his stock to the drapers in Hon-chō and bought a supply of north country silk and cotton for sale on his return. By plying this two-way trade, like a sawyer who relaxes neither pulling nor pushing, in under ten years he made a fortune of more than one thousand kanme.

Kikyōya employed a large number of clerks, and to them he now left the practical matters of business. Meantime he enjoyed life to the full, as compensation for the weary years of labour in his youth. This surely is proper conduct. What use to a man is even a fortune of ten thousand kanme if he never ceases to work, but tires his body and racks his brains far into old age? He is dead before he knows that life is passing.

A man in his family trade is like a samurai in service. For daimyō who inherit whole provinces from their forbears there is little more to gain, but it was never intended that the rank and file of retainers should read the revenues inscribed on their fathers' tombstones [21] and contentedly continue at that level throughout life. Only if they perform meritorious services themselves and earn promotion to higher office and reward can they be said to have lived successfully. The case of a townsman is no different. There are those who are content to think of money-making as their father's department, and who, when they have inherited everything by a simple deed of legacy, suffer the family business to prosper as best it can on the reserves of goodwill accumulated in the past. Or there are those who live lives of utter uselessness and indolence on steady incomes from property-rents or the never-failing interest from loans. These people have risen above themselves and care no longer what the world may think—from the age of twenty they lean on walking-sticks, affect the flat-caps of master-merchants, [22] and oblige their servants to follow them through the streets with long-poled sunshades—but, even granting that this money which they spend is theirs by law, they live in ignorance of the dispensations of heaven. A man, it is decreed, is lacking in all discrimination till the age of thirteen; from then until the age of twenty-four or twenty-five he must abide by the guidance of his parents; thereafter he must earn his living by his own efforts, on his own responsibility, and if, by the age of forty-five, he has laid firm the foundations of his household's prosperity in his own life-time, he may then take time for pleasure. Premature pensioners, retiring from work in the prime of manhood, giving notice to a host of family retainers and obliging them to seek new masters, betray the trust placed in them for the future, and bring distress to everyone. To consider the welfare of those in one's charge, to share the family inheritance, [23] to establish

Kikyōya and his wife in prosperity

senior clerks in branches of the family business—this is the meaning of townsman success, the true way of a master.

Feeding three people is not called 'supporting a household'. That is reserved for those who earn enough for five and above. No more do we give the title 'master of an establishment' to a man without a single servant. If there is none to call him 'sir', if his meals are not brought on a serving tray, if he takes each dish direct from his wife's hands, and his wife acts as table maid, his belly may swell to great proportions, but no one can envy him his lot. He is 'keeping himself alive', but there are immense differences of degree contained in that one phrase. With this in mind, let none of you rest idle and content for a moment. Money is ever on the move, and, if you devote your whole strength to its pursuit, there is no reason why you should not collect a great heap of it.

Kikyōya had started his career in a household of two—himself and his wife—but now he was commander-in-chief of a domestic army [24] of seventy-five. The mansion in which he lived was the answer to a merchant's prayer: there were seven storehouses for treasure, nine reception rooms, and a garden where, besides hundreds and thousands of the usual trees and flowers, there were a number of those famous trees which money grows on. [25] The name of his district was Millionaire-machi. [26]

2. *A subterfuge behind a literary screen*

SAILING only in winds which are fair and steady, each ship with its experienced look-out, able to give three days' warning of the impending storm when 'one foot eighter' clouds [1] are spotted on the Kyūshū coast—a voyage in these days need arouse no fears. Thanks to ships—ships which skim across a hundred leagues of sea a day, a thousand leagues in ten—all the world's ten thousand needs are promptly met. A great merchant should model his mind on an ocean-going ship. The man whose life is bounded by the drainage channels round his house, who never risks the soaring leap from door to lands of treasure overseas, [2] will never tap his balance [3] with a magic wishing mallet. [4] It is a pitiful thing to pass a lifetime going round and round the pans of the shop scales, and to know nothing of the wide world which lies beyond.

To turn from Japan to risky speculations [5] in the China trade, sending one's money clean out of sight, needs boldness and imagination. But at least a Chinese merchant is an honest man, and keeps squarely to his promise: the insides of his rolls of silk are the same as the outsides, his medical herbs are not weighted with worthless ballast, his wood is wood, his silver is silver,[6] and none of it changes as the years go by. For sheer duplicity one need go no farther than Japan, where the length of needles is made shorter at each delivery, the breadth of cloth grows narrower and narrower, and even paper umbrellas are sold without waterproof. Penny wisdom is the ruling principle in our country. If an umbrella is sold what happens thereafter is no concern of the supplier: it is not he who gets wet. And he is so close-fisted that he would sooner see his own father go naked through a cloudburst than lend him an umbrella free of charge.

Many years ago a thriving business was conducted in the export of small boxes of tobacco to Korea.[7] The cutting and packing was done by workmen in Ōsaka, and one year, calculating that there was no immediate fear of detection, the manufacturers arranged for the lower layers of boxes to be loosely filled, and then soaked in water to make up the weight. During the subsequent voyage across the seas the tobacco became as hard as rocks and completely lost its virtue as a source of pipe-smoke. Although the Chinese were deeply incensed at this, in the next year they placed an order for ten times the previous amount, and the manufacturers, too eager for profits to suspect a trick, worked in feverish haste to get the goods down to Nagasaki before it was too late. When the boxes were ready and stacked on the dockside, the Chinese rejected them all.

'Your method of soaking last year's tobacco with cold water was unsatisfactory', they said. 'This year try pickling it in hot water, or in the sea.'

The tobacco rotted where it stood, and became part of the mud along the foreshore. Swindling, as one may observe from this, has no permanent success. If a man is honest the gods assist his plans,[8] and if he is pure the Buddhas enlighten and guide him.

In Hakata, in Chikuzen province,[9] trusting all to the whims of heaven, there lived a man called Kanaya (or something like that),[10] a backer of overseas ventures at Nagasaki. Fate on the high seas was against him, and three great storms in one year brought disaster to the expeditions on which he had gambled his life's savings. He was left with nothing but his house, his empty store-sheds, and the melancholy sound of the wind moaning through the pines in his garden. His servants were given their dismissal, and to his wife and children fell the unhappy lot of never knowing how they might live through the next day. Kanaya, cast suddenly into these troubled waters, with no land in sight, trembled at the mere sound of a wave, and vowed in his heart to the god of seafarers [11] that he would suffer no descendant of his ever to put anything aboard a ship.

One evening he sat on the verandah, longing for a cool breeze, and gazed at the clouds which towered above him in every quarter, peak upon peak. It seemed that at any moment a dragon might soar into them and unleash a summer storm. [12] Man's possessions, he reflected, were no more permanent than those threatening skies. Now that his household was poor even the garden had disappeared beneath a thick layer of dead leaves, and the house itself had changed, almost without his noticing it, to a weed-covered ruin. Thousands of summer insects were treating its rooms as wastelands in which to sing in desolate chorus. From a large bamboo projecting over the garden wall a spider was spinning a single thread to the twigs of a cryptomeria, and he watched it crossing. When it had reached halfway, a sudden gust of wind broke the thread, and the spider hurtled downwards in peril of its life. Once more it began spinning, and once more the thread broke. Three times he saw it meet with disaster, but at last, at the fourth attempt, it made the crossing safely, spun it's spider house, and took its supper on the flies which flew in.

'If an insect like that can be so patient,' he thought, after watching the spider respinning its thread again and again, [13] 'and can cheerfully persevere until its nest is built, how much less excuse has a human being for hasty despair! All is not lost yet.'

The example of the spider had given him new heart. He sold his house and everything in it, and bought in a small stock of merchandise, [14] choosing the goods with an eye on current price fluctuations. There were no clerks to do his business for him as in the old days, so he took his load down to Nagasaki himself. Mingling with the crowds in the import market, passing before piles of other people's treasures, [15] he saw Chinese textiles, medical herbs, shark skin, [16] and tea implements of every kind—all of them, as he knew, destined to rise in price before long. But he had no money for expensive purchases, and he was obliged to leave all these splendid opportunities to the buyers from Kyōto and Sakai. In experience and natural cunning he was a match for the best of them, but there was nothing he could do now. His leather money satchel contained a mere fifty ryō. [17] Without bothering either to join the merchants bidding here, or to consider any alternative scheme for his paltry capital, he gave himself up for lost, and went to the brothel quarter at Maruyama.[18]

There was a certain first-grade courtesan with whom he had been intimate in the heyday of his wealth, and he was determined that for this one night, if it was for the last time in his life, he would enjoy himself in the old way. Kachō was the girl's name,[19] and with the assistance of their former go-between the two were brought together again. From the very first meeting they had felt a genuine affection for each other, and tonight, as they shared their pillow for the last time, they experienced a depth of passion which they had never known before. At the head of the pillow Kanaya noticed a folding screen.[20] On both faces it was lacquered in silver, and over the whole surface, with hardly a space between, were pasted specimens of old calligraphy. Not one of these was of inconsiderable merit, and in particular he noted that there were a number of poem sheets of the 'Ogura Hundred Poets'[21] in Fujiwara Teika's handwriting, six of which had not even been recorded in the collectors' catalogues. The more he looked at them the more he became convinced that they were on genuine antique paper in Teika's original hand. Who on earth could have given such a screen to this courtesan, he wondered? And now that his greed was thoroughly roused the delights of love-making dropped into second place. After this night he visited Kachō frequently, with great regularity, and so cleverly did he play upon her feelings that before long the courtesan cried every minute that he was away, and reached the point where she would have shorn her head of its ebony locks if he had asked for them. When he finally asked for her screen she gave it without seeking a word of explanation. At once, hardly stopping to say good-bye, he set off for the home provinces, where he obtained the services of an agent, offered the screen for sale to daimyō,[22] and received an enormous price for it. Once more he

Kanaya leaves Kachō

became a great merchant, employing as many assistants as in the old days.

After his success Kanaya went down to Nagasaki and bought Kachō her freedom.[23] Since she had set her mind on a young man from a seaside village in Buzen province,[24] he sent a handsome dowry to the man's home, together with a complete bridal trousseau and household set, and settled the two in marriage. Kachō's joy knew no bounds, and she vowed that she could never forget her obligations to him.

It was true that he made his money by playing a heartless trick on a courtesan, but there are worse methods. And his genius for sizing up an antique, in any situation, won universal admiration.

3. *Showers of zeni*

HONEST dealing among men is a tradition which originated in Ise, the province of the gods. Besides the two main shrines at Ise,[1] of course, there are one hundred and twenty flimsy-looking side-shrines, each of which displays a picture of its god on a paper poster. These shrines are not in the best of taste, perhaps, but in the hearts of the deities themselves, as in their crystal mirrors, there is no trace of deceit. In the attendants' hearts too there is nothing but innocence and purity; and it is in this knowledge that people from every quarter of our Land of Autumn Harvests[2] make the pilgrimage to Ise. But who, one wonders, was the petty-minded genius who started the custom of 'pigeons' eyes'[3] those curious lead zeni which are sold to pilgrims, sixty on a 'hundred string', as offering money on their tour? What stingy creatures men are! The wealthy gods of luck would laugh outright at such an offering.

The business done at this place, I need hardly say, is a roaring one. Contributions flow in without a moment's pause: mountains of gold and silver for ritual dances,[4] thousands of dozens of monme for answers to prayers.[5] Souvenir dealers, making their livings by selling toy whistles, sea-shell spoons, and edible seaweed, are as countless as the grains of sand on the seashore. Besides this, the lesser pilgrim-agents,[6] men without private scribes, pay a zeni a copy to anyone who will write out the routine New Year messages they must carry round to their patrons in the provinces, and there are hundreds of people who support wives and families throughout the year by this alone. No one fails to get a living of some sort here. Salesmanship by courting the customer is the speciality of the people of Ise province. Even the female beggars [7] along the Ai-no-yama [8] road are patient practitioners of this art, and by making eyes at every passing pilgrim they never go cold or hungry. Dressed in gay silks, strumming samisens in time with their neighbour, they sing their one and only song—'Oh, how sad to be single!' [9] No one has ever heard them sing a new one, and the three-mile road from the outer to the inner shrine would lose its special flavour if they did.

A zeni is a delightful thing. No one had ever given these beggars their fill of them, though crowds of pilgrims had passed their way.

'It's a small enough sacrifice, and you would think that someone would feel the urge to make us happy', grumbled one old man, a vendor of souvenir pebbles. [10] 'Kyōto people give fantastic New Year tips at the Shimabara brothels, [11] but when they come here they're the stingiest of the lot.'

Once a certain townsman from Edo made the pilgrimage to Ise. His baggage, strapped on a hired mule, [12] was of no particular distinction; the cushions in his palanquin were of the plainest purple; and his attendants numbered no more than two or three. One of the usual pilgrim-agents had been entrusted by him with all the arrangements for his visit. Before leaving Yamada [13] for the inner shrine the merchant bought two hundred thousand zeni of genuine copper, which he set across the backs of a team of light baggage mules, [14] and as he moved along the twenty odd furlongs of the Ai-no-yama road he scattered the coins in every direction. The surface of the highway disappeared from sight, and you might have thought that every tree by the wayside was the celebrated 'pine of a million zeni'. [15] The beggars rose from their haunches and gathered all they could, till zeni overflowed from capacious Matsubara dancing sleeves [16] or dripped over the rims of bean-paste sieves. [17] For a moment their singing and strumming was stilled. They wondered what sort of a millionaire this man could be, and they asked the attendants his name. It was Fundōya something-or-other, [18] they gathered, and he lived somewhere near Sakai-chō in Edo. [19] He was one of those rich men of whom no one ever hears.

The world offers many examples of shaky businesses blown up to daimyō proportions, but with this man the case was reversed: behind an unimpressive façade he concealed a fortune of such massive solidity that one might sooner catch slippery demons in the dark than budge it an inch. Spring after spring luck had kept the devils from his door, [20] and now, after making his own way in the world for thirty-four years,

Fundōya and the beggars

from twenty-one to fifty-five, [21] he had retired and passed on to his only son a capital of seven thousand ryō. His initial venture in trade had been to rent a three-yard wide stall near the Miyako Dennai Theatre [22] and set up a zeni shop [23] to provide small change for purchasers of side-show tickets. When weighing customers' silver he allowed himself a commission of a half to one fun in every two or three monme, and, although his trade at first gave trifling returns, as his capital slowly grew he was able to make much larger profits. In time he rose to be a fully-fledged money broker. He was truly 'as sound as a camphor tree', [24] and nothing could shake the foundations of his fortune.

Next door to his zeni shop there had lived an extremely clever showman, a man who could pass off a crow as a white heron. One year, when he exhibited a 'Bird of Hell' [25] of consummate workmanship, his takings reached fifty thousand zeni every day; and another year he made mountains of money from a queer-shaped thing which he named 'The Berabō Beast'. But he was not the man to hurry and get himself a house and store-shed. He turned his mind instead to distant mountains and ocean gulfs, dreaming of the day when he should discover a monkey of a naturally pale blue complexion, or a bream with hands and feet. Looking for his livelihood he floated about like a bubble on a river, liable to burst and vanish at any moment.

The takings of actors and boy players, too, are momentary blossoms which bear no fruit. In the Kabuki play 'Visits to Kawachi' [26] Tamagawa Sennojō, [27] as the heroine, received a fixed salary for every performance of one gold koban, so that in a single year he made three hundred and sixty ryō. But when he died in retirement in Ise he owned not so much as an old theatrical robe, and his only consolation in his old age had been the memory of his days of glory. He had had no conception of how to save money and use it for trade. A man must know his way about the world, whatever his calling.

In the late year of the Cock, [28] when even pots and pans went up in smoke, everyone alike was obliged to start life again from naked poverty, but things were very soon exactly as before. The saké shops reappeared, with the familiar cedar brooms of the trade over their doors, the drapers of Hon-chō [29] were displaying materials as fine as ever, the Tenma-chō silk and cotton stores were rebuilt with the same distinctive shop-fronts, [30] and the street through Sakuma-chō was lined once more with its multitudinous paper-merchants. Business in the Funa-chō fish market, the Kome-gashi rice market, the Amadana wholesale lacquer shops, and everywhere along Tōri-chō was well on the way to the prosperity we know today. When the wind had dropped and the clouds were stilled makers of clogs and sandals reappeared in Furetere-chō, silversmiths' hammers were heard again in Shirogane-chō, and everywhere it was the same people one had seen before, plying the same trades. The day-labourers' bodies, the begging priests' [31] faces, the voices of vendors of ointments for boils and cuts—all were the old familiar ones. Not a single person, it seemed, had changed his mode of life. The old poor, even, were the new poor; and the old rich had become rich again.

Fundōya toured the city after the fire, and he noted all this in amazement.

'In all the districts and streets in Edo,' he said, 'only one man changed his trade. Perhaps he had picked up some capital in the fire—at any rate, he gave up the rosary business he had run all his life and opened a sword and dagger shop at Nakabashi. [32] He looked to have set himself up splendidly for life, but no customers came, and his shiny new swords were soon as rusty as ancient kitchen knives. [33] In time he realised that rosaries were his only hope of salvation, and he returned to his old shop to pick up the broken threads of his livelihood. A man does well to keep to the path of life he knows.'

4. *All the goodness gone from tea*

ONE gold bankin [1] a day—that, they say, is the average toll levied on cargoes landed at the port of Tsuruga in Echizen. [2] The daily toll on freighters up and down the river Yodo [3] is no greater. Tsuruga is a place where wholesalers of every kind flourish, but its period of greatest activity is in the autumn, when rows of temporary shops are erected for the annual market. The streets take on a truly metropolitan air, and to look at the women, strolling at ease amid crowds of men, and bearing themselves with feminine grace and restraint, you might think that a new Kyōto had sprung up in the north. This is also the season for travelling players to converge on the town, and for pickpockets to gather in strength. But people have learnt to keep their wits about them: they have altogether abandoned the practice of hanging valuable ornaments [4] from their belts, and money wallets are thrust far out of reach in the folds of their kimono. These are hard times indeed, if even the brotherhood of thieves can no longer make a dishonest penny in a crowd the size of this. But honesty still reaps its reward, and a skilful tradesman, humbly inviting buyers to inspect his wares, treating each customer with courtesy and respect, need not despair of making a livelihood.

On the outskirts of the town lived a man called Kobashi no Risuke. [5] With no wife or children to support, his only care each day was to provide a living for himself. In his approach to this he displayed considerable ingenuity. He had built a smart portable tea-server, and early every morning, before the town was astir, he set the contraption across his shoulders and set out for the market streets. His sleeves were strapped back with bright ribbon, he wore formal divided skirts, tightly bound at each ankle—the picture of efficiency—and on his head he set a quaint eboshi cap. [6] He might have passed for the god Ebisu himself. When he cried 'Ebisu tea! A morning cup of Ebisu tea!' the superstitious merchants felt obliged to buy a drink for luck, even if they were not at all thirsty, and from force of habit they tossed him twelve zeni for each cup. [7] His luck never changed, day after day, and before long he had enough capital to open a retail tea shop and do business on a larger scale. Later he came to employ a great number of assistants, and he rose to be a leading merchant in the wholesale trade.

So far, as a man who had made a fortune by his own efforts, he had earned nothing but admiration and respect. He even received, and rejected, requests from influential citizens to marry their daughters.

'I shall take no wife before I have ten thousand ryō', he used to say, calculating that matrimony might involve inconvenient expenses at the moment. 'There is plenty of time left before I pass forty.'

For the time being he found sufficient pleasure in watching his money grow, and he lived on in solitary bachelorhood. As time passed he became less scrupulous in his business methods: sending his assistants to all parts of Etchū and Echigo provinces[8] he bought up used tea leaves, on the pretext that they were needed for Kyōto dyes, and he mixed these with the fresh leaves in his stock. People could see no difference, and his sales brought tremendous profits. For a period, at least, his household enjoyed great prosperity, but heaven, so it would seem, did not approve. Risuke became stark mad, gratuitously revealing his private affairs to the whole province, babbling of tea dregs wherever he went. People cut him dead: they would have no dealings with a man whose fortune was so disreputably made. Even when he summoned a doctor no one would come. Left to himself he grew steadily weaker, till he had not even the strength to drink hot or cold water. Once, towards the end, he begged tearfully for a mouthful of tea to cleanse him of worldly thoughts, but, although they held the cup before him, a barrier of retribution was firmly settled in his throat. Then, scarcely able to breathe, he bade his servants bring the money from his strong-room and lay it about his body, from head to foot.

'To think that all this gold and silver will be someone else's when I die!' he sobbed. 'What a sad and dreadful thought that is!'

He clasped the money to his breast; he clenched it between his teeth; his tears trailed crimson streaks across his ashen face, and he needed only horns to be the image of a white devil. In his madness he leapt wildly about the room, a shadow of his former self, and even though he sank down again and again in exhaustion no one could hold him still for long: he revived and started searching for his money once more. Thirty-four or -five times he repeated this performance. By then even his own servants could find no more pity for him. They were terrified, and one by one they gathered in the kitchen, grasping sticks and clubs to defend themselves. They waited for two or three days, and when no further sounds could be heard they rose together and peeped into the room. Risuke lay there with staring eyes, still clutching his money. Nearly dead with fright they bundled his body, just as it was, into a palanquin, and set off for the cremation ground.

It was a mild spring day, but suddenly black clouds swirled into view, sheets of rain sent torrents racing across the flat fields, gusts of

The dying tea dealer leaps wildly about the room

wind snapped withered branches from the trees, and lightning lit the skies. Perhaps it was the lightning which stole away the corpse, even before they had a chance to burn it. At all events, nothing remained now except the empty palanquin. With their own eyes they had witnessed the terrible truth that this world of the senses is a world of fire.[9] They turned and fled, and every one of them became a devout follower of the Buddha.

Later all Risuke's distant relatives were summoned and asked to settle the division of the deceased's property, but when they heard what had happened they shook with fright, and not one of them would take so much as an odd chopstick. They told the servants to split the property amongst themselves. But the servants showed no enthusiasm at all: on the contrary, they quit the house, and they even left behind the articles of clothing which Risuke had given them during their service. Since the laity, trained in the world of greed, had shown themselves so stupid, there was nothing for it but to sell the whole property at a loss and present the proceeds to the local temple. The priests were delighted with their windfall. The money could hardly be used for sacred purposes, so they went up to Kyōto, where they had the time of their lives with boy actors, and brought smiles of happiness to the faces of Higashiyama brothel keepers.[10]

Strangely enough, even after his death Risuke made regular rounds of the various wholesale stores to collect his dues on previous credit sales. The proprietors knew well enough that he was dead, but from sheer terror at seeing him in his old form they settled their accounts at once, without attempting to give him short weight. The news of his reappearance caused wide alarm. They called Risuke's old house 'ghost mansion', and as nobody would take it even as a gift, it was left to crumble and become a wilderness.

It is easy enough, as may be observed, to make money by shady practices. Pawning other people's property, dealing in counterfeit goods, plotting with confidence tricksters to catch a wife with a large dowry, borrowing piecemeal from the funds of innumerable temples, and defaulting wholesale on a plea of bankruptcy, joining gangs of gambling sharks, hawking quack medicines to country bumpkins,[11] terrorising people into buying paltry ginseng roots,[12] conniving with your wife to extort money from her lovers, trapping pet dogs for skins, charging to adopt unweaned babies and starving them to death, collecting the hair from drowned corpses[13]—all these are ways of supporting life. But if we live by subhuman means we might as well never have had the good fortune to be born human. Evil leaves its mark deep in a man's heart, so that no kind of villainy seems evil to him any longer; and when he has reached that stage he is indeed in a pitiful state of degradation. The only way to be a man is to earn your livelihood by means not unfitted to a man. Life, after all, is a dream of little more than fifty years, and, whatever one does for a living, it is not difficult to stay so brief a course.

5. *Extortionate prices for Ise lobsters*

In a world where nothing is granted life without means to support it,[1] worrying too much over how to make a living is a waste of precious time. Every year we complain how difficult things have become, telling each other that we shall never manage, but when it comes to getting ready for New Year there is not a household where rice-cakes are not prepared, not one of us too poor to buy a pickled herring roe.[2] We even see prosperous well-managed households where stocks are laid in to last till the third moon—rows of Tango yellow-fish[3] and pheasants hanging in the kitchen, piles of firewood in the lumber shed, stacks of rice-bales in the yard—or places where all paying is finished by the twentieth, with the rest of the year for receiving only. At the same time, it must be admitted, there are households where the margin could hardly be more slender, where the accounts balance on paper but every due on sales must be in before debts on purchases can be paid, and where the buying of clogs and socks for servants' presents must wait till after midnight on the thirtieth—so hard pressed are such people by the world's insistence that debts must be settled first. Then there are the employers who have scraped through by economising on the new outfits for their articled maids and apprentices,[4] sewing plain blue linings on the cheapest ready-dyed material they can find in the shops—New Year's Day is the day when the world gets its first visible evidence of how shaky these businesses really are. Still, economy is undoubtedly the watchword for New Year. Replacing cups and bowls which will serve longer, repairing the house, changing the tops of tatami mats, painting the kitchen stove, touching up here, there, and everywhere—each item is trifling enough in itself, perhaps, but together they add up to an outlay which lies heavy on the account-books for the rest of the year. A wise man will leave most of this till later, when the longer days of spring or summer have come.

One year Ise lobsters[5] and eternity oranges[6] were in short supply. In Edo, where daimyō needed these things for their New Year celebrations, the shops in Setomono-chō, Suda-chō, Kōji-machi,[7] and anywhere else one looked, were selling lobsters at five gold koban each, and eternity oranges at three. That year they were short in the home provinces too, and even in places like Ōsaka an Ise lobster was two and a half monme of silver, and an eternity orange seven or eight fun. But spring would not be the same without them, and people felt obliged to buy, in order to decorate their Hōrai trays[8] in the traditional way.

In Edo, of course, the townspeople are singularly lacking in moderation, and have little thought for the morrow. In Sakai, however, in the neighbourhood of Ōshōji,[9] on the border-line between Settsu and Izumi provinces, there was a man called Hinokuchiya[10] who kept a sharp eye on all matters affecting his livelihood and had spent a lifetime avoiding unnecessary expenses, and, for his part, even if the Hōrai tray was a custom inherited from the age of the gods he could see no purpose in decorating it with goods bought at such extortionate prices. Instead of Ise lobsters he bought cartwheel shrimps.[11] In place of eternity oranges he displayed a pile of nine-year lemons.

'Under the circumstances,' he argued, 'the goddess Amaterasu herself could hardly blame me.'

The essential flavour of spring seemed in no way diminished, and Hinokuchiya's device was praised as worthy of a man of true ingenuity. That year the whole of Sakai made its New Year preparations without buying a single Ise lobster or eternity orange.

The people of Sakai have a quiet mode of life, but they are the reverse of dreamy when they use an abacus.[12] And though they keep a careful check in private, they nevertheless have a sense of proper style, maintaining considerable outward state and strictly observing their social obligations. Still, it is a town with a suggestion of old age, and people from other parts find it difficult to settle here. Its citizens fix their budgets for the whole period from New Year to New Year's Eve at one stroke, and they will not spend a penny more without good reason, nor buy a single item not strictly needed for that year. Everything is firmly under control. A man will keep a striped cloak of homespun silk for thirty-four or -five years without once having to send it to the wash, or will cool himself summer after summer with the same fragile folding fan. A mother will give her marriage trousseau to her daughter in a state as good as new, and it will be passed on to her daughter's daughter without a crease in the wrong place. Seven miles away from Sakai is Ōsaka, another world, where they live for the day and let the morrow care for itself. There it is the rule to be extravagant whenever the chance arises, and plans are made and changed on a moment's inspiration. This, after all, is natural, since fortunes are so rapidly made in Ōsaka. The women are even more open-handed than the men. Not content with a change of clothes at New Year, Bon, summer, and winter,[13] they buy new dresses for every occasion which offers an excuse, discard them after a brief spell of merciless treatment and use the material as scrap for the sewing box. It is amusing to observe how differently the people of these two places behave: Sakai standing solidly on thrift, Ōsaka living adventurously.

A prosperous man, however, is respected in any town. A man without a fortune, no matter how intelligent his looks, receives a hearing nowhere. When everything which even the stupidest of rich men does is accepted as clever, it makes the position of an intelligent man who fails to make a living all the more unbearable. The god Daikoku, who does not usually tell lies, has declared that a man who cudgels his brains and tires his strength in youth will early taste the pleasures of old age—but we must remember, all the same, that the chances for success have never been so slim as they are today. The amount of gold and silver in the world has increased tremendously since ancient times, but where people have taken and hidden it is an unsolved mystery. If money is so precious that people can hardly bring themselves to show it to the light of day, it should certainly not be spent, not a penny of it, on unnecessary things. Making a fortune takes a long, long time; spending it takes no time at all.

Late one night a man wanting to buy some vinegar came knocking at Hinokuchiya's shop door. His shouts, which could be heard faintly in the inner part of the house, behind the partition dividing it from the shop, roused a man-servant from his slumbers.

'How much do you want?' he shouted back.

'Just a zeni's worth, if it's not too much trouble.'

At this the servant pretended to fall asleep again, and the customer, who could get no further reply, went away. Next morning the master summoned this servant and told him, for no apparent purpose, to dig a hole three feet deep in front of the gateway. Obediently the man stripped to the waist, fetched a pick, and worked away strenuously at the stony ground, digging deeper and deeper, dripping with sweat.

'I've dug three feet', he said at last.

'I thought there might be some zeni there', said the master. 'Haven't you found any yet?'

'I can't see anything except stones and broken shells.'

'Then take a lesson from the fact that, after all this labour, you haven't found a single zeni. Perhaps you will think a zeni's worth of trade more valuable in future.

'Back in the old days,' Hinokuchiya went on, 'when the linked verse master Sōgi Hōshi [14] was visiting Sakai, and poetry was all the rage, there was a poor druggist here who was an amateur of these things, and he invited Sōgi and others up to his best room, over the shop, to hold a linked verse session. [15] Just when it came to the host's turn to make a verse a customer called at the shop to buy some pepper. [16] The host begged the company to excuse him a moment, went downstairs, weighed out two drams of pepper, took three zeni, returned, gave quiet consideration to his verse, and recited it. Sōgi, it is said, was lost in admiration at his composure. This is the proper way for men to attend to their duties.

'When I myself started I was a mere petty tradesman, and the secret of how I became rich in a single lifetime has lain solely in my careful approach to money matters. It will do you no harm to hear about this

Hinokuchiya's idle servant digs a pit

and try to imitate me. First, a man who lives in lodgings should calculate the rent on a daily basis, and set aside that amount each day. He should use the same methods with borrowed money, never allowing the interest to get ahead of him by a single month; and when he uses the money it will be doing business for no one except himself. The method for repaying the borrowed money itself is carefully to set aside, in a separate place, one half of one's profits whenever they occur, and if you put only one hundred monme away each year towards a debt of one kanme, you will have a clean slate in ten years. People who make the books balance by leaving such money jumbled up with their own are on the road to ruin. Even for purely private expenses you should note everything in a petty cash book. Mistakes often occur when you are shopping, and if you have no check you will never notice them. On days when you do no business, spend absolutely no money. Do not get into the habit of buying on credit. Since these expenses make no immediate impression they accumulate all the more rapidly, and when it comes to paying you will be horrified at the bill. If you ever reach the stage where you are ready to offer your whole house as security for a loan, do no such thing. Sell the house instead, no matter how much face you lose. I have never heard of anyone redeeming such a pledge—

your house gets hopelessly involved in the monthly interest and is finally taken from you free of charge. If you change your mind in time and leave the district, at least you may salvage a cupboard's worth of property, and a living of some sorts is possible.' [17]

In Sakai newly-rich are rare. It is a place where fortunes have deep, firm roots, stretching back for three generations or more, and where goods bought on speculation centuries ago are still kept in stock, awaiting the favourable moment for sale. The red ink corporation [18] is secure in its monopoly, the fire-arms manufacturers [19] have government patronage, and the finances of the drug merchants' association are so sound that outside assistance to cover the Nagasaki bills of exchange is never sought. The people ordinarily conduct themselves with restraint, but there are occasions when they do things which might be thought impossible elsewhere. It was no mean feat, for instance, for a single man to cover the cost of the whole Nanshūji temple, [20] from sanctuary to kitchen. There may be differences at heart, but the customs of Sakai people resemble those of Kyōto. That they are enthusiastic culture-seekers is evident from the fact that when Kanze-dayū [21] staged his benefit performance of Noh [22] some time ago, at Kitano Shichihon-matsu [23] in Kyōto, with the price of each family box at one gold bankin, reservations from Sakai were fewer only than those from Kyōto and Ōsaka. In population Sakai is much the same as Nara, Ōtsu, or Fushimi, but no one from these places reserved a single box. A bankin is easily said, but spending it is a different matter. And when even worldly-wise townsmen compete for theatre seats at that price, and pack the house to capacity, we are indeed living in an age which deserves, as the Noh plays say, to last 'a thousand autumns—nay, ten thousand years'. [24]

BOOK V

I

MAKING A CLOCK IN SLOW MOTION

An inventive citizen celebrated in Nagasaki
A genuine fire-eater

2

YODO FISH FOR FORTUNE BUILDING

Money-making mallets in Yamazaki
The water-wheel of fortune turns

3

A SOLITARY BEAN WHICH LIGHTED THE WAY

A cotton dealer celebrated in Yamato
A remarkable will of debts

4

SALT IN THE MORNING, OIL IN THE AFTERNOON

A rich man celebrated in Hitachi
All achieve their hearts' desires

5

A HANDFUL OF SILVER AT DAWN

A jealous wife celebrated in Mimasaka
Zōgō, the merchant with nine storehouses

BOOK V

I. *Making a clock in slow motion* [1]

THE Chinese are a self-composed people, and will never be rushed, even to make a living. They spend their time strumming the koto, playing chess, making verses, and drinking wine. In autumn they stand by the sea admiring the moon, and in spring—for the reckoning day before the third moon [2] is unknown in China—they make trips to the mountains to view the wild apple [3] in bloom. In Japan, however, only a fool would try to imitate the lackadaisical Chinese approach to earning a living. The clock was invented in China. Year after year a man thought about it, with mechanisms ticking by his side day and night, and when he left the task unfinished, his son took over, in a leisurely way, and after him the grandson. At long last, after three lifetimes, the invention was completed [4] and became a boon to all mankind. But this is hardly the way to make a successful living.

When Konpeitō sugar-balls [5] were first imported from Nanking, people examined them with infinite care and tried all kinds of experiments to discover the secret of their manufacture, but to no avail. At that time a pound of Konpeitō cost five monme, but now that the women of Nagasaki have acquired the knack of making them themselves, the price has fallen steadily. The Nagasaki method is now widely known and has been copied even in the home provinces. The Kyōto confectioners had tried a thousand approaches, but had never guessed that Konpeitō could be made so simply, with the sesame seed as the key to the process. The first man in Japan to tumble to it was a poor townsman of Nagasaki. For more than two years he puzzled over the problem, and when he asked the Chinese themselves and none of them had the slightest idea, he grew very disconsolate. Even in straight-dealing foreign lands, it seemed, profitable secrets were closely guarded. He remembered the case of the imported peppercorns. Before being sent to Japan they had been soaked in hot water, and no one had ever seen what sort of tree they grew on. No matter how many of these peppercorns were sown, nothing ever sprouted from them. It was not until fifteen bushels were scattered at the same time, in some temple or other on Mount Kōya, that two seeds took root and sprouted leaves. Now pepper bushes were fairly common. [6]

It occurred to him that these Konpeitō, too, had seeds inside them, and he tried coating sesame seeds with sugar and moulding them into balls. Then he wondered whether the trick might not lie rather in the preparation of the seed itself.

He boiled a quantity of sesame seeds in sugar solution, and after leaving them to dry for several days he scattered them in a pan and heated them. As the heat penetrated the seeds it forced out frothy bubbles of sugar, and these grew of their own accord into Konpeitō. Two quarts of sesame seeds, used as centres, produced two hundred and sixty pounds of Konpeitō.[7] It cost him four fun to prepare one pound of these sweets, and by selling each pound at five monme he made an overall profit of two hundred kanme in less than a year. Later, when people had learnt his methods and making Konpeitō had become a routine part of every Nagasaki housewife's work, he abandoned the confectionery trade and opened a fancy goods store. Continuing to exercise his gifts to good purpose, and working hard at his trade, he eventually found himself the owner of one thousand kanme—all made within his own lifetime.

Nagasaki, first city of Japan for fabulous treasure, is a busy sight when the autumn shipping[8] calls and bidding starts for the bales of raw silk, rolls of cloth, medicinal herbs, shark skins, aloes wood, and curios of all kinds. Year after year there is a mountain of merchandise, and not a thing is left unsold. Whatever it is—the underpants of a thunder-clap, or knick-knacks carved from demons' horns[9]—it finds a buyer. No one who stands in this market can doubt that the world is wide. Chief among the merchants gathering here from all Japan are the sharp-witted dealers from Kyōto, Ōsaka, Edo, and Sakai, men who think in terms of loss as well as gain, ready to send their money[10] chasing after clouds in a foreign ship,[11] but seldom losing in the long run. Each is a master in his own line, assessing an article at a moment's glance, and never changing his mind. The clerks who make the biggest gains are those who can spend and still keep the books balanced. The conscientious man who thinks too long of the expense always misses the money-making. Good opportunities seldom wait.

The money from the home provinces would have a better chance of returning safely to its masters if there were no Maruyama quarter[12] in Nagasaki. What may happen on the high seas is only one of the worries of merchants trading through this port: the tempests of love, which blow up without a moment's notice, in winter, summer, spring or autumn, are no less disastrous.

Chinese traders land their wares at Nagasaki

One comfortless wet evening a number of clerks of different firms gathered together and passed the time telling how their respective employers had made their fortunes. Not one of these had grown into a rich man from nothing: there was always a seed which had started the process. The first to speak was an Edo man.

'My master started as a small trader in Tenma-chō,' [13] he said, 'but one day he picked up four hundred and thirty ryō, dropped in the street by a daimyō as an "evil year" offering. [14] After that he went on steadily to make a fortune.'

'My master was not doing very well at first either,' said a clerk from Kyōto, 'but he had a good head for business, and he made up his mind that the only thing was to change to a line that no one else had tried. He bought in a stock of funeral accessories—eboshi caps, [15] pure white suits, plain unpatterned overskirts, and even palanquins for coffins—and he kept them ready for hire at a moment's notice. His takings soon mounted up. In time he gave up the business and settled himself in a cosy retreat on Higashi-yama. [16] People judge that he's now worth about three thousand kanme—and they're not far wrong.'

'My chief was different from most men in that he had settled on no wife to run his house', said an Ōsaka clerk. 'And if you think he refrained because of the expense, you're mistaken. He made exhaustive enquiries about widows, particularly if they seemed well satisfied to remain single. Most of them had grown a little unsightly here and there over the years but he was not particular about that: his sole concern was to discover one who kept an ancient heirloom-box. When he married, things turned out as he had calculated. His wife had a private nest-egg of thirty kanme. With this to help him he found it an easy matter to change his line of business from selling paper to dealing in imported herbs, and now he trades with a capital of two thousand kanme. He seized his opportunity and he went on to make a fat fortune; and now, as a successful townsman, no one dreams of criticising him for the way he did it.'

From these stories it was evident that to become a man of truly great wealth was hardly possible unless you had more than the usual start. All of them, in their different ways, had done something extraordinary.

People who buy imported goods at Nagasaki when the market prices are really low are sure of making a profit in good time—provided the goods are not the sort which deteriorate as the years go by. One man bought a baby alligator [17] here for twenty ryō. It was about two feet long at the time, but within ten years it had grown unmanageably bulky and fierce, and it proved a constant source of trouble to its owner. Another man bought a fire-bird's egg [18] for one bankin, and when it was hatched, sure enough, the chick ate burning charcoal. Nevertheless, rare though such things may be, to buy them is a waste of the country's money.

2. *Yodo fish for fortune building*

MAN'S work to make his living must run on and on, day and night, like a water-wheel harnessed to a swiftly flowing stream. [1] In a day and a night, they say, a stream may flow seventy-five leagues. The speed of the advancing tide of years and months has likewise been calculated by our men of science, but although it is known in the moonlit nights of autumn that the last night of the year will be black as pitch, people are invariably unprepared for it when it comes. Tradesmen sharpen their wits well in advance, and craftsmen press on quicker with the various orders in hand, but it is always the same: when the days have slipped by they are short of the goal.

With sales on account a man should calculate on receiving only one-third of his dues by New Year. If it is a debt of ten kanme, he should spend on the assumption that he will get three kanme back to pay his own debts. It is in things like this that a man should exercise his ingenuity, out-foxing the fox in concealments, and never being caught with his tail exposed.

'Collect your debts [2] from the easiest places first', a skilled tradesman advised. 'If you put it off, thinking the money is yours whenever you care to take it, when the time comes you may find it takes much longer than you thought, or you may arrive when the man is out, and have to go back to his house again and again. As a first principle, a debt collector must never grow philosophic about life. [3] Even when the evening bells are sounding from the temples he must keep his thoughts on his purse, speak as sharply as ever, and in no way soften his expression. Seating himself on the kitchen step he accepts no tobacco and drinks no tea. If the lady smiles and starts a conversation, he gives no sign that he sees or hears her. He fixes his gaze on the rows of yellow-tails and pheasants hanging in the kitchen. "You seem to have done well with the New Year preparations", he says. "I saw three koku of rice in the yard—best local produce, too, it seemed. The rice for the rice-cakes is already pounded, I see. Even earlier than usual. Everything here looks new, right down to the lid on that saucepan. Is that your daughter's spring outfit, with the red silk lining and the dappled purple pattern? This is the way to celebrate New Year! Personally—the way my heart keeps jumping up and down like a dancer—I feel more as if it were Bon. Not that, as the song goes, 'dancing over the pine-clad fields' [4] I've found myself a single bunch of fern to decorate the front door. I haven't bought a herring-roe yet, either. A new outfit for my son is unlikely, I'm afraid. I'd thought that at least I should be able to get some fresh cotton wool to pad the home-made striped kimono he had last year, but even that is going to be difficult. When I look at the way you've managed things here I can't help thinking you must be millionaires. Perhaps they do their New Year preparations on this scale in Edo—I wouldn't know—but I've seen nothing like it in Kyōto." If he persists in this way, talking of nothing but the house's prosperity, making a thorough nuisance of himself, they will leave the other accounts and settle his first. But, above all, no matter how chilly the day is, he must take care never to accept a cup of saké, or even a bowl of rice and hot water, from the house he is picketing.'

The other side of the question was put by a man who had waded up to his neck through many a pool of debts, and who had considerable experience in shooting the rapids at the year's end.

'In buying on credit certain things are accepted as a matter of course by both parties', he said. 'If you ask for fresh rice at a time when the market price per koku is sixty monme, you are charged sixty-five and given stale rice into the bargain. If a quart of cooking oil is two monme you are charged two monme three fun, and when the same thing happens with bean-paste, saké, firewood, and everything else, it means that you spend your whole year working to fill someone else's pocket, and you never have any money for your own needs. As for the way to settle debts, you should pay the little ones first, putting off the big ones till next year. Even if you have saved and have the money ready, never pay until late on New Year's Eve. The collector is generally weary by that time, resigned to accept excuses about paying the rest "before the decorations are down".[5] He won't bother to check whether the coppers are short or the silver is under-weight, but will rush for the gate clutching his money as though he'd picked up something which didn't belong to him. He will complain later, of course, and swear to have no further dealings with a house like yours; but trade must go on, and when New Year has passed he will have forgotten, and things will be the same as before. These methods are not strictly honest, I know; but when a man can't make ends meet it is surprising how his nature changes for the worse.'

In the village of Yodo[6] in Yamashiro province there was a man called Yamazakiya,[7] an oil merchant. His father had sown the seeds[8] of the household's prosperity, but the son detested his inherited trade. The sound of the pounding of his mallets was odious to him. Moreover he insisted on keeping his shop so unnecessarily spick and span that the family god of luck, who had always hidden himself in the dust on the floor, took fright at the brooms and fled. Custom dwindled and the shop took on a deserted air. Year by year the stocks of money grew lower, and soon the sound of mallet and mortar was stilled, and even the household lamps went out through lack of oil. In desperation, and to no avail, Yamazakiya prayed at the nearby 'Treasure Temple'[9] for the return of his vanished fortune. Left with little except his two hands he found it difficult to think of any scheme which could provide him with more than the shakiest of livelihoods. There were, however, fish in the pools beneath Ko bridge.[10] Gazing idly into their depths without a net[11] would naturally not improve his prospects—without a net he could not even catch enlightenment, as 'Holy Jirō'[12] had done—but if he really put heart and soul into the task of making this his living, there was no reason (for the slowest ox reached Yodo in the end, [13] and the wheel of fortune, like the Yodo water-wheel, was always turning) why he and his household should not prosper a second time. So he changed his line of trade and made daily trips to Kyōto with a load of carp and gibel [14] across his shoulders. 'Fish from the Yodo!' he cried, and, Yodo fish being noted for their excellent flavour, he used to have no difficulty in selling his stock. When people came to know him by sight they gave him the nickname of 'Jirō the Buddha from Yodo', [15] and whenever they needed carp or gibel they would wait specially for him to appear. At this point he stopped carrying fish all the way from Yodo and bought his carp and gibel in Kyōto, from the supplies brought from Tanba and Ōmi. [16] He still sold out every day, because people maintained that his fish had a distinctive flavour, and although other merchants were selling the identical fish they would buy nothing from anyone but Yamazakiya. An established reputation can work wonders for a tradesman. Next he took to preparing raw fish-slices, [17] setting them out on plates and providing whatever quantity the customer required, even if it was only five or three fun's worth, and Kyōto people being what they are—always ready to economise on food—they made do with these dishes of ready-sliced fish even for entertaining guests. Gradually his shop grew fashionable, and it was not long before he was a rich man. He invested his money here and there, opened a money exchange business, and came to employ a great number of assistants; and now that his house was so prosperous no one ever mentioned the matter of his former fish trade. Living in Kyōto his tastes in clothes inevitably became more refined, and he tended to copy the styles of the professional set in Shinzaike. [18] When he appeared in pure Aburaya silks with crests of Kenbō brown, [19] stiffened the cuffs of his three layers of

Yamazakiya hawks fish in Kyōto

sleeves with a little padding, wore his neck-line not a fraction too high, hung his skirts fashionably low, and graced his shoulders with a cloak of the same silk, adjusted with the same care, it was plain to all —without their being told—that he was a personage of distinction.

A man may be related to a court noble, or he may be the descendant of a daimyō—but if he has sold his ancient sword to buy a meal, if his luck has gone to heaven and his armour to the pawnshop, [20] neither lineage, sword, nor armour will serve him when he needs them. The only things which matter, they say, are wisdom and wit—though these too are nothing unless you keep them by you while making your living.

Of all the crises in a man's life there is none more terrible than the reckoning day at the end of the year. If you treat its approach casually, and start thinking about it only after half the twelfth moon has gone, you will be too late. If even the most insignificant shrines and temples trouble to have their paper charms and New Year fans ready on time, craftsmen and merchants who sit back with a complacent thirteen-moon expression on their faces, watching the flowers of poverty grow, can hardly complain when they find them suddenly in full bloom. If you wind up the old year with tolerable success the feeling of the new spring is wonderful. But when you are so hard pressed that it is necessary to avoid paying the doctor's bill, or to give the apprentices their old cotton garments to wear again, re-vamped with washy home-made dyes—even if you scrape through, the spirit of spring is lost. In Kyōto the townsmen meet the New Year in a variety of ways, but although the customs which one most readily associates with the Emperor's capital are things like meditating a poem about the first day of spring, the people with leisure to do this are rare. The great majority have time for nothing but the weary struggle to pay their bills.

An assistant in Yamazakiya's fishmonger business set up on his own by opening a small rice shop. His capital was a meagre five kanme, but he scattered credit sales in every direction, like ground beans caught in a wind, and when it came to collecting his debts and he saw the conditions in his debtors' tiny houses, he felt too much sympathy to press his demands. In one household, although it was already the twenty-eighth of the last moon—and a short moon this year, [21] with only today and tomorrow left—they were still snatching odd moments between a host of chores to weave a length of cotton cloth on a loom, intending to sell it cheaply to pay for the hundred things needed for New Year. As he reached another house they had just called in an old-iron dealer to value a metal mirror-frame, a rat trap with bronze netting, a small rake, and a kettle-stand with a broken leg. But the man rejected them all. They were worth no more than one hundred and thirty zeni altogether, he said, and it would be a waste of his time to buy them. After he had gone, the husband and wife spoke to each other, without realising that someone was listening.

'Paying any part of our debts is out of the question this year', they said. 'If only five hundred zeni would fall from heaven! With that amount we could get through easily, and even afford to scatter a few beans for luck.'

When they were joined by their daughter, a little girl at the most charming age, he felt all the more sorry for them.

'How many more nights do I sleep before it's New Year's Day?' she asked.

'It will be New Year when we have some rice to eat', they replied.

Noticing the debt collector's presence at last, they glared at him with such hostility that he retreated from the door in alarm without saying a word about his money.

At the next house he was confronted by an argumentative woman who lost no time in giving him a piece of her mind.

'We are always getting people from your shop asking for their rice money', she shouted. 'There's nothing wrong with borrowing money—everybody does it—but you people say the most dreadful things to us. One of you said he'd take his money now if he had to pull my husband's head off. My husband shook till he dropped, and he hasn't moved from his bed since. It's really shameful, having your head pulled off for four or five fun!'

She went on shouting and sobbing, and he saw that it would be too much trouble to argue with her.

'Look after him well', he said as he turned to go. 'If he's still alive, I'll discuss matters with him in the spring.'

At another house, apparently highly pleased with himself, a man was setting out an offering of saké before an old kimono. The under-parts of its sleeves were patched, and beneath its faded green dye traces of an erstwhile light blue were visible.

'What a splendid constitution this kimono has!' he was saying. 'For the last seventeen or eighteen years it has spent summer and winter alike in the pawnshop, but now it has come home to keep New Year with its master. This will really be a Happy New Year!'

'Well then,' said the rice dealer, coming forward at that point, 'let's settle our accounts.'

The man took the bill, and against the entry of '18 monme 2 fun' he wrote 'Paid: 1 monme 6 fun'. He produced a dubious-looking silver coin.

'I weighed this one and put it by specially for you. But if you don't want it, say so.'

He turned his attention to his cat's fleas, and took no further notice of the visitor. There was no choice. To refuse the money was only to increase the loss. So the dealer took it and went his way.

Later, calling at another house, he found that the master was not at home. The lady of the house, a tolerably attractive woman who had arranged her coiffure with particular care and changed into an unusually fine sash for the occasion, was sitting with copies of 'The Romance of Lady Usuyuki'[22] and 'The Tales of Ise' open before her, surrounded by a crowd of debt collectors. With an air of great composure she was discussing which plays would be most popular this spring.

'Where has your husband gone?' they asked.

'He found his wife too old for his taste', she replied, laughing gaily. 'He has deserted me.'

'Make him give you a divorce!' they cried. 'There are plenty of us willing to take care of you.'

A few more jests of this sort and their hearts had erased the entries in their account-books. They went away empty-handed.

No creature can rival man in his combination of intelligence and stupidity. Be constantly on the alert, for there are tricksters of every kind even in the poorest of debtors' houses. In credit sales the secret is to guard against the growth of friendly relationships with your customers, no matter how frequently you have done business with them. There may be times when intimacy does no harm, but they are rare. Even if you have been given a deposit, if your customer's debts start to mount up higher than ever before, cut him dead and give him back his money as a sign that you have finished with him. Merchants who allow themselves to be drawn on and on, and swell their losses to huge proportions, are victims of nothing but their own short-sighted greed.

This rice merchant, too, now changed to ready cash deals, and sold only by small measures. For four or five years his luck grew better and better, but one year he started supplying rice in bulk to certain silk-weaving firms in Nishijin,[23] and although there was an agreement that payment should be made for the last consignment before the next was delivered, payments were overdue year after year. The accounts balanced on paper, but the money was never at hand and served no useful purpose. In time the grinding of his hulling-mortars was heard no more, and he had nothing left except the small wooden boxes with which he had once measured out his rice sales. Selling on credit needs to be approached with the greatest caution.

3. *A solitary bean which lighted the way*

In the village of Asahi,[1] living wretchedly in a mean hut with horn-like outhouses[2]—but with not an ox to his name—was a small farm-holder called Kawabata no Kusuke.[3] He tilled the land unaided, driving his hoe into the ore-laden[4] earth, while his wife sat weaving hemp, from early dawn, at a towering Yamato loom. Autumn after autumn he measured out the same one and a quarter koku of tax-rice for the lord. Every New Year's Eve until past his fiftieth year—though without any visible improvement in his fortunes—he hung his narrow windows with holly sprigs and sardine heads,[5] as careful as any to bar entrance to invisible demons, and scattered parched beans over the floor with fervent prayers for luck. One year, on the morning after Setsubun, when he was gathering up these beans, he took one and planted it in some wasteland. Miracles sometimes happen, he thought, and he waited to see whether even a toasted bean could bear flowers.[6] There was no denying the results. That summer it sprouted green stalks and leaves, and when autumn came and the pods were filled he gathered more than two handfuls of beans. He scattered these along the water channels on his land, carefully resowing the yield each year and cutting back the stalks. The number of plants grew steadily larger and larger, and after ten years had passed they bore a crop of eighty-eight koku.[7] When he had sold these beans he had a great stone lantern constructed, and set it by the Hase highroad[8] to light the way at night. Known as 'The Lantern of Beans' it shines to this day, telling us of Kusuke's success. All things grow bigger in time, and our largest ambitions are not beyond hope of ultimate fulfilment. In this spirit Kusuke gradually increased his household's prosperity, bought more and more land, and eventually became a farmer of the first magnitude.

Manuring, weeding, and watering the soil for every crop in every season, he watched the ripening ears of rice grow fat and full, and the cotton plants blossom with numberless flowers. If his harvests were richer than his neighbours' it was no chance of fate, but the result of

Kawabata no Kusuke's farm in Yamato

unremitting toil, from morn to dusk, till spade and hoe were worn to stumps. He was also a man of great inventiveness, and he thought out many devices which have proved a boon to mankind. He invented the rake,[9] with its row of iron teeth, and nothing has ever been found of greater assistance to man in breaking the surface of soil. Next followed the Tōmino Winnowing Fan and the Thousand Koku Sifter; and since threshing purely by hand was a time-consuming labour, he devised an implement with a row of pointed bamboo prongs, which he called 'The Widow's Downfall', and whereas two people had formerly been required to thresh his grain, when this implement was used one person could manage it all conveniently and without effort. The labours of the women in preparing cotton were slow, too—particularly the whipping of the ginned cotton, which they did at the rate of barely five kin in a whole day. After puzzling over this problem, and making enquiries about Chinese methods, he devised 'The Chinese Bow'[10] and experimented with it in secret, using a novel type of wooden plucker for the string. When he discovered that with one bow he could manage three kanme a day, he bought vast snowy mountains of ginned cotton, trained a host of operatives, and forwarded bale after bale of whipped cotton to Edo.[11] In four or five years he became a man of great wealth, one of the foremost cotton dealers of Yamato province. Through each of the cotton brokers at Hirano-mura [12] and Ōsaka's Kyōbashi [13]—such firms as Tondaya, Zeniya, [14] and Tennōjiya [15]—he daily bought countless hundreds of kanme of ginned cotton from Settsu and Kawachi provinces, [16] and he made such profits every year, in the short whipping season from autumn to winter, [17] that at his death a little more than thirty years later he bequeathed a fortune of a thousand kanme. Throughout his life he had known no relaxation, having spent every moment working for his descendants. He died at the age of eighty-eight.

Since he died like a saint—and died, moreover, on the anniversary of Amida's enlightenment [18]—his prayers for salvation in the Western Paradise must certainly have been answered. His remains were turned to smoke over the funeral ground, and one hundred days later, when the head priest of the Ariwara temple [19] had been summoned as a witness, in accordance with Kusuke's last wishes, and had been offered a suitably frugal meal, the box containing the will was opened.

All my money, one thousand seven hundred kanme, I give to my only son, Kunosuke. Likewise my house, land, and effects—which I need not here specify.

Next, the list of parting gifts to each of his relatives:

To my aunt in the village of Miwa: [20] one hand-woven cotton kimono of criss-cross pattern; one neck-cloth of pongee; one mulberry walking-stick. [21]

To my younger brother in Shimoichi, [22] Yoshino: my cotton coat, of a three-star stencil pattern, and my rough-woven shoulder pieces.

To my younger sister in Okadera: [23] one dark blue cotton gown with black neck-band attached; and one vest of unbleached hemp. To her only son, my nephew: the striped mattress which was under me during my illness; and one pair of brown leather socks. (He must first stitch these to a smaller size.)

Two articles—my bamboo tobacco pipe and my muffler of Hino silk—I bequeathe to my doctor, Nakabayashi Dōhakurō.

My summer cloak of persimmon-juice dye (the sleeves a little rat-bitten, but he can patch them up) I confer on my temple-going companion, Nizaemon.

There were two clerks who had faithfully served the household for many years, and to one he bequeathed an old discarded abacus, and to the other the scales the clerk had always used. Before the contents of the will were known everyone had entertained high hopes for themselves, and they could hardly wait for their names to be read. They were dumbfounded when they discovered that not a penny of the actual money was to be theirs.

'When you can't even count on money from your rich relatives, things are pretty bad', they grumbled.

They dried the tears which they had been producing so readily up to this point, and returned in disgust to their native villages. To amass this one thousand seven hundred kanme Kusuke had spent a whole lifetime in economising, and he could hardly have been expected to be lavish with his money now, no matter how keen his relatives were to have it.

When Kusuke's effects were examined it became evident that throughout his life he had never worn silk next his skin. In his 'evil year' [24] of forty-two he had purchased, for the first time in his life, a silken loin-cloth, but it now remained as new, innocent of any trace of use. The outer garments which the old man had worn were found to be no more than those mentioned in the will. Of ornamental accessories there were only a dagger, with a wisteria-coil handle and a walnut hilt-pin, a leather purse with a carved button of deer-horn, and a plain black drug-container.

Kunosuke felt rather ashamed of his father's stinginess, and he soon disregarded the will, giving a share of his inheritance to various relatives and even to the clerks. All were naturally delighted. They declared that he was a much more understanding person than his father, and they started to visit his house once more. For a while Kunosuke carried on the business much as in the old days. One day, however, an acquaintance induced him to visit a small village called Niōdō, [25] at the foot of Tafu-no-mine, where touring bands of boy actors [26] from Kyōto and Ōsaka often took secret lodgings, and after this he returned to the place with steadily increasing frequency. He developed a taste for the other way of love, too, and started affairs in Kitsuji, [27] the Nara brothel quarter. When these no longer interested him he went up to Kyōto regularly, and there he hired every courtesan the go-betweens [28] recommended, drifting on the tide of love from the present Madam Japan as far as Lady China. [29] His mother, greatly distressed at this endless dissipation, arranged for him to marry a particularly attractive girl from Tōichi village. [30] But a man who had become accustomed to the fine ladies of the quarters could never content himself with a country wife, and his mother's anxieties continued, until, very soon, she followed her husband to the grave. There was now no one left to remonstrate with Kunosuke, and he thought of nothing, year after year, but his riotous pleasures. Even his employees lost all respect for him, and took no further interest in their work. However, in the course of time his wife bore him three sons, and at least he had no worries on the score of succession. Drink and women between them steadily undermined Kunosuke's health, and after eight or nine years he was in an almost hopeless state. At the age of thirty-four, suddenly—but to no one's great surprise—he passed away, and his remains were borne to the burial ground.

Kunosuke had been well aware of his state of health, and had drawn up a will in readiness for death. His sons, however, were still very young, and the clerks were rather worried about this.

'Perhaps it would be best if their money were entrusted to our charge', they said. 'We can surrender it to each of them later, as they come of age.'

Their anxiety did credit to their hearts, and the local people greatly admired this demonstration of faithfulness towards the departed master. There were loud exclamations of surprise, however, when the will itself was opened. And well there might have been, for the whole fortune of one thousand seven hundred kanme had gone, and this was a statement and formal bequest of debts. It quite dampened the company's spirits.

To Izutsuya Kichizaburō of Kyōto I owe two hundred and fifty ryō. Since I borrowed this when desperately in need of money in a shameful place, and thereby avoided disgrace, this is a debt which involves a moral obligation. My son and heir Kutarō, therefore, when he reaches manhood, must work hard at some occupation in order to repay it.

Attached is a list of outstanding debts for my entertainments in Dōtonbori, Ōsaka.[31] These are to be paid by my second son, Kujirō.

In addition I have purchased goods on credit from various places. These debts amount to only thirty kanme, and they may be paid by my third son, Kuzaburō, as occasion offers.

As for the house, land, and household effects, it is best to declare bankruptcy and surrender these to my local creditors.

The expenses for the funeral and mourning shall be the responsibility of my widow.

This is my last will and testament, to be carried out in accordance with the above clauses.

4. *Salt in the morning, oil in the afternoon*

'MAY I trouble you a moment?' says the Kashima soothsayer[1] at your door. 'I have an oracle from the god of Kashima. "Earthquakes will rage in the fortunes of men," it says, "but as long as the god of trade exists the pivot-stone[2] will never be dislodged." And the sense of this divine revelation is that all must pay proper heed to their means of livelihood, and that poverty never gets the better of a busy man.'[3]

Let these words sink into the ears of honest folk, and let none of them spend a zeni on useless things. Long ago, when Aoto Saemon[4] dropped ten coppers in the Kamakura river he had costly pine-torches lit to help him recover them, so deep was his concern that none of the world's treasure should be left to rot away unused. That was in the days of Hōjō Tokiyori,[5] when even a man who sold dwarf pine, cherry, or plum for firewood[6] could make a fortune with ease. Nowadays, when fortunes only grow from capital, the man who treats money casually has not the slightest chance of success.

In Hitachi province, in the village of Kogane-ga-hara,[7] there lived a man called Higurashi something-or-other[8] who had made a fortune of a hundred thousand ryō in a single lifetime. His house was surmounted by lofty sloping roofs, he had men and horses in abundance, he farmed more than two hundred acres of land, his household prospered, and he wanted for nothing. Deeply sympathetic and charitable towards the lesser farmers in the village, he was looked upon as the treasure of the community. Even the village trees and grasses bowed before him. When he started in life things had been very different. Living in a mean cottage thatched with bamboo grass, his evening meals had summoned the barest wisps of smoke from the kitchen, and his breakfasts had been served without rice. His clothes had been the same at New Year and midsummer, and though he was scrupulously honest and hard-working, many were the years of distress and poverty which he and his wife had borne together. In the mornings he sold vinegar and soy sauce; in the afternoons he peddled salt in baskets hung from his shoulders; in the evenings he changed the baskets to buckets and the salt to cooking oil; and late at night he made straw hoof-covers for sale to pack-horse drivers. From his early youth not a moment had been spent in sitting down and doing nothing. His position grew a little better every year, and by the time he was fifty he had increased his capital to thirty-seven thousand zeni.[9] He never lost a zeni from the moment he started in trade, and year after year he made a profit—but his original capital had been so small that the process of raising it to one hundred ryō was painfully difficult. It was only after the laborious accumulation of this first one hundred that he really began his steady advance to the position of a leading millionaire of the eastern provinces. And now, with four sons in his family, his good fortune was complete.

The rōnin in their house on Higurashi's farm

His house was not far from Edo, and some long-unemployed rōnin,[10] finding it difficult to remain in hiding in the city, and hearing that he was a likely person to help them, came to Kogane village armed with letters of introduction from relations, and earnestly begged his assistance. Higurashi, being a sympathetic man, presented them with a straw-thatched cottage and provided each with a fixed ration. There were seven or eight of them, and it was not long before they became boisterous and discontented; but it is hard for a rōnin to sell his services in these peaceful days, and since none of them had any alternative they remained in the village for several years.

One of their number, Morishima Gonroku, who was a tolerably intelligent man and something of a scholar, thought—being mindful of his Confucian training—that at least he should do something to show his gratitude for his benefactor's trouble, and accordingly he taught the four boys how to recite passages from the Four Books.[11] This was most praiseworthy. Another of the men, Kizuka Shinzaemon, took the second boy in charge, taught him love-play in the New Yoshiwara quarter,[12] and got him to spend a great deal of money. One, called Miyaguchi Hannai, was clever at carving little objects with a penknife, and he made ear-picks and toy rats from Utsugi wood. All day long he chiselled with enthusiasm, and by sending his wares to Tōri-chō in Edo for sale, in five or six years he made a considerable pile of money.

His was the talent most suited to the situation. Another, a man called Ō-ura Jinpachi, turned his mind to learning popular songs and little dances, and in due course he developed such a feel for rhythm that there was nothing in the amateur repertoire too difficult for him to master. Another, Iwane Banzaemon, was a man of surpassingly large bulk who, with his bristling moustache and fearsome eyeballs, would have been worth a salary of three hundred koku even as a sentry, but his disposition contradicted his looks. Versed in the Way of Buddha, he could neither kill a flea which bit him nor squash a worm underfoot. He was an upright and god-fearing man, and it was only his face which was terrible. Lastly there was a man called Akabori Uzaemon. Poor though he was he still preserved his musket and his samurai pride, and now he poached game, shot wolves, and swaggered about picking quarrels at imaginary slights. The master, however, reproved none of them.

'It's only natural for human beings to have different outlooks on life', he used to say.

One year there was a general investigation of rōnin,[13] and all these men were expelled from the village.

It is interesting to look closely into their subsequent careers, and to note the variety of callings they adopted to keep themselves alive. Gonroku, the one who had a taste for literature, earned his living as a street story-teller, reciting excerpts from the military romances[14] on Sujikai bridge in Kanda.[15] Shinzaemon, the expert on the art of love, opened a tea house in Ta-machi,[16] where he was known to all as 'Sour-faced Shinyoshi', and later he became a professional entertainer in the quarter, employing his natural gifts for making 'chin-chiri-ton' sounds like a samisen.[17] Hannai, the one who was clever at wood-work, sold knick-knacks spread out on a sheet of waterproof paper before the Shiba Jinmei shrine.[18] He was a curious sight, sitting there beneath his broad-rimmed samurai hat. Jinpachi, the amateur musician, joined Matakurō's theatre company,[19] and eventually graduated to minor speaking roles. Morning, afternoon, and evening he took the parts of the characters who said 'Yes, sir' or 'No, sir', and this earned him enough to keep alive. Uzaemon, the one who could not refrain from martial exhibitions, achieved his heart's desire, riding on horse-back with an attendant to carry his spear, and he now had a salary of five hundred koku, no less than he had earned in the old days. The salvation-minded Banzaemon soon assumed the black robes of a priest, and—looking like a massive Buddha himself—he stood before the Great Buddhas at Shiba[20] and reproved himself for his wickedness, chanting prayers to Amida in an ear-splitting voice. In almost every case they had fallen pitifully low. If even men who once enjoyed salaries as samurai can bear to live on in these conditions, it must indeed be difficult to die.

With their examples in mind, let none of you grow over-fond of arts and accomplishments, and allow your proper business to suffer neglect. These people became what they had always fancied they would prefer to be. When a man is told that he has outstanding talent for this or that, it does him nothing but harm.

'Poetry is for court nobles, and horsemanship and archery are for the military class', the rich man of Kogane told his numerous children. 'The art for townsmen is accurate calculation. They should keep their eyes on the needle of the scales, and take care to note down everything in their books without a moment's delay.'

5. *A handful of silver at dawn*

CHECKING affinities in an almanac[1] reveals amazing coincidences and disconcerting differences; but in modern marriages neither harmony of elements nor even good looks enter into the question. Everyone alike is in favour of girls who bring the element of gold with them. Accordingly the matchmaker of our day first enquires into the marriage portion, and only then asks whether the lady has any physical deformity. The customs of ancient times are gone. With the growth of greed even men's desires have changed, and the stream of love has lost itself in shallows.

By the upper reaches of the Waké,[2] where its waters flow—as human love has flowed—from deep pools into shallow rapids, in Sarayama village in the district of Kume,[3] there lived a man who had risen slowly and surely from a humble marriage to become a millionaire of unfathomable wealth, acknowledged in Mimasaka province to be second only to the celebrated Zōgō.[4] His name was Yorozuya.[5] He had amassed mountains of silver in a single lifetime, but though their captive spirits moaned the whole night long, he suffered the sound to disturb no poor man's rest. For Yorozuya disdained all ostentation: the gables of his house rose no higher than those of his neighbours, and even on New Year's Day for forty years he had made his social calls wearing an overskirt of hemp which had been tailored for him at the time of his marriage. Regardless of current fashions in design or colour, spring after spring he wore gowns printed with the same pattern of lemon-coloured spots, bearing the same black-ringed crests. As for his other clothes, no shade of maple or wisteria disturbed their everlasting blue.

The wealthy and distinguished Zōgō household, with its array of nine storehouses, was truly an ornament to the province. Yorozuya, on the other hand, did all he could to conceal the fact that he was rich. He had an only son called Kichitarō, and when he caught him, at the age of thirteen, wiping his nose with a piece of fine Kosugi paper, he disinherited him. He sent him to his aunt's house in Aboshi in Harima, and told him to learn better habits by watching a wealthy merchant called Nabaya.[6] After thus disposing of his own boy he next adopted his younger sister's only son. Up to the age of twenty-five or -six he made him work like any of the other clerks, but when he observed that his frugality was such that he even collected worn-out straw sandals and sent them to his old home as manure for the melons, he took a personal liking to the young man, and made him his heir. After surrendering the management of the business to him, he began enquiries for a suitable daughter-in-law. His wishes in this matter were rather out of the ordinary.

'I should like my son to have the most violently jealous wife obtainable', he said.

The world is broad: a girl was found to suit his taste, and the marriage ceremony was concluded. The old couple now went into retirement, handing over everything they possessed to the young man. The heir, feeling more at ease now that he had money of his own, immediately took a little for his private use and procured himself a concubine. He had in mind a further project for hiring boy actors,[7] but at that his wife could contain her jealousy no longer, and—as had been foreseen—lifted cries of reproach which shook the mountains. Having no desire to become the focus of local gossip he abandoned his plans for a gay life and contented himself with saké after supper and early nights. Since the master never left the premises, everyone else had to stay at home, the clerks sitting in the light of the lamp, running through the account-books to amuse themselves, the apprentice boys practising elementary additions and subtractions on the abacus—all admirable pursuits, calculated to further the interests of the firm. At first people had laughed at the wife's violent jealousy, but now everyone thought again.

In general, when parents are too lenient towards their sons it is the beginning of trouble for the house. Even if the father treats them

Yorozuya's wife does some sightseeing

strictly, the mother frequently takes their side, finding them means of evasion, and they acquire the habit of spending more money than they can afford on idle pastimes. Harshness is for the good of a boy, soft-heartedness will ruin him.

After the death of Yorozuya and his wife, their daughter-in-law made a pilgrimage to Ise, and on her return did some sightseeing in Kyōto and Ōsaka. Observing the elegant attire of the people, she remodelled her own dress in imitation. Her heart, too, suffered a change. To show jealousy, she now learned, was not fashionable. As she became more moderate in this respect, her husband, realising that this was his opportunity, decided to enjoy himself. Feigning an illness, and claiming that the local air was not good for his recovery, he went up to the home provinces, and spent his whole time practising one or the other of the arts of love with courtesans or actors. So freely did he scatter money every day that his love affairs soon tore a gaping hole in his finances, and if koban had been as easily come by as sewing-needles he would never have made ends meet.[8] The gold and silver in his house, so long accustomed to lying undisturbed, took an active dislike to him, and the god of luck in his strong-room moved his quarters elsewhere. At length Yorozuya awoke from his dream, astonished at what had happened. Changing his trade to more flexible lines, he enlarged the business premises and added banking and money-changing to his activities. As people's deposits poured in, he invested them here, there, and everywhere, aiming to recover his position by the end of the year. What passes for solid wealth is often no more than paper and paste,[9] and the procession of paper lanterns on this New Year's Eve, borne by clients coming to draw their deposits, filled Yorozuya with terror.

'If I can only survive tonight's business, from tomorrow I shall be out of danger', he thought.

When the last out-going zeni had been noted down and he had balanced his books, the bells were already striking the hour before dawn.[10] A man was selling New Year prints of Ebisu[11] in the street, but Yorozuya had not a copper left to buy one. All the same, for appearances' sake he called the man over.

'Sorry', he said, sending him away again. 'I wanted a picture of Ebisu without his hat.'

Not long after this there was a knock at the door and a merchant called Hyōgoya entered, and handed him a leather bag.

'Here are one thousand five hundred gold koban which I wish to deposit for next year', said the merchant, producing the money. 'And in the interest I received from you last night'—he continued, producing some more money—'were these three monme five fun[12] of bad silver coins.'

The young Yorozuya had nothing left with which to change them. The truth was out.

BOOK VI

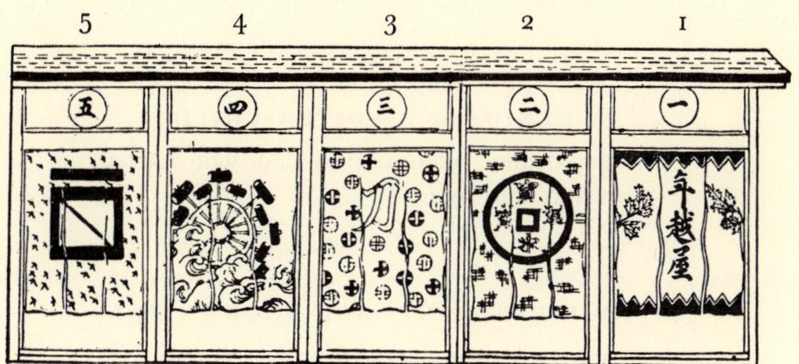

1

SPRIGS OF HOLLY FROM A MONEY TREE

Toshigoshiya, celebrated in Tsuruga

2

A GENIUS AS A FOSTER-CHILD

A money dealer, celebrated in Edo, who started with only one zeni

3

SOUND INVESTMENTS AND GOOD FRIENDS

A present for the doctor from Kogatanaya, celebrated in Sakai

4

A SOLID FORTUNE FLOATING DOWN THE YODO

The water-wheel of Yozaemon, celebrated in Yamazaki

5

RATIONS OF WORLDLY WISDOM FROM A MAN OF EIGHTY-EIGHT

Congratulations for the Three Couples, celebrated in present-day Kyōto

1. *Sprigs of holly from a money tree*

KING Wên of China,[1] they say, had a garden seventy leagues square. But in viewing his forests of trees and shrubs he could have felt no more pleasure than a man who looks at a holly bush in a spare two-yard plot and thinks of it as his private estate.

In the large port of Tsuruga,[2] in Echizen province, there lived a certain Toshigoshiya.[3] He was a maker of bean-paste and soy sauce, a man of great wealth who had lived his life in this locality, starting as a very small tradesman and gradually rising to his present prosperity. He was a shrewd business man, and the foundations of his success were laid early, in the following manner. For daily sales of bean-paste to customers from outside the town it was usual for each dealer to provide, at considerable expense, small wooden pails or straw bags. Toshigoshiya, however, had an original idea, and one year, when the Bon festival[4] was over and each family had taken down its array of offerings to the departed spirits, he went to a river bank where the cast away peaches and persimmons were floating by in the shallows, and fished out all the lotus leaves which had been used as offering plates. For the whole of the next year he made use of these as wrappers for his small sales of bean-paste. Others copied his ingenious device, and now there is not a province in the land where bean-paste is not sold in lotus-leaf wrappers.

When, in due time, Toshigoshiya bought himself a house with a large garden, the trees he planted were chosen as much for what they bore as how they looked. As hedgerows he grew tea bushes[5] and medicinal boxthorn.[6] He tore up flowering lespedeza[7] by the roots, and in places where there had once been windmill blossoms[8] he planted rows of green-pea[9]—both were attractive climbing plants, but he preferred the one with a practical advantage. He even found a use for discarded jelly-fish preserving tubs[10] by growing water-pepper[11] in them. Nothing the eye could see was there for any idle purpose. A holly sprig he had once planted, and which grew in time into a large bush, became the symbol of his house, and everyone knew it as the trade mark of the Toshigoshiya. On the night of Setsubun he picked bunches of this to

Toshigoshiya shows his presents

hang over his doors and windows, [12] and although a spray was only a zeni to buy, he estimated that the total savings in a lifetime would be considerable.

Until his fortune reached thirteen thousand ryō in gold he continued to live in an unpretentious house roofed with wooden shingles. From the time a suitable bride was found for his son and heir, however, things began to change. The go-between and the mistress of the house agreed, behind the master's back, that for the betrothal presents fashionable clothes and rolls of silk should be ordered from Kyōto, and that enough barrels of saké should be sent to the bride's home to ensure that the neighbours were given no excuse for laughing at them. Twenty-five porters were employed to carry the saké, each with a barrel across his shoulders, but the only betrothal presents the mistress and her son showed to the old master were two light saké casks, a pair of salted bream, and a silver chōgin. He pulled a long face even at this, and said that instead of the silver chōgin they should send the equivalent in copper—three thousand zeni—which would increase the bulk and look better. In matters of etiquette like this he had no conception of what was expected. [13] During his whole life of more than sixty years he had had no time for anything outside the honest prosecution of his trade.

The sending of the betrothal presents was the first step to a more luxurious mode of life.[14] The next was when the son conceived a plan for rebuilding the main section of the house. His father would not listen to him, but he canvassed support from kindly-disposed people in his ward, and even enlisted the influence of his father's temple-going group—sworn companions unto death and the hereafter—and of the abbot of the family temple. At length he had his way, and set to the work of construction. After he had built a splendid lofty-roofed mansion in the place where the old house had stood, with every detail arranged to his taste, he had the whole place scrubbed and polished daily so that it glistened as never before. But the woodcutters from the hills and the neighbouring farmers no longer dared enter such a place, and trade suddenly came to a standstill. Faced with the prospect of throwing away his stocks of bean-paste and emptying his pails of soy sauce into the river, the young Toshigoshiya sent numbers of travelling salesmen out from the house to do business for him. But, although his products were of as high a quality as ever, people now claimed that their flavour had deteriorated, and even this device failed to improve his sales. In time he changed his line of business—but there is always a risk in trying something for which you have had no training, and he lost a great deal of money every year. He bought goods on speculation, and the bottom fell out of the market; he gambled his capital on mining investments, and lost; and it was not long before his house was his only worldly possession. Eventually he sold this and the land for a mere thirty-five kanme. The old man was deeply grieved, but his son took a foolish pride in the way he had managed things.

'It's lucky I had the house improved when times were good', he said. 'It made it more valuable for selling.'

The father had worked for his fortune for forty years, and the son had disposed of it in six. Money, as can be seen, is made with difficulty and spent with ease. Never for one moment, between waking and sleeping, let your attention wander from the abacus.

The correct appearance for a shop differs according to type. If you are dealing in shark skin, books, perfumery, or silks, your shop should be decorated tastefully and have an air of spaciousness. But if you run a pawnbroker's or a grocery store, a cramped interior and a suggestion of disorder is more suitable. Moreover, in the words of a certain millionaire of great experience, 'Long established business premises, with which customers have become familiar, should never be enlarged and improved.'

This young bean-paste dealer now divorced the wife he had taken in Tsuruga, and opened a small shop in a village near the coast. Finding that even here someone was needed to manage the household affairs, he chose a second wife from among the local women, and on a suitably propitious day he forwarded his betrothal presents to her home—two light saké casks, a pair of salted bream, and a string of one thousand zeni. He had come to appreciate the wisdom of his father's remarks, made in happier days, on the present he had once shown him. Etiquette was a minor point; the essential thing, after all, was to understand how to make a living.

2. *A genius as a foster-child*[1]

'UPON my oath,' declares the Japanese shopkeeper in the course of his sales talk, 'I am not making a penny in selling at this price.'

At this the customer hesitates no more, but buys, whether the article is worth it or not. These lies are an accepted part of business technique.

A certain rōnin of distinguished family was living in quiet seclusion opposite the Myōjin shrine at Kanda.[2] Having already reached the age when a man may use a stick[3]—indoors, at least—without impropriety, he no longer entertained any ambition for service under a new lord. With a boy to attend upon him, and with sufficient savings to last his lifetime, he managed well enough from day to day without undue exertion; but others resented the fact that he sat around and did nothing, and when he could bear their talk no longer he opened a crockery shop —just for appearances' sake.[4] If a customer enquired about his prices, for articles worth a hundred zeni he asked a hundred zeni. When the customer tried to bargain with him, he refused to be beaten down. His original stock had consisted of nine earthenware mortars, thirteen fish platters, forty-five small plates, twenty tea bowls, seven saké servers, and two oil jugs; and not a thing did he manage to sell in three years. A technique of salesmanship, as may be seen, is important in trade.

Complete absolution for any false oaths made during the year is obtainable on the twentieth of the tenth moon at the feast of Ebisu.[5] On that day every tradesman declares a holiday, and, having bought whatever kind of fish or bird he can afford, holds a family feast and exchanges cups of saké with the assembled household. Employees, taking heart at the master's temporary display of good humour, sing popular songs and give recitations of Jōruri. All the temples, shrines, and theatres in Edo, not to mention the excursion spots, enjoy a day of splendid business. Where Edo differs from the home provinces is in the absence of silver. Instead, golden one-bu pieces are scattered like showers of blossom—no scales are needed to test their weight:[6] no better coinage could be found. Open-handedness being second nature to the whole population, the citizens do their everyday shopping like daimyō, with a wonderful disregard for cost. For today's festival of Ebisu everyone was naturally intent on buying fish, but it so happened that there had been storms at sea, and the shops had even fewer fresh fish to offer than on normal days. Sea-bream, in particular, were selling at one ryō two bu each, and these were of no more than medium size, one foot two or three inches from head to tail. Ordinary townsmen could hardly be expected to use fish like this for an informal family supper, but the merchants of Edo, being merchants of Edo, ate their sea-bream none the less. In Muromachi[7] in Kyōto, where bream were on sale at a twentieth of the Edo price,[8] each fish was divided into five slices and people were buying single cuts by weight. The ways of the capital look ridiculous beside those of Edo.

The apprentice boy at the feast of Ebisu

Here in Edo, near Nakabashi[9] in Tōri-chō, there was a zeni exchange dealer[10] who employed a large staff of assistants in his shop. On normal days he was scrupulously careful in matters of economy, but today he too bought sea-bream at the current price of one ryō two bu to set before the image of Ebisu. When portions of the offering had been distributed to all, the company duly settled down to the auspicious supper. Amongst the crowd of assistants was a boy from Yamada in Ise,[11] a young apprentice of fourteen whom the master had lately taken into his household for a ten-year term of service. When his tray was set before him he raised it ceremoniously to his head two, three times, and before eating took out his abacus and made some calculations.

'If I had gone anywhere except to Edo for my apprenticeship,' he murmured to himself, 'I should never have known luxuries like this.'

The master noticed him sitting there with such a happy expression, and asked him the reason.

'It's like this, sir', said the boy. 'Today's broiled bream cost one ryō two bu, and has been cut crosswise into eleven slices. That means that the price of each portion comes to seven monme nine fun eight rin. When I had worked it out like that, taking the exchange rate as fifty-eight monme five fun to the koban,[12] it was like crunching mouthfuls of silver. But even salted or dried bream were fresh once, and they would have suited the spirit of the day equally well. And, after all, now that we have all finished, our stomachs feel no better than they do on ordinary days.'

'Really, what a bright boy this is!' cried the master, clapping his hands in amazement. 'Even my senior assistants here, for all their years of discretion, ate their supper as though the food was nothing out of the ordinary. Their minds merely registered the fact that the chopsticks were there to be grasped in the right hand. They were not even aware that they owed their master any gratitude. But here is a youngster, not yet of age, who can already see beneath the surface of things. Heaven will surely look with favour on this boy.'

He summoned together all his relatives, and after he had given a full account of the episode, he and his wife and the others were of one mind, determined that the boy should be adopted into the family and made heir to the business. A messenger was about to be sent to his home in Ise, to arrange matters with his parents, when the boy came respectfully into their midst and addressed the master.

'I am truly grateful for your kind intentions towards one who has yet given you no cause for such confidence', he began. 'However, I venture to suggest that by sending a messenger to my home you may be putting your respected self to unnecessary trouble. At a time when the position at this end is not fully clarified, you might do well to avoid such expenses. In particular—for what looks like wealth is often, as they say, mere paper and paste[13]—I am yet uninformed on the true state of your finances. It is possible that your business is based upon clever investments of other people's money. Until you have kindly allowed me to make a thorough investigation of the books, it will be difficult for me to agree to the deed of adoption.'

'Your anxiety is only natural,' replied the master, much impressed with the young boy's words, 'but I have not borrowed a zeni from a soul.'

He showed him the account-books for each year, and demonstrated that he had two thousand eight hundred ryō of gold in hand.

'Besides this, five years ago I put by a hundred ryō for my wife's use on temple visits when she retires', he continued, and he showed the boy where it lay—still in its original package, with the year, month, and day written across the seal.

'Dear me!' said the boy when he saw it. 'This is no way to do business. Gold coins wrapped up and left are hardly likely to multiply, not by so much as a single ryō. Tucking away a clever interest-making koban,[14] putting it at the bottom of a deep trunk, and keeping it from outside contacts all these years is not what we expect from a true merchant. If these are your methods, sir, you will never become a millionaire. To live in a city like Edo till your head goes bald, and to make scarcely three thousand ryō is no justification at all for the large airs you have permitted yourself. Should you adopt me as your son, in four or five years your house will rank among the top three exchange brokers of Edo. Please live long, that you may see it happen.

'First, as from now—since I shall relieve you of your responsibilities in the shop—kindly take your wife every day to a temple where a sermon[15] is being given. Before you return please speak to the priest in the temple office and buy all the zeni collected in the offering box. This will be improving your worldly and heavenly prospects at the same time.[16] A boy attendant will be necessary to create a good impression on your journeys to and fro, of course, and I shall require him to take a supply of pepper rolls[17] with him in his satchel. Before the sermon starts he will sell these to the congregation as sleep-preventers. Most of the people will have come without attendants of their own, and he must offer to guard their umbrellas, walking-sticks, and sandals until the sermon is over. He will charge one zeni per article.'

By sending off apprentices with these instructions he contrived that they should never miss a day's profit-making, even when on duty as the master's attendant.

In everything which he did the boy from Ise exercised the same meticulous care. As the years went by he developed into a man of surprising intelligence and resource. By a variety of original devices—by providing bath-house boats[18] for the convenience of large ships calling into port, by selling seaweed ready cut for cooking, in exactly the required quantities, and by making oil jars proofed with pitch and tobacco pouches of paper crêpe—he increased the family fortune to thirty thousand ryō in less than fifteen years. He then retired to Reiganjima [19] and devoted himself to filial attendance upon his foster-parents.

Even in a prosperous place like Edo it is difficult to become a millionaire by following the ordinary lines of trade. There was a man called Sanmonjiya. [20] He started with an invention—pocket raincoats. [21] Next he sold riding capes for travellers. As his capital steadily grew larger he bought in stocks of Japanese silks and, in time, textiles from abroad. Next he bought furs—a four hundred yard length of scarlet orang-outang, [22] and a thousand tiger skins. Everything you wanted was always there, and you would find high-class yellow [23] and purple woollen fabrics in his shop which were unobtainable even in Kyōto. He was rumoured to be fabulously rich, and his house at Nakabashi, with its nine storehouses, is famous. Men who make such a fortune in a single lifetime are in a class apart. For the ordinary man outstanding wealth is beyond reach unless he stands on a fortune inherited from his parents.

In Kyōto there was a man whose father had been a rich and distinguished merchant of Muromachi. The son, however, followed no trade at all. He supported himself by lending large sums of his inherited capital to investors like Zengorō. [24] The interest from this alone brought him an average daily income of two hundred and thirty-five monme, [25] but somehow—and no one can say exactly how he managed it—within fifteen years he had gone clean through his whole inheritance. He then set off for Edo to find work. His accomplishments were superb. He could recite the whole Noh canon of three hundred and fifty plays [26] by heart; he was in the second grade at chess, [27] and for his prowess at kickball he had been granted the right to wear a purple overskirt; [28] in miniature archery he was a holder of the gold medal; [29] his samisen technique in popular songs had won him a reputation as a maestro of the orthodox school; [30] his Jōruri recitations were compared with those of Yamamoto Kaku-dayū; [31] in the tea ceremony he had drunk deep of the Rikyū [32] stream; when it came to a well-turned epigram at a party, even Kagura and Gansai [33] shed their shoes and fled before his wit; his ability to withdraw a wooden pillow from a pile without disturbing the balance [34] had drawn gasps of admiration from Inishie Dennai himself; [35] he was a student of the most modern trends in linked verse; [36] his discernment in matters of perfume was unparalleled even in Kyōto; he could air his views at length in company; and with his own hand he could draw up a formal application. In all these things he was fully qualified. The vital gap in his knowledge lay in the field of earning a living. When he went down to Edo, with no particular occupation in mind, and was asked by prospective employers whether he could judge a bad coin or do a sum on the abacus, he was obliged to admit that at the moment he could do neither. Since his varied attainments in the arts had failed to meet the needs of the moment, he made the journey back to Kyōto again, deciding that it was best, after all, to stay in the place he had grown to understand. With the assistance of friends who had been his intimates in the old days he set up as a teacher of Noh recitation and drums, and he managed to make enough at this to support himself, if no one else. When business looked up every year at the time of the spring Noh festivals [37] he was able to relax his normally straitened mode of life, and even to redeem his pawns; and it was easy enough to put them back again when times grew bad. But he wondered how long a man could go on living like this. Human bodies, he knew, were liable to sickness, and even if he reached old age his prospects of enjoying it seemed none too good.

'If it is merely a question of living, most people can stay alive for the usual sixty years', said a certain millionaire. 'Making a decent livelihood, even for six days, is altogether more difficult. Bear this in mind before you neglect your proper businesses.'

3. *Sound investments and good friends*

IN Izumi province, in the town of Sakai, [1] there lived a dealer in Nagasaki goods called Kogatanaya. [2] Habitually, on each New Year's Day, he revised his will; for not only did he know the law of life's decline after forty, [3] but so honestly did he apply himself to his trade that his fortune grew surely and steadily larger year by year.

Sakai is a city of millionaires in hiding. No one knows how many rich men live there, nor where the roots of their wealth end. Among them are men whose strong-rooms house celebrated tea antiques, [4] imported fabrics and other luxuries, all of which were bought on speculation by their ancestors and have lain undisturbed for five generations. Some have been making money steadily since Kanei times, [5] but have not yet had occasion to spend a penny of it. Others, on settling their daughters in marriage, have sent them off to their husbands with the identical fifty kanme dowry which their own wives brought them when married at the age of fourteen [6]—the money

Kogatanaya's storehouse in Sakai

untouched in its original box, the seals of the box unbroken. They are closer with money in Sakai than anywhere else, and their fortunes are vaster. Kogatanaya was not in the same class as these long-established and distinguished merchants: his first will was for a mere three and a half kanme. But every year for twenty-five years, during which time he had nothing to help him except his native ability and industry, the number of kanme recorded increased, and in his very last will, made out to his only son, he bequeathed a sum of eight hundred and fifty.

He was well liked by others, and it was thanks to this that he received his first chance to make a fortune. One year, after the arrival in Japan of an unusually large number of foreign ships, silk cloth quotations dropped severely, and even the finest vermilion figured satin [7] was selling at eighteen monme a roll. Kogatanaya judged that such prices were not likely to recur, and after confiding his hopes of trade to a group of kind friends he borrowed five kanme from each of them—from ten people a total of fifty kanme—and bought a stock of this figured satin. Next year he sold it at a great profit and made thirty-five kanme more than he had borrowed. However, even as he was rejoicing over this success, his only son fell desperately ill. He did all he could to nurse him back to health—he would willingly have sacrificed his fortune—

but nothing had any effect. While he was in this unhappy state, with every conceivable remedy already tried, he heard from someone of a poor carriageless doctor [8] who, in spite of his unimpressive appearance, had often treated his patients with success. His informant introduced the doctor to him, and after this his son revived and made good progress until he was seven parts cured of his dangerous malady. From this point, however, the improvement was slow, and after a consultation with his relatives Kogatanaya decided to change to one of the more reputable physicians. But his son now weakened rapidly and when he was almost at death's door the husband and wife agreed, on the off chance that he might be able to do something, that the earlier doctor should be asked in again. Without troubling about loss of face they begged for his services through the man who had first introduced him. By now they had given up their son for lost, but the doctor came and administered his medicines again, and in a little more than half a year he made their son as sound as a devil in his prime. The feat earned him wide acclaim.

As for the parents, they were overcome with joy. They visited the house of the man who had referred the doctor to them.

'Today being a suitably auspicious day,' they said, 'we wish to offer the doctor his dues, in gratitude for his splendid services. And we beg you to present it to him.'

When they were gone the man and his wife gossiped together on the matter.

'Since they have asked us to act as intermediaries it must be a fairly large thank-offering', said the husband. 'About five silver chōgin, I should imagine.'

'Hardly as much as that!' objected his wife. 'Three chōgin should be enough.'

While they were still arguing, the doctor's payment arrived—one hundred chōgin, [9] twenty bundles of silk wadding, two barrels of saké, and a box of fish. Two or three times the doctor declined to accept this amazing return for his services, but the go-between pressed it upon him, and even lent him another hundred chōgin and persuaded him to buy a house and land. In time the doctor acquired a fashionable practice, and was soon making his calls in a palanquin.

It sounds little enough, perhaps, but when Kogatanaya, whose fortune was scarcely forty kanme, rewarded his doctor with a hundred chōgin he did something which no townsman in Sakai had done since the city began. This liberal spirit paid handsome dividends, they say, and his household prospered.

4. *A solid fortune floating down the Yodo*[1]

In earning his living a man should no more take a moment's respite than does a water-wheel harnessed to a swiftly flowing stream.[2] In a day and a night a rushing river will flow for seventy-five leagues, and as rapidly as such waters reach their appointed end do the longest of human lives cover their brief course. The waves of old age[3] soon ruffle the smooth waters of youth.

The lump of lacquer in the river Yodo

In Yodo village, by the waters of the Yodo river, lived a man called Yozaemon.[4] He had been a poor tradesman once, with meagre capital, but a chance discovery completely changed his circumstances. It was at the time of the summer rains. They had been falling steadily for days on end, and the high waves on the river were already lapping over the long embankments. The villagers had sounded alarm drums, and gathered together gangs of labourers, but although the waters had been checked, the pool beneath Ko bridge[5]—always deep—today presented a terrifying spectacle, with swirling eddies and counter-eddies reminiscent of the Awa whirlpool.[6] From the centre of one of these a huge black object, a miniature mountain, rose into view, and was carried along downstream in the swiftly moving current. Those who saw it pointed and guessed that it was an ox from one of the carts going to Toba.[7] To Yozaemon's mind it was far too big for an ox. He kept it carefully in sight, following along behind until it came to a stop, entangled in a pine which protruded from the bank. On coming closer he discovered that it was the solidified sap of lacquer trees,[8] washed down miraculously from innumerable river valleys.

'A gift from heaven!' he cried in delight.

Later he took it to his home, piece by piece, in a small lighter, and when he had sold it secretly, making more than a thousand kanme from this one lump, he became the millionaire of his village. He acquired his wealth by no exercise of ability, but through a chance stroke of luck, and since his money automatically made more money, his fame soon spread far and wide.

Inheriting your father's fortune, making money at gambling, dealing in fakes, marrying a rich widow, re-loaning money borrowed at easy rates from the temples on Mount Kōya, [9] or begging loans in Eta villages [10] because no one will guess where the money comes from—all these are ways of getting rich, but they are not good ways. True success is when a man earns his riches by orthodox means. It is wrong to laugh at people's stinginess. They are stingy on principle, and each has a good reason. We live shoulder to shoulder with people whose principles are far worse—if they do not pick pockets, what they do is the same in essence. When an honest man, for instance, finds that he has fallen so heavily in debt that he can risk no further investments, and that no kind of shift will improve things, he naturally dissolves his business, concealing nothing of his true circumstances, and offers up a true and detailed account to his creditors. People suffer from his bankruptcy, it is true, but there is no ill feeling. This, however, is not the current fashion among merchants. Their tastes being too grand for their means, they pay for them day and night with other people's money, and at the end of the year the deficit amazes them. From then on they make deliberate preparation for bankruptcy. To bolster credit by an impressive outward show they buy the neighbour's house and make it one with their own, invite people from the ward to boating picnics, hire koto players [11] for entertainments in honour of their wives' relations, buy early mushrooms and Yamato persimmons with apparent disregard for cost, standing well to the fore of the shop where all may see, and—though it has never been their custom to hold tea gatherings—lay out a guest path from the shop to the main porch shortly before the time for opening the winter's first tea-jars, [12] and get an odd job man to do the paving daily in full view. By a studied arrangement of the gold-lacquered screens in the inner rooms they make certain that the gleam can be detected from outside. Before long the house will be up for sale, but they change the walls of the garden well from wood to stone to suggest that they are staying another thousand years or so. After borrowing as much as anyone will lend they surreptitiously invest in the purchase of farm land, making every provision for a decent livelihood during the remainder of their days. They even put aside sums for the children's education. When they have totted everything up and arranged that their ostensible property shall cover thirty-five per cent of their debts, [13] they surrender that much to their creditors, and if the creditors at first demand more, in time they weary with asking and settle for what they have. For a while the bankrupts creep about with penitent looks in clothes of cotton, but they soon cast off the colds [14] of their disgrace and wrap themselves once more in draught-proof suits of silk. It seems as if the stormy weather has merely cemented the ground they stand on, [15] and they are now seen about the streets with all the paraphernalia of umbrella bearers, bamboo walking-sticks, and flat caps in purple dyes. [16] Their conversation turns on the exchange rate of the koban—'Is this the best time to sell, do you think?'—and the only conclusion to be drawn is that they had more money than they declared.

The world is a dreadful place. Never lend money casually, nor, when you marry off your daughter, leave the marriage broker to arrange matters as he pleases. There are enough ways of losing money even if you take proper care. Long ago when there was a bankrupt in Ōtsu [17] whose liabilities were calculated at one thousand kanme, people talked as though nothing like it could ever happen again; but nowadays in Kyōto and Ōsaka even bankruptcies of three thousand five hundred or four thousand kanme are not rated as all that extraordinary. Standards vary with age, and everything has grown bigger. There is more money than there used to be, and both making it and losing it are done on a grander scale. Now, if ever, trade is an exciting venture. So let none of you risk slipshod methods in earning your livings. 'Sell what you begrudge, and refrain from buying what you fancy' was the rule laid down by a certain millionaire, [18] and if you work in this spirit, with no concessions to the urge for display, it will surely be to your ultimate profit. Strong roots and steady growth—that is the secret of success in trade.

The merchant of Yodo copied the extravagances he saw in the capital. He pumped water from the great river into ornamental garden springs, summoning hosts of carpenters from Kyōto to build him a water-wheel. Round and round it went, like the wheel in the song, and in and in flocked the guests it was there to entertain. [19] The clatter of bowls and dishes was heard as far away as Fushimi, [20] the smell of broiled bream drifted to Hashimoto [21] and Kuzuwa, [22] a living bridge of tea porters linked the house with Uji, [23] and rivers of spilt saké flowed all the way to the brewers' shrine at Matsu-no-o. [24] The pace showed never a sign of slackening. One year Yozaemon humbly solicited the privilege of leading the fasting rite at the Iwa-shimizu Hachiman shrine,[25] and when his request was granted it seemed that his good fortune had now been crowned with the blessing of the gods. In these ceremonies the state of mind of the leading celebrant is of vital importance, and if he performs any of his manifold duties in a begrudging spirit the efficacy of the rites is lost at once. Perhaps it was an omen of impending ruin—but when, at the peak of the ceremonies, the great heap of reeds beneath Yozaemon's kitchen furnace began to burn low, not one of the crowd of people in his garden did anything to replenish it. When the master realised what was happening, it was already too late. Not long after this his household's fortunes crumbled, and his name now only survives in dancing songs.[26]

5. *Rations of worldly wisdom from a man of eighty-eight*

We have now seen that our world, after all, is wide. 'There are no prospects in trade these days'—we and our neighbours alike have voiced this same complaint for the last forty-five years,[1] but while people like us were bemoaning trade's demise, others—large numbers of them—were starting new businesses from naked nothingness and working their way towards wealth and fame. The fault lies in ourselves, it seems: when a whole koku of rice can be had for fourteen and a half monme[2] there are still beggars.

On looking more closely into the way people have managed we find that over these years each family has steadily enlarged its stock of household equipment, and that in all respects lives are less restricted than in the old days. There are people whose homes and fortunes have crumbled to ruin, of course, but they are outnumbered by those whose homes and fortunes have been newly built. Not only in Kyōto but all around the outskirts of Edo and Ōsaka vacant plots and even expanses of wasteland have disappeared without trace, and rows of dwelling houses now stretch over them in unbroken succession. How these people support themselves is not clear, but they present their families of three or five children with freshly padded kimono at New Year, and not only make them dancing gowns[3] for Bon but improve the effect with dapple-dyed waistbands, bound at the back in the latest style. The fathers are day labourers, perhaps, or well-rope twisters, or they weave the straw windmills sold by street pedlars.[4] The mothers, never sure whether their husbands will bring home a profit on a day's work, or—if they do—whether it will be thirty-seven, forty-five, or as much as fifty zeni, must grapple alone with the problem of how to feed their families of four or five and clothe them against the cold. In other families, of equal size, the daily income may be more than five or ten times this amount.[5] Every household has its own way of managing on the housekeeping money. The differences are as many and varied as degrees of success in making a living. Sometimes a husband and wife working together will fail even to support themselves, and sometimes—though this is no common case, even amongst townsmen, and marks the possessor of genius—a man by his single-handed labours will support a multitude.

All human beings have eyes and noses, and all alike are born with hands and feet. But in one respect the ordinary townsman is different from the nobility, the great military families,[6] and the practitioners of the various arts—his hopes of worldly fame rest solely on the acquisition of money. It is a pitiful thing for him if he works from early youth and dies without the reputation of a man of wealth. Birth and lineage mean nothing: money is the only family tree for a townsman. A man may be descended from the noblest of the Fujiwara,[7] but if he dwells among shopkeepers and lives in poverty he is lower than a vagabond monkey-trainer.[8] There is no alternative for a townsman: he must pray for wealth and aim to be a millionaire. To be a millionaire he must have the will of a hero, the heart to climb a great mountain. He must also, even to rise to middling wealth,[9] employ good clerks.

To take the successes in Ōsaka alone, there is the man who pioneered the brewing of saké for shipment to Edo,[10] whose whole family now shares his prosperity; the man who made his fortune overnight in copper mining;[11] the dealers in Yoshino lacquer,[12] with more money hidden away than anyone cares to guess; the builder of the first light freighters for the Edo run,[13] now famed as a shipping agent; the men who have made vast fortunes by lending on the security of property; or those who have risen slowly and steadily to wealth by buying iron mines. All these are examples of recently established merchant houses, starting and rising to success in the last thirty years. If others hope to rival them, they must live in one of the three great cities. There are plenty of rich merchants in distant provincial places, but few of them are ever talked about. The millionaires of the capital, on the other hand, are known everywhere. Not only do they have money, but they hand down within their families ornaments and curios which are acknowledged treasures.

The anniversary celebration

There is the example of the tea canister [14] which belonged to the house of Kameya, bought by the merchant Itoya at a price of three hundred kanme of silver. Again, in Kyōto there are, they say, exchange brokers who have recovered from bankruptcies of two hundred thousand ryō, paying off the debt in yearly instalments. Indeed, the stories one hears about the capital tell of things which could happen nowhere else. As the older millionaires fade away new ones appear, and the city's prosperity grows and grows.

But an ordinary man who enjoys good health and makes a living sufficient to his needs and station can be yet more fortunate than the greatest of millionaires. A household may be rich and prosperous, but if it lacks a son to succeed, or if death has separated master and mistress, its happiness is not complete. Disappointments of this and many other kinds are common enough in our world.

In a village at the foot of the hills to the north of Kyōto lived a celebrated family, the envy of all, known as 'The Three Couples'. First there were the grandfather and grandmother, still safely together after all the years; then there was their son, with the wife he had taken; and lastly the grandson, and he too had grown up and was married. The three husbands and three wives lived together in the same house, and in each case the man and his wife had been childhood friends before their marriage. Few parallels could be found for such good fortune. When the grandfather reached the age of eighty-eight,[15] his wife was eighty-one; the second couple were fifty-seven and forty-nine; the third were twenty-six and eighteen. Not once in their lives had any of them suffered the slightest illness, and, what is more, they had always lived together in perfect harmony. They were farmers, and their paddy fields, tilled land, cattle, horses, and rows of adjoining houses for men and women helpers were such as farmers dream of; and since they had been granted tax exemption,[16] every harvest they reaped was for themselves alone. Living thus in perfect contentment, worshipping the gods and holding the Buddhas in deep reverence, their hearts came naturally to be endowed with every virtue. At the beginning of the grandfather's eighty-eighth year someone—no one knew who was the first to ask—persuaded the old man to cut him a bamboo grain-level.[17] As the word passed quickly around whole forests of straight bamboo were cut to the ground, and merchants of every variety in Kyōto sought a similar favour. Their trade improved at once, and as the demand grew greater and greater, and more merchants used these 'Three Couple' levels to measure their bales of grain, good fortune spilled everywhere over the rims of measuring boxes. A certain millionaire of northern Kyōto is said to have used one of these bamboo levels to share out the silver which he bequeathed to his three sons.

Money is still to be found in certain places, and where it lies it lies in abundance. Whenever I heard stories[18] about it I noted them in my great national stock-book,[19] and, in order that future generations might study them and profit thereby, I placed them in a storehouse to serve each family's posterity. Here they now rest, as securely guarded as the peace of Japan.[20]

COMMENTARY

ABBREVIATIONS OF REFERENCES

1. When reference is made to certain modern Japanese editions of *Nippon Eitai-gura* the following abbreviations are used:

Satō	*Nippon Eitai-gura Hyōshaku* (Satō Tsurukichi, 1930).
Fujii	*Saikaku Meisaku Shū* (Fujii Otoo, 1935).
Ōyabu	*Nippon Eitai-gura Shinkō* (Ōyabu Torasuke, 1937).
Shuzui	*Kōchū Nippon Eitai-gura*, I (Shuzui Kenji, 1937).
TSZ	*Teihon Saikaku Zenshū*, VII (Ehara Taizō, Teruoka Yasutaka and Noma Kōshin, 1950).
Shuzui II	*Nippon Eitai-gura Seikō* (Shuzui Kenji, 1953).

2. Note also:

Edo Chiri	*Saikaku to Edo Chiri* (Mayama Seika, posth. 1952).
Eitai-gura	*Nippon Eitai-gura.*
Goi Kōshō	*Saikaku Goi Kōshō* (Mayama Seika, posth. 1952).
Kōken Roku	*Chōnin Kōken Roku* (Mitsui Takafusa, 1726–33).
Kinmō Zui	*Jinrin Kinmō Zui* (1690).
Sansai Zue	*Wakan Sansai Zue* (Terajima Ryōan, 1715).

An alphabetical list of all works cited, together with their characters and dates, will be found in Appendix 4, pp. 251–5.

3. References to the various sections of the present volume are abbreviated as follows:

Intro.	Introduction.
Tr.	Translation (e.g. Tr. I, 2 indicates the translation of Book One, Story Two).
Com.	Commentary (e.g. Com. I, 2, n. 3 refers to Note Three of the Commentary on Book One, Story Two).
App.	Appendix.

COMMENTARY

BOOK I, 1 (pp. 13–16)

[1] *Tendō mono iwazu:* an echo of a passage from the Chinese classic *Lun-yü*, *Yang Ho P'ien:* 'Does heaven speak? The four seasons come and go, and the earth yields its fruits. Does heaven speak?' References to this passage of *Lun-yü* were fairly common in contemporary *kana-zōshi* (e.g. *Ukiyo Monogatari* (*c.* 1661), v; *Kashō Ki* (1642), 1).

[2] *Sono shin wa moto kyo ni shite:* a translation of a Chinese poem by Ch'êng I included in *Kobun Shinpō Gōshū* (compiled *c.* 1391–1500), 'Ch'êng Chêng Shu—Shih chên'.

[3] *Sugu naru ima no onyo wo...wataru:* the phrase combines two distinct meanings. (1) 'To make an honest living'; (2) 'To live through the present glorious era of honest government'. The latter, a passing compliment to the Tokugawa rulers, has no bearing upon the logic of the argument, and I have thought it best, for clarity's sake, to omit it from the translation.

[4] *Futa-oya no hoka ni inochi no oya:* lit. 'besides one's natural parents, the parent of life'. There is a play upon the proverbial expression for the person who saves one's life—*inochi no oya*—and the more usual sense of *oya*, 'parent'.

[5] *Tenchi wa banbutsu no gekiryo:* a translation of a poem by the Chinese poet Li Po, included in *Kobun Shinpō Goshū*, 'Hsü lei'.

[6] *Itsutsu ari:* the 'five things' mentioned here are possibly the 'five borrowed things' (*itsutsu no kari-mono*) to which Saikaku refers in *Kōshoku Ichidai Otoko* (1682), iv, 3. These are elements of life borrowed from various Buddhas at birth, and returned at death. According to one source they are bones, flesh, blood, sinews, and breath; according to another, they are heart, liver, spleen, lungs, and kidney. Other theories have been advanced by commentators to explain the 'five things' (see *Ōyabu* (1937), pp. 6–8), but the matter remains conjectural.

[7] *Takara-bune:* wood-block prints sold in the streets at *Setsubun* (the first night of spring, corresponding—in the old Japanese calendar—with the last night of the year), which depicted a ship laden with a variety of treasures, bales of rice, bags of money, coral, spices, and many magic implements. The prints were placed under the pillow to induce lucky dreams. Unlucky dreams were quickly eaten by a *Baku* monster, whose picture was likewise placed under the pillow. (See *Hinami Kiji* (1676), 'Setsubun no yoru'.) These customs are still observed to a limited extent.

More literally translated this sentence would run: 'What treasure-ship print is more desirable than money?' Saikaku used the phrase, with the licence of a *haikai* poet, to give the required meaning of 'treasure' in a broad sense, and to open the way to the subsequent remarks on the particular treasures of a *takara-bune*.

[8] *Kakure-gasa, kakure-mino:* these reed hats and straw capes were not only worn by devils on the mythical *Oni-ga-shima* (Devils' Island) but were among the traditional magic implements depicted on 'treasure ship' prints.

[9] *Hatsu-muma no hi:* in the old Japanese calendar the days of the year, like the years themselves, were named by a combination of ten calendar signs (*jik-kan*) and twelve signs of the zodiac (*jū-ni-shi*), in a cycle of sixty. The system was independent of month and year divisions, and the first day of the Horse (one of the *jū-ni-shi*) in the second moon would thus fall on a different date each year.

Throughout the translation I use 'moon' to indicate a Japanese lunar month, which was of thirty or twenty-nine days (see also Com. v, 2, n. 21).

[10] *Mizuma-dera:* Ryōkonzan Mizuma-*dera*, a temple of the Tendai sect in the country south of the present Kaizuka-*shi*, Ōsaka-*fu*. The festival on the first day of the second moon was called *hatsu-muma-mairi*, or *fuku-mairi* (lucky pilgrimage).

[11] *Kari-zeni: zeni* were copper coins of small value. It was usual to thread them on strings in collections of 96 or 960 (in theory 100 or 1000, see App. I, p. 237, n. 5).

[12] *Fūzoku ritsugi:* in *Shikidō Ōkagami* (1678), II, 'Ifuku', rules of dress are laid down for the guidance of fashionable clients at the Shimabara brothel quarter: 'Skirts should hang loose about the body...sleeves should be long ...a patternless dye of deep blue is too naïve...reinforced collar bands are for country bumpkins only....'

[13] In translating ages I give the figures in the text. It should be borne in mind, however, that the old Japanese method of calculating ages indicated the number of the years in which a person had lived rather than the strict length of time. In the year of his birth he was 'one', and on the following New Year's Day (even if he was born the day before) he became 'two'.

[14] *Ueda-jima no haori:* a *haori* is a short gown with sleeves, worn over the *kimono*. *Ueda-jima*, a product of Ueda in Shinano province, was a striped pongee cloth of exceptional durability. It earned the name *mi-ura* (three linings) for its ability to last out three changes of lining. (*Mankin Sangyō-bukuro* (1732), IV, 'Kyō-ori Rui'.)

[15] *Chū-wakizashi:* daggers were worn by civilians largely as dress ornaments. It was not unusual to cover them with dust-protectors during travel, but the word sometimes used for these protectors—*sechiben-bukuro* (stingy wrappers)—suggests that, being ornaments, the daggers were better displayed.

[16] *Koami-chō:* the present Koami-*chō*, Chūō-*ku*, Tōkyō-*to*, extending along the north bank of the Nihonbashi river.

[17] *Funa-doiya:* an agent for the transmission of goods by sea, a middleman between the cargo owner and the shipping company, receiving a commission for his services. There were a number of shipping agencies in Koami-*chō* in the Edo period (see *Kinsei Fūzoku Shi* (*c.* 1837–53), I, 'Seigyō I: Koami-*chō*').

[18] *Kake-suzuri:* a miniature chest of drawers, designed to hold writing materials and small articles of value. Its lid opened on a hinge, and was lockable.

[19] *Tōkai-dō:* the principal highway of Tokugawa Japan, linking Edo and Kyōto. The money would presumably be carried from Kyōto to Mizuma-*dera* via Ōsaka.

[20] *Tōshi-muma:* baggage horses which covered the whole journey to Mizuma-*dera*, without being changed at the usual relay points. A method of ensuring safe delivery.

[21] *Jōtō:* lamps continually replenished with oil, set in the strong-room to honour the family god of luck. In *Seken Munesanyō* (1692), IV, I, Saikaku indicates that the practice was confined to merchants who possessed more than 1000 *kanme* in silver.

[22] *Amiya:* in *Kokka Manyō Ki* (1697) is the entry *Amiya, Koami-chō*. The trade is not specified, but there is possibly a connection with the Amiya of the present story (*Kokka Manyō Ki*, 'Edo').

[23] *Gin gohyaku kanme:* 1 *kanme* = 1000 *monme*. For the silver coinage see App. I, pp. 235–8.

[24] *Bungen...chōja:* the distinction here drawn between *bungen* and *chōja* is not strictly observed elsewhere in *Eitai-gura*. The *furi-gana* in this passage indicates the pronunciation *bungen*, but *bugen* is equally common.

[25] *Kono gin no iki yori wa iku-senmanzairaku to iwaeri: iki* has the double sense of 'interest on loans' and 'the moaning breath' of stocks of money. (Money was reputed to have a spirit and voice: for a further reference to this superstition see Tr. V, 5, p. 123.) *Iku-senmanzairaku* is a pivot phrase composed of *iku senman*, 'how many thousands and tens of thousands of silver *kanme*!'; *iku-senmanzai*, 'how many thousands and tens of thousands of years!'; and finally *manzairaku* (a form of congratulatory song and dance, performed before a person's house to wish him long life and prosperity).

BOOK I, 2 (pp. 16–20)

[1] *Hito no ie ni aritaki wa:* a reference to *Tsurezure-gusa* (*c.* 1330), 139: 'The trees I should like in my home are pine and cherry...' (*Ie ni aritaki ki wa matsu, sakura...*).

[2] *Kiken-jō:* the castle in which the god Taishaku-*ten*, guardian of the law of Buddhism, lives. Outside each of its four gates is a spacious pleasure-garden.

[3] *Shijō no hashi wo higashi e:* immediately east of the bridge was Gion-*machi*; east, and a little to the south were Ishigake-*chō* and Miyakawa-*chō*; to the north was Nawate street. All these districts are now *geisha* or brothel quarters. In Saikaku's time it seems that they were no more than 'low haunts' on the outskirts of the town, in quite a different category from the splendid Shimabara quarter. Their speciality was male prostitution, and they are introduced here to point a contrast with the other way of love as practised in the Shimabara. (See *Goi Kōshō* (posth. 1952), 'Shijō no hashi wo higashi e...'.)

[4] *Tanba-guchi* is the entrance from Ōmiya street on to the main road to Tanba province, which runs westwards out of Kyōto. The district west of Tanba-*guchi* is the Shimabara licensed brothel quarter. The Shimabara, in contrast to the Gion quarter, has now fallen on evil days.

[5] *Shukke...rōnin:* priests sought contributions for their temples, and *rōnin* were often clever swindlers or spongers. For the latter, see Tr. v, 4, p. 121.

[6] *Masu-kaki:* a bamboo stick used to level the surface of rice in a grain-measure (*masu*). It was a custom among townsmen to ask a person who had reached the auspicious age of eighty-eight to cut them lengths of bamboo as grain-levels. These levels were reputed to bring luck. The age of eighty-eight was called *beiju* (rice longevity), since the Japanese numeral eighty-eight is similar in form to the character for 'rice'. (See also Tr. vi, 5, p. 146.)

[7] *Nijū-ni nen iki tamaeba chō-hyaku nari:* the Japanese commentators, without exception, assume that '22' is a misprint or Saikaku's error, and they substitute '12'. Their interpretation then runs: 'If he had lived another twelve years he would have reached his century. To die so young was a great loss.' The 'loss' must then be taken to exist purely in the mind of the speaker, who is parsimoniously obsessed with tidy figures.

My own interpretation seems to me to be justified by the text, and to give a rather more tangible explanation of the 'loss'. If '22' is correct, it means that the father had first started wearing the cloth at the age of 10, and having worn it during the subsequent 78 years, died 22 years before it had given him a century of service. This, too, may seem a little far-fetched, and an emendation of the figure '22' to the figure '32' would lessen the strain on the imagination.

The word used here for 'century', *chō-hyaku*, is appropriately financial, signifying 'a complete hundred' of *zeni* as opposed to the usual 'hundred', which was really ninety-six (see App. I, p. 237, n. 5).

[8] *Murasakino:* a district in the northern suburbs of Kyōto, between Funaoka-*yama* and Daitoku-*ji*. In Tokugawa times herbs for medicinal use in the imperial palace were grown here.

[9] *Nisan* (Two-three) would be the *nom d'amour* of someone called Gobei, Goemon, or any name including the figure 'five'. It was customary for

patrons of the brothel quarters to assume such names to conceal their identity. In *Shikidō Ōkagami*, VI, where it explains how a courtesan should tattoo her lover's name on her skin, it says, 'For Jūbei (a name containing the figure "ten") they should write *Nigo-no-mikoto* (Lord Twice-five), and for Gobei *Nisan-no-mikoto* (Lord Two-three)'.

[10] *Go Dairiki Bosatsu:* 'The Five Dairiki Bodhisattvas'—a formula written on a letter as a prayer for its safe delivery.

[11] *Tsubone jorō:* a prostitute of the lowest class, also called *hashi-geisei*. There were four grades inside the Shimabara—*tayū*, *tenjin*, *kakoi*, *tsubone*—just as there were four classes outside in normal Japanese society.

[12] *Sugiwara hongo ichi-mai:* Sugiwara paper was originally manufactured in Sugiwara-*mura*, Harima province, but was later manufactured in many places throughout Japan. It was a form of thin, soft paper, used for special occasions (see *Sansai Zue* (1715), XV).

[13] *Ichibu:* the smallest gold coin. The usual currency in Kyōto was silver (see App. I, pp. 235–8).

[14] *Haru-giri-mai:* it is assumed by most commentators that the writer of the letter is a *samurai*, and that *haru-giri-mai* is the spring payment of his stipend, transmuted from rice into cash. The difficulty is that, if this is so, he should just have received his stipend for the winter (issued in the tenth moon)—this episode taking place on the anniversary of the old man's death —and it should not be 'a difficult time' for a *samurai*. Mayama Seika points out that *kiri-mai* is, in fact, not necessarily a *samurai*'s salary, but is a general term for payments of all kinds, whether for services rendered by business clerks, artisans' apprentices, or hired concubines. The writer of the letter is probably some Kyōto clerk (see *Goi Kōshō*, 'Haru-giri-mai').

[15] *Ōzakaya no Nokaze: Ōzakaya* was the name of one of the *yūjoya* in Shimabara, i.e. a place where the courtesans of a particular firm were housed, as opposed to the *ageya* where they went to entertain clients (see map of Shimabara in *Shikidō Ōkagami*, XII). Nokaze was a celebrated *tayū* (first-grade courtesan) in this establishment.

[16] *Kiku no sekku:* ninth day of the ninth moon. On this day the Shimabara courtesans donned new clothes and decorated their rooms in the *ageya* with special care. The expenses for the courtesans were considerable and they wrote for contributions to customers with whom they were particularly intimate (see *Shimabara Yamato-Goyomi* (1683), I, 'Kugatsu kokonoka').

[17] *Ageya yori sake tori ni yuku:* for *ageya* see n. 15, above. Catering for *ageya* was generally done by *chaya* (tea houses) in the vicinity of the Shimabara (see *Kinmō Zui*, VII, 'Shimabara no chaya').

[18] *Amigasa:* a broad hat of sedge or raffia, which concealed the customer's face. At Shimabara, it was *de rigueur* to wear one. The character in this story, not knowing the rules, takes his off.

[19] *De-guchi no chaya:* the *chaya* (tea houses) just inside the entrance

were used as *ageya* for the lowest grade of courtesan. For a description of the functions of the various *chaya* of Shimabara, see *Kinmō Zui*, VII, 'Shimabara no chaya'.

[20] *Ichimonjiya no ima Morokoshi dekake-sugata ni:* a *tayū*, setting out from her *yūjoya* to meet a client in an *ageya*, moved through the streets of the quarter in full state, with various attendants. Ichimonjiya Shichirōbei was a noted *yūjoya* proprietor of Naka-*no-machi*, Shimabara (see map of Shimabara in *Sujaku Tōmegane*, 1681). The titles of *tayū* were hereditary, but this is probably the lady *Morokoshi* (China) mentioned in Tr. v, 3, p. 118.

[21] *Ao-nōren:* the doorways of the houses of the fourth-grade courtesans were draped with dark blue curtains. In Tayū-*machi*, the curtains were dyed light brown with persimmon juice.

[22] *Fujiya Hikoemon:* the *chaya* of Fujiya Hikoemon, just inside the entrance to the Shimabara, is marked on the maps in *Shikidō Ōkagami*, XII and *Sujaku Tōmegane*.

[23] *Kyū monme no o-kata:* nine *monme* was the price paid for a *hanya*, a special type of *kakoi* (third-grade prostitute) who worked in twelve-hour shifts. Their charge was half that of a *kakoi* (see *Shikidō Ōkagami*, I, 'Hanya'; XII, 'Rakuyō Keisei-machi').

[24] *Shi-tennō*, a Buddhist term, came to be used in the sense of the four brightest pupils in some particular following. Here it means the four outstanding *taiko-mochi*, or brothel entertainers, of this period in Kyōto. These four are frequently mentioned in Saikaku's works. Their full names were Gansai no Yashichi, Kagura no Shōzaemon, Ōmu no Kichibyōe, and Ranshu no Yozaemon, and they specialised in witty conversation, mimicry, and drinking-party pastimes and etiquette (see *Kōshoku Ichidai Onna* (1686), v, 1; also Tr. VI, 2, p. 136).

[25] *Ōgiya* (fan-shop) was the name of his business. *Ōgi* is here followed, in *haikai* fashion, by several associated words and phrases—*kaze* (wind), *fuki-age* (to blow money about in hiring courtesans), *hifuku chikara naku* (to have no strength left to blow on the embers of a dying fire).

[26] *Mi no hodo wo utai-utaite: utai* (or *utai-utai*) was a type of singing beggar (see *Kinmō Zui*, VII, 'Kanjin-morai').

[27] *Kamadaya no nanigashi:* this is possibly a reference to the Kamadaya of *Chōja Kyō* (1627). (For a complete translation of *Chōja Kyō*, see App. 2, pp. 239–44.)

BOOK I, 3 (pp. 21–25)

[1] *Nami-kaze shizuka ni Jinzū Maru:* the title derives from a brief passage of seemingly little significance, and has been criticised as inappropriate. In *Shuzui* (1937), p. 47, it is suggested that Saikaku, after settling on the title, was involuntarily carried away by his interest in the arising topics. But the title here is truly inappropriate only if one regards the last episode—the

success story of the old woman and her son—as the core of the whole, and all that precedes as a diffuse introduction to this.

The essential unity of the story appears to lie in the theme of the prosperity of Kitahama rice-exchange on the banks of the Yodo at Ōsaka. Every episode or descriptive passage, with the exception of the short introduction on *daimyō* differences, centres around this locality and theme; and it was possibly in relation to this that the title was selected, referring, as it does, to an example of an enterprising and successful merchant in the rice trade at Kitahama. See Intro., pp. xxxv–vi for further analysis of this story. (For a useful commentary on this story see *Nippon Eitai-gura Kōgi* (1952).)

[2] *Shaka nyorai go-nyūmetsu:* it is estimated that there are even now some fifty-two versions of the date of the Buddha's death, and in Saikaku's time there were possibly more. If the year 486 B.C. (as given in *Bukkyō Daijiten*, 1917) is accepted, then Saikaku's arithmetic is correct. (For a few contemporary estimates of the date see *Goi Kōshō*, 'Shaka Nyorai go-nyūmetsu konokata'; see also *Iguchi Monogatari* (1662), VIII, 7.)

[3] *Hyakuni jūman koku:* the revenue of Lord Maeda of Kaga, the most wealthy of the *daimyō*, was at this time approximately 1,020,000 *koku*. In former times it had approached the figure Saikaku gives, and it may still have been the popular belief in *chōnin* circles that this figure was correct.

[4] *Chigai kakubetsu, sekai wa hiroshi:* 'the world is broad' serves not only to conclude the opening remarks but to introduce the next section, suggesting the vast distances sailed by the *Jinzū Maru*.

[5] *Kindai Senshū ni Karakaneya tote:* presumably 'the famous shipowner Karakaneya Yomozō of Sano in Izumi province' mentioned in *Setsuyō Kikan* (1833), XVIII, which gives a long account of the activities of this family, and of the magnificence of the family mansion and estate.

[6] *Jinzū Maru:* in *Setsuyō Kikan*, Karakaneya's largest ship is called *Ōtsu Maru*, and carries a cargo of 4800 *koku*. According to the same passage, the ship was built in the Kanbun era (1661–73), and became one of the wonders of Ōsaka. It was broken up after being damaged by a tidal wave in the opening years of the eighteenth century. If *Ōtsu Maru* is correct, it is not clear why Saikaku has changed it to *Jinzū Maru*—though *jinzū*, a Buddhist term meaning 'divine power', is more propitious. (N.B. *Setsuyō Kikan* is not a direct contemporary source: it was compiled in 1833.)

It seems that until the eighties of the seventeenth century the normal cargo vessel for rice carried a load of 500–600 *koku* (1 *koku* = approx. 5 bushels), but that much larger vessels carrying 1000 *koku* became more common after the opening of the northern sea route to Ōsaka, from the rice-producing areas facing the Japan sea. (*Nippon Eitai-gura Kōgi*, p. 162.)

[7] *Hokkoku no umi:* the 'northern coast' is that of the Japan sea. Rice from this area was transported to Ōsaka via the Shimo-no-seki straits and Seto inland sea.

[8] *Kitahama no kome-ichi:* present Kitahama-*chō*, Higashi-*ku*, Ōsaka-*shi*, a district on the south bank of the Tosa-*borigawa*, facing Naka-no-shima. It is now an important stock exchange. The founder of the famous Yodoya fortune, Yodoya Saburō Tsuneyasu, took up residence here in the early years of the seventeenth century, and it was largely due to his influence that the area developed as a rice mart. In 1697 the rice merchants began to move to the newly reclaimed area of Dōjima, on the opposite bank of the Yodo, and the rice mart at Kitahama dwindled to insignificance.

[9] *Hiyori wo miawase:* the price of rice fluctuated considerably from week to week, and the possible effect of the weather on the season's crop was a major factor in determining the current value.

[10] *Naniwa-bashi:* Naniwa bridge lies between Yodoya bridge and Tenjin bridge, spanning the river Yodo just above Naka-no-shima. The following passage—a parody on 'The Hundred Views' of various noted scenic spots in Japan—is in typical *Danrin haikai* vein.

[11] *Sore hodo no yo wo wataru, Naniwa-bashi...:* *wataru* is here used in the sense of 'making a living' and 'spanning a river', and forms a pivot, concluding one sentence and starting the next. The same word was used earlier in this story, in connection with Karakaneya and his ship, to suggest 'making a living' and 'crossing the ocean'.

[12] *Uwani, cha-bune:* vessels used to transport cargo from sea-going ships to the wharves, or for general transport purposes on rivers (see *Sansai Zue*, XXXIV, 'Uwani-bune').

[13] *Kome-sashi:* the porters at Kitahama carried short sharpened bamboo shafts (*kome-sashi*) which they inserted into each bale of rice they handled, withdrawing a quantity of rice in the hollow of the shaft. Ostensibly this was to test the contents for possible deterioration in transit or other defects, but the samples also served as payment for the porters, who received no other wages. It became the practice to make two insertions—one portion was kept by the porters themselves, and the other was handed over to the examiners, who subsequently distributed the accumulated rice amongst their subordinates. The owners of the rice complained about this, and the practice was officially prohibited; but it nevertheless continued (see *Ōyabu*, pp. 57–8).

[14] *Tenbin ni roku jichū no kane ni hibiki-masatte:* the *tenbin* balance was used mainly for weighing money, and the arm of the balance was tapped with a small mallet in rechecking (see Com. IV, 2, n. 3, for further details). According to *Nippon Eitai-gura Kōgi*, p. 171, the Kitahama hour bell was installed to commemorate the exemption of the citizens of Ōsaka from land tax by the *Shōgun* Iemitsu, on the occasion of his visit to Ōsaka in 1633.

[15] *Naka-no-shima ni:* the merchants in the list are presumably authentic contemporaries, but their precise identity is difficult to determine. The lengthy identifications attempted by the commentators lack sufficient substantiation (see *Nippon Eitai-gura Kōgi*, p. 173).

[16] *Shōbai wo yamete:* it was a common practice for a merchant who had made a tolerable fortune in his own business to retire, and to concentrate on making a really big fortune by loaning money or renting property. The carefree, magnificent lives of these retired merchants (*shimotaya*) is enviously described by Ogyū Sorai in *Seidan* (1720) (see *Goi Kōshō*, 'Shōbai wo yamete...').

[17] *Yamato, Kawachi, Tsu no kuni, Izumi:* the provinces in and around Ōsaka.

[18] *O-shikise:* apprentices received no wages—only board, lodging, and gifts of clothes presented on certain festival days, such as New Year and *Bon.*

[19] *Yuku mizu ni kazu kaku:* a reference to the poem in *Kokin Shū* (905), Koi, I: 'More hopeless even than writing numbers on a flowing stream is to feel love for one who loves not in return' (*Yuku mizu ni kazu kaku yori mo hakanaki wa omowanu hito wo omou narikeri*). Here it is merely a decorative pivot phrase linking boating excursions with practice in characters and arithmetic. Teaching an apprentice to write in a sand-box was one way of economising on paper.

[20] *Sumi-mae* (square-in-front): a popular style of hair-cut for the early teen-ager, the last to be adopted before the more manly styles which would follow his 'coming of age', at fifteen or sixteen.

[21] *Ninai-akinai no mi no yuku sue:* if a clerk was convicted of dishonesty and dismissed, no other merchant would employ him. This was a mutual arrangement among merchants to safeguard themselves, since a clerk had access to considerable confidential information which could be used to the disadvantage of his former employer (*Nippon Eitai-gura Kōgi*, p. 177).

[22] *Shiika, kemari, yōkyū, koto, fue, tsuzumi, kōgai, cha-no-yu:*

Shiika (poetry), here, is not the popular *haikai* but formal Chinese verse and *tanka.*

Kemari (kickball) is an ancient court game for four, six, or eight players. The object of the game is to keep a small leather ball ballooning in the air, within a prescribed area, by skilful kicking. The foremost exponents were the members of the noble court family of Asukai.

Yōkyū: a form of miniature archery, in which arrows about ten inches long were used (see also Com. VI, 2, n. 29).

Koto: a multi-stringed musical instrument, laid horizontally on the floor and plucked with plectra on thumb and forefinger. The number of strings varied, according to the type of *koto*, from six to thirteen.

Fue, tsuzumi (flute, drums): instruments used as accompaniment to Noh performances.

Kōgai (incense blending): the appreciation of various types of incense, or —sometimes—a game of guessing the names of different types of incense burning together.

Cha-no-yu (tea ceremony): the ritual connected with drinking green tea in company.

Such accomplishments were part of the traditional culture of court nobles or *samurai*, and in the seventeenth century they became increasingly popular in *chōnin* circles. There were many professional instructors for these arts in Ōsaka, Kyōto, and Edo (cf. Com. II, 3, n. 22, and Tr. pp. 47 and 136).

[23] *Atarashiya Tennōjiya:* both Atarashiya and Tennōjiya were great exchange-brokers (*jūnin-ryōgaeya*) of the time (see n. 29, below).

[24] *Sugiwae wa kusa-bōki no tane:* a parody of the proverb, *Sugiwae wa kusa no tane*—'Ways of making a living are as numerous as seeds of grass.'

[25] *Tsutsu-o-gome wo haki-atsumete, sono hi wo kuraseru rōjo:* the rice-sweepers of Kitahama, like the porters (see n. 13, above) formed a corporation of closed membership, and had their own methods of earning a living. They worked in close co-operation with the porters, and the latter did their best to spill as much rice as they could for the sweepers to gather, presumably claiming a proportion for themselves. The sweepers were officially expected to gather only sufficient for their own daily needs, and it was forbidden for them to sell the rice. For that reason the old woman disposes of her store 'secretly' (see *Nippon Eitai-gura Kōgi*, pp. 182–3).

[26] *Shokoku kaimen:* the 'revision' may possibly be that of Hideyoshi in 1586 (see *Ōyabu*, p. 74), but this seems rather early, as Ōsaka castle was completed only the previous year, and the Kitahama rice-exchange was in its infancy. The phrase itself is not clear, and is open to various interpretations.

[27] *Itto shi-go shō:*

10 *shō* = 1 *to* (about 4 gallons)
10 *to* = 1 *koku* (about 5 bushels)

[28] *Zeni-sashi:* cords for stringing together small copper coins (see App. 1, p. 237, n. 5).

[29] *Zeni-mise:* a shop changing gold and silver coins to *zeni*, taking a small commission. It was the humblest form of *ryōgaeya*. On *ryōgaeya* in general I quote *Ōyabu*, pp. 77–8:

> Strictly speaking, the function of a *ryōgaeya* was the exchange of gold, silver, and copper currency, and his livelihood was derived from charging a commission for these services. However, by the time of the publication of *Eitai-gura* this original function had already split into roughly three main divisions. Among the *ryōgaeya* of the great cities, those of Ōsaka had reached the highest degree of development, and the *ryōgaeya* in that city were divided into three grades: *jūnin-ryōgaeya, hon-ryōgaeya*, and *zeni-ryōgaeya*. The *jūnin-ryōgaeya* were the ten houses with the oldest tradition in the trade—such houses as Tennōjiya, Hiranoya, and Kōnoikeya—and they exercised control over the *hon-ryōgaeya*, having the right to approve or veto the establishment of new exchange businesses. They changed currency on behalf of the government, and also handled government bills of exchange.... The main functions of the *hon-ryōgaeya* were the issue of loans or the handling of private bills of exchange, and they

corresponded roughly to the ordinary modern bank. *Zeni-ryōgaeya* were principally concerned with the exchange of *zeni*, but, as a sideline, they sold rice, *sake*, soy sauce, or other provisions.... Over their shop-front they displayed a sign in the form of a *zeni*. Being merely *zeniya*, their capital was small. They were outside the jurisdiction of the *jūnin-ryōgaeya*. The *hon-ryōgaeya* were divided into twenty-two groups, by district ... and were classified, according to the extent of their transactions, as great, middle, and small. The *dai-ryōgaeya* (great exchange-brokers) advanced loans chiefly to *daimyō*, in the same way as the *jūnin-ryōgaeya*, and became agents (*gin-kakeya*) for the various fiefs. The middle and small *ryōgaeya* generally advanced loans to merchants.

It should be noted that a *ryōgaeya* could also increase his profits by speculating in the purchase and sale of currency at favourable opportunities. The hero of the present story increases his fortune by this means. (For fluctuations in the rates of exchange, see App. 1, p. 238.)

[30] *Imabashi no kata-kage:* Imabashi-*chō*, west of Ima bridge, and adjoining the southern side of Kitahama-*chō*. The district contained several *ryōgaeya*.

[31] *Chōgin, komagane,... koban, mame-ita:* for these coins see App. 1, pp. 235–6.

[32] *Daimyō-shū no kakeya:* a *kakeya* or *gin-kakeya* was a financial expert of the merchant class who raised funds on behalf of certain *daimyō* to whom he was accredited. He took charge of the disposal of the products which the *daimyō* sent to Ōsaka from their fiefs for sale, and on occasions lent money to them on the security of these goods. A single merchant could become the agent for several fiefs, and—in addition to a commission for his services, and the interest on his loans—was granted a regular stipend. He was also permitted to carry a sword like a *samurai*, and became, in fact, a form of retainer. Usually the position was a reserve of the *dai-ryōgaeya* (see n. 29, above), and it would be a great achievement for an outsider like the hero of this story—a mere *zeni-ryōgaeya*—to reach such heights.

BOOK I, 4 (pp. 26–29)

[1] *Osoroshiki* is a pivot word, referring backwards to 'punishment' and forwards to 'the nobility'.

[2] *Kōke kinin:* it is possible that *kōke* is here used in the technical sense of certain celebrated military families who performed the duties of liaison between the *Bakufu* and the imperial court (see *Fujii* (1935), p. 446), but I here follow the broader interpretation suggested in *Goi Kōshō*, 'Kōke kinin'.

[3] *Habutae:* a type of smooth, strong silk, widely manufactured in Japan. In the present case it is woven in the Nishijin district of Kyōto, the centre of the weaving industry in Tokugawa times.

[4] *Kuroki mono ni sadamatte no itsudokoro-mon:* at an audience with the *shōgun* it was the custom for every *samurai*, regardless of rank, to wear the

same formal black dress. The five crests (*itsudokoro-mon*) on the cloak (*haori*) were arranged one on each sleeve, one on each lapel, and one on the back.

[5] *Ukiyo komon...gosho no momo-iro-zome, toki-sute no arai-kanoko: komon* designs are produced by a stencil process, and consist of extremely fine white lines, straight or curved, on a coloured base. It is not clear whether *ukiyo komon* is a specific subdivision of this type of design, or whether *ukiyo* has merely the sense of '*à la mode*'.

Gosho-zome, 'imperial designs', 'took their name from the fact that this type of multi-coloured design for *kimono* was popular with palace ladies in the early days of the Tokugawa era.

Kanoko, 'dapple pattern', is produced by dipping cloth into a dye while small portions of its surface are drawn tightly together with thread. When the thread is removed small, star-shaped, undyed patches are revealed. If the cloth is dipped into water immediately, the colour runs into the patches, giving a more subtle contrast.

[6] *Muromachi:* Muromachi street, in Kyōto, runs parallel to Karasuma street, a little to the west. It was a centre for drapers' businesses in Tokugawa times, and also contained the houses of many wealthy citizens.

[7] *Kinukake-yama*, more commonly known as *Kinugasa-yama*, a hill on the north-western outskirts of Kyōto, just west of the Tōji-*in*, Kamikyō-*ku*. Its nickname of *Kinukake* derived from the traditional story that a certain emperor had once ordered its summit to be draped with white cloth that he might enjoy the spectacle of a snow-capped mountain in midsummer.

[8] *Koromo-gae:* the first day of the fourth moon marked the beginning of summer, and on this day it was customary to change from padded to unpadded garments (from *wata-ire* to *awase*).

[9] *Machikane-yama:* a non-existent mountain (lit. 'cannot-wait-mountain'), frequently used as a pivot word in poetry, and often associated with a cuckoo, the symbol of yearning. Saikaku, in *haikai* style, here elaborates this traditional association of words and ideas.

[10] *Ishō hatto:* clothing edicts, setting out lists of materials deemed suitable for the clothes of the various classes, and prescribing penalties for extravagant display, were issued regularly by the *shōgun*'s government. Numerous examples of these throughout the Edo period may be found in *Tokugawa Jidai Kinrei Kō* (1894). About five were issued in the thirteen years before the publication of *Eitai-gura*. It would seem from this passage that they had little effect, and Saikaku's phrase *ima omoi-atarite* (now, on second thoughts) suggests that the wisdom of those who promulgated them was not immediately appreciated in *chōnin* society.

[11] *Tokiwa-bashi:* Tokiwa bridge spanned the outer moat of Edo castle, leading from Ōte gate on to the first section of Hon-*chō*. The name means 'imperishable as a rock', and it is here used partly as an introduction to the drapers in nearby Hon-*chō*, but chiefly for its propitious sound, echoing the

preceding compliments about the peaceful and changeless rule of the Tokugawa family in Edo. Hon-*chō*, in the present Chūō-*ku*, near Nihon bridge, was at that time a centre for drapers' establishments.

[12] *Iki-ushi... Tora-no-gomon... senri:* 'Bull... Tiger... a thousand miles' are all related words, in *haikai* style. A tiger was traditionally said to 'roam a thousand miles at night'. There were thirty-six gates to Edo castle, and the Tiger gate (*Tora-no-gomon*) was one of those on the outer perimeter, in the south.

Iki-ushi no me wo mukujiri (gouging the eyes from a living bull) is a variation on the proverbial expression for smart dealing, *Iki-uma no me wo nuku*, 'Stealing the eyes of a living horse'.

[13] Edo was situated on the plain of Musashi province.

[14] *Kurai-zume ni narite:* for this interpretation of the phrase see *Goi Kōshō*, 'Kurai-zume'.

[15] *Ashi-moto no akai uchi ni hon-momi no iro kaete to:* in Saikaku's text there is a word play which I have been unable to reproduce. The original is, literally, 'thinking, while the ground before them was still clear, to change their scarlet silks'. The word for 'clear' is *akai*, which also means 'red', and therefore forms a neat introduction (to a *haikai*-trained mind) to the following 'scarlet silks'.

[16] *Mukashi koban no Suruga-chō:* the *koban* current in Saikaku's day, the *Keichō koban*, were first minted in the sixth year of the Keichō era (1601). The *koban* previously in circulation had been produced at two Edo mints during the Bunroku era (1592–5), and one of these series, produced at the Suruga mint, bore the characters for *Suruga* marked in black ink on the face. The latter coins were commonly known as *Suruga koban*. (For *koban*, see App. 1, pp. 235–6.) Suruga-*chō* is a district adjoining Hon-*chō*, and was in Saikaku's time a centre for *ryōgaeya*.

[17] *Mitsui Kurōemon to iu otoko: Mitsui Kurōemon* is evidently Mitsui Takahira Hachirōemon (1655–1737), the eldest son of the head of the Mitsui household at that time, Mitsui Takatoshi Hachirōbei (1615–94). The draper's store in Suruga-*chō*, Edo, to which Saikaku here refers, was called *Echigoya Hachirōemon*, and was opened in 1683 (see *Ōyabu*, p. 101).

In modern times the Mitsui family, members of the powerful *zaibatsu* group of business concerns (officially disbanded in 1945), have exercised considerable influence upon politics in Japan. The founder of the family business, a man of *samurai* stock, settled in Matsuzaka in Ise province in the early seventeenth century and established himself as a *sake* brewer and pawnbroker, adopting the trade name of *Echigoya*. Takatoshi, the second in the line, opened a draper's store in Hon-*chō*, Edo, in 1673, as a branch of a similar store in Kyōto, and also commenced activities as a *ryōgaeya* in Edo, Kyōto, and Ōsaka. He rose to undertake business on behalf of the *Bakufu* and the imperial household, and it was largely as a result of these connections that the Mitsui house enjoyed official patronage after the Meiji restoration (see *Nihon Shi Jiten* (1954), pp. 478–9). When the Edo draper's store was moved from Hon-*chō* to Suruga-*chō* in 1683 its management was entrusted to Takahira, Takatoshi's eldest son, and the new business was immediately successful. An account of Takahira's 'cash only' innovation and of the subsequent popularity of the Echigoya is to be found in *Waga Koromo* (1825) (see *Shuzui*, p. 86).

Mitsui Takahira Hachirōemon drew up the first formal household code of the Mitsui family, the 'Sōjiku Testament' (*Sōjiku yuisho*) which remained unaltered until 1900. He may also be regarded as part author of the *Kōken Roku* (compiled 1726–33), in that it is largely his own recollections of the careers of contemporary merchants which comprise that work. (The actual compiler, however, was his son.) By codifying the house law of his family, and by supervising the production of the *Kōken Roku*, he considerably influenced the practical business methods and morality of later Tokugawa *chōnin*, both within the Mitsui household and more generally (see *Chōnin Shisō to Chōnin Kōken Roku* (1940), and *Kōken Roku*, 'Batsu-bun').

[18] *Omote kyū ken ni shijū ken:* the dimensions of this shop are given elsewhere as twelve yards frontage and twenty yards depth. In view of the fact that the depth of Suruga-*chō* itself was the customary forty yards, a shop of eighty yards depth, such as Saikaku describes, could hardly have been built there (see *Edo Chiri* (1952), 'Suruga-chō').

[19] *Hino Gunnai kinu-rui:* silks from Hino, a district in Shinano province, and Gunnai, a district in Kai province.

[20] *Asa-bakama: hakama* are pleated overskirts, worn over the *kimono* on formal occasions.

[21] *Ryūmon:* a thick, strong silk, rather like *habutae*, often used for summer *kimono* (*awase*) and sashes (*obi*).

[22] *Noshime:* a vest worn on formal occasions in conjunction with starched jacket and overskirts (*kataginu* and *hakama*).

[23] *Iroha-tsuki no hiki-dashi:* drawers marked with all the syllables of the Japanese language, in the order of the syllabic poem commencing *Iro ha nihohedo*.

[24] *Chūjō-hime no te-ori...:* the articles in the list are, of course, nonsensical.

Chūjō-hime: a pious lady of the Nara period, daughter of Fujiwara no Toyonari (703–65). At Taima-*dera* in Nara-*ken* there is a picture of Amida in his heaven (*Taima no mandara*) which Chūjō-*hime* is reputed to have woven —with divine assistance—from lotus-root fibres.

Hitomaro: a well-known verse by this celebrated ancient poet, about a boat fading into the mist off Akashi, is included in the *Kokin Shū*. Akashi, in Harima province, was also associated with the crêpe industry.

Amida's bib is difficult to explain. A bib is associated with Jizō rather than Amida.

Asahina: Asahina Saburō Yoshihide was a general of the Kamakura period, and in the popular theatre of Saikaku's time his *kimono* were customarily adorned with 'flying-crane' crests. In Kiyomizu-*dera* in Kyōto there was a celebrated votive picture (*ema*) in which the artist had carelessly painted a 'flying-crane' crest across a gap in Asahina's *hakama* (see *Saikaku Oritome* (posth. 1694), IV, 2).

Daruma-Taishi meditated for nine years facing a blank wall when he visited China.

Rin Wasei was a Chinese hermit of the Sung dynasty. It is not clear why he has a 'bonnet'.

Sanjō Kokaji was a sword-maker of the ninth century, celebrated in the Noh play *Kokaji* (*c.* 1363–1443).

BOOK I, 5 (pp. 29–32)

[1] *Kuni ni nusubito, ie ni nezumi...:* a parody of *Tsurezure-gusa*, 97, 'There are endless numbers of things which, being attached to other things, undermine and destroy them. On bodies there are lice, in houses there are rats, in kingdoms there are bandits, for small men there is wealth....' The concluding episode in this story concerns a widow, and Saikaku opens with a very brief preliminary reference to the subject. However, he promptly digresses into a lengthy discussion of marriage in general.

[2] *Ko-tsuzumi uteba, bakuchi uchi:* the parallelism in the original depends upon the repetition of the verb *utsu*, the same word meaning both 'to beat' a drum, and 'to throw' dice. (For Noh drums see Com. III, 1, n. 4 (3).)

[3] *Yarō-asobi:* hiring young boys, usually members of the theatrical profession, for homosexual purposes. The term *yarō* originally described a type of hair-style (*yarō-atama*) which *kabuki* actors were obliged to adopt by government edict. The front of the head was closely shaved, and it was hoped that the resulting loss of attraction would serve to discourage the fashion of homosexuality in theatrical circles.

[4] *Go sekku:* the five festival days were the seventh day of the first moon, third of the third, fifth of the fifth, seventh of the seventh, and ninth of the ninth (*Wakana no sekku*, *Momo no sekku*, *Ayame no sekku*, *Tanabata-matsuri*, *Kiku no sekku*—though there are variants for most of these names).

[5] *Kataginu:* brief jackets with stiffly starched, elongated shoulder points, worn on formal occasions in conjunction with overskirts (*hakama*).

[6] *Itsuwari no yo-no-naka ni shigure furi-yuku Nara-zaka ya:* Saikaku effects a smooth and rapid transition from the general discussion of human deceit to the particular location of the main story which is to follow, by adroitly intertwining phrases from two well-known poems on the subject of autumn rain. One cites the autumn rain as an example of nature's constancy (*Zoku-Goshūi Shū* (*c.* 1325, Fujiwara Sadaie): *Itsuwari no naki yo narikeri...*). The

other refers to the autumn rain falling on the oaks of Nara (*Kokin Shū*, Fumiya Arisue: *Kaminazuki shigure furi-okeru Nara no ha...*). Such literary allusions are an essential element in Saikaku's style, and would be readily appreciated by contemporaries.

[7] *Matsuya no nanigashi:* amongst the twenty-two principal agencies for the Nara bleaching industry listed in *Nara-zarashi Kokin Rigen Shū* (1748) appears the name *Matsuya Sakubei*. The list is for the Jōkyō period, i.e. contemporary with *Eitai-gura*.

[8] *Akitaya, Kureya:* the above list mentions *Akitaya Kubei*. For *Kureya* see *Goi Kōshō*, 'Nara no Kureya'.

[9] *Fuka no sashimi: fuka* is the *kansai* word for all species of *same* (shark). Raw slices of shark in vinegar were a special dish associated with Nara.

[10] *Tenmei wo shiru toshi ni narite:* according to a classical Chinese theory a man 'understood the laws of heaven' at the age of fifty (*Lun-yü*, *Wei Chêng*).

[11] *Tanomoshi* in this case means no more than 'a lottery'. In the Edo period the word was more usually associated with a form of mutual contract whereby a sum of money contributed to a common pool was lent to subscribers for investment over a limited period. The subscribers drew lots for the temporary use of the money.

BOOK II, 1 (pp. 35–39)

[1] *Fuji-ichi:* an abbreviated form of the name *Fujiya Ichibei*. Fujiya Ichibei, a celebrated merchant of Goike-*machi*, Muromachi street, Kyōto, died about twenty years before the publication of *Eitai-gura*. A brief account of his career, and of the subsequent downfall of his house in the third generation, is given in *Kōken Roku*, II. In the same passage is written: 'His mode of life was severe, and everybody knows the "Tales of Thrift" connected with this Ichibei. Moreover they are contained in such works as *Eitai-gura*.' Ichibei started as an apprentice and clerk in the house of Fujiya Kiyobei of Muromachi street in Kyōto, but as people were impressed by his business ability he was able to borrow sufficient capital to speculate on his own in the purchase of imported goods at Nagasaki. On one occasion, noting that the bidding at Nagasaki was running very high, he decided to use the money he had brought with him to buy a large stock of rice instead, and when he sold this at a favourable time in Ōsaka he reaped a huge profit (see *Kōken Roku*, II). As it was considered rather shameful in Nagasaki traders' circles to refuse to bid, this episode may be taken as yet another example of the independence of judgement which Saikaku illustrates in his story. The thriftiness of Fuji-ichi finds passing comment in *Saikaku Ōyakazu* (1681), 30, and *Kōshoku Ichidai Otoko*, VII, 'Gojissai'.

[2] *Karasumaru:* the formal reading for the characters, but the Kyōto pronunciation is *Karasuma.* A long street running north and south through the centre of Kyōto.

[3] *Zeni-koban no sōba:* for some of the fluctuations in the ratio of gold to copper, see App. 1, p. 238.

[4] *Kigusuriya, gofukuya:* herbs for use in Chinese-style medicinal concoctions, and quantities of high-class silk cloths, were imported through Nagasaki. The prices fetched by the bidding in the Nagasaki market would affect the prices of similar commodities throughout Japan.

[5] *Sanbyaku me irite:* 'padded with 300 *monme* of cotton wool'. The usual amount seems to have been about 120–130 *monme.* The padding would be removed in spring and summer.

[6] *Sode-fukurin:* narrow strips of cloth sewn over the cuffs of *kimono* sleeves to prevent them from fraying. They are mentioned in Tr. I, 4, p. 28. They seem to have been invented in the early seventeenth century, and it is improbable that Fuji-ichi was the inventor.

[7] *Toribe-yama:* an old cremation ground in the vicinity of Kiyomizu-*dera*, Higashiyama-*ku*, Kyōto-*shi. Rokuhara* was a vaguely defined area of open land between Toribe-*yama* and Hōkō-*ji*.

[8] *Mochi:* sticky rice-cakes or dumplings formed, then as now, an essential part of the New Year celebrations. Their preparation involves the heavy and prolonged pounding in a mortar of a special variety of glutinous rice. For all business concerns the end of the year was a particularly hectic period, as it was necessary to collect debts and balance the books before the final reckoning day on the last day of the twelfth moon.

[9] *Daibutsu no mae:* a famous rice-cake shop in front of the *Daibutsu* (Great Buddha) of the Hōkō-*ji*, present Higashiyama-*ku*, Kyōto-*shi.* The name of the shop was *Daibutsu Mochi* (*Kinmō Zui*, VI, 'Mochi-shi').

[10] *Tō-ji:* a temple of the Shingon sect, at Kujō-Ōmiya, present Shimogyō-*ku*, Kyōto-*shi.* Its five-storied pagoda is one of the landmarks of the city. In the seventeenth century it stood in open country.

[11] *Yanagi, hiiragi, yuzuri-ha, momo no ki, hana-shōbu, juzu-dama:* the first five were useful as decorations at New Year and other festivals. The last was used for making toy beads.

[12] *Genji, Ise Monogatari: Genji Monogatari* (1001–20) was the work of the court lady Murasaki Shikibu. The author of *Ise Monogatari* (*c.* 905–50) is not known.

[13] *Tada no kana-yama:* in Settsu province, present Tada-*mura*, Kawabe-*gun*, Hyōgo-*ken.* The mines were first opened under Toyotomi Hideyoshi, and continued to produce silver and copper well into the Tokugawa era.

[14] *Iroha-uta:* poems of forty-eight verses, each one of which commenced with a different syllable in the order of the famed *Iro ha nihohedo*... poem. (A complete instructional poem of this nature is quoted in *Ōyabu*, pp. 148–9;

a mid-nineteenth century one, *Shōnin kokoroe iroha-uta*, appears in *Tsūzoku Keizai Bunko* (1916–17), II, pp. 169–73.)

[15] *Ehi mo sezu-kyō no kashiko-musume...:* another example of Saikaku's literary dexterity. The phrase *ehi mo sezu-kyō* is the end of the *iroha* alphabet, and is used here to signify 'finally'. But *kyō* is also used in the sense of 'Kyōto, the capital'. Moreover, the succeeding phrase *kashiko-musume* has not only the meaning of 'clever girl', but also contains—in the word *kashiko*, which is appended at the end of ladies' letters, meaning 'yours in all humility' —further suggestions of 'conclusion' and an additional sense of 'a proper attitude of womanly humility'.

[16] *Sekku no hina-asobi...Bon ni odorazu:* the Doll festival (*Hina-matsuri*) was on the third of the third moon. The Buddhist festival of *Bon* (an abbreviation of *Urabon*) was on the fifteenth of the seventh moon, and special dances were held in the streets at that time. The custom is still widely observed.

[17] *Zōni:* a traditional New Year dish. In Kyōto, a thick soup of bean-paste (*miso*), vegetables, and rice-dumplings (*mochi*). The grinding sound would be the mixing of the bean-paste.

[18] *Nanakusa:* on the festival day of the seventh of the first moon rice-gruel is served flavoured with the 'Seven herbs of spring'. According to *Hinami Kiji*, 'Shōgatsu nanuka', substitutes were often used for the traditional Seven Herbs, which were difficult to obtain. The concoction was reputed to ward off sickness.

[19] *Kake-dai:* a pair of salted bream on a wooden spit, decorated with ferns, was hung over the kitchen range from New Year's Day until the first of the sixth moon, as an offering to the god Kōjin. Sampō Kōjin was originally a guardian of the Three Treasures of Buddhism, but he was popularly worshipped as a god who warded off starvation and fire. He was therefore installed as a god of the kitchen range.

[20] *Daifuku-chō no uwagami:* for the custom in merchant houses of binding a new account book for each year see Com. II, 4, n. 14.

BOOK II, 2 (pp. 39–43)

[1] *Ōmi no mizu-umi ni shizumete mo isshō hairu tsubo wa sono tōri nari:* a variation of the proverb, *Isshō hairu fukuro wa umi-kawa de mo isshō*, 'A one-*shō* bag holds one *shō* even in the sea or in a river'. The sentence forms a general introduction to the examples of 'pint-size' men which follow, and the reference to Lake Biwa sets the scene of the whole story.

[2] *Ōtsu:* a town at the southern extremity of Lake Biwa. In early Tokugawa times it was a fairly important inland port, since goods were often transported from the northern coastal regions via Tsuruga, Lake Biwa, and Ōtsu, to Ōsaka. It was also the fifty-third station on the Tōkai-*dō*, the last before Kyōto. (See also Com, IV, 4, n. 2.)

[3] *Ja no sushi, oni no tsuno-zaiku:* imaginary goods. See Tr. v, 1, p. 106: 'the underpants of a thunder-clap, or knick-knacks carved from demons' horns'.

[4] *Toiya-machi:* a district in Ōtsu where many wealthy men had their homes (see *Goi Kōshō*, 'Ōtsu no Toiya-machi'). There is a proverb: *Toiya chōja ni nitari, tamago ni nitari*, 'A broker is like a millionaire and like an egg' (i.e. impressive but easily broken), and the association here of Toiya-*machi* and millionaires plays upon this.

[5] *Shibaya-machi:* the brothel quarter of Ōtsu was known as *Shibaya-machi*, but was actually situated in Baba-*machi* (see *Shikidō Ōkagami*, XII, 4).

[6] *Yonomiya no emuma:* votive pictures at Yonomiya-*daimyōjin*, present Yonomiya-*machi*, Ōtsu-*shi*. It had been the custom in ancient times to present real horses or small model horses to *Shintō* shrines, but these were gradually superseded by pictures of horses. By Tokugawa times these pictures, though still called 'Painted Horses' (*ema* or *emuma*), depicted a great variety of subjects. They were presented to *Shintō* shrines and Buddhist temples alike.

[7] *Taka-gannon:* probably the high platform of the Kannon-*dō* (Shōhō-*ji*, Mii-*dera*), which overlooks the town of Ōtsu and commands an extensive view of Lake Biwa. The 'Eight Views of Ōmi province' are all grouped about these southern shores. Kannon-*dō* was commonly called *Taka-gannon* in Saikaku's day. The name *Taka-gannon* is now used only in connection with Gonshō-*ji*, another temple attached to Mii-*dera*, but since Gonshō-*ji* has no platform, the many modern commentators who assume that Genkō climbed to Gonshō-*ji* appear to be in error (see *Goi Kōshō*, 'Taka-gannon').

[8] *Go-kai:* 'a *go* club'.

[9] *Mumaya-machi:* there is no place of this name in modern Ōtsu, and no reference to it can be found in topographical records.

[10] *Ototo:* there seems to be a slight discrepancy here. Nibei is an 'only son' (*hitori no ko*), but he apparently has a younger brother.

[11] *Matsumoto no machi:* there is now a district called *Matsumoto-machi* in Ōtsu, at the eastern end of Kyōmachi street. In Saikaku's time it was a locality distinct from Ōtsu (see *Ōyabu*, p. 170).

[12] *Nuke-mairi no mono:* in the Edo period young people often made a secret pilgrimage to Ise, without the consent of parents or employers, and the practice, though illegal, was popularly condoned and even admired. There is an example of such a runaway pilgrimage in Saikaku's *Kōshoku Gonin Onna* (1686), II.

[13] *Ike-no-kawa no hariya:* 'Ike-no-kawa needles' were a noted product of Ōtsu, though Ike-no-kawa itself was a district near Fushimi, in Yamashiro province. The needle makers were reputed to have moved thence to Ōtsu in ancient times.

[14] *Gin nisen-mai:* the value of 'one *chōgin*' on such occasions was interpreted as forty-three *monme* in silver, and if the *chōgin* itself was short of that, the value was made up with lesser coins. Thus two thousand *chōgin* would be eighty-six *kanme*. This in itself was a large sum, but it was in the interest of the marriage broker, who took a commission of ten per cent of the dowry (see Tr. I, 5, p. 29), to make it even larger. (For *chōgin* see App. I, p. 236.)

[15] *Hangi de oshitaru yō na kono ie no waka-ebisu:* the phrase 'as if stamped by a wood-block' serves the secondary purpose of introducing the *waka-ebisu*—a small wood-block print of Ebisu, a god of luck. These prints were sold, together with similar pictures of Bishamon-*ten* (another god of luck) on the last night of the year. People pasted them on the gateway or hung them on the god-shelf, and prayed to them for wealth. (See *Hinami Kiji*, 'Ōmisoka; Ganjitsu'.)

BOOK II, 3 (pp. 43–49)

[1] *Ichi ni tawara...:* the trade names of the principal characters in this story, father and son, being respectively *Daikokuya* and *Kasa-Daikokuya*, Saikaku opens with a variation on the traditional verses of the Daikoku dance. Daikoku is one of the gods of luck, customarily depicted sitting smiling on two bales of rice, a mallet in one hand, and a sack over his shoulders. At New Year companies of begging street performers, wearing Daikoku masks and carrying mallets, moved from house to house serenading the inmates with the words and dance of the *Daikoku-mai*. There was a traditional pattern for the words, but variations were extemporised to fit individual cases. The present example is adapted to the case of Daikokuya of Kyōto. The *Daikoku-mai* flourished chiefly in the Kyōto-Ōsaka area in the first half of the Tokugawa period. It later enjoyed a fresh lease of life as a New Year custom in the Yoshiwara brothel quarter of Edo.

The pattern of the verses may be observed from one example quoted in *Sabishiki-za no Nagusame* (1676): 'He has come, he has come! Leading the gods of luck, Lord Daikoku has come! Observe his clever ways: one, he squats on bales of rice; two, he smiles contentedly; three, he's a brewer of *saké*; four, his business flourishes; five, he never grows old; six, he's free from sickness and disaster; seven, he never suffers loss; eight, his mansion grows bigger and bigger; nine, he builds rows of storehouses; ten, he lives in perfect peace—and ten is the very end. See the Daikoku dance, the Daikoku dance!' In the original each line contains a simple alliterative jingle with the numeral. (See *Shuzui*, p. 149.)

[2] *Gojō no hashi:* Gojō bridge, one of the bridges across the river Kamo in Kyōto, was changed from wood to stone in 1645. (It was destroyed in the great Kyōto earthquake of 1662, and reconstructed in wood once more.) For the custom of making Daikoku images from bridge planks, see *Chōnin-bukuro* (1719), I, 11.

[3] *Shinjin ni toku ari:* 'In faith there is profit', a well-known proverb, reflecting the current utilitarian attitude towards religion.

[4] *Daikokuya Shinbei: Daikokuya* was, and is, a common trade name, and it is difficult to identify *Daikokuya Shinbei.* The careers of Daikokuya Tokuzaemon, and Daikokuya Kuzaemon, both of Kyōto, and roughly contemporary with the present character, are outlined in *Kōken Roku.* Saikaku sometimes alters the names of contemporary merchants a little, possibly to avoid the accusation of libel.

[5] *Shichi-gatsu mae:* the audit day before the *Bon* festival (seventh of the seventh moon). Books were set in order before each of the five principal festival days of the year, though the most important and thorough examination was reserved for the last day of the twelfth moon.

[6] *Inari-no-miya:* Inari-*jinsha*, Fushimi, south of Kyōto. 'Fox-tail' is here introduced as an associated word with the Inari-*jinsha* (Fox shrine).

[7] *Kyūri wo kitte:* in a formal disinheritance it was necessary to observe a strict procedure: (*a*) inform the neighbourhood group (*gonin-gumi*); (*b*) obtain the signature (*han*) of a representative of one's relations; (*c*) submit the documents to the headman of the ward (*nanushi*) and obtain his signature; (*d*) submit the application, in the presence of the neighbourhood group, at the office of the *shōgun*'s representative (*machi-bugyō*). The disinherited person's name was removed from the census rolls, and he was evicted from his ward, becoming a homeless person. (See *Ōyabu*, pp. 180–1.)

[8] *Fuji-no-mori:* South Fushimi, in the present Fukakusa-*mura*, Fushimi-*ku*, Kyōto-*shi*. On his journey to Edo, Shinroku sets off along the Fushimi-*kaidō*, joining the Tōkai-*dō* a few miles east of Kyōto. He follows the Tōkai-*dō* through Ōtsu to Kusatsu, and there branches north along the Nakasen-*dō* for about ten miles. In the region of Sekigahara he turns south again along a road through Mino and Owari provinces, and rejoins the Tōkai-*dō* near Nagoya. He then proceeds along the Tōkai-*dō* to Shinagawa and Edo. The length of the Tōkai-*dō* itself, from Sanjō bridge in Kyōto to Nihon bridge in Edo, was roughly 305 miles, and Shinroku's route would be about 350 miles.

For convenience, the places along Shinroku's route which are referred to in the text are listed below:

Ōkamedani. Present Fukakusa Ōkamedani-*machi*, Fushimi-*ku*, Kyōto-*shi*. At that time a lonely stretch of mountain road.

Kanshuji. Present Yamashiro Kanshuji-*machi*, Higashiyama-*ku*, Kyōto-*shi*.

Ono. Present Yamashiro Ono-*machi*, Higashiyama-*ku*, Kyōto-*shi*.

Otowa-*yama*. A hill about 1500 feet high, three miles north-east of Ono.

Oiwake. The junction of the Fushimi-*kaidō* and the Tōkai-*dō*.

Ōsaka-*no-seki*. On the western outskirts of Ōtsu, at the foot of Ōsaka-*yama*. It was one of the three barriers erected in ancient times to guard the approaches to the imperial capital of Kyōto, and was set on the boundary between Yamashiro and Ōmi provinces.

Hat-*chō*. A district in Ōtsu, where the road from Kyōto enters the town.

Seta bridge. A long bridge crossing the Seta river, at the southern extremity of lake Biwa. It was, in fact, comprised of two separate bridges, meeting on an island in midstream.

Kusatsu. Present Kusatsu-*machi*, ten miles east of Ōtsu. The junction of the Tōkai-*dō* and the Nakasen-*dō*.

Kagami-*yama*. A famous landmark, reputed to look like the face of a mirror when viewed from the west. Gamō-*gun*, Shiga-*ken*.

Sakura-*yama*. A small hill near Mikami-*yama*, Yasu-*gun*, Shiga-*ken*.

Oiso. The present Oiso-*mura*, Gamō-*gun*, Shiga-*ken*. In a nearby wood stood Oiso-*jinsha*.

Fuwa-*no-sekido*. One of the three barriers guarding the approaches to Kyōto (see Ōsaka-*no-seki*, above). Sekigahara-*mura*, Fuwa-*gun*, Gifu-*ken*.

Mino road. A road through Mino and Owari provinces, linking the Nakasen-*dō* and the Tōkai-*dō*.

Shinagawa. The first stage on the Tōkai-*dō*, five miles from Nihon bridge, Edo, in the present Shinagawa-*ku*, Tōkyō-*to*.

[9] *Kuroyaki:* concoctions made from the ash of plants, birds, beasts, fishes etc. were popular at this time as medicines or ointments, for internal or external use. A special technique was required to make the ash black instead of white or grey.

[10] *Yuku mo kaeru mo no seki koete shiru mo shiranu mo ni tsuki-tsuke-akinai:* Saikaku weaves into his text a quotation from a celebrated poem by Semimaru: *Koreya kono iku mo kaeru mo wakarete wa, shiru mo shiranu mo Ōsaka-no-seki.* The poem is included in *Ogura Hyakunin Isshu* (*c.* 1200). (For Osaka-*no-seki* see n. 7, above.)

[11] *Kusatsu no hito yado . . . Mino-ji Owari wo sugite:* the passage describing the forty miles of Shinroku's journey from Seta bridge through Kusatsu to the barrier at Fuwa contains no verbs of motion. The physical movement is suggested incidentally by the place-names, but Saikaku's object is to describe psychological motion—Shinroku's gradual change of mood from melancholy homesickness, to blossoming hope, to a realisation of the strength of youth, and optimism for the future. The place-names mentioned are selected for their appropriate allusive qualities, and are interwoven into the syntax supra-grammatically, sometimes in the manner of interjections, sometimes as pivot words. It is a miniature *tour de force* in the traditional style of Japanese poetic prose, and I have not attempted a literal translation in the text. The following more literal rendering may serve to give an idea of the style, though even this one is more grammatical than the original:

'In lodgings at Kusatsu he passed New Year, comparing *Uba*[1] cakes with

[1] *Uba* cakes were a speciality of Kusatsu.

old Kagami[1] hill. Soon in his heart the early-blossoming Sakura[2] hill, the colour and fragrance of full-flowering youth! Working and in his prime, no god of poverty could overtake him. The god was a weak-kneed Oiso[3] wood even, its groves hung with New Year festoons, was spring-like, and even the autumn-sad moon was cheerful. At Fuwa the barrier was up[4] and down, day and night, he followed the Mino road....'

The literary techniques employed in this passage are not uncommon in *Eitai-gura*, but they are seldom used in such concentration. In a way Saikaku is here merely following in the well-established tradition of the travel scenes (*michi-yuki*) of the old military romances, such as *Heike Monogatari* (*c.* 1219) and *Taihei Ki* (1370), in which the description of the journey is related to the inner emotions of the protagonist. Similar passages, with a wealth of play upon place-names, were common in the *jōruri* drama of Saikaku's day.

[12] *Rokujū nichi-me ni Shinagawa ni tsukinu:* Shinroku's journey seems to have been leisurely. Supposing that he travelled 350 miles in all, his daily average is not much above five miles.

[13] *Tōkai-ji:* a temple of the Rinsai sect, in present North Shinagawa, Shinagawa-*ku*, Tōkyō-*to*. With the construction of embankments along the shore, the location of the temple is now about 700 yards from the sea, and even in Saikaku's day it was nearly as far. This seems to conflict with the text, but it is possible that the gate mentioned here is one several hundred yards north of the temple precincts, specially constructed for the convenience of the *Shōgun* Iemitsu. This gate was within sound of the sea (see *Goi Kōshō*, 'Tōkai-ji Monzen').

[14] *Hinin:* beneath the four classes of *samurai*, farmers, artisans, and merchants, which formed the socially recognised components of the state, there were communities of outcasts such as the *eta* and the *hinin.* These generally lived in hutments on the outskirts of towns and cities. The *eta* had existed as a separate class with their own way of life, ostracised from contact with the main body of Japanese society, for centuries; but the emergence of *hinin* as a recognisably separate community seems to have been brought

[1] *Kagami* cakes are the large *mochi* used as decorations at New Year. The logical sense indicates 'the old *kagami* cakes of home', but Saikaku substitutes the locality 'old Kagami hill'.

[2] Sakura-*yama*, 'cherry hill', is introduced for its connotations of blossoming hope and the spring of life.

[3] 'Oiso', the place-name, is used as a pivot word. The first two syllables, *oi*, mean 'old man', and thus round off the remarks about the god of poverty—'a weak-kneed old man'. The complete word is then used to indicate the journey past Oiso wood, and a contrast is suggested between the old-sounding name and the spring-like appearance of the trees bedecked with New Year festoons.

[4] *Ake-kure* means literally 'morn and night', but it is used here as a pivot word. *Ake* also means 'open', and refers back to the place-name 'Fuwa barrier gates' (the gates of this former barrier survived only in name). *Ake-kure* as a complete phrase refers to the subsequent journey along the Mino road.

about largely by the urban developments of the Tokugawa period and the tightening of class distinctions under the Tokugawa shogunate. There were two categories of *hinin*. The first lived in hutment communities under the supervision of *hinin-gashira* (*hinin* chiefs), who kept a register of their names and were responsible to the shogunate for their behaviour. These were the genuine *hinin*, irrevocably committed to their degraded status, and they lived by casual employment in various low-grade occupations, often connected with the punishment of criminals. The second category was of *hinin* beggars. These had no fixed lodgings and were registered on no form of census roll. They were known in the Kyōto area as *kojiki* (food-beggars), and in Edo as *yado-nashi* (homeless-people).

The characters in this story would appear to belong to the second category. A straw cape had come to be regarded as the distinctive dress of their class. (See *Ōyabu*, p. 189; see also *Nihon Shi Jiten*, p. 51, *Eta*, *hinin*; and *Kinsei Fūzoku Shi*, I, 6.)

[15] *Suji naki kotsujiki:* a reference to the proverb, *Kojiki ni suji nashi*, 'If you become a beggar, your lineage no longer counts'. Saikaku's meaning, however, is different in this context.

[16] *Yamato no Tatsuta:* present Tatsuta-*machi*, Nara-*ken*.

[17] *Gofuku-chō:* a commercial district east of the present Gofuku bridge, Chūō-*ku*, Tōkyō-*to*. At that time the merchants in the locality were principally *sake* retailers, fishmongers, and greengrocers, but the first were the most numerous.

[18] *Kōnoike*, *Itami*, *Ikeda*, *Nanto:* the first three are localities in Hyōgo-*ken*, near Ōsaka, and each produced a much-esteemed brew of *sake* which was exported by sea to all parts of Japan. Nara (*Nanto*, 'the southern capital'), in Yamato province, had produced high-class *sake* since very early times.

[19] *Momiji no nishiki:* the word for 'scarlet' (*momiji*) here signifies the colour of maple leaves. This is a reference to the celebrated maple leaves of Tatsuta.

[20] *Sakai:* the port adjoining Ōsaka, to the south. For about one century, from late Muromachi times until the beginning of the Tokugawa period, it had been the most prosperous port in Japan. Though it was now eclipsed by its neighbour Ōsaka, it remained the home of many celebrated merchant families, and boasted considerable prowess in the arts (see Tr. IV, 5, p. 101).

[21] *Te wa Hirano Chūan ni...:* the names in the following passage are those of contemporary scholars, aesthetes, actors, etc., mostly from Kyōto and Ōsaka. Exact identification is difficult in some cases.

Hirano Chūan: (dates uncertain), an artist and calligraphy master of Kyōto.

Kanamori Sōwa: (1584–1656), founder of the Kanamori style of tea ceremony, and *daimyō* of Takayama castle in Hida province. Later, on being dismissed his fief, he settled in Kyōto.

Gensei: (1623–68), a scholar-priest of the Nichiren sect. His Chinese verse is not very highly rated. Originally a *samurai*, at the age of twenty-five he entered the Zuikō-*ji* in Fukakusa, Fushimi, Kyōto.

Nishiyama Sōin: (1605–82), founder of the *Danrin* school of *haikai* of which Saikaku himself was a disciple. Originally a *samurai* of Higo province, he became a professional *haikai* master in Ōsaka.

Kobatake: (dates uncertain), possibly Kobotake Ryōtatsu of Kyōto, a master of the Noh drums.

Shōda Yoemon: (dates uncertain), a Kyōto master of the Noh drums.

Itō Genkichi: (1627–1705), more usually known as Itō Jinsai. A celebrated scholar of the Chinese classics, teaching at Horikawa in Kyōto.

Asukai: the Asukai family, members of the ancient court nobility, were the foremost exponents and teachers of the art of kickball (*kemari*). (See Tr. 1, 3, n. 22.)

Gensai: (dates uncertain), possibly Terai Gensai, a member of one of the *go* families officially accredited to the shogunate.

Yatsuhashi: (1614–85), Yatsuhashi Kengyō, founder of the Yatsuhashi style of *koto* playing, also a master of the *samisen*, taught in Kyōto.

Sōsan: (dates uncertain), Nakamura Sōsan, a blind master of the *hitoyogiri* flute, a form of *shakuhachi*.

Uji Kadayū: (1635–1711), a famous *jōruri* singer of Kyōto.

Yamatoya no Jinbei: (d. 1704), a popular *kabuki* actor of Kyōto and Ōsaka, renowned for his skill in dancing.

Takahashi: a *tayū* of the Shimabara brothel quarter, in the Ōzakaya establishment.

Suzuki Heihachi: (1664–86), a celebrated young *kabuki* actor of Kyōto. Died in early youth.

[22] *Tōri-chō:* a district on either side of the main street running north and south from Nihon bridge, Edo, between Kyō bridge and Sujikai bridge (see *Edo Chiri*, 'Tōri-chō jū-ni ken').

[23] *Kuruma Zenshichi ga nakama:* Kuruma Zenshichi of Asakusa was the hereditary chief of the *hinin* community north of Nihon bridge in Edo. The *hinin* south of Nihon bridge were under the supervision of Shōemon of Shinagawa. The first Kuruma Zenshichi was a *samurai* who attempted to assassinate the *Shōgun* Hidetada to avenge his elder brother. He was reprieved from the death sentence, but assigned to the duties of supervising the *hinin* of Edo, and his descendants throughout the Tokugawa period inherited the position and the name. Kuruma Zenshichi's romantic history made him far more well-known than his counterpart in Shinagawa, and his name appears frequently in popular Tokugawa literature. (See *Kinsei Fūzoku Shi*, 1, 6, 'Edo hinin no chō'; also n. 14, above.)

[24] *Reigan-jima:* a district in the present Chūō-*ku*, Tōkyō, near Eitai bridge. It forms an island, bounded by canals on three sides, and the Sumida river on the other.

[25] *Tenma-chō:* the present Dai-temma-*chō*, Chūō-*ku*, a district then noted for its cotton and silk merchants.

[26] *Shitaya no Tenjin:* the Ushi-tenjin-*jinsha* (Ox *Tenjin*), at the foot of Ueno-*yama* (present Ueno park, Daitō-*ku*). The shrine was moved in 1697, and became known as *Ushi-gojō-tenjin.*

[27] *Kōte no saiwai to:* proverb, *Kōte no saiwai, utte no shiawase,* 'Happiness for the buyer, luck for the seller'. The saying was particularly associated with the street vendors hawking prints of Ebisu at New Year.

[28] *Yatsu yashiki-kata ni...:* the Daikoku dance (see n. 1, above) is this time adapted to fit Shinroku. (For '*daimyō*'s agent' see Com. I, 3, n. 30.) 'Nuggets of gold in stock' is a rather free translation of *koban no kai-oki*—speculations in the purchase of gold currency for resale at a profit, should the market prices prove favourable.

BOOK II, 4 (pp. 49–52)

[1] *Rakuten:* a poet of the T'ang dynasty. The reference here is to the story of the Noh play *Hakurakuten* (*c.* 1400):

> Po Chü-i receives an imperial order to cross the seas to Japan to estimate the sagacity of its inhabitants. On arriving at Hirado he meets the god Sumiyoshi, disguised as an old fisherman. The god demonstrates his skill in both Chinese and Japanese verse, and Po Chü-i, amazed that even an old fisherman should possess such accomplishments, turns back to China in consternation.

[2] *Yokote-bushi* possibly means 'The Hand-clap Tune'. There are occasional references in contemporary works to a *Yokote-bushi* connected with this coastal area, but neither words nor tune are known to have survived.

[3] *Taiji:* a fishing village near the southern extremity of the Kii peninsula, present Higashi Muro-*gun*, Wakayama-*ken*. An important centre for the whaling industry during the Tokugawa period.

[4] *Kujira-ebisu no miya:* Ebisu is a god of luck. There is no shrine of Whale-Ebisu (*Kujira-ebisu*) in present-day Taiji.

[5] *Tengu Gennai:* no record of a person by the name of *Tengu Gennai* survives. According to the inscription on his 'shop curtain', as illustrated in the list of contents to Book II, p. 33, his trade name was *Aburaya.* It remains in doubt whether Tengu Gennai is a real person, or an invention of Saikaku's. There is also the possibility that he is a composite personage, devised to cover the activities of several people connected with the whaling industry in Taiji.

Tengu, in any case, appears to be a nickname. *Tengu* are supernatural creatures of the Japanese country-side, whose characteristic physical feature is an enormously long nose. They are noted for their agility, and the name would not not unnaturally be applied to a skilled harpoonist. (Cf. the proverbial expression *Tengu no ya-tori*, 'catching arrows like a Tengu'.)

[6] *Kono hama ni kujira-tsuki no ha-zashi:* the time with which Saikaku deals is the pioneer period of whaling at Taiji, and the descriptions contained in such nineteenth-century compilations as *Kii Zoku Fudoki* (1839) and *Gei Shikō* (*c.* 1840) relate to a later stage of development, when the use of whale-nets, for instance (the invention of which Saikaku attributes to Tengu Gennai), was an accepted part of whaling technique. Nevertheless many features were doubtless common to both periods.

According to *Kii Zoku Fudoki*, LXXVIII, whaling was first introduced to Taiji in 1606 by Wada Chūbei Yorimoto. As regards whale-nets, it is stated that these were invented by a descendant, Sōemon Yoriharu, in 1677. According to *Gei Shikō* (quoted in *Shuzui*, p. 178), whale-nets were first used at Taiji by a member of another well-known local family, Ōike Kakuemon, in the Enpō era (1673–81). The original inventor is said to have been Fukazawa Gidayū of Ōmura in Hizen province, Kyūshū; and Kakuemon, who was then the headman of Taiji-mura, made a special journey to Ōmura in order to learn the technique of their use. Both sources agree roughly on the date, and on the fact that thereafter whale-nets came into use in all the whaling centres of Japan, and to this extent they corroborate Saikaku's account. It is not impossible that these later sources record rival traditions of the leading families of Taiji, and that—if Tengu Gennai really existed—Saikaku's contemporary account may be nearer the truth of the matter. More probably, however, Gennai is a fictional person.

In later days a whaling fleet consisted of two types of boat: (i) *Tsuki-bune* (pursuit boats, carrying the harpoon thrower), and (ii) *Ami-bune* (net boats). These were organised into groups called *kumi*. When Tengu Gennai captured his monstrous whale, only pursuit boats were in use, and it appears from the illustration in the text, that each was manned by a crew of four. This is corroborated by the section on 'Whalers' in *Kinmō Zui*, III, where it is also stated that one *kumi* was made up of twelve such boats, and that in each *kumi* there was a leader, called the *ha-zashi*, who was also the harpoon thrower. In Saikaku's text, too, Gennai is described as a *ha-zashi*. His function would appear to have been not only the aiming of the harpoon, but also the direction of the manœuvres of the twelve boats in his group in the chase which preceded and followed the lodging of the harpoon in the whale's flesh. If a hit was registered with the first, second, or third throw, this was regarded as a great feat, and flags showing the crest of the *ha-zashi* were immediately raised in each boat. The operations often took place several miles out at sea, and whale-spotters with telescopes, posted at vantage points along the coast, signalled the whereabouts of whales to the fleets by sounding horns, waving flags, or lighting bonfires. When the whale was exhausted by the chase one of the fishermen, leaping on to its back, cut a hole in the flesh, through which a hawser was passed and attached to a formation of boats on either side. The whale was then rowed slowly back to the shore to the accompaniment of a triumphal chorus. The animated scene of this final procession—each boat gaily painted with dragons, lions, and flowers, its flag fluttering in the breeze, and the whole flotilla keeping strict martial formation—is described in *Kii Zoku Fudoki* as 'the grandest spectacle of our sea-faring nation'.

When the whale was grounded in shallow water, unable to move, the slaughter and dismemberment commenced. Large slices of flesh were hewn from the body and dragged to the shore by ropes attached to a winch. The sea, sand, and rocks for a large area round about became red with blood.

[7] *Kaza-guruma:* a large eight-petalled garden flower, resembling a windmill. A formalised version of it was a common crest. (For the significance of hoisting flags on whaling boats see n. 6, above.)

[8] *Sanjū-san hiro ni shaku roku sun semi: semi,* more correctly *sebi,* is Balaena Glacialis Bonnaterre, a large black-backed whale of high-quality flesh and blubber.

Saikaku's whale is approximately sixty-six yards long, but the popular notion of 'thirty-three fathom whales' is dismissed as ludicrous in *Sansai Zue,* LI. The same authority gives the length of the very largest *semi* whales as approximately thirty-three yards, the normal being twenty-five yards. It is possible that Saikaku intends his figure to be taken humorously. 'Thirty-three' was a popular round number, frequently found in Buddhist phrases (e.g. *sanjū-san shin, sanjū-san so, sanjū-san sho,* etc.), and the addition of the precise 'two feet six inches' savours of the ridiculous.

[9] *Nanasato no nigiwai:* a play on the proverbial expression, *Kujira ippiki toreba nanasato no nigiwai,* 'One whale means prosperity for seven villages'.

[10] *Takao:* a beauty-spot celebrated for its autumn tints, at the foot of Atago-*yama,* Ukyō-*ku,* Kyōto-*shi.*

[11] *Kujira-ami:* for the invention of whale-nets see n. 6, above.

[12] *Kusunoki-bungen:* the phrase 'sound as a camphor tree' reappears in Tr. IV, 3, p. 91. In the fifteenth century *Tako Shinkei Kakun,* a compilation of precepts to be observed by young *samurai* of the Tako household, the following passage occurs: 'A plum tree spreads its branches three yards in one year. A camphor tree grows one inch in one year. However, amongst camphor trees, which grow taller inch by inch, there are very large trees. Amongst plums, which increase by yards, there are no large trees. So it is with men.' See also Nabaya's speech in *Chōja Kyō* (App. 2, p. 240) for a close parallel.

[13] *Shin areba toku ari:* a common proverb (see also Tr. II, 3, p. 43).

[14] *Nishi-no-miya:* Nishi-no-miya-*jinsha,* in the present Nishi-no-miya-*shi,* Hyōgo-*ken.* Its most popular festival was the *Tōka-Ebisu*—the festival of Ebisu, the merchants' god of luck, on the tenth of the first moon.

[15] *Chō-toji no sake ni:* drinking and feasting to honour the occasion of the binding of the new account-book for the coming year was a regular feature of the New Year celebrations in most merchant households. There seems to have been no universally accepted day for this observance. In the present passage it is obviously the ninth, the day before *Tōka-Ebisu. Hinami Kiji* describes the custom under both 'Fourth day' and 'Eleventh day' of the first moon. *Seken Munesanyō*, v, 2 gives the tenth day.

[16] *Chōchin hodo na hi ga furau:* the metaphor of 'falling sparks as large as lanterns' seems to have been commonly used at this time to describe a condition of extreme poverty. The reason is not clear. A similar phrase is found in the opening of *Kōshoku Ichidai Otoko*, III, 4.

[17] *Hirota no hama:* the beach in front of Nishi-no-miya-*jinsha*. The shrine is now set far back from the coast. Gennai's boat must have travelled very rapidly to cover the distance of one hundred and fifty miles from Taiji to Hirota in only twelve hours. An average speed of ten to eleven knots would be required.

[18] *O-kagura:* a sacred dance performed in *Shintō* shrines at festivals by young virgins (*miko*). The dance usually takes place on a raised platform to the accompaniment of flute (*fue*), big drum (*dadaiko*), and a variety of other percussion. Worshippers pay a small sum for a performance on their behalf, and the *miko* jingles a wand of bells (*suzu*) over their heads at the conclusion.

[19] *Eboshi no nugeru mo kamawazu:* Ebisu is always depicted wearing a tall black hat of lacquered paper or stiff cloth (*eboshi*). For a reference to the inseparable nature of Ebisu and his hat, see also Tr. v, 5, p. 126.

[20] *Uojima-toki:* 'the Uojima Season' was the period in early spring when fish, especially sea-bream, gathered in their greatest numbers off the southern coasts of the *kansai* area. The term is still in use in the *kansai*, and may have originally derived from the small island of Uojima just south of Tomo (a once important harbour in the Seto inland sea) where particularly large quantities of sea-bream are caught at this season.

The advice comes appropriately from the Ebisu of Nishi-no-miya, since the waters off this shrine were likewise noted sea-bream fisheries. Possibly Saikaku's account is an adaptation of a Nishi-no-miya-*jinsha* tradition.

BOOK II, 5 (pp. 53–56)

[1] *Yuki-zao:* notched bamboo poles placed by the roadside to indicate to travellers the depth of the snow. They were a special feature of the north country.

[2] *Nehan:* celebrated on the fifteenth day of the second moon.

[3] *Sakata:* one of the largest ports on the Japan sea. It is situated at the mouth of the Mogami river in Akumi-*gun*, Yamagata-*ken* (Dewa province in Saikaku's time).

[4] *Abumiya to ieru ō-doiya:* from a passage in the topographical records of Akumi-*gun* (quoted in *Shuzui*, pp. 189–90) it appears that generation after generation of Abumiya's flourished as rice brokers in Sakata from early Tokugawa days until the Meiji restoration. The earliest in the line was holding the post of *toshi-yori* (senior representative of his district) of Sakata town in 1638. Sakata was an important centre for the export of rice from the north to Ōsaka, and Saikaku mentions the numbers and prosperity of its brokers in *Kōshoku Ichidai Otoko*, III, 6.

[5] *Toiya:* (sometimes *tonya* or *toimaru*) were a combination of lodging house and broker's agency. The original form of the word appears to have been *tsutoi-ya*, literally 'a gathering place' (see *Kiyū Shōran* (1830), 'Toiya'). There are numerous references to varieties of *toiya* throughout *Eitai-gura* (see Index).

[6] *Hasuwa-onna* (lotus-leaf girls) are mentioned in a passage on Ōsaka brokers in *Kōshoku Ichidai Onna*, V, 4. Saikaku describes their gaudy attire, mincing step, and brazen manners, and suggests that the name is possibly derived from *hasu-no-ha-mono*, meaning an article of little worth. Their duties, which they interpreted broadly, were to attend to the refreshment and sleeping arrangements of the clients. (For common uses of lotus-leaves see Tr. VI, 1, p. 129.)

[7] *Shaku to ieru onna:* in Saikaku's estimation (*Kōshoku Ichidai Otoko*, III, 6) the *shaku* or 'service girls' of the Sakata brokers were in the same moral category as their counterparts, the *hasuwa-onna*, in Ōsaka. He thinks the name may have the sense of 'playing up to the customer'.

[8] *Jū-nin yoreba tokuni no kyaku:* a common proverb, with *kyaku* (clients) substituted for the more general *mono* (people).

[9] *Banshū Aboshi:* Aboshi in Harima province, a small port on the Seto inland sea, a few miles south-west of Himeji. Also mentioned in Tr. V, 5, p. 124.

[10] *Tsuzura wo agete:* commentators universally assume that the reading *agete* in the text is a mistake for *akete* (opening the trunk). I take *agete* to have the sense of 'lifting' off the horse and into the house.

[11] *Hiki-hada tori-sute:* I have adopted Mayama Seika's interpretation (in *Goi Kōshō*, 'Hiki-hada'). Most commentators follow Satō, and assume that *hiki-hada* is a form of traveller's footwear (see *Satō* (1930), p. 128).

[12] *Nihyaku nichi wo matazu ni kaze:* most commentators assume that this is a reference to the storms which were usually expected to arrive after the 210th day from the beginning of spring. If they broke earlier it meant damage to crops—and a rise in prices. This interpretation is denied in *Goi Kōshō*, 'Nihyaku nichi wo matazu ni', and it is suggested that the clerk is worrying about the weather two hundred days hence, when the rice is shipped from Sakata in the early summer.

[13] *Beni-no-ha*, 'safflower', was used for the preparation of a red dye.

Aoso, 'green hemp', was used for green dyes. Both plants were noted products of the Sakata area.

[14] *Kara-sake no nuke-me no nai otoko:* the pun in the original, 'their eyes firmly screwed in like those of a dried salmon', is slightly different from that in the translation. Dried salmon were a speciality of Sakata, and their eyeballs were not removed for the process. *Nuke-me no nai otoko* is a common expression in Saikaku for a wily character.

[15] *Toiya chōja ni nite:* a reference to the proverb, *Toiya chōja ni nite, tamago ni nitari*, 'A broker is like a millionaire, and like an egg'. A broker's establishment, crammed with other people's merchandise, gave an outward appearance of immense prosperity, but its true condition was as fragile as an egg. (See also Com. II, 2, n. 4.)

[16] *Itsutsu mae:* 'the time before five', which means the period stretching for roughly two hours after dawn.

In the old system of reckoning the hours of the day, the time from midnight to midnight was divided into twelve periods, each of which was designated by a Japanese numeral (and also by a sign of the zodiac). The numerals descended from 9 to 4 for the period from midnight to midday, and from 9 to 4 again for the period from midday to midnight. Division 6 (*mutsu*) always began at sunrise or at sunset, whatever the time of year, so that it was only at the autumn and spring equinoxes that the six divisions of the day were the same length as those of the night. The Japanese time divisions and their corresponding modern times, at these equinoxes, were as follows:

a.m.	p.m.
9 (12 midnight–2 a.m.)	9 (12 noon–2 p.m.)
8 (2 a.m.–4 a.m.)	8 (2 p.m.–4 p.m.)
7 (4 a.m.–6 a.m.)	7 (4 p.m.–6 p.m.)
6 (6 a.m.–8 a.m.)	6 (6 p.m.–8 p.m.)
5 (8 a.m.–10 a.m.)	5 (8 p.m.–10 p.m.)
4 (10 a.m.–12 noon)	4 (10 p.m.–12 midnight)

BOOK III, 1 (pp. 59–63)

[1] *Shihyaku-shi byō:* according to the traditional medical theory each of the four elements of which the human body was compounded—earth, air, fire and water—could give rise to a hundred and one diseases, making a total of four hundred and four.

[2] *Hin-byō no kurushimi:* the metaphor of the 'poverty disease' appears frequently in pre-Saikaku works. The opening passage of this story bears a close resemblance to a short passage in *Kashō Ki*, II (*Tokugawa Bungei Ruijū* (1914–15), II, p. 59).

[3] *Shijū no in made:* the life of a human male was thought to be governed by the *shō-in* (lesser negative) principle, which operated in octennial periods. See *Chōnin-bukuro*, IV, opening passage: 'A male follows the *shō-in* series: from

eight onwards the broad lines of character and constitution are firmly settled; at sixteen semen is passed; thereafter, in each octennium, there are developments in character and constitution, and by the end of the fifth octennium, at the age of forty, a man is at the zenith of his vigour. But from forty-one onwards his vitality slowly declines, so that forty is regarded as the beginning of old age.' (A woman develops according to the *shō-yō* series—the 'lesser positive'—which operates in periods of seven years. She passes her prime at the age of thirty-five.)

The division of life into two parts—unremitting toil until forty, increasing relaxation thereafter—which underlay much *chōnin* thought, was presumably influenced by this theory.

I prefer to take *shijū no in* in the general sense of 'the shady side of forty' rather than in the particular sense, favoured by some commentators, of 'the *shō-in* ending at forty' (i.e. the fifth octennium).

[4] *Doku-tachi ari:* below I give notes of explanation on certain of the items in this 'black list'. Broadly speaking it is a prohibition of wasting money, or of wasting time which should be devoted to making money. Money is wasted through ostentation, unnecessary luxuries, or risky speculations, and time is wasted in religious observances, and idle or un-townsmanlike pastimes.

(2) *Zensei musume ni koto uta-garuta:* like a knowledge of the tea ceremony which was (and, in many cases, still is) a prerequisite for the would-be bride, tolerable skill in *koto* playing or in the New Year game of poem-cards (*uta-garuta*) was calculated to improve a young lady's chances on the marriage market. It was Saikaku's contention, however (see Tr. I, 5, p. 30, and II, I, p. 38), that, for townsmen's daughters at least, a practical education was preferable. In the present context the custom is probably cited as an example of needless expense through ostentation—parallel with the practice of buying a palanquin for the wife instead of making her walk.

(3) *Yorozu no uchi-bayashi:* the art of playing the various drums used in Noh performances (*taiko*; *ō-tsuzumi*; *ko-tsuzumi*). The lessons would be a source of expense for the father. The son too—like the beggar from Sakai in Tr. II, 3, p. 47—might live to regret the time wasted on such pursuits.

(4) *Mari*, *yōkyū*, *kōgai*, *renpai:* for 'kickball, miniature archery, perfume appreciation', see Com. I, 3, n. 22. 'Poetry gatherings' is a free translation of *renpai* (i.e. *renga* and *haikai*). *Renga* was the traditional linked verse, jointly composed by groups of poets, and *haikai* was the seventeenth-century or 'modern' form of this, very fashionable in *chōnin* society. Like every other artistic accomplishment it was dismissed by Saikaku (himself a lifelong exponent of 'modern' *renga*) as a waste of time for business men.

(5) *Zashiki-bushin*, *cha-no-yu-zuki:* a study of the severe canon of tea aesthetics, based on *Zen* asceticism, was likely to breed dissatisfaction with supposed vulgarities in the interior decoration. This might lead to the em-

ployment of a tea master to supervise necessary alterations. See *Nippon Shin Eitai-gura* (1713), VI, 3.

(7) *Yo-ariki...go, sugoroku:* here *yo-ariki*, 'evenings out'—probably means going out with bad friends to bad places. In *Shimai Sōshitsu no Yuikun Jūshichi-ka-jō* (1610), Article 14 (App. 3, p. 249), the identical phrase occurs with the more innocent sense of 'social calls after dark', but the after-dark entertainments which awaited townsmen in Ōsaka in 1688 were considerably more varied and expensive than those worrying Shimai in Hakata in 1610.

Go and *sugoroku* ('backgammon' is, of course, only an approximate translation for the latter) are not gambling games, but they consume precious time. See the proverb: *Go-uchi, oya no shinime ni awanu*, 'a *go* player is late for his father's funeral'. The modern *sugoroku* is a children's pastime, similar to Snakes and Ladders, but at that time it was a game akin to Japanese chess (*shōgi*), much simpler and shorter than *go*, but still time-consuming.

(8) *Chōnin no iai, hyōhō:* 'sword-drawing' and 'duelling'. The former was the art of drawing a sword quickly, in any position. The latter was the general art of sword fighting. Both arts, essential to *samurai*, were becoming increasingly popular as pastimes for young townsmen, who attended classes held by *rōnin* teachers. The government, no less than Saikaku (though for different reasons), looked with disfavour upon this usurpation of *samurai* techniques by the townsman class, and edicts were frequently issued threatening punishment to teachers and pupils alike (see *Ōyabu*, pp. 236–7). Saikaku's objection is mainly that the time could be better spent in making money.

(9) *Mono-mōde, goshō-gokoro:* for this train of thought in the townsman's philosophy, not necessarily anti-religious, see *Shimai Sōshitsu no Yuikun Jūshichi-ka-jō*, Article 2 (App. 3, p. 245). Religion was regarded as a good thing for old men, but if taken seriously by the young it claimed too much valuable time, and might encourage a negative attitude towards money matters. The present story aptly illustrates the townsman's conception of the proper time for religion in practical life.

(11) *Shinden no soshō-goto, kana-yama no nakama-iri:* 'lawsuits over reclaimed land' were usually expensive; see *Jikata Hanrei Roku* (1871), II:

> In reclaimed land...strictly speaking there are the distinctions of new rice-fields, new dry-fields, and ground for building....Having selected some land at the mouth of a river, low-lying marshland, high moorland, or reedy wastes which can be made into cultivable land, an inhabitant of a neighbouring or distant village may submit an application for permission to develop it. If, after careful investigation into possible disadvantages to older fields or neighbouring villages, no objection is apparent, he is granted the right of development.

A considerable amount of bribery seems to have been necessary during the course of the investigations (see *Ōyabu*, pp. 237–8).

'New mining projects' were a notoriously risky form of speculation, as it was impossible to test the truth of the land agent's claims until you had actually bought and dug the land concerned. Land agents dealing with mining had a very bad reputation.

(12) *Ke-zake:* Saikaku does not advocate teetotalism—the drinking of *sake* was an essential part of social etiquette for business men—but merely moderation.

(14) *Kin no hanashi-menuki:* 'fancy sword-accessories', more precisely the small ornamental heads of the metal pins used to keep the blade of a sword firmly fixed to the hilt.

[5] *Hanmyō:* for the contemporary use of dried 'blister-flies' in medicine, made illegal by government edict, see *Goi Kōshō*, 'Hanmyō'.

[6] *Nihon-bashi:* a bridge across Nihonbashi river (present Chūō-*ku*, Tōkyō-*to*) upon which all the principal routes into Edo converged, and from which all distances from Edo were measured.

[7] *Kyō no Gion no e, Ōsaka no Tenma-matsuri:* festivals of Yasaka-*jinsha*, Kyōto, and Tenman-*gū*, Ōsaka, respectively. Both were observed in the sixth moon, and were (and are) the most popular summer festivals of the *kansai* area.

[8] *Tōri-chō no daidō:* strictly speaking, the highway running north through the centre of Edo, from Kanasugi bridge (in the present Minato-*ku*) across Nihon bridge, terminating at Sujikai bridge (present Mansei bridge, Chiyoda-*ku*). Whenever Saikaku uses the name, however, he seems to mean only the section from Kyō bridge (present Chūō-*ku*) to Sujikai bridge. For a discussion of this, and of the width of the road in Saikaku's time, see *Edo Chiri*, 'Tōri-*chō* jū-ni ken'.

[9] *Suruga-chō no tsuji:* the first cross-roads along Tōri-*chō* north of Nihon bridge. For Sujikai bridge see n. 8, above.

[10] *Suda-chō Setomono-chō no aomonoya: Suda-chō* is still a district for greengrocers. For the varied trades of Setomono-*chō* see *Edo Chiri*, 'Setomono-*chō*'. Suda-*chō* is the present Chiyoda-*ku*; Setomono-*chō* is in Chūō-*ku*. It seems strange to us that greengrocers should deal in chopsticks, but that was apparently the practice. I have translated as 'grocers' to avoid the awkwardness for English readers.

[11] *Hashiya Jinbei*, 'Chopstick Jinbei', is possibly the earlier trade name of *Kamakuraya Jinbei*, a leading Edo timber merchant who flourished about the middle of the seventeenth century. Kamakuraya Jinbei purchased tracts of forest land adjoining the Tenryū river, in Shinano province (in the present Shimo Ina-*gun*, Nagano-*ken*), and acted as supervisor of the group of timber merchants accredited to the shogunate. His house was in Zaimoku-*chō*, Edo. Numerous other identifications have been attempted by commentators, but the *Kamakuraya Jinbei* theory, first advanced by Mayama Seika (*Edo Chiri*, 'Kamakura-gashi no Hashiya Jinbei') is now widely accepted.

[12] *Zaimoku-chō:* (lit. Timber block) present Hon-zaimoku-*chō*, Hatchō-*bori*, Chūō-*ku*, Tōkyō-*to*. There were many timber merchants living in this district in the Edo period.

[13] *Kawamura, Kashiwagi, Fushimiya:* Kawamura Zuiken (1618–1700), a celebrated merchant who laid the foundations of his fortune at the time of the Great Fire of Edo in 1657 by transporting timber from the Kiso river area for the rebuilding of the city. He later performed many public services, including the construction of dykes and the opening up of an all-sea route from the northern areas of Japan to Ōsaka and Edo.

Kashiwagi Taemon, a prosperous broker of Kayaba-*chō*, Edo, dealing in cypress timber from Kiso.

Fushimiya Shirōbei, timber merchant of Sakuma-*chō*, Edo. For the collapse of the Fushimiya fortunes in the second generation, see *Kōken Roku* 'Fushimiya Shirōbei'.

[14] *Kokoro no umi-hiroku, shindai matomo no kaze, ho-bashira no kai-oki ni:* the remark on Jinbei's transactions in ship-mast timber is preceded by nautical metaphors, in *haikai* style. Timber for ships' masts was extremely expensive, and very few merchants would be bold enough, or rich enough, to buy in a large stock of it on speculation (see *Goi Kōshō*, 'Ho-bashira no kai-oki').

[15] *Tsukiji no Monzeki:* the Nishi Hongan-*ji* of Tsukiji, Edo (present Tsukiji, Chūō-*ku*), was a branch temple of the Nishi Hongan-*ji* of Kyōto, Shinshū sect. Kobiki-*chō*, a short distance north of the Nishi Hongan-*ji*, contained in Saikaku's time two large *kabuki* theatres and a variety of smaller houses of entertainment.

[16] *Tsubo no kuchi wo kiri:* in the tenth moon, it was customary to hold social gatherings at which the first tea-jars of the new season's crop were opened. These meetings were called *kuchi-kiri*, 'cutting the covers' (see *Hinami Kiji*, 'Jū-gatsu'; also Tr. VI, 4, p. 141).

[17] *Nageire-bana:* one of the many styles of Japanese flower arrangement.

[18] *Hashiba no keburi:* Hashiba was a cremation ground on the northern outskirts of Edo, near Asakusa. The phrase 'smoke above Hashiba' was a commonplace of contemporary literature. For a discussion of the exact location of Hashiba see *Edo Chiri*, 'Hashiba no keburi'.

[19] *Hachijū-hachi no toki:* for the significance of the eighty-eighth birthday and for the customs connected therewith, see Com. I, 2, n. 6.

BOOK III, 2 (pp. 63–66)

[1] *Matsugo no mizu ima zo, shō-ji no umi, hamaguri-gai nite...:* there is evidence to suggest that the custom existed in Saikaku's day of offering water in a clam-shell to a dying man (see *Ōyabu*, p. 258), though the origin of the

custom is not clear. Here Saikaku introduces the 'clam-shell' for two further reasons: first, to extend his *haikai*-inspired chain of related words—water, seas of death, clam-shell; secondly, to indicate the hopelessness of the situation by indirect reference to the proverbial expression for an impossibility: *Hamaguri-gai nite umi wo kaeru*, 'To empty the ocean with a clam-shell'.

[2] *Enma:* the king presiding over the Buddhist underworld. Note the sustained metaphor of accountancy in this dying speech, realism being sacrificed for *haikai* dexterity. The concluding phrase *tane wo wasure-na*, 'never forget the seeds of livelihood', has a double significance which appears later. *Tane* not only has its basic meaning of 'seeds', but also signifies 'the basis', 'the start', 'the cause', or 'business capital'.

[3] *Shijū-ku nichi:* in Buddhist theory seven times seven days elapsed between a man's death and his entry into the next world.

[4] *Jigoku no muma:* 'hell-horses' were human-headed four-legged beasts which inhabited the Buddhist underworld. There is no evidence that they were available for hire by travellers along the road to hell—this is a Saikaku conceit based on the facilities of the Tōkai-*dō* and similar highways.

[5] *Bungo no Funai:* the present Ōita-*shi*, on Beppu bay in north-east Kyūshū. The old province of Bungo corresponded roughly with the present Ōita-*ken*.

[6] *Yorozuya Sanya tote nadakashi:* the problem of the identity of Yorozuya Sanya has possibly an important bearing upon the interpretation of the present story, and it is necessary to discuss it at some length. A closer examination of the contemporary documents is long overdue, but I give here the two principal theories so far advanced by commentators, followed by some remarks of my own.

Theory I. Yorozuya Sanya is the Yorozuya Sanyasuke Ujisada whose history is recorded in *Ōita-shi Shi* (1937) (History of Ōita city). The outline of the facts as therein stated is as follows: Yorozuya Sanyasuke was a merchant of Funai in Bungo province, reputed to be the richest merchant of Kyūshū in his day. The family business was founded by Morita Denzaemon, a *samurai* of Buzen province who moved to Funai at the invitation of the castle-lord, Takenaka Shigetaka (1553–89), built himself a very large house (occupying the whole of the districts now known as *Yorozuya-chō* and *Ebisu-chō*) and adopted the trade name of *Yorozuya.* Sanyasuke was the third in the line. Sanyasuke's principal activities were mining and the sale of goods imported through Nagasaki. For the former he installed a smelting furnace, casting moulds, and a refinery in his own house, where he extracted pure gold and silver from mineral-ore transported overland from his mines on the borders of Hyūga and Bungo provinces. The expression *Sanyā-dokkoi!*, still used in Ōita by people lifting heavy weights, is supposed to have originated with the labourers employed in this work. Little is known of Sanyasuke's activities in the Nagasaki trade, but he appears to have been well known amongst the

Portuguese (*sic*), Spanish (*sic*) and Chinese merchants, and to have used an alternative trade name, *Ebisuya* (*ebisu* = foreigner), in these transactions. On the third of the tenth moon in Shōtoku 4 (1714) Sanyasuke, together with his four sons, was publicly executed in Funai. The reasons for his downfall are not clear, though there are various traditional explanations. Possibly he was charged with illegal overseas trade, or with Christian beliefs or sympathies. Possibly he became involved in local political intrigue, or his downfall was engineered by the *Bakufu* as a means of their appropriating his enormous wealth. (See *Shuzui*, pp. 225–6; *Fujii*, App. p. 772; *TSZ*. p. 78.)

Theory II. The name *Yorozuya Sanya* was invented by Saikaku. It is a combination of Man no Chōja (*Man*, 萬, is also read *Yorozu*) and Sanro, the two principal personages in a well-known legend (recounted, for example, in the *kōwaka-mai Eboshi-ori* (15th century?). Man no Chōja, more commonly called *Mano no Chōja*, was a millionaire of ancient times, living in Bungo province in Kyūshū, and *Sanro* was the name assumed by the young Emperor Yōmei when he visited Mano, in the disguise of a shepherd boy, to woo his beautiful daughter. In all essentials Saikaku's plot and the legend are completely different, but there are a succession of similarities in detail, such as the occurrence in both of episodes connected with fans and with the sowing of seeds, which—when coupled with the above-mentioned coincidence of names, and of locality (Bungo and Kyōto), and with one unequivocal reference by Saikaku to Mano no Chōja—all combine to give the impression that Saikaku was writing with the older story in mind. (See *Ōyabu*, pp. 260, 268–70, 273.) (Note: *Ōyabu* makes no mention of the possible existence of a historical Yorozuya Sanya, though *Fujii* had been published two years earlier.)

Translator's Comment. The obvious objection to Theory I (so obvious, it seems, that not one commentator bothers to draw our attention to it) is that Saikaku writing before 1688 could hardly have described events, such as Yorozuya's downfall and death, which were not to take place until 1714. If it were not for the date, however, one would be inclined to accept the identification at once, for the similarities of name and location are striking, and even the substitution of the *kamigata* shipping trade for the China trade, of bath-boilers for smelting-furnaces, of barrels of water transported from Kyōto for loads of ore transported from the Hyūga borders, only serves to strengthen the impression that there is a close connection between Saikaku's story and the career of the personage described in *Ōita-shi Shi*.

One way out of the dilemma is to assume that the date given in *Ōita-shi Shi* is incorrect; and there are various passages in the excerpt quoted by commentators (e.g. *Shuzui*, pp. 225–6) which suggest to the translator that this may be so. For instance: (i) the date is taken from a tombstone in Ōita city which the compiler admits to be strangely large and magnificent for that of an executed criminal; (ii) if the first generation Yorozuya moved to

Funai some time in the decades before 1589 (see Theory I, above), it is unlikely that the third generation would be still alive in 1714; (iii) the compiler of *Ōita-shi Shi* seems to imply that Sanyasuke was well known by Spanish and Portuguese traders. If this is the truth, and not a slip for 'Dutch traders', then Sanyasuke must have been active in the period before 1640, before all European traders, with the exception of the Dutch, were excluded from the country. A more likely date for the downfall and death of Sanyasuke would be the middle or the third quarter of the seventeenth century, and if a re-examination of the *Ōita-shi Shi* sources were to confirm this, we could feel reasonably certain that the model for Saikaku's Yorozuya Sanya is Yorozuya Sanyasuke Ujisada of Funai.

If we accept Theory I, with reservations about the date, it would seem that Theory II is unnecessary. But the correspondences with the story of Mano no Chōja are curious, and very possibly intentional. Saikaku could be writing with both the contemporary history and the legend in mind, though none of his principal episodes are necessarily 'borrowed' from either, but are merely the author's fictions, calculated to do no more than 'remind' his readers of this or that episode in the Yorozuya scandal or the story of Mano no Chōja. If the downfall of Yorozuya was very recent (one is tempted to think that the date Shōtoku 4 might be a mistake for Jōkyō 4, i.e. 1687) Saikaku could safely assume that his *chōnin* public would be well informed on the true facts of the Yorozuya history—and its memories of a legendary millionaire of the same locality would have been sharpened at the same time. To give a few examples of the relationship between Saikaku's story and these possible sources:

(1) Mano's enforced tribute to the emperor of 10,000 *koku* of poppy seeds becomes the episode wherein Yorozuya, inspired by his father's dying reference to 'seeds', makes a small fortune by planting rape-seeds in waste ground.

(2) The Emperor Yōmei's visit to Bungo to find a wife becomes Yorozuya's visit to Kyōto to see the 'walking blossoms'. Yōmei returns to Kyōto with Mano's daughter and Yorozuya returns to Bungo with 'twelve comely concubines'.

(3) The historical Yorozuya's profitable experiment of installing a smelting furnace in his house, transporting gold and silver ore from his mines on the Hyūga borders, becomes the Saikaku Yorozuya's ruinous fancy for building bathrooms all over the house, and for shipping water from Kyōto for his private boilers.

(4) The Emperor Yōmei's distribution of fans throughout every province, adorned with a painting of his ideal woman, becomes Yorozuya's 'War of the Fans', waged by his comely serving-maids.

It should also be noted that the bath water episode, and the description of Yorozuya's garden and pond, have possibly a third source of inspiration—

the story of Minamoto no Tōru, the ninth-century courtier to whom Saikaku refers towards the close (see n. 17, below).

The creation of reminiscences in the reader's mind—the momentary multiplication of a line of thought into a number of parallel lines, all but one of which dissipate into nothingness—is a common device of *haikai* verse. Saikaku makes frequent use of it in his prose, but it is normally confined to individual phrases recalling brief classical poems or popular proverbs. In the present case, it seems, a whole story is constructed on this principle. Although the story without the undertones is entertaining enough in itself, its literary effect is heightened for a reader who appreciates the reminiscent qualities. With the example of the relationship of *Kōshoku Ichidai Otoko* to *Genji Monogarati* in mind, of *Saikaku Oritome* to Asai Ryōi's *Kannin Ki* (1661) or even, perhaps of *Eitai-gura* itself to *Chōja Kyō*, we are tempted to wonder how many of the careers of other merchants featured in *Eitai-gura* are *haikai* perversions of this nature (cf. the case of Higurashi, Com. v, 4, n. 8).

[7] *Shinden:* for 'reclaimed land' cf. Com. III, 1, n. 4 (11). An exemption of land-tax for the initial ten years was not unusual in Saikaku's time (see *Goi Kōshō*, 'Jū nen wa munengu').

[8] *Yama mo kawa mo chiranu hana no ariku wo mite:* a more literal translation might be: 'He gazed at blossoms walking—blossoms such as were never scattered on hillsides or running rivers.'

[9] *San no ji...shi hō ni san kai:* the numeral 'three', i.e. the first character of the name *Sanya*. There is a little mathematical by-play here, with the first 'three' followed quickly by 'four' walls and 'three-storied' storehouses.

[10] *Ō-shoin:* 'great library'. A *shoin* was originally a room for study and contemplation in the houses of *Zen* devotees, but imitation *shoin* were incorporated in the houses of wealthy *chōnin* as reception rooms for visitors.

[11] *Seiko:* a Chinese lake, west of Hangchow, Chekiang province.

[12] *Sesshū:* (1420–1506), a famous artist of the Muromachi period.

[13] *Gensō no hana-ikusa:* to amuse the Empress the T'ang Emperor Hsüan Tsung (713–756) is reputed to have arranged 'flower battles' between his ladies-in-waiting. There was a well-known scene in a contemporary *kyōgen* play, performed in Kyōto in the Kanbun era (1661–72), depicting one such contest at Hsüan Tsung's court. (See *Shuzui*, p. 232.)

[14] *Magetaru kata no ōgi:* most editions emend *magetaru* to the simpler *maketaru*. I have attempted to translate the sense of the former.

[15] *Mukashi no Mano no Chōja:* for the legend of *Mano no Chōja*, and its possible relationship to the present story, see n. 6, above.

[16] *Otowa no taki:* a waterfall near Kiyomizu-*dera*, Higashi-*yama*, Kyōto-*shi*. The name *Kiyomizu* (clear-water) is possibly derived from the purity of the Otowa stream—or *vice versa*.

[17] *Shiogama no daijin* (the salt-kiln minister) was the nickname given to Minamoto no Tōru (822–95), also known as *Kawara Sadaijin*, a son of the

Emperor Saga. In the grounds of his magnificent mansion in the sixth ward of Kyōto he had pagodas, springs, landscape rocks, and a pond in which he kept exotic varieties of fish and shellfish. He was particularly renowned for the practice—here referred to—of having sea-water transported to Kyōto monthly from Ōsaka bay, in order that he might boil it in salt-kilns in the section of his garden which reproduced scenes of the salt industry in the northern provinces. (See the Noh play *Tōru* (*c.* 1363–1443); *Dai Jinmei Jiten* (1953), 'Minamoto no Tōru'; see also n. 6, above.) The Chika coast is the coast near the present Shiogama-*machi*, Miyaji-*ken* (near Sendai-*shi*).

[18] *Keburi taenishi koto:* smoke ceasing to rise from the kitchen at meal-times is a frequent metaphor in Saikaku for the ruin of a household (see e.g. Tr. II, 1, p. 36; III, 3, p. 68).

[19] *Gosen kanme...:* the exact meaning of this sentence is not clear to me. 'Five thousand *kanme*' (five times the amount needed to become a *chōja*) is a fantastic amount to be spent in one year, if that is the sense. The expression *hongin*, which I have translated as 'firm's capital', is also ambiguous.

[20] *Sen jō no tsutsumi mo...:* cf. *Han Fei-tzu* (3rd century B.C.), XIX: 'A dyke one thousand *chang* long is destroyed by the hole of a burrowing cricket or ant.'

BOOK III, 3 (pp. 67–70)

[1] *Fushimi:* a small town between the Uji river and Kyōto, on the main road from Kyōto to Ōsaka—a section of the present Fushimi-*ku*, the southernmost suburb of Kyōto-*shi*.

[2] *Fushimi no go-jōdai no toki:* the castle at Fushimi was erected upon the orders of Toyotomi Hideyoshi, and he himself resided there for a period of about three years, until his death in 1598. The castle was dismantled, by order of the *Bakufu*, in 1620. Saikaku's phrase *go-jōdai no toki*, which I have translated as 'when Hideyoshi was lord of the castle', is perhaps purposely ambiguous, since the gate of the lord of Echizen, subsequently described, cannot be strictly dated to this period. At no other time, however, were there mansions of 'assembled *daimyō*' at the foot of Fushimi castle.

[3] *O-nari-mon* were gateways used only on ceremonial occasions, particularly for the reception of distinguished visitors.

[4] *Uta-nenbutsu no higurashi to iu wa: Higurashi* (day-dreamer) *no uta-nenbutsu* was the name given to a particular type of street performer of the early Tokugawa period. The nature of their performance is not clear, though the name *uta-nenbutsu* suggests that, originally at least, it involved the singing of Buddhist invocations. They normally carried gongs and dressed themselves as priests. There appears to be some connection between *uta-nenbutsu* and the form of popular dramatic art known as *sekkyō-jōruri*, which was performed in Kyōto in Saikaku's day. The chief exponents of this latter art also took the name of *Higurashi*, e.g. Higurashi Kodayū, Higurashi Hachidayū.

[5] *Echizen no dono:* at the time of Hideyoshi's residence in Fushimi there was no 'lord of Echizen', since the Echizen fief was split up amongst several small lords. Tokugawa Hideyasu (1574–1607), who became *Echizen no dono* in 1601, was previously the impoverished lord of the fifteen thousand *koku* fief of Yūki, and, although resident in Fushimi at the time in question, he was in no position to build magnificent gateways. However, after his appointment to the rich fief of Echizen he remained in Fushimi until 1607, and old maps show the position of his mansion. (See *Goi Kōshō*, 'Fushimi no go-jōdai no toki'; 'Fushimi no Higurashi-mon'.)

Saikaku's figure for the revenue of the Echizen fief is not accurate—in Hideyasu's time it was 670,000 *koku* (the figure of 750,000 *koku* sometimes appears in documents, but this is apparently an error). After the disgrace of Hideyasu's son in 1623, the fief was bestowed, in a reduced form, on another family, and its revenue was then 525,000 *koku.* At the time of the composition of *Eitai-gura* this last figure held good, though the fief was no longer in the possession of any single lord, and Saikaku's '550,000 *koku*' may represent the popular approximation. (See *Goi Kōshō*, 'Gojūgoman koku sannen no mononari'.)

[6] *Morokoshi no ni jū-shi kō:* twenty-four examples of perfect filial behaviour, drawn from Chinese legend and history. An illustrated booklet, *Nijū-shi Kō* (Jap. trans. 1596–1614), relating these various stories, was printed in Keichō times (1596–1614), and frequently reprinted in subsequent years. For the stories in detail see *Nijū-shi Kō* (*Nihon Bungaku Taikei*, XIX), but I give below the episodes to which Saikaku later refers.

(*a*) Ta Shun: 'Ta Shun's father was an obstinate old man; his mother was noisy and untruthful; and his younger brothers were very boastful and ill-behaved. Nevertheless Ta Shun gladly performed the duties of a filial son. Once he was ploughing his field at a place called Lishan when great elephants, admiring his filial piety, came and broke up the earth for him, and birds flew down to pull up the weeds.... When the ruler heard of Ta Shun's filial piety he gave him his daughter's hand in marriage, and bequeathed the kingdom to him.' (*Nijū-shi Kō*, 'Dai Shun'.)

(*b*) Lao Lai-tzu: 'Lao Lai-tzu cherished both his parents. When he was seventy years old he used to dress himself in gay clothes, making himself up to look like a young boy, and dance about and play the fool. Sometimes, when he was serving things to his parents, he would purposely trip, roll over on the floor, and burst into childish tears. The reason behind this behaviour was his anxiety lest his parents, should they ever see him as he really was—an ugly old man of seventy—might feel sad for him, or be reminded of their own extreme age.' (*Nijū-shi Kō*, 'Rōrai-shi'.)

(*c*) Kuo Chü: 'Kuo Chü's family was poor, and he supported his old mother. His wife had borne him a son, who was now three years old. Kuo Chü noticed that his old mother, who was much attached to her grandson, used to share her portion of food with him, so one day he said to his wife: "We are poor, and it seems to me that the food we give my mother is not sufficient as it is, and if she gives a part of even this to our son she will not live. This is all because we have a son. Since I am married to you I can have another son, but I cannot have another mother—so it is my intention to bury the child and preserve my mother." His wife was very sad, but obeyed her husband's orders, and together they took their son out to bury him. Restraining his tears Kuo Chü started to dig, but before long he uncovered a golden cooking pot. On it he noted the surprising inscription: "Heaven gives this to the filial son Kuo Chü. Officials must not appropriate it. People must not steal it." Overjoyed at this discovery, Kuo Chü did not bury his boy, but returned home, and thereafter fulfilled his filial duties towards his mother with even greater care.' (*Nijū-shi Kō*, 'Kaku-kyo'.)

[7] *O-nari-mon:* there were a large number of gates known as *Higurashi-mon* in Edo, Kyōto, and elsewhere, and many of them are preserved to this day. It is possible, in view of the lord of Echizen's close connection with Fushimi, that the *Higurashi-mon* in Fushimi Gokō-no-miya-*jinsha*, which is decorated with scenes of the Twenty-four Filial Sons and Daughters, is the one here described, and that it was bequeathed to the shrine by Hideyasu. (See *Goi Kōshō*, 'Fushimi no Higurashi-mon'—though the note is unfinished.) There is a theory that Saikaku's description of this gate is merely an adaptation of Asai Ryōi's description of a similar gate in Edo castle (*Tōkai-dō Meisho Ki*), but this seems an unnecessary supposition.

[8] *Toba* is the district now divided into Kami-Toba and Shimo-Toba, Fushimi-*ku*, Kyōto-*shi*. The town of Yodo is the present Yodo-*machi*, Kuse-*gun*, Kyōto-*fu*. At Yodo the Uji river, flowing south, changes its name to the Yodo river.

[9] *Tsuzura, fuki-ya:* in Saikaku's travel book *Hitome Tamaboko* (1689), III is the entry: 'Fushimi-*no-mura*...wicker baskets, blow-pipes, tea-whisks (*cha-sen*), bamboo brooms, and special peach-wood products.' *Tsuzura* (wicker baskets) were used mainly for travellers' luggage. *Fuki-ya* were toy blow-pipes of bamboo with paper darts.

[10] *Torifuki no yane:* roofing of strips of wood or bark, held down by bamboo poles and occasional heavy stones. The 'hoops' (*wa*) were to hold the stones in place.

[11] *Kikuya no Zenzō:* Saikaku's account here is possibly based upon fact, but—as is frequently the case when he is dealing with a comparatively insignificant person—no corroboratory evidence is available.

[12] *Okite no tōri:* regulations governing the acceptance of pawns were posted from time to time by the *Bakufu*. Public Notice of 1648: 'The acceptance of pawns: if there is no guarantor, pawns must not be accepted. Even if a guarantor is cited, a careful examination must be made before even articles of small value are accepted. A person who accepts stolen articles in pawn is liable to confiscation of his property or to imprisonment.' (See *Ōyabu*, p. 286.)

[13] *Kōsen Oshō no tera:* Fukkoku-*ji*, Fukakusa Ōkamedani-*machi*, Fushimi-*ku* (on the north-eastern edge of the site of Fushimi castle), founded in 1678 by the Chinese priest Kōsen.

[14] *Gokō no miya:* Gokō-no-miya-*jinsha*, Gokō-no-miya-monzen-*machi*, Fushimi-*ku*. (For its Higurashi-*mon*, now designated a 'national treasure', see n. 7, above.)

[15] *Hatsuse no Kannon:* the eleven-faced Kannon Buddha (*jū-ichi men Kannon*) of Hatsuse-*dera* (now more commonly called Hase-*dera*), Hase-*machi*, Shiki-*gun*, Nara-*ken*. The temple is about thirty miles from Fushimi.

[16] *Bankin ichi-mai:* 1 *bankin* (or *ōban*) was roughly equivalent to 8–9 *ryō* in Saikaku's day (see App. 1, n. 4). If 1 *ryō* is taken at the value of 60 *monme*, 3 *bankin* were 1440 to 1620 *monme*, i.e. over two-thirds of Kikuya's fortune at that time.

[17] *Kyō-bashi:* Kyō bridge spans one stream of the Uji river, on the road from Fushimi to Yodo. The passenger boats coming up the river Yodo on the Ōsaka–Kyōto service went no farther than this bridge—hence its name: 'Kyōto bridge'.

[18] *Amai mo karai mo hito wa yowasarenu yo ya:* in this concluding sentence the phrase *amai mo karai mo* (sweet or bitter) conveys the dual sense of types of *sake* and methods of salesmanship. The word *yowasarenu* is likewise to be taken in the two senses of 'being made to drink' *sake* and 'being befuddled or deceived'.

BOOK III, 4 (pp. 71–74)

[1] *Kōya-san shakusen-zuka no seshu:* this story is constructed from a series of rather loosely connected topics and episodes (cf. also Tr. I, 3; II, 2; V, 1; VI, 2; also Com. V, 1, n. 1). There is, however, a general unity of place—Ōsaka—and a certain logic behind the movement of thought. Briefly, the structure might be explained as follows:

(i) The doctrine that moderation brings long life is contrasted with the actual case of an Ōsaka miser, in which moderation did no such thing.

(ii) The workings of fate, illustrated in the story above of the miser who was fated to wealth and stinginess, leads on to a discussion of the unfair distribution of luck in this world.

(iii) In contrast to honest people who are poor, there are dishonest people —like those who borrow with the intention of going bankrupt—who do very well.

(iv) From this point the general topic of bankruptcy is the connecting theme:

(*a*) The creditors who argued too long over their shares.

(*b*) The increasing scale of bankruptcies (bringing the general discussion to a close, and reintroducing the Ōsaka locality).

(*c*) The story of an honest bankrupt of Ōsaka who recovered his fortune and paid all his debts.

It will be noted that the title refers only to this last episode, and the two subtitles, in the list of contents to Book III, p. 58, only to the opening episode of the miser.

[2] *Fugu* (swell fish) are still an expensive delicacy in Japan, eaten principally as *sashimi* or in soups. The blood from the offal of certain varieties is poisonous, and unless the fish is carefully prepared and washed it can be highly dangerous.

[3] *Mo-uo:* (rock-cod), a species of *hata.*

[4] *Ima-bashi:* a small bridge over the Higashi-yoko-*borigawa*, where the latter joins the Yodo river just east of Naniwa bridge. Imabashi street (*Imabashi-suji*) was presumably the road crossing this bridge. It was in a quiet corner of this district that the *ryōgaeya* hero of *Eitai-gura*, I, 3 (Tr., p. 25), first opened his shop.

[5] *Kuken-chō:* a block of *ageya* houses in the Shin-*machi* brothel quarter of Ōsaka. It was the custom for *ageya* in all parts of Japan to settle their tradesmen's bills on the second of each moon (*futsuka-barai*). (See *Fujii*, app., p. 774, 'Kuken no futsuka-barai'.)

[6] *Dōtonbori:* district along the south bank of Dōton-*borigawa*, a canal in Minami-*ku*, Ōsaka-*shi*. It is still the entertainment centre of Ōsaka.

[7] *Takara to iu ji:* lit. 'the character for Treasure' (which was stamped on the surface of silver *chōgin* minted in the Keichō era).

[8] *Mizunoto no tatsu no toshi, tatsu no hi no tatsu no koku:* years were named by a combination of the ten calendar signs (*jik-kan*) and the twelve signs of the zodiac (*jū-ni shi*), in a cycle of sixty, and the same system was applied to days. There is, however, no such combination as *mizunoto-tatsu*, and—even if there were—a man who is born and who dies in years of the identical designation should be sixty, not fifty-seven. It would be a strange mistake for Saikaku to make—perhaps it is intentional nonsense.

The 'Dragon hour' is *itsutsu-doki*, approximately 8–10 a.m. (see Com. II, 5, n. 16).

[9] *Sanzesō-meikan*, lit. 'The Mirror of the Three Phases of Existence' (past, present, and future), was one of the many contemporary almanacs of occult lore. These works became popular after the publication, in 1667, of the *Meikan Sanzesō Tenmon Sō* (1667), an annotated edition of a Chinese work of the T'ang period.

[10] *Kogane no neko:* the story of how Minamoto Yoritomo presented the priest Saigyō (1118–90) with a silver cat, in appreciation of some lectures he had given on the military art, appears in *Azuma Kagami* (1180–1266), 'Bunji 2, Hachi gatsu, jū-go nichi'. Saikaku's substitution of gold for silver is possibly a variation derived from some other source.

[11] *Sanmen no Daikoku:* a large figure of Daikoku-*ten*, flanked by two smaller figures of Bishamon-*ten*, and Benzai-*ten*—all deities of luck.

[12] *Tamon-ten:* also called *Bishamon-ten.* One of the *shi-tennō* (guardians

of the four quarters and of the Buddhist scriptures) and the principal deity worshipped at Kurama-*dera*, a temple on a hill north of Kyōto (Kurama-*mura*, Atago-*gun*, Kyōto-*fu*). Saikaku introduces the rather far-fetched centipede simile because centipedes were traditionally regarded as messengers of Bishamon-*ten*.

[13] *Shiri mo musubanu ito no gotoku, hari wo kura ni tsumite mo tamaranu naishō:* Saikaku here employs two proverbial expressions in juxtaposition, the 'stitches' of the first suggesting the 'needles' of the second: (i) *shiri mo musubanu ito no gotoku*, 'like a stitch with its end unfastened', i.e. something slovenly and unfinished; (ii) *Hari wo kura ni tsumite mo tamaranu*, 'Even if one pours money into the storehouse like needles it makes no difference', i.e. a chronic state of expenditure exceeding income.

[14] *Zaigō no shinrui:* compare Tr. 1, 3, p. 23: 'In Ōsaka even persons who started life with very little...have risen to be addressed as "Master".... Generally they are all sons of nearby farming people from Yamato, Kawachi, Settsu, and Izumi provinces.'

[15] *Chōshū:* e.g. the *toshi-yori* and *gonin-gumi*.

[16] *Momo no sekku:* presumably the bankruptcy was settled at the year's end. The next reckoning day would therefore be the *Momo no sekku* (Peach festival), on the third of the third moon, at which time it was customary to drink *sake* flavoured with peach leaves. I have used the term 'quarter day', but strictly speaking the Tokugawa financial year was divided into fifths.

[17] *Bunsan:* the type of bankruptcy case to which Saikaku refers in this story, and in all other examples in *Eitai-gura*, is the *bunsan* (lit. 'division and distribution' of effects). The *bunsan* of the Tokugawa period was a purely temporary settlement, arranged without recourse to law by private agreement between the debtor and his creditors. It should not be confused with the other common form of Tokugawa bankruptcy case, the *shindai-kagiri*, which involved the confiscation and auction of the complete effects of the debtor by the authorities. *Bunsan* was essentially 'a gentleman's agreement' based upon the mutual trust of the parties concerned. The private effects of the debtor's wife were traditionally exempted from the assessment (a tradition which encouraged dishonest debtors to buy their wives handsome presents—see *Seken Munesanyō*, 1, 1), and the debtor was morally obliged to pay the remainder of his debts should he ever recover sufficiently—though this was generally a remote possibility.

It seems that the value of a debtor's property at the time of its surrender was usually expected to amount to thirty to forty per cent of the total debts. Twenty per cent was the lowest acceptable figure. The property of the bankrupt in the last episode of the present story amounted to sixty-five per cent of his debts—a most exceptional case. (See *Fujii*, App. p. 763, 'Bunsan'; p. 774, 'Roku bu han ari'; p. 774, 'Shiawase-shidai ni'.)

[18] *Undon, soba-giri:* the present *udon* and *soba*.

[19] *Shi fun go rin:* this is a very small sum, 0·45 *monme.*

[20] *Mukashi Ōtsu nite...:* for a further reference to this Ōtsu bankruptcy, and a similar passage on Kyōto and Ōsaka bankruptcies, see Com. VI, 4, n. 17, and Tr. p. 142.

[21] *Naniwa Enoko-jima:* the present Enoko-jima-*chō*, Nishi-*ku*, Ōsaka-*shi.*

[22] *Izu no Ōshima:* the largest of the group of seven islands off the south-east coast of Izu peninsula, present Ōshima-*gun*, Tōkyō-*fu.* Formerly these islands were a part of Izu province.

[23] *Amaterasu-ō-mi-kami.*

[24] *Kōya-san:* a high plateau in the Kii peninsula on which many temples of the Shingon sect were founded. The first century of the Tokugawa era was its period of greatest prosperity. There are still about one hundred and twenty temples on the mountain.

BOOK III, 5 (pp. 74–78)

[1] *Hidari-mae* (lit. putting the left lapel across before the right, i.e. the reverse of the usual practice), a metaphor from clothing, is here aptly used to describe a draper who has reversed the fortunes of his family.

[2] *Hana-bishi:* a flower arranged as a parallelogram.

[3] *Suruga no Hon-chō: Hon-chō* is the present Gofuku-*chō* (drapers' block), Shizuoka-*shi* (see *Goi Kōshō*, 'Suruga no Hon-chō'). Saikaku here gives only the name of the province, *Suruga*, omitting the name of the provincial capital which was at that time called *Sunpu* (an abbreviation of *Suruga Fuchū*), or simply *Fuchū*. The name *Fuchū* is introduced in the concluding section of the story.

[4] *Fuji no keburi:* smoke no longer rose from Fuji-*san* in Saikaku's time, but it was common literary practice to pretend that it did.

[5] *Shimo-bashira:* small pillars of ice which push up from the ground on very cold days, especially in places which are normally damp.

[6] *Abegawa kami-ko:* the districts along the valley of the river Abe, present Abe-*gun*, Shizuoka-*ken*, were celebrated for the manufacture of crêpe paper kimono (*Abegawa kami-ko*). The invention of the crêping process is attributed by Saikaku, in *Saikaku Zoku Tsurezure* (posth. 1695), IV, 1, to a certain *samurai* of Echizen. The true originator of the process—if it was any one man—was very likely not known, and Saikaku possibly takes the liberty of selecting any person who is convenient in a given story.

[7] *Sanjū nen amari kanjō nashi:* 'ten years' is my own emendation of the text's 'thirty years' which, if left, would imply that Chūsuke took as long to lose the fortune as his father had taken to make it. This is difficult to reconcile with Saikaku's subsequent comment that 'if making money is a slow process, losing it is quickly done'. What is more, it is revealed later in the story that Chūsuke himself, at the time of his downfall, was only thirty-

nine. There is no doubt that the text of 1688 has 'thirty years', but it may have been a slip—perhaps an unintentional repetition of the 'thirty years' in the previous line.

[8] *Soroban no tama ni mo nukete, haru no yanagi no kaze ni temae midarete:* a reference to the poem attributed to Sōjō Henjō (*Kokin Shū*, Haru, 1): *Asa-midori ito yori-kakete shira-tsuyu wo tama ni mo nukeru haru no yanagi ka*, 'The willows of spring, weaving their pale green branches into strings, threading white dew-drops like beads'. Saikaku's very similar phrase has an entirely different significance. The *tama* are the beads of an abacus, not of a necklace, and *nukete* means not 'threading' but 'being slovenly with'. *Haru* is coupled with *kaze* to imply the winds which blow on the great reckoning day before New Year. The introduction of *kaze* and the subsequent *temae midarete* seems to be an intentional allusion to yet another poem in *Kokin Shū*, Haru 1, this time by Ki no Tsurayuki: *Ao-yagi no ito yori-kakuru haru shi mo zo, midarete hana no hokorobinikeru.*

[9] *Sengen no miya:* the present Sengen-*jinsha*, Miyagazaki-*chō*, Shizuoka-*shi*.

[10] *Sashi-saba:* salted mackerel, skewered in pairs on a stick, eaten at *Bon*.

[11] *Ehō higashi yara minami:* the 'lucky quarter' (*ehō*) is the direction whence the year's luck-god (*toshi-toku-jin*) arrives on the first day of the year. The god chooses a different quarter of approach each year.

[12] *Tōtōmi no Nissaka:* Nissaka was one of the stages on the Tōkai-*dō*, in the present Ogasa-*gun*, Shizuoka-*ken*. It was about twenty-five miles from Fuchū.

[13] *Se ni kawaru Ōi-gawa:* the river Ōi, marking the boundary between the old provinces of Suruga and Tōtōmi, was one of the most difficult obstacles in the path of the Tōkai-*dō* traveller. The river bed was wide, containing a number of separate streams whose course changed from time to time. The Tokugawa government, regarding the river as a convenient strategic obstacle, forbade the construction of any bridge across it.

[14] *Sayo-no-naka-yama...no Kannon:* west of the river Ōi the Tōkai-*dō* entered the hills, and one of the steepest gradients was the pass of Sayo-*no-naka-yama* (also called Saya-*no-naka-yama*) between the stages of Kanaya and Nissaka (see n. 11, above). About three miles to the north of the pass, on the peak of Awa-*ga-mine*, stood a small temple called Kannon-*ji*.

[15] *Muken no kane:* Muken was the eighth and lowest of the 'Eight Hot Hells' of Buddhism, where sinners were tortured with fire. The 'Bell of Muken' was in the Kannon-*ji* (though, as Saikaku says, it had been buried long ago) and there was a tradition that whoever struck it would gain riches in this life, but that after death he would descend to hell, and his descendants would become beggars. The tradition seems to have been widely known in Saikaku's time. (See *Ōyabu*, pp. 315–17.)

[16] *Sue no yo ni ja ni naru:* it was popularly supposed that people who could not bear to be parted from their money came back to look for it after

death in the form of snakes. There is a story on this theme in the *hiragana* version of *Inga Monogatari* (*c.* 1660), II, 3 (see *Ōyabu*, p. 318).

[17] *Hiru no jigoku:* there is a story, recorded in *Honchō Koji Inen Shū* (1689), II, 55, that when a certain merchant visited the Kannon-*ji*, with the intention of striking the Bell of Muken, the head priest attempted to dissuade him by dwelling upon the terrors of hell. To demonstrate his point he threw a piece of cooked meat into a pond near the temple, and immediately thousands of leeches rose to attack it. 'That is how devils will torture you if you fall into hell', he said (see *Ōyabu*, pp. 315–16). Saikaku is possibly thinking of this story—leeches do not seem to have been a special feature of the Muken hell. However, the allusion to *hiru no jigoku* (leech-hell) is also 'appropriate', in the limited *haikai* sense, in that there was a cave near the Kannon-*ji* called *Hiru no jigoku.*

[18] *Mime wa kahō no hitotsu:* 'Good looks are a part of karma'—proverb.

[19] *Abegawa no yūjo:* the Abegawa prostitute quarter, in the western outskirts of Fuchū, is reputed to have been founded on the orders of Tokugawa Ieyasu. In *Tōkai-dō Meisho Ki*, III, is the entry: 'Abegawa: the river is easily fordable. There are many prostitutes here. It is a noted place for paper *kimono.*'

[20] *Morokoshi Hō-koji:* a Confucian scholar of the T'ang period who threw all his wealth in the sea, became a beggar, and eventually—together with his daughter Ling Chao—achieved enlightenment in *Zen.* The story of how he earned his living by making baskets, which his daughter sold, is recounted in *Iguchi Monogatari*, v, 18. It seems that 'Ling Chao's Baskets', made of bamboo, were a speciality of the craftsmen of Fuchū at this time, and also that in *haikai* any reference to baskets was liable to be capped by a reference to Ling Chao (see *Shuzui*, p. 284).

BOOK IV, 1 (pp. 81–85)

[1] *Ō-emuma:* for the pictures dedicated to shrines and temples, called *ema* (painted horses) see Com. II, 2, n. 6.

[2] *Gofukusho:* firms of drapers accredited to the imperial court in Kyōto, to noble families, or to *daimyō.* An ordinary draper's firm was called *gofukuya* or, on a smaller scale, *kireya.*

[3] *Muromachi:* for Muromachi street, the drapers' street of Kyōto, see Com. I, 4, n. 6.

[4] *Waka-ebisu*, *Daikoku-dono*, *Bishamon*, *Benzai-ten:* four gods of luck. For Ebisu Saikaku uses the term *waka-ebisu*, which is strictly speaking the 'New Year Ebisu', the block-printed picture of the god sold as a lucky charm on the first day of the year.

[5] *Kikyōya:* possibly Kikyōya Jinzaburō (see n. 19, below).

[6] *Shōjiki no kōbe warashite:* Saikaku's phrase recalls the proverb, *Shōjiki*

no kōbe ni kami yadoru, 'The gods lodge in honest heads'. The phrase would suggest to the reader that Kikyōya and his wife were exactly the sort of people entitled to some assistance from the gods.

[7] *Mochi-tsuki osoku, sakana-gake ni buri mo nakute:* for the New Year custom of pounding rice for *mochi* see Com. II, 1, n. 8. Hanging salted and dried *buri* (a fish usually translated as 'yellow-tail') on a row of hooks in the kitchen (*sakana-gake*) was another of the season's customs. Such fish were frequently used as New Year presents.

[8] *Takara-bune wo shiki-ne shite:* for 'treasure-ship' charms see Com. I, 1, n. 7.

[9] *Setsubun mame:* in the old calendar *Setsubun* (the dividing point between winter and spring) was the night before New Year's Day, and at this time it was customary for all members of a family to scatter beans about their house as a form of exorcism of evil spirits, shouting at the same time: *Fuku wa uchi, oni wa soto!* (Luck come in, devils go out!). The custom is still widely observed, though *Setsubun* itself now occurs some time in the early months of each year.

[10] *Binbō-gami*, the god who attaches himself to the poor or those destined to be poor, finds frequent mention in Edo literature. He appears to have been a popular invention of the time, a rather disreputable god who, unlike the gods of luck, received no official backing from either *Shintō* or Buddhism. He appears in *Chōja Kyō* (see App. 2, pp. 243–4).

[11] *Nanakusa:* see Com. II, 1, n. 18.

[12] *Binbō-gami-me to ategoto wo iware:* the original gives the insulting word itself: *Binbō-gami-me!* (*-me* is a common suffix in insults, e.g. *baka-me! chikushō-me!*).

[13] *Kamo-namasu, sugi-yaki:* the first, *kamo-namasu*, was a preparation of raw duck flavoured with vinegar and *sake*. The second, *sugi-yaki* (not to be confused with the post-Meiji *suki-yaki*), was a form of fish or shellfish stew cooked and served in boxes of cryptomeria wood (*sugi*). The fish was boiled in a soup of white bean-paste (*shiro-miso*). Of course, other ingredients could be added to taste. (For the contemporary recipes in detail see *Ōyabu*, pp. 330–1.)

[14] *Tsuri-yagi:* coverlets (*kake-buton*) suspended from the ceiling to reduce the weight on the body.

[15] *Panya no kukuri-makura:* pillow-cases stuffed with cotton wool, in contrast with the usual head-rest which was made of wood. *Panya* is the Portuguese word 'panha', meaning (in its original sense) a special type of cotton substitute which we now call 'kapok'. Whether the Tokugawa Japanese used it in this sense, or merely in the sense of 'imported cotton', seems to be in doubt.

[16] *Momi-zome:* 'redflower dyes', prepared from the petals of *beni-bana*, 'safflower' or 'dyers' saffron'.

[17] *Kobeniya to iu hito:* there were various firms of Kyōto dyers at this time called *Kobeniya.* (See *Kyō Habutae Oritome* (1689), 'Kobeniya'.) The name is evidently connected with *beni-bana* (see n. 16, above).

[18] *Satō-zome* (translated as 'sugar-red-dyes') are presumably dyes of a brown-sugar colour. Brown sugar was sometimes called *murasaki-zatō* (purple sugar). The meaning is not certain, but at least it seems unlikely that any glutinous sugary substance could have been used as a dye ingredient. (See *Ōyabu*, pp. 334–5.)

[19] *Suō-gi no shita-zome:* shavings from the roots of sapan-wood trees (*suō-gi*) had been used as a material in dyes in Japan from ancient times. Kikyōya's original contribution would seem to be the vinegar processing.

There is no reliable contemporary evidence connecting the name of Kikyōya with the invention of a new dye, but a passage in *Honchō Seji Danki* (1733) (quoted in *Ōyabu*, p. 336) gives some substantiation: 'Jinza-*momi*: a man called Kikyōya Jinzaburō of Chōja-*machi*, Kyōto, discovered this dye in the Shōō period (1652–5). Using *akane* he produced a colour similar to that of *momi*. This is also called *chū-momi*. There is a tradition that this Jinzaburō achieved great wealth by praying to the god of poverty.' Whether Saikaku himself was the source of this last tradition is a question which cannot be decided without further evidence.

[20] *Edo ni kudari:* possibly the reason why Kikyōya takes his goods to Edo is that the drapers there were less likely to notice the inferiority of his product to the genuine article. The people of Kyōto, as he himself had remarked, were discriminating in such matters.

[21] *Ihai-chigyō* (mortuary-tablet stipends) was a derogatory term for the inherited livings of *samurai*. The mortuary-tablets (*ihai*) of one's ancestors were placed in the family Buddhist altar (*butsu-dan*) as objects of worship: hence an *ihai* stipend has the sense of something sacrosanct from the past.

[22] *Oki-zukin:* a flat cloth cap much worn by elderly and rich *chōnin*. It is mentioned in Tr. 1, 3, p. 23, as part of the dress of successful business men of Ōsaka.

[23] *Sono ie wo amata ni shi-wakuru:* the usual expression for the practice of providing senior clerks with capital to set up as the masters of branch shops, using the name of the parent business, though independent of it financially, was *nōren wo shi-wakeru*, 'dividing the shop-curtain'.

[24] *Kamado-shōgun:* 'kitchen stove *shōgun*'.

[25] *Kane no naru meiboku:* a variation on the proverbial expression for money which multiplies itself by interest, *kane no naru ki*, 'a tree which grows money'. It has similarities with the English expression, 'Do you think money grows on trees?'—except for the English implication that it never does.

[26] *Chōja-machi:* present Chōja-*machi*, west of the imperial palace, Kamikyō-*ku*, Kyōto-*shi*.

BOOK IV, 2 (pp. 85–89)

[1] *Isshaku hassun to ieru kumo-yuki:* a variety of explanations have been offered by commentators on why these clouds are called 'one *shaku* eight *sun*' clouds and what sort of clouds they are. The cloud caps which sometimes form over Fuji-*san* are still given this name by local people, in which case 'one *shaku* eight *sun*' is to be taken as the diameter of a certain type of Tokugawa reed hat (see *Goi Kōshō*, 'Isshaku hassun to ieru kumo-yuki'). Fuji-*san*, however, is not in Kyūshū, and a number of alternative explanations seem equally possible (for these see *Ōyabu*, pp. 244–6).

[2] *Takara no shima:* I take *shima* here to mean not 'an island', but more broadly 'overseas lands'. This seems to be in accordance with usage in Tokugawa times. (Cf. *shima* meaning a striped cloth, originally imported from abroad: *Wakun Shiori* (1883), II.) I know of no tradition in Japan of the existence of any specific 'Treasure Island', to which Saikaku might be alluding.

[3] *Tenbin:* an accurate balance used for weighing money, part of the standard equipment of a *ryōgaeya*. The exact coincidence of two needle points at the central pivot indicated that the coin in one pan and the weight in the other were equally balanced. To ensure that there was no mistake the beam of the balance was set in motion again by the light tap of a hammer (*kozuchi*) on the pivot. This is the 'tap-tap on the scales' to which Saikaku frequently refers (e.g. Tr. I, 3, p. 22; II, 2, p. 40; IV, 1, p. 82). *Tenbin* are shown in various illustrations in *Eitai-gura*: possibly the clearest is that in V, 2, p. 111.

There were two other principal types of weighing instrument: *chigi* and *hakari*. Both were of the single pan variety, with a graduated scale on the arm to indicate weights. The former, *chigi*, was used for comparatively bulky objects (it is mentioned in Tr. II, 1, p. 37), and the latter, *hakari* (or *sao-bakari*) was a much smaller version of the same thing, the pivot of which was held in one hand. (It is mentioned as part of the equipment of drapers' clerks in Tr. I, 4, p. 27.)

[4] *Takara no shima...uchide no kozuchi:* following upon the mention of *takara no shima*, with its suggestion of *takara-bune* (treasure-ship charms, see Com. I, 1, n. 7), Saikaku introduces one of the traditional treasures associated with the latter, namely *uchide no kozuchi* (small mallets which tap out whatever one desires. The god Daikoku is usually depicted holding one in his right hand.) This, in turn, suggests the mallets used on a balance (see n. 3, above).

[5] *Nage-gane* (lit. 'money thrown', meaning, possibly, into space or into the sea) was a technical term for a particular type of investment in overseas trading ventures in the late sixteenth and early seventeenth centuries. It was money lent by a third party to swell the joint capital of the Japanese partici-

pant in a trading project and the foreign master of a ship. The third party's profits were purely in the form of a fixed interest on his loan, and he was in no way a shareholder entitled to a return in proportion to the success of the venture. The rate of interest was extremely high, but offsetting this was the provision that, in the event of the ship failing to return, the borrower was under no obligation to repay either the original loan or the interest. For the borrower it was a form of marine insurance, reducing his own share in any loss, and for the lender it was a gamble. The rate of interest varied from thirty to eighty per cent per voyage in accordance with the credit of the borrower and the ship's master (the latter, of course, played a vital part in these ventures, not only in the navigation of the ship but in the supervision of the business at the foreign ports). A general explanation of *nage-gane*, and examples of contracts drawn up by merchants of this time, is to be found in *Shuin-sen Bōeki Shi*, XI, pp. 148–69. (See also *Fujii*, app., p. 775, 'Tō e nage-gane'). It should be noted, however, that the attribution of the term *nage-gane* to this particular type of investment is found only in a rather late source, *Zenkai Yōshi* (1757), and it is possible that Saikaku and his contemporaries use it in a more general sense to mean any rash investment in the Nagasaki trade.

In spite of Saikaku's reassuring words at the opening of this story, trade by sea—particularly with foreign countries—remained extremely risky. The dangers included not only the navigational hazards of adverse winds, storms, and uncharted rocks, but also pirates. Expeditions were usually away for six months, leaving for the Philippines and ports in south-east Asia in the winter, on the north-east monsoon, and returning in the summer on the south-west monsoon.

[6] *Ki wa ki, kane wa kane:* 'wood is wood, and silver is silver', a proverbial expression suggesting the clear distinctions which must be drawn between things of a different nature, is here used verbatim by Saikaku, but—as is often the case—with a different meaning.

[7] *Shima-yuki no tabako:* the reading indicated by the *furi-gana* here is *shima*, but the characters are those for *Tsushima*, two large islands between Kyūshū and Korea. Saikaku's phrase does not necessarily imply that the tobacco was bound any farther than Tsushima itself, but as Tsushima was the regular entrepôt in Tokugawa times for the Japan–Korea trade, it seems justifiable to assume that the 'flourishing trade' was not aimed primarily at consumers in those sparsely populated islands, but at the larger market in Korea.

[8] *Shōjiki no atama ni kami yadoru:* lit. 'The gods lodge in honest heads'—proverb.

[9] *Chikuzen no kuni Hakata:* Hakata is now the section of Fukuoka-*shi* east of the Naka river. It had once been an important port for overseas trade, but foreign ships ceased to call there after 1552. It continued to

flourish as a business centre, however, throughout the Tokugawa period, and was the home of many celebrated merchant families.

[10] *Kanaya to ka ya ieru hito:* Saikaku, when he mentions a principal character by name, does not often refer to him in such vague terms as this. Perhaps it is a concealed reference to a real person which meant more to Saikaku's contemporaries than it does to us. There was a celebrated merchant family of Hakata called Kamiya, and Kamiya Sōtan (1553–1635) made his fortune in overseas trade. The fact that he was also a connoisseur of tea implements might lead one to suppose that there was a possible connection between him and Saikaku's Kanaya. This, however, is purely the present translator's surmise. No identification is attempted by the commentators.

[11] *Sumiyoshi-daimyōjin:* Sumiyoshi is the god who protects voyagers and fishermen. He is also called Suminoe-*no-kami*.

[12] *Tatsu mo noborubeki fusei:* dragons were reputed to drive clouds along and, by flying through them, to cause storms.

[13] *Nao-nao ito kuri-kaesu wo mite:* this episode bears a strong family likeness to that of Robert the Bruce and the spider. There is no need to infer that it is a foreign import into Japan, but the fact that it is here related in a Nagasaki setting encourages speculation.

[14] *Sukoshi no nimotsu wo shi-ire:* Kanaya appears to buy in a stock of goods for sale in Nagasaki, in order that he may use the money for speculative purchases of imported goods. Such, at least, seems to be the only possible interpretation of this sentence. But there is no mention hereafter of his selling his goods, unless the 'fifty *ryō*' which appears in his purse is the proceeds from such a sale.

[15] *Hito no takara no ichi:* this can be translated simply as 'a market where other people's goods were on sale', meaning the import market at Nagasaki—*takara* (treasure) and imported luxury goods being the same thing to Tokugawa Japanese—but a further significance of *hito no* may be to point a contrast with the famous *Takara no ichi*—Treasure market festival—celebrated at the Sumiyoshi-*jinsha* (present Sumiyoshi-*ku*, Ōsaka-*shi*) on the thirteenth of the ninth moon. In this case there is a belated *haikai* reference to the previously introduced Sumiyoshi-*daimyōjin*.

[16] *Same* here means *same-gawa*, shark skin. This was often used as a covering for sword hilts.

[17] *Gojū ryō:* fifty *ryō* are roughly three *kanme* of silver (see App. 1, p. 238).

[18] *Maruyama no yūjo-machi:* Maruyama-*machi* was the principal brothel quarter of Nagasaki, in the eastern section of the city. It was one of the earliest licensed quarters to be established in Japan, dating from the Bunroku era (1592–6).

[19] *Kachō to ieru:* the Maruyama *tayū* Kachō is one of the thirty-six women poets mentioned in Saikaku's *Kokin Haikai Nyo-kasen* (1684): 'She recites Chinese verse for Chinese, and *uta* for Japanese. She has composed

one work of *haikai*, and her *hokku* have appeared in several compilations.' Since the name was possibly hereditary it is not certain whether this bluestocking of the *demi-monde* is the person to whom Saikaku here refers. In *Nagasaki Miyage*, a work on the Maruyama brothel quarter published in 1680, Kachō is mentioned as a *tayū* in the employment of a certain Bungoya Gorōbei.

[20] *Makura-byōbu:* a screen placed above the pillow to keep off draughts. *Makura* (pillow) is here used as a pivot word, effecting an ingenious and surprising switch of interest from the passion in the bed to the screen at the top of it.

[21] *Ogura shikishi:* sheets of elegantly coloured paper on each of which was inscribed one verse of the celebrated compilation of one hundred poems known as the *Ogura Hyakunin Isshu.* The compiler of these poems was Fujiwara Teika (1162–1241). There was a tradition (see *Ōyabu*, p. 356) that the original hundred *shikishi* were once preserved on a screen in Ise province. According to this same source, *Rōjin Zatsuwa* (1710), only thirty of these survived by Saikaku's time. It is possible that Saikaku's idea for this episode owes something to the above tradition.

[22] *Daimyō-shū e agete:* there would be few *daimyō* in the *kamigata* (Kyōto–Ōsaka area), but many art dealers or connoisseurs with *daimyō* connections.

[23] *Kachō wo uke-dashi:* it was possible for a customer, after coming to an agreement with the brothel keeper concerned, to buy a courtesan and take her away from the brothel quarter for good. This was called *uke-dashi* or *mi-uke*.

[24] *Buzen no ura-sato:* Buzen was a province in the north of Kyūshū, its coastline running east from the Shimo-no-seki straits.

BOOK IV, 3 (pp. 89–92)

[1] *Ise no yashiro:* the Ise-*jingū* at Uji-Yamada-*shi*, Mie-*ken*. There are two principal shrines at Ise. The outer (*gegū*) is dedicated to Toyouke-*hime*, the goddess of food, and the inner (*naigū*), about three miles to the south, is dedicated to Amaterasu-*ō-mi-kami*, the great goddess of the heavens. Around the outer shrine are forty side-shrines (*massha*), dedicated to a variety of gods, and a further eighty are grouped around the inner shrine.

[2] *Aki-tsu-su:* one of the early names for the main island of Japan, later applied to the whole country.

[3] *Miya-meguri no maki-sen ni hato-me to iu okashige naru namari-zeni:* at most shrines it was the custom to make offerings of rice (*sanmai*), but at Ise it was usual to offer *zeni*. Few pilgrims, however, offered real *zeni* at the side-shrines: instead they bought strings of imitation lead coins (*hato-no-me* or 'pigeons' eyes') which were offered for sale in the vicinity. The price of

a thousand of these was approximately one *monme* five *fun* of silver, about one-tenth of the price of real *zeni*. The practice, which lessened the shrines' takings considerably, seems to have been officially forbidden soon after Saikaku wrote *Eitai-gura* (see *Saikaku Oritome*, IV, 3).

[4] *Dai-dai-kagura:* see Com. II, 4, n. 17, 'O-kagura'.

[5] *Sho-gan jōju jū-ni kanme:* the price for a prayer for the fulfilment of all one's prayers was twelve *monme* of silver.

[6] *Oshi:* agents for Ise pilgrims, chiefly concerned with arranging their lodgings. Each *oshi* had his regular patrons in various parts of Japan, and once a year, during the last month, he set out to visit them, carrying paper charms (*o-harai*) from the two Ise shrines. The charms were carried inside small boxes (*o-harai-bako*) which also contained various small presents—Ise specialities such as seaweed, face powder, or fans—and a formal letter of greetings from the *oshi* himself. The patrons gave a certain amount of money in return, according to their means.

[7] *Sode-goi:* the various types of beggar along the Ai-*no-yama* road are described in *Saikaku Oritome*, IV, 3, and also in *Kōshoku Tabi Nikki* (1687), IV. Many were mere children, but the type to which Saikaku here refers seem to be a mixture of beggar and prostitute.

[8] *Ai-no-yama* (the hill between) was the name of the hill between the outer and inner shrines.

[9] *Asamashi ya, kokoro hitotsu to:* this is possibly the *Ise-bushi* referred to in *Saikaku Oritome*, IV, 3, or the *Ai-no-yama-bushi* of *Kōshoku Ichidai Onna*, VI, 2, but little is known about the words or music of either.

[10] *O-shiroishi maku oyaji:* this possibly means an old man who scatters gravel around a shrine when it is moved to a new position (see *Fujii*, p. 507; *Ōyabu*, p. 370). I have followed the interpretation given in *Goi Kōshō*, 'O-shiroishi', though it is not entirely convincing.

[11] *Shimabara shōgatsu-kai no niwa-sen:* a customer at the Shimabara brothel quarter on any of the five main festival days (see Com. I, 5, n. 4) was obliged to give a fixed gratuity to the courtesan he hired—the amount varying from fifteen thousand *zeni* to four thousand *zeni* according to the grade of courtesan. This money was called *niwa-sen*.

[12] *Nori-kake:* a type of baggage horse supplied on hire along the principal highroads, which carried a mount in addition to light baggage. The weight of baggage was not permitted to exceed twenty *kanme*. For various regulations governing charges and baggage weights see *Ōyabu*, pp. 371–2.

[13] *Yamada:* present Uji-Yamada-*shi*, Mie-*ken*, the town where the outer Ise shrine was situated.

[14] *Kara-jiri-muma:* another type of light baggage horse. With a mount the limit of baggage weight was five *kanme*; without a mount, the limit was twenty *kanme*. Nine of these horses would be required to carry Fundōya's two hundred thousand *zeni*.

[15] *Zeni-kake-matsu:* the name given to a pine which stood by the pilgrim's route at Toyokuno, north of Tsu-*shi*, Mie-*ken*. It was the custom to hang *zeni* on its branches as a distant offering to the Ise shrines. It was also called *sen-kan-matsu* (million *zeni* pine).

[16] *Matsubara-odori no sode:* the baggy sleeves of *kimono* are commonly used as pockets, and the sleeves of dancing *kimono*, which have flowing cuffs reaching nearly to the ground, are more than usually capacious.

[17] *Miso-koshi* (sieves for preparing bean-paste, '*miso*') were used by the Ai-*no-yama* beggars as begging bowls (see *Saikaku Oritome*, IV, 3).

[18] *Fundōya no nanigashi:* no identification of Fundōya has been attempted by commentators.

[19] *Sakai-chō:* a district of small theatres and side-shows in Edo—the modern Kakigara-*chō*, Chūō-*ku*, Tōkyō-*to*.

[20] *Oni...toshi-goshi...shiawase:* 'demons...spring...luck' are related words, in *haikai* fashion, all connected with the custom of exorcising demons and inviting in luck at *Setsubun*.

[21] *Sanjū-shi nen ware to kasegi-dashi:* cf. Tr. IV, 1, p. 84, where it states that a man should 'work on his own' from about twenty-five to forty-five. Fundōya starts earlier and retires much later.

[22] *Miyako Dennai to iu shibai:* Miyako Dennai was the manager of the Miyako-*za kabuki* theatre in Sakai-*chō*, Edo. The theatre was built in 1633, but destroyed in the Great Fire of 1657. Thereafter the company moved to another district in Edo.

[23] *Zeni-mise:* Saikaku here seems to differentiate between *zeni-mise* and *ryōgaeya*. (For *zeni-mise* and *ryōgaeya*, see Com. I, 3, n. 29.)

[24] *Kusunoki-bungen:* see Com. II, 4, n. 12.

[25] *Enma-chō Berabō:* both are mentioned in other works of the time as popular exhibits at side-shows in Ōsaka, Kyōto, and Edo. The *Enma-chō* (Bird of Hell) seems to have been an outsize cockerel. The *Berabō* was of human shape, with a pointed head, large round red eyes, and a receding chin.

[26] *Narihira Kawachi-gayoi* (1694): a play by Tominaga Heibei, based on an episode from the *Ise Monogatari* (see *TSZ* (1950), p. 110).

[27] *Tamagawa Sennojō:* a celebrated female-impersonator in early *kabuki*, who died *c.* 1680. He started his career at a very early age in the Kyōto Murayama-*za*, a troupe of boy actors specialising in feminine roles. In the Shōō era (1652–5) he moved to the Jinzaburō-*za*, Sakai-*chō*, Edo, and for three years played the role of Narihira's wife, Izutsu, in the *kabuki Kawachi-gayoi*, earning wide acclaim. Later he moved to Ise, where he became the manager of a theatre on the Ai-*no-yama* road, between the outer and inner shrines.

[28] *Suginishi Tori no toshi:* the Great Fire of Edo in the third year of the Myōreki era (1657).

[29] *Hon-chō... Tenma-chō... Sakuma-no-omote... Funa-chō... Kome-gashi ... Amadana... Tōri-chō... Furetere-chō... Shirogane-chō:* the localities of Edo mentioned in this section are listed below:

Hon-chō: north-east of Nihon bridge, present Chūō-*ku*, Tōkyō-*to*.

Tenma-chō: present Dai-tenma-*chō* and Shō-tenma-*chō*, Chūō-*ku*.

Sakuma-no-omote: a section of Dai-tenma-*chō*, Chūō-*ku*, renowned at that time for its wholesale paper dealers.

Funa-chō: present Hon-funa-*chō*, Chūō-*ku*.

Kome-gashi: present Kawagishi-*dōri*, Ise-*chō*, Chūō-*ku*.

Amadana: an abbreviation of *Amagasaki no tana*, 'the stores of Amagasaki-*chō*', present Urakawa-*gishi*, Chūō-*ku*.

Tōri-chō: the highway crossing Nihon bridge (see Com. III, 1, n. 8).

Furetere-chō: present Terifuri-*chō*, Chūō-*ku*.

Shirogane-chō: present Hon-shirogane-*chō*, Chūō-*ku*.

For more exact locations see *Edo Chiri*: 'Amadana'; 'Funa-chō'; 'Kome-gashi'; 'Tenma-chō'; 'Sakuma-no-omote'; 'Furetere-chō'.

[30] *Tenma-chō no kinuya... onaji tana-tsuki:* for the peculiar roof structures of the shops in Tenma-*chō* see *Edo Chiri*, 'Tenma-chō ni kinuya wataya'.

[31] *Yamabushi:* begging ascetics, followers of the part Buddhist part *Shintō* sect called Jugen-dō. The sect stressed the virtues of a rigorous asceticism as against the study of the scriptures.

[32] *Nakabashi:* present Nakabashi Hiro-*koji*, Chūō-*ku*.

[33] *Ima no tsurugi, mukashi no na-gatana:* an inversion of the proverb, *Mukashi no tsurugi, ima no na-gatana*, 'Ancient swords, modern kitchen knives'. The proverb's meaning was that even famous ancient swords rusted and lost all usefulness, except as knives for cutting up vegetables.

BOOK IV, 4 (pp. 93–96)

[1] *Bankin ichi-mai:* approx. eight *ryō* of gold, or five hundred *monme* of silver (see App. I, p. 236).

[2] *Echizen no kuni Tsuruga no minato:* present Tsuruga-*shi*, Fukui-*ken*. Tsuruga bay affords one of the finest natural harbours along the Japan sea-coast, and in early Tokugawa days it was used extensively as a terminus for shipping bringing cargoes for Kyōto and Ōsaka from the northernmost regions of Japan. The cargoes were carried overland from Tsuruga to Kaizu, a port at the northern extremity of Lake Biwa, trans-shipped thence to Ōtsu at the southern end of Lake Biwa, and moved by land to various destinations in the *kansai* area. The toll here mentioned (*uwa-mai*) is that levied by the feudal lord of the Tsuruga area on goods transported through his domains.

Zoku Shoshū-meguri (*c.* 1685), I:

> Tsuruga is a town on the coast of the northern sea. It is a harbour where ships call from every province on the northern coast of Japan—from Ōshū, from Dewa,

and from the Sanin-*dō* areas—and amongst these the ships from Akita, Sakata, Tsugaru, and Takada are especially numerous. Consequently Tsuruga has a large population and many rich merchants. Most of them deal in rice, beans, or timber, and when goods such as these are sent to the Kyōto area they are transported by horse overland to Kaizu in Ōmi province, and sent by ship from Kaizu to Ōtsu. Again, all sorts of goods are sent from Kyōto to Tsuruga by this same route, and the traffic of men and horses along the road from Kaizu to Tsuruga is dense and never-ending. Ships arrive at Tsuruga port in their greatest numbers in the fourth, fifth, and sixth moons.

Since the north of Japan is too cold for the production of tea, large quantities of it are brought here from the Kyōto area, and from the provinces of Ōmi, Mino, and Owari. The tea is sold at Tsuruga and then dispatched to the various provinces in the north. Before the merchants [from the *kansai*, and from the north] return to their homes they purchase great quantities of merchandise here to take with them. The tea business quarter, which stretches a great distance, contains the homes of many great merchants and also many wholesale tea firms....

A transport charge of three *shō* five *go* of rice is levied by the castle lord on each baggage animal passing between Tsuruga and Kaizu. For a baggage animal bearing a mount (*nori-kake*) the charge is five *shō*. When this charge has been paid, transmuted to cash in accordance with rice quotations at Ōtsu, to the lord's official representative in the town, the man in charge of the horses receives a ticket, which he surrenders when he passes the watch-point on the road leading out of the lords' domains. If he has no ticket he may not pass. There are hundreds of horses passing to Kaizu every day, and in the old days the daily profit from these levies is said to have amounted to one *bankin*. Since twenty-four or five years ago, however, ships bearing rice from the north have not called at Tsuruga, but have made the voyage direct to Ōsaka, passing along the northern coast and rounding the mainland through the Shimo-no-seki straits, and the revenue at Tsuruga has decreased. This is the result of the charges being too high, it is said. (*Ōyabu*, pp. 389–90.)

The autumn market which Saikaku mentions was possibly held when the tea merchants from distant parts had gathered in Tsuruga to sell tea and buy goods for the return journey.

[3] *Yodo no kawa-bune:* light cargo vessels plying between Ōsaka and Yodo.

[4] *Inrō:* small boxes for medicine, frequently worn at the waist for ornamental purposes alone.

[5] *Kobashi no Risuke*, if he ever existed, has not been identified. It has been pointed out that various episodes in his story have similarities with passages in the *hiragana* version of *Inga Monogatari*, and that Saikaku himself, in *Honchō Nijū Fukō* (1686), IV, 3, had related a story concerning a farmer's son of Tsuruga who met a similar end. *Inga Monogatari*, IV, 6, also tells how divine punishment was visited upon a man of Tsuruga—a rice wholesaler's clerk. On the evidence so far presented by commentators, however (see e.g. *Ōyabu*, p. 404), one can say little more than that the present story *may* owe its inspiration in a few details to a vague Tsuruga tradition or to a recollection of tales from *Inga Monogatari*.

[6] *Tama-dasuki wo agete...eboshi okashige ni:* Ebisu, the merchants' favourite god of luck, invariably wore an *eboshi*, a tall black cap of lacquered paper or stiffened cloth. In Tr. II, 4, p. 52, bright sleeve ribbons (*tama-dasuki*) also appear as a feature of Ebisu's dress.

[7] *Ebisu no asa-cha...jū-ni mon zutsu:* worshipping Ebisu early in the morning (*asa-ebisu*) was a common practice among merchants. The reason why they gave twelve *zeni* for each cup of tea—a large sum for so trifling a thing—is possibly connected with the custom of offering twelve incense tapers to a Buddha. The price for this was twelve *zeni*—the figure 'twelve' being interpreted to represent either the twelve moons of a year, or the twelve karma of Buddhism (*jū-ni innen*).

[8] *Etchū Echigo:* the two provinces north-east of Echizen, corresponding roughly with the present Toyama-*ken* and Niigata-*ken*.

[9] *Mokuzen ni kataku no kurushimi:* the present existence, being insecure and subject to change, was likened in the Buddhist scriptures to a 'house afire' (*kataku*).

[10] *Higashiyama no chaya:* these were the small unlicensed brothel houses east of Shijō bridge (see Com. I, 2, n. 3) at the foot of Higashi-*yama*. Their speciality was male prostitution, and it seems that it was in this that the priests were chiefly interested.

[11] *Yama-uri:* the usual interpretation of this is 'selling land for mining which you know is useless for that purpose'. I follow the interpretation in *Goi Kōshō*, 'Yama-uri', as being more in keeping with the items which immediately precede and follow it—all are means of swindling simple people, and to introduce an element of high finance seems incongruous.

[12] *Ninjin* (ginseng) was noted for its medicinal virtues.

[13] *Kawa-nagare no kami:* this was sold to wig makers.

BOOK IV, 5 (pp. 96–101)

[1] *Shō areba jiki ari:* 'Where there is life there is food'—a proverb.

[2] *Kazunoko:* hard roe of herring, salted. A delicacy associated with New Year.

[3] *Tango buri:* the 'yellow-tail fish' from the province of Tango (the northern part of the present Kyōto-*fu*, facing on to the Japan sea) were thought to be of superior quality. (For *buri* see also Com. IV, 1, n. 7.)

[4] *Shikise:* gifts of clothing presented to apprentices at the end of each of the four seasons, in the third, sixth, ninth, and twelfth moons.

[5] *Ise-ebi:* a species of spiny lobster caught off the Pacific coast of central and south Japan. The foremost fishing ground is off the coast of Mie-*ken*, the old Ise province, hence the name *Ise-ebi*. These lobsters are still used as decorations at New Year.

[6] *Daidai:* a type of bitter orange used mainly as a decoration at New Year. The name means 'generation after generation'.

[7] *Setomono-chō, Suda-chō, Kōji-machi:* for the first two see Com. III, 1, n. 10. Kōji-*machi* was the district lining the highway from Edo castle to Kōfu, and was specially noted for its poulterers and fishmongers (see *Edo Chiri*, 'Kōji-machi').

[8] *Hōrai:* an abbreviation of *hōrai-kazari*, a tray decorated with articles representing the blessings bestowed by the land and the sea—rice, oranges, millet, persimmons, edible seaweed, Ise lobsters, etc. It was the custom to display it in the house from the first to the fourteenth day.

[9] *Ōshōji no hotori ni:* Ōshōji *no tsuji* (street) in Sakai ran along the border-line between Settsu and Izumi provinces. (For Sakai see Com. II, 3, n. 20.)

[10] *Hinokuchiya to iu hito:* Hinokuchiya of Sakai is mentioned in *Saikaku Ōyakazu*, XIX, from which it appears that he was celebrated for his stinginess, and that by 1681 his household had gone bankrupt. The Hinokuchiya family had evidently been long associated with Sakai, since the name appears several times in early sixteenth-century documents of that town. In *Shison Daikoku-bashira* (1709), V, there is a story of how Hinokuchiya of Sakai, 'the foremost economiser in the land' (*tenka ichiban no kanryakusha*) once sent a letter written on a persimmon leaf. It seems that stories of thrift gathered around the name of Hinokuchiya much as they did around that of Fujiya Ichibei of Kyōto (see Com. II, 1, n. 1; also *Goi Kōshō*, 'Hinokuchiya'). Nothing is known of Hinokuchiya's trade, although we gather from the present story that he sold vinegar.

[11] *Kuruma-ebi:* large prawns, five or six inches long; their name (according to *Sansai Zue*, LI) derives from the cartwheel (*kuruma*) shape into which they bend when boiled. *Kunenbo* are a citrous fruit similar in appearance to *daidai* oranges, but sweeter to the taste. The characters for *kunenbo* read 'nine year mother' but they are in fact merely used for their phonetic values, approximating to the Indian word 'kumlanebu'.

[12] *Soroban utsutsu ni mo wasurezu:* Saikaku here uses the phrase *utsutsu ni mo* (even when awake) instead of the *yume ni mo* (even in their dreams) which one would expect. It may be a joke without significance, but I have attempted to provide a logical sense in my translation.

[13] *Koromo-gae:* new suits of clothes were prepared for the first of the fourth moon (the beginning of summer) and the first of the tenth moon (the beginning of winter).

[14] *Sōgi Hōshi:* (1421–1502), a celebrated poet-priest of the fifteenth century.

[15] *Renga.*

[16] *Koshō:* pepper was an imported commodity, brought to Japan usually in Dutch ships (see *Sansai Zue*, LXXXIX).

[17] *Nariwai no tosei wa okuru mono nari:* there is no indication in the text that Hinokuchiya's speech stops at this point. The following remarks, however, read more like the author's comments than those of the parsimonious Hinokuchiya.

[18] *Shuza:* a group of merchants in Sakai who had been granted monopoly rights by the *Bakufu* in the manufacture of red printer's ink, widely used for signature stamps. The materials for the manufacture of the ink were imported through Nagasaki.

[19] *Teppōya:* fire-arms were a noted product of Sakai.

[20] *Nanshū-ji:* a large temple of the Rinsai sect, in Minami Hatago-*machi*, Sakai-*shi*. It was founded in 1556.

[21] *Kanze-dayū:* a leader of the Kanze school of Noh.

[22] *Issei ichidai no kanjin-nō:* a public performance, for the leading actor's benefit. Most Noh performances were private, since the actors were in the service of various feudal lords. Special permission from the *Bakufu* was necessary to hold a grand benefit performance, and it was granted only once in a leading actor's career.

[23] *Kyō no Kitano Shichihonmatsu:* a locality near the present Shichihonmatsu-*dōri*, south-east of the Kitano Tenman-*gū*, Kamikyō-*ku*, Kyōto-*shi*. It is known that a benefit performance of Noh was staged there in 1599 by the ninth Kanze-*dayū*, Kanze Tadachika, and it is possibly this to which Saikaku refers. However, it is equally possible that Saikaku refers to the tenth or eleventh Kanze-*dayū*, who may have staged similar performances at Shichihonmatsu in their respective times.

[24] *Senshu banzei* (a thousand autumns, ten thousand years) is a phrase frequently found at the conclusion of Noh plays (e.g. *Shunei* (1363–1443); *Shakkyō* (1363–1443). It comes aptly as a propitious conclusion to Saikaku's own story after the previous references to Noh.

BOOK V, I (pp. 105–108)

[1] *Mawari-dōki wa tokei saiku:* this story follows the pattern observable in, for example, Tr. I, 3, p. 21; II, 2, p. 39; III, 4, p. 71; IV, 5, p. 96; and VI, 2, p. 132, of a collection of seemingly disconnected anecdotes welded into one by unity of location. In I, 3, it is Ōsaka; in II, 2, Ōtsu; in III, 4, Ōsaka; in IV, 5, Sakai; in VI, 2, Edo, and here it is Nagasaki. As in the other cases, however, the unity does not depend solely upon location: there is a common theme, which is in the present case the proper approach to making a successful living. First, the wrong—the unpractical Chinese—approach is given. Then follows an example of how inventiveness should be turned to practical use, to the making of a fortune in a single generation. Next, after a brief introductory description of trading at Nagasaki, come stories of Nagasaki dealers, illustrating the point that ingenuity is essential for making a fortune.

Then there is a short conclusion giving right and wrong methods of buying imported goods at Nagasaki.

Saikaku does not labour his points, however. He proceeds rapidly from topic to topic, expecting his readers to follow as best they can—and if his readers were already schooled in the twists and turns of rapid *haikai* verse, they probably experienced little difficulty. The moral is there for the curious, but it does not seem likely that either Saikaku or his readers were interested in it for its own sake. It is a part of the pattern.

[2] *Sangatsu no sekku-mae to mo shiranu:* the first reckoning day after New Year was on the last day of the second moon.

[3] *Kaidō:* Malus Haliana Koehne, much admired in China for its blossoms.

[4] *Tokei no saiku...sandai-me ni jōju shite:* Saikaku here attributes the invention of the clock to *Morokoshi-bito*, a term which strictly means the Chinese but which Saikaku may possibly be using in the wide sense of foreigners. In *Sōshi Hen* (1745) there is an account of the invention of the clock as told to a Japanese by a Dutchman at Nagasaki. The scene is obviously some European country, though the name is not given, and it is noteworthy that the invention is said to have been the work of three generations of the same family (see *Goi Kōshō*, 'Sandai-me ni jōju shite').

[5] *Konpeitō* is derived from the Portuguese 'confeitos', and the sweets were presumably of Portuguese origin. Possibly they were manufactured at Macao and shipped to Japan by the Chinese. The term *Nankin*, which Saikaku uses, seems to have included, for the Japanese at least, the area of Shanghai. For the process of making *Konpeitō*, see *Sansai Zue*, CV.

[6] *Ima sejō ni ōshi:* Saikaku is exaggerating when he says that pepper plants became 'common' (*ōshi*) in Japan. It is true, however, that some were grown (see *Sansai Zue*, LXXXIX).

[7] *Goma isshō...Konpeitō nihyaku kin:* I have given rough equivalents for the Japanese weights.

[8] *Aki-bune:* the shipping sailing from south-east Asia, the Philippines, and China on the summer monsoon, arriving in Japan in the early autumn (see Com. IV, 2, n. 5).

[9] *Kaminari no fundoshi, oni no tsuno-saiku:* cf. a similar use of nonsensical examples in Tr. II, 2, p. 39: 'Even a shopkeeper who specialised in snake-meat rice-rolls, miniatures carved from devils' horns, or similar rarities, would have no difficulty here in finding customers.'

[10] *Nage-gane:* see Com. IV, 2, n. 5.

[11] *Kumo wo shirushi no ikoku-bune:* i.e. foreign ships which steer far out to sea where only clouds can be used as landmarks.

[12] *Maruyama to iu tokoro:* the Nagasaki brothel quarter. See Com. IV, 2, n. 18.

[13] *Tenma-chō:* present Dai-tenma-*chō* and Shō-tenma-*chō*, Chūō-*ku*,

Tōkyō-*to*. If he worked in Tenma-*chō* he was possibly a dealer in cotton goods (see *Edo Chiri*, 'Tenma-chō').

[14] *Yaku-otoshi:* dropping money or beans in the street on the eve of one's 'evil year' to ward off disaster. A man's 'evil years' (*yakunen*) were the ages of twenty-five, forty-two, and sixty-one; a woman's were the ages of nineteen, thirty-three, and thirty-seven; and among these the most dangerous were forty-two and thirty-three. The years before and after the *yakunen* were also considered dangerous. It was customary to drop one bean or coin for each year of one's age, and sometimes one extra. In the present case the *daimyō* drops four hundred and thirty *ryō*, i.e. ten *ryō* for each of forty-two years, with ten *ryō* extra.

[15] *Eboshi* here signifies *hitai-eboshi*, a small triangular cap worn on the front of the head. It was worn only at funerals.

[16] *Higashi-yama:* the hills running along the eastern side of Kyōto.

[17] *Ryū no ko:* possibly a kind of alligator. The name means literally 'baby dragon', but there seems little doubt that Saikaku is speaking of a genuine creature, and is not talking intentional nonsense. It is presumably the same as the *ama-ryū no ko* mentioned in *Seken Munesanyō*, IV, 4. There is a story in *Saiyū Ki* (1795) of a Nagasaki interpreter who purchased an *ama-ryū* from the Dutch in the early eighteenth century. This one was four feet long, very fierce: it eventually killed the interpreter. In 1759 an *ama-ryū* was exhibited, pickled in a bottle, at a medical meeting in Edo. It was two feet long, and had been imported by the Dutch *c.* 1680, and kept in their factory at Nagasaki for many years until its death (see *Goi Kōshō*, 'Hikui-dori to Ama-ryū').

[18] *Hikui-dori*, 'fire-eating bird', was also a creature imported by the Dutch, a speciality of the island of Ceram. It ate stones and burning charcoal, in addition to the more usual fare of plants and insects (see *Sansai Zue*, XLIV). Engelbert Kaempfer, the German physician of the Dutch East India Company's factory at Nagasaki, recording his impressions of the exhibitions of 'uncommon or monstrous animals' in Ōsaka, when visiting that city in 1691, says: 'Some years ago our East India company sent over from Batavia a *Casuar* (a large East India bird, who would swallow stones and hot coals) as a present to the Emperor. This bird having had the ill luck not to please our rigid censors, the governors of Nagasaki, to whom it belongs to determine what presents might be the most acceptable to the Emperor, and we having thereupon been ordered to send him back to Batavia, a rich Japanese and a great lover of these curiosities assured us that, if he could have obtained leave to buy him, he would willingly have given a thousand *Thails* for him, as being sure within a year's time to get double that money only by shewing him at Osacca.' (E. Kaempfer, *The History of Japan* (1727), V, 9.)

BOOK V, 2 (pp. 108–115)

[1] *Hito no kasegi wa haya-kawa no mizu-guruma no gotoku:* the opening phrase, repeated verbatim in a later story about Yodo (Tr. VI, 4, p. 140), contains an indirect reference to the large irrigation water-wheel of Yodo castle.

[2] *Kake-gin:* the collection of debts at New Year in Kyōto is the principal topic of the present story. The section on the rise of the oil merchant Yamazakiya, though occupying a central position, has no close connection with the main theme.

[3] *Mujō wo kan-zuru koto nakare:* lit. 'do not reflect on the impermanence of this life'. Cf. *Tsurezure-gusa*, 217, where a rich man gives the identical advice: *kari ni mo mujō wo kan-zuru koto nakare.*

[4] *Matsubara koete:* a phrase from the song of the *Ise-odori*, which was perhaps used for the dancing at *Bon.*

[5] *Matsu no uchi:* at this time it was customary to display the pine decorations at the door from New Year's Day until the fifteenth.

[6] *Yodo no sato:* present Yodo-*machi*, Kuse-*gun*, Kyōto-*fu.*

[7] *Yamazakiya tote:* nothing is known of Yamazakiya. His trade name is presumably taken from Yamazaki-*mura* (present Ō-yamazaki-*mura*), a few miles south-west of Yodo, which was noted for the manufacture of oil.

[8] *Misugi no tane...kashoku no tsuchi:* mallets pounding rape-seeds for oil. There is a play in this passage on the word *tane*, which means 'seeds', 'a start in life' or 'business capital'. Saikaku frequently plays upon the various meanings of *tane*—see e.g. Tr. V, 1, p. 107 (see also Com. III, 2, n. 2).

[9] *Takara-dera:* the popular name for the Hōshaku-*ji*, Ō-yamazaki-*mura*, Kyōto-*fu.*

[10] *Ko-bashi:* the smaller of the two bridges at Yodo. It spanned the Uji river (the northern continuation of the Yodo river).

[11] *Ami nōte fuchi wo nozoki:* a reference to the proverb, *Ami nōte fuchi wo nozoku na*, 'If you have no net, don't gaze into pools'.

[12] *Mida Jirō:* an abbreviation of *Amida Jirō*, here used as the name of the fisherman Jirō. It is also used to mean the bronze Amida Buddha which Jirō caught in his net, and which became the principal Buddha of the Saihō-*ji*, a temple near the present Uji-*shi*, Kyōto-*fu.* Jirō was a disreputable character who had earned himself the name of 'Wicked Jirō' (*Aku-Jirō*), but after catching his Buddha he even repented of killing fish, and became a priest. (See *Ōyabu*, p. 454.)

[13] *Oso-ushi mo Yodo-guruma no mawari:* a reference to the proverb, *Oso-ushi mo Yodo, haya-ushi mo Yodo*, 'Slow oxen reach Yodo, quick oxen reach Yodo'. *Yodo* is here used as a pivot word, serving to conclude the above proverb and start the reference to the Yodo water-wheel. (For the water-wheel see n. 1, above.)

[14] *Koi-funa:* carp and gibel (or 'crucian') were both noted products of Yodo.

[15] *Yodo no Shaka-Jirō:* a variation on Amida Jirō (see n. 12, above).

[16] *Tanba, Ōmi yori...koi-funa:* carp from the Ōi river, which rose in Tanba province, and from lake Biwa in Ōmi province. The carp of both these places were noted for their excellent flavour, but came second to those caught in the Yodo river.

[17] *Sashimi.*

[18] *Shinzaike:* the name of a district west of the emperor's palace, near the present Chōja-*machi*. At this time it was a district of doctors, *renga* teachers, and Noh musicians.

[19] *Aburaya-ginu...Kenbō zome:* the first is not clear. *Kenbō-zome* was a type of dark brown dye, the process for which appears to have been invented by a Kyōto dyer called *Kenbō*.

[20] *Un wa ten ni, gusoku wa shichiya ni:* a verbal play on the proverb, *Un wa ten ni ari*, 'Luck is in heaven', i.e. luck is beyond our control.

[21] *Shō no tsugomori:* the last day of a twenty-nine-day month. In the Japanese lunar calendar there were two types of month, *dai no tsuki* (thirty days) and *shō no tsuki* (twenty-nine days), but their times of occurrence varied from year to year.

[22] *Usuyuki, Ise Monogatari no sōshi:* the *Usuyuki Monogatari*, first published in 1632 and frequently republished in the seventeenth century, described the love affair between a young *samurai* and the daughter of a court noble, Usuyuki-*hime*. The heroine dies while her lover is away on a journey, and the young man retires from the world heart-broken. The author is unknown. The greater part of the story is told in the form of letters between Usuyuki and her lover, and the work is the earliest example in Japanese literature of the epistolary novel. It is interesting to note that it antedates Richardson's *Pamela* (1740) by more than a hundred years.

For *Ise Monogatari*, see Com. II, 1, n. 11.

[23] *Nishijin no kinu-ori-ya:* Nishijin is a district in Kamikyō-*ku*, Kyōto-*shi*. Its importance as a centre for the silk-weaving industry dates from the latter part of the sixteenth century, and has been maintained to this day.

BOOK V, 3 (pp. 115–119)

[1] *Higashi-akari no Asahi no sato:* Asahi is part of the present Asawa-*mura*, Yamabe-*gun*, Nara-*ken*. I have not translated the epithet *higashi-akari no* (of eastern light) which is prefixed to *Asahi no sato*, as this is a play upon the meaning of *asahi* (morning sun) which would be lost in English. The phrase *higashi-akari no asahi* also refers to the work on the Yamato loom, suggesting that it starts as soon as the sun rises.

[2] *Tsuno-ya-zukuri*, 'a horn-shaped structure', presumably refers to the

common arrangement of farm buildings in which the main house has sheds or barns protruding from either end like horns. The word *tsuno* (horns) has a *haikai* significance here as a related-word (*engo*) to oxen.

[3] *Kawabata no Kusuke:* nothing is known of the man himself. *Kawabata* is the name of a district in Asahi, Asawa-*mura*. There is a stone lantern on the Hase-*kaidō* known as the *Mamen-tōrō* which is possibly the *Mame-tōrō* (Lantern of Beans) of Kusuke. As for his 'inventions', there is no corroboration from any source that Kusuke was the originator of the agricultural implements mentioned in this story—though Saikaku is possibly faithfully following a local tradition. (See *Goi-Kōshō*, 'Hase-kaidō no Mame-tōrō'.)

[4] *Arakane...ashibiki:* the epithets prefixed to 'earth' and *Yamato* are traditional *makura-kotoba*—a form of 'Homeric epithet' commonly used in Japanese poetry from the very earliest days. The precise meanings of most of these *makura-kotoba* are not known.

[5] *Iwashi no kashira, hiragi:* on the night of *Setsubun* (corresponding to New Year's Eve) it was customary to hang holly or the heads of dried sardines before the windows and doors to ward off evil spirits. The holly was said to pierce the devils' eyes, but it is not clear what function the sardine heads performed. For the throwing of beans at *Setsubun* see Com. IV, 1, n. 9.

[6] *Moshi iri-mame ni hana no saku koto mo ya:* proverb, *Iri-mame ni hana no saku*, 'Blossoms from a toasted bean', i.e. a miracle, or a distinct improbability.

[7] *Hachijū-hachi koku:* for the auspicious nature of the figure eighty-eight, see Com. I, 2, n. 6. Kusuke also dies at the age of eighty-eight.

[8] *Hase-kaidō:* the road from Nara-*shi* to Hase-*machi*, Shiki-*gun*, Nara-*ken*. It was the route frequently followed by pilgrims to Hase-*dera*. (For Hase-*dera* see Com. III, 3, n. 15.)

[9] *Komazarae... Tōmino, Sengoku-dōshi... Goke-daoshi:* for details and illustrations of these various agricultural instruments see *Sansai Zue*, XXXV, 'Komazarae'; 'Tōmi'; 'Sengoku-dōshi'; 'Goke-daoshi'. The 'Widow's Downfall' (*Goke-daoshi*) is so named because it reduces the opportunities of employment for women. (See *Goi Kōshō*, 'Goke-daoshi'.) The 'whipping' process—sometimes called 'bowing'—removed foreign matter from the ginned cotton, and to a certain extent separated the fibres.

[10] *Tō-yumi:* see *Sansai Zue*, XXXVI, where it is stated that the implement may have been introduced into Japan, via Nagasaki, by a Chinese in the Myōreki era (1655–8).

[11] *Uchi-wata iku-maru ka Edo ni mawashi:* presumably through the brokers at Kyōbashi, Ōsaka (see n. 13, below).

[12] *Hirano-mura:* the present Hirano-gō-*machi*, Sumiyoshi-*ku*, Ōsaka-*shi*. In Tokugawa times it was outside the Ōsaka boundary, situated at a point where roads from Yamato and Kawachi provinces into Ōsaka converged. It was noted for its cotton brokers, and the special scale of weights used in Japan for cotton was called *Hirano-me*.

[13] *Ōsaka no Kyōbashi:* the present Kyōbashi-*chō*, Higashi-*ku*, Ōsaka-*shi*. Cotton brought down the Yodo river into Ōsaka from Ōmi, Yamato, Kawachi and other nearby provinces was dealt with by the brokers of this district. Cotton for Edo was usually forwarded through the brokers of Kyōbashi.

[14] *Tondaya, Zeniya:* in *Naniwa Suzume* (1679) Tondaya Kurōbei and Zeniya Jinbei are listed as cotton brokers of Kyōbashi.

[15] *Tennōjiya:* possibly a cotton broker offshoot of the famous *ryōgaeya* firm of Tennōjiya (see Tr. I, 3, p. 24).

[16] *Sekka ryōgoku no kiwata:* Settsu province cotton was recognised as of superlative quality. That of Kawachi stood third in the list (see *Sansai Zue*, XCIV, 'Kusa-wata').

[17] *Aki-fuyu sukoshi no ma ni:* the cotton was gathered in autumn, and the 'whipping' (*wata wo utsu*) season would last from then until winter.

[18] *Jū gatsu jū-go nichi:* the fifteenth of the tenth moon was the end of the ten nights of the *nenbutsu* changing (*jū-ya nenbutsu*) performed by members of the Jōdo sect of Buddhism in celebration of Amida Buddha's attainment of enlightenment.

[19] *Ariwara-dera:* the present Honkōmyō-*ji*, Tanba-ichi-*machi*, Yamabe-*gun*, Nara-*ken*, a few miles north of Asahi.

[20] *Miwa no mura:* present Miwa-*machi*, Shiki-*gun*, Nara-*ken*.

[21] *Kuwa no ki no shumoku-zue:* the use of mulberry wood walking-sticks or chopsticks was reputed to be beneficial for palsy sufferers.

[22] *Shimo-ichi:* present Shimo-ichi-*machi*, Yoshimo-*gun*, Nara-*ken*.

[23] *Oka-dera:* the vicinity of the Ryūgai-*ji* (Oka-*dera*), Taka-ichi-*mura*, Taka-ichi-*gun*, Nara-*ken*.

[24] *Yakunen:* for the 'evil years' of a man's life see Com. V, I, n. 13. Presumably the urge to buy silk underwear is one of the temptations which beset a man at the dangerous age of forty-two.

[25] *Tafu-no-mine no fumoto-mura, Niōdō to iu tokoro:* the present Niōdō-*mura*, west of Sakurai-*machi*, Shiki-*gun*, Nara-*ken*. It is some miles from the foot of Tafu-*no-mine* (now pronounced *Tō-no-mine*). In *Kōshoku Ichidai Otoko*, II, I, it is mentioned as a haunt of *tobi-ko* (see n. 26, below).

[26] *Tobi-ko:* lit. 'jumping boys'. These young boys were nominally trainees for the *kabuki* stage, but in reality they were male prostitutes, travelling about the country in troupes.

[27] *Nara Kitsuji:* present Higashi-Kitsuji-*machi*, a southern district of Nara-*shi*. It was a well-known licensed quarter in Tokugawa times.

[28] *Hiki-bune:* lit. 'boats in tow'—courtesans of the third grade detailed to attend upon a *tayū*. The term also suggests, here, being towed in a boat from Japan to China—or from the *tayū* called 'Japan' to the one called 'China'.

[29] *Ima no miyako no Wakoku, Morokoshi:* 'the Kyōto *tayū* at present holding the names of *Wakoku* (Japan) and *Morokoshi* (China)'. This part of the story is evidently near-contemporary with the time of writing, since a *tayū* would not hold her hereditary name for much more than ten years. They are, perhaps the Wakoku and Morokoshi whose charms and accomplishments are outlined respectively in the Shimabara guide-books *Sujaku Tōmegane* (1681) and *Sujaku Shinobu-zuri* (1687). Both were in the establishment of Ichimonjiya Shichirōbei. For Madam Morokoshi see also Tr. I, 2, p. 19.

[30] *Tō-ichi no mura:* present Tō-ichi-*mura*, Shiki-*gun*, Nara-*ken*.

[31] *Ōsaka no Dōtonbori:* for the Ōsaka entertainment centre of Dōtonbori see Com. III, 4, n. 6.

BOOK V, 4 (pp. 120–123)

[1] *Koto-bure: Shintō* priests of the Kashima-*jingū* who toured the country collecting funds for the shrine in return for forecasts of disasters, good harvests, etc., which were reputed to have been made by the god of Kashima at New Year. By Saikaku's time, however, the majority of people calling themselves *Kashima no koto-bure* were probably beggars unconnected with the shrine, collecting funds for themselves. (See *Kinmō Zui*, 'Kanjin-morai no bu': 'koto-bure'.)

Kashima-*jingū* is in the present Kashima-*machi*, Kashima-*gun*, Ibaraki-*ken*. The god worshipped at the shrine is Take-mikazuchi-*no-kami*.

[2] *Kaname-ishi:* the 'pivot-stone' (also called *mimashi-ishi*, 'the august sitting stone') still exists in the grounds of Kashima-*jingū*. The god of the shrine is reputed to have alighted on it when he first descended from the heavens. Saikaku here parodies a song connected with this stone: 'Earthquakes may rage, but as long as the god of Kashima exists the pivot-stone will never be dislodged.' (See *Sansai Zue*, LXVI, 'Kaname-ishi'.)

[3] *Kasegu ni oi-tsuku binbō nashi:* 'No poverty can overtake work'—a proverb.

[4] *Aoto Saemon:* Saemon-no-jō Fujitsuna, a military administrator of the Kamakura shogunate. His exploits are mentioned frequently in such semi-fictional works as *Taihei Ki*, but his name does not appear in any historical records of the time. The story to which Saikaku alludes is to be found in *Taihei Ki*, XXV.

[5] *Saimyōji:* Saimyōji Hōjō Tokiyori (1227–63), the fifth of the Hōjō regents of the Kamakura period.

[6] *Matsu, sakura, mume wo kitte:* a reference to the Noh play *Hachi no Ki* (*c.* 1363–1443), which relates how Hōjō Tokiyori, disguised as a priest, sought shelter in a snow-storm at the house of Sano Tsuneyo. As it was snowing too hard to gather firewood, Tsuneyo used instead the valuable potted dwarf trees inside his house. He was later richly rewarded with land by Tokiyori.

[7] *Hitachi no kuni ni...Kogane-ga-hara:* present Kogane-*machi*, Higashi Katsushika-*gun*, Chiba-*ken*. Saikaku is mistaken in saying that it was in Hitachi province. It was in the neighbouring province of Shimōsa.

[8] *Higurashi no nanigashi:* the name *Higurashi* appears on the death-roll of a temple in Kogane-*machi* for the year 1706. It is also the name of a neighbouring district. The career of Higurashi, as related by Saikaku, has several parallels with that of a celebrated *chōja* of fiction, Bunshō the salt merchant of Kashima-*jingū*, whose success story is told in the Muromachi romance *Bunshō-zōshi* (see *Ōyabu*, pp. 511–12). It seems probable that this is another instance of the *haikai* technique of oblique reference noted in Com. III, 2, n. 6.

[9] *Zeni sanjū-shichi kan:* 37,000 *zeni* = approximately 9 *ryō* or 540 *monme*. (See App. I, p. 238.)

[10] *Rōnin:* former *samurai* no longer on the pay-roll of a feudal lord. It is estimated that as a result of the redistribution or confiscation of fiefs by the *Bakufu*, the number of *rōnin* had reached about four hundred thousand by the middle of the seventeenth century (*Nihon Shi Jiten*, 'Rōnin'). Some of these, particularly the more literate, adapted themselves to their new civilian surroundings (see, e.g., the number of ex-*samurai* in the list of professional teachers of the arts in Com. II, 3, n. 21), but the majority remained without regular employment. They were naturally ill-disposed towards the Tokugawa family, who had deprived them of their livings, and there was a constant danger that they might engineer a revolt. They had already fought against *Bakufu* forces in large numbers at the Ōsaka campaign (1615) and the Shimabara insurrection (1637). After the abortive *rōnin* plot of Yui Shōsetsu in 1651, the *Bakufu* issued strict regulations that no *rōnin* was to be afforded lodgings in the cities.

[11] *Shi-sho: Ssu-shu*, the four classical Confucianist texts: *Ta-hsüeh* (The Great Learning); *Lun-yü* (The Analects); *Chung-yung* (The Doctrine of the Mean); *Mêng-tzŭ* (The Book of Mencius).

[12] *Sanya:* the site of the new Yoshiwara brothel quarter in Edo, erected in 1657, after the destruction of the old Yoshiwara quarter in the great fire of that year. Present Asakusa Sanya-*chō*, Daitō-*ku*, Tōkyō-*to*.

[13] *Rōnin-aratame:* these examinations and expulsions (also called *rōnin-barai*) were carried out periodically by the *Bakufu* or by individual *daimyō* in their domains.

[14] *Taiheiki no kanjin-yomi:* a type of beggar who recited passages from the *Taihei Ki* or similar military romances. Also called *Taiheiki-yomi*. (See *Jinrin Kinmō Zui*, VII, 'Kanjin-morai no bu': 'Taiheiki-yomi'.)

[15] *Kanda no Sujikai-bashi:* present Mansei bridge, Chiyoda-*ku*.

[16] *Ta-machi:* present Asukusa Ta-*machi*, Daitō-*ku*.

[17] *Kuchi-zamisen:* nasal intonation of a *samisen* accompaniment, employing the appropriate *iroha* syllable or syllables for each note. These

syllables, when sung with the correct pitch and exact time-values, form a precise musical notation for the *samisen*. By themselves (i.e. when not sung) they indicate which of the three strings to play, whether the string is open or stopped, approximate time-values, rests, 'portamento', and whether to pluck with finger or plectrum, or use the plectrum (as is most frequent) in a downward stroke.

[18] *Shiba no Jinmei:* the Shiba-*dai-jingū*, present Jinmei-*chō*, Minato-*ku*, Tōkyō-*to*. The shrine is dedicated to Amaterasu-*ō-mi-kami*.

[19] *Matakurō ga shibai:* Bandō Matakurō, the leader of a theatrical troupe in Sakai-*chō*, Edo.

[20] *Ō-botoke:* a group of large Buddhas before the Nyorai-*ji*, a temple in the southern precincts of the Sengaku-*ji*, present Minato-*ku*, Tōkyō-*to*.

BOOK V, 5 (pp. 123–126)

[1] *Mannen-goyomi:* (lit. ten-thousand-year calendars) almanacs from which predictions for any year could be calculated. Since each year was assigned to one of the five elements (*go-gyō*)—wood, fire, earth, gold, water—a harmonious marriage could be predicted if the birth-year elements of the parties concerned were not mutually antagonistic (as, for instance, are fire and wood). Editions of these almanacs are frequently named in seventeenth-century book catalogues. (See *Ōyabu*, p. 513.)

[2] *Koi no kawa:* the river Waké. *Koi* (love) suggests *wake*, which is the word for services rendered in a brothel. The upper reaches of the river Waké (more commonly known as the river Yoshii) are in the north-east of the present Okayama-*ken*. The northern section of Okayama-*ken* is the old Mimasaka province.

[3] *Kume no Sarayama:* present Sara-*mura*, south-west of Tsuyama-*shi*, Kume-*gun*, Okayama-*ken*.

[4] *Zōgō:* a rich merchant of Tsuyama (present Tsuyama-*shi*, Okayama-*ken*). (See *Goi Kōshō*, 'Zōgō'.)

[5] *Yorozuya to iu mono:* nothing is known of this Yorozuya.

[6] *Nabaya-dono:* presumably a reference to the parent house of the well-known Nabaya family of merchants who were active in Kyōto approximately 1630 to 1730. The founder of the family fortune was Nabaya Kurōzaemon, a native of Naba harbour in Harima province (part of the present Aioi-*shi*, Hyōgo-*ken*). The rise and fall of the Nabaya fortunes is outlined in *Kōken Roku*, 'Nabaya'. Aboshi is about eight miles east of Naba harbour.

The *Nabaya* who features as one of the three millionaires of *Chōja Kyō* is possibly Nabaya Kurōzaemon (see App. 2, pp. 239–40).

[7] *Tabi-ko:* (lit. travelling boys). These are the same as *tobi-ko* (see Com. v, 3, n. 26).

[8] *Koi ni hokorobi, hari wo kura: hokorobi* (to tear) and *hari* (a sewing-needle) are related-words (*engo*). For the proverbial expression *Hari wo kura ni tsumite mo tamarazu*, see Com. III, 4, n. 13.

[9] *Hito no naishō wa harimono:* 'People's finances are things of paper and paste', i.e. a hollow show—proverb (cf. Com. VI, 2, n. 13). 'Paper and paste' leads on to the remarks about paper lanterns.

[10] *Nanatsu no kane:* bells indicating the beginning of number 7 time-division. Roughly 4 a.m. (see Com. II, 5, n. 16).

[11] *Waka-ebisu:* wood-block prints of Ebisu, sold in the streets at New Year. Ebisu is invariably depicted with an *eboshi* hat (see Com. II, 4, n. 19).

[12] *San monme go fun no mame-ita:* about two hundred *zeni*'s worth of silver. (See App. I, p. 238.)

BOOK VI, 1 (pp. 129–132)

[1] *Morokoshi Fun-ō:* that king Wên of the Chou dynasty kept birds and beasts in a large reserve, seventy leagues square, is mentioned by Mencius (*Meng-tzŭ, Liang Hui Wang*, II).

[2] *Echizen no kuni Tsuruga:* present Tsuruga-*shi*, Fukui-*ken*. See Com. IV, 4, n. 2.

[3] *Toshigoshiya no nanigashi:* no identification is attempted by commentators. *Toshi-goshi* means 'passing from the old year into the new', and the name presumably derived from the holly tree in his garden. For the connection between holly and New Year's Eve see n. 12, below.

[4] *Tama-matsuri:* 'the festival of departed spirits' in the seventh moon: *Bon*. At this time each household placed offerings of food before the family Buddhist shrine. The offerings—boiled rice, rice-cakes, various fruits, beans, etc.—were set out on lotus leaves (*hasu-no-ha*).

[5] *Kuko:* a common shrub with a pale purple flower. Its berries were used for medicinal purposes. Its leaves could be eaten or used as a substitute for tea. Toshigoshiya's attitude to gardens is very similar to that of Fuji-ichi in Tr. II, 1, p. 38.

[6] *Ukogi:* a bush with pale green flowers, often used for hedgerows. Its leaves could be eaten or used as a tea-substitute, and its roots were said to have medicinal virtues.

[7] *Hagi:* 'lespedeza', a flowering bush with no practical application.

[8] *Kaza-guruma:* 'windmill flower', a garden vine bearing large eight-petalled flowers resembling toy windmills.

[9] *Jū-hachi-sasage:* 'eighteen-pea', a leguminous plant noted for the length of its pods, some of which may contain as many as eighteen peas.

[10] *Kurage-oke:* certain types of jelly-fish (*kurage*) were dried and preserved in salt as a food. After being soaked in water and softened, they were cut into fine strips and served with vinegar.

[11] *Tadebo:* also called *hosoba-tade*, a type of smartweed used as a pungent flavouring in various Japanese dishes.

[12] *Oni no me-tsuko:* lit. 'let's pierce the devils' eyes', a popular name for holly (*hiiragi*). Holly and sardine heads were hung over the doors and windows of houses at *Setsubun* (New Year's Eve) to bar the entrance of evil spirits (cf. Tr. v, 3, p. 115).

[13] *Seken wo shiranedomo:* a rich man would normally be expected to present at least a gold *koban* to his son's bride, but Toshigoshiya thinks that even a silver *chōgin* is too much, and further suggests that *zeni* might create a better impression. The contrast suggested in *shiranedomo*, 'he knew nothing of etiquette, but...', is not logically pursued in the remainder of the sentence, and I have accordingly omitted it.

[14] *Kono ie yori tanomi wo ogori no hajime toshite:* it is apparent that soon after the son's marriage the old man retires from business and his son becomes the active head of the Toshigoshiya firm. This step in the story is omitted by Saikaku.

BOOK VI, 2 (pp. 132–137)

[1] *Mi-tatete yōshi ga rihatsu:* the title refers to the central episode, but it is a mistake to regard this as the crux of the whole, and the remainder as 'padding'. The structure follows the complex pattern we have observed in other stories in *Eitai-gura* (see Com. v, 1, n. 1), and the transitions from topic to topic are reminiscent of the transitions of *haikai* linked verse. There is a unity of place—Edo; and a broad unity of theme—the methods and approach necessary if one is to succeed in Edo. The internal movement may be outlined as follows:

(i) Remarks on the necessity for a certain amount of deceit in business introduce the story of an Edo *rōnin* who was consistently truthful.

(ii) The topic of false statements leads on naturally to a story connected with the festival of Ebisu—the festival at which merchants seek absolution for the year's false statements. The scene is Edo, and the story introduces the 'boy from Ise', who demonstrates to his master that the opportunities for making money in Edo are far greater than he had assumed.

(iii) The episode of the 'boy from Ise' ends, and a short parallel success story, that of a man who lived in the same district in Edo, further points the moral that the opportunities exist for those who have the genius to seize them. But it is emphasised that for the ordinary man, unlike the hero of this last story, the only hope of acquiring such wealth is to start with a moderate inherited fortune.

(iv) A man in Kyōto starts with an inherited fortune, but whereas the 'boy from Ise' increased his tenfold in fifteen years, this man loses his completely in the same time. He is a typical Kyōto aesthete—not an Edo man at all, as he discovers when he comes to Edo to find employment.

(v) The Kyōto man has neglected trade for artistic accomplishments, and the story is rounded off with a moral in the *Chōja Kyō* tradition, spoken by an unnamed millionaire.

The story, it should be noted, begins and ends with failures. This outline, of course, conveys no impression of the story itself. It merely shows the mechanism which maintains the flow, and even the morals—which figure so largely in a bald outline of the structure—are little more than convenient aids to inspiration.

[2] *Kanda no Myōjin:* present Kanda-*jinsha*, Kanda, Miyamoto-*chō*, Chiyoda-*ku*, Tōkyō-*to*.

[3] *Ie ni tsue tsuku koro:* the age of fifty, when it is permissible, according to the Chinese rules of etiquette set out in the 'Record of Rites' (*Li Chi*, *Wang chih*, v), for a man to start using a stick within the privacy of his own home. Not until sixty may he use one in public.

[4] *Setomono-mise bakari:* the word *mise* here performs a dual function, first as the termination of *setomono-mise*, 'a crockery shop', and secondly as the opening of the phrase *mise-bakari*, 'for appearances' sake only'.

[5] *Ebisu-kō:* the festival of the merchants' god Ebisu Saburō-*dono*, celebrated in Edo on the twentieth days of the tenth and first moons (hence called *Hatsuka-Ebisu*, 'twentieth-day-Ebisu'). In Kyōto and Ōsaka the first moon celebration was held on the tenth day (see *Tōka-Ebisu*, Com. II, 4, n. 14). These days were trade holidays, and in Edo, where there was no particular shrine associated with the festival, each merchant arranged a ceremony and entertainment in his own house for his employees and friends.

The purpose of the festival was to obtain absolution from Ebisu for the various false declarations which merchants were obliged to make in the course of daily business. Hence the festival was also known as *Seimon-barai* (purification from false oaths).

[6] *Hakari irazu ni:* the gold coinage of Edo was based on monetary units (*bankin*, *koban*, one-*bu* pieces), whilst the silver coinage of the *kansai* was based on weight (*kanme*, *monme*, *fun*, *rin*). (See App. I, pp. 235–6.)

[7] *Kyō no Muromachi:* Muromachi street, Kyōto-*shi*, which then contained the houses of many rich men. It is mentioned here to show that even in Muromachi street, where people could well have afforded to pay more, the proverbially stingy citizens of Kyōto were buying little slices of bream by weight. The district appears later in the story as the home of a *reki-reki hito*, 'a rich and distinguished merchant'.

[8] *Ni monme shi-go fun:* 'one-twentieth of the Edo price'. I have not translated the figures as they stand, but have given the rough proportion to the Edo price of 1 *ryō* 2 *bu*. If 1 *ryō* is taken to be 60 *monme* of silver, then 2 *monme* 5 *fun* is $\frac{1}{24}$ of 1 *ryō* 2 *bu*.

[9] *Tōri-chō Nakabashi:* the present Nakabashi Hiro-*koji*, Chūō-*ku*.

[10] *Zeni-mise:* the humblest form of *ryōgaeya*, selling *zeni* in exchange for silver or gold (see Com. I, 3, n. 29).

[11] *Ise no Yamada:* present Uji-Yamada-*shi*, Mie-*ken*, where the outer Ise shrine is situated. Since merchants coming originally from the province of Ise (*Ise-shōnin*) were celebrated in the Edo period for their business ability, diligence, and thriftiness, this precocious young boy is presumably offered by Saikaku as a representative type. The famous Mitsui family was of Ise extraction.

[12] *Gojū-hachi monme go fun:* the usual exchange rates in the seventeenth century, in Ōsaka at least, seem to have been rather higher, varying between sixty and sixty-three *monme* of silver to the gold *ryō* (see App. I, p. 238). There appears to be no exact information available for Edo exchange rates of this period.

[13] *Yo wa harimono:* 'The things of this world are of paper and paste', i.e. appearances are deceptive—proverb. Cf. Com. V, 5, n. 9.

[14] *Rihatsu naru koban:* the surface meaning of *rihatsu* is simply 'clever'; but here it is probably to be taken to imply an additional sense of 'interest-making'—the sense of the two Chinese characters which form the compound.

[15] *Dangi:* sermons elucidating passages from Buddhist sutras became extremely popular in Tokugawa times. They were delivered at temples of all sects, but most frequently at those of the Jōdo sect. (See *Ōyabu*, p. 547.)

[16] *Setai-buppō:* a reference to the proverb, *Setai-buppō, hara-nenbutsu*, 'Buddhism for worldly ends, prayers for the stomach'.

[17] *Ukiyo sanshō:* possibly *sanshō* (an aromatic condiment, similar to pepper) wrapped in rolls of edible seaweed (*kobu-maki*). See *Shōgatsu-zoroi* (1688), VII: 'Spiced seaweed: useful for keeping the eyes open during sermons.' *Ukiyo* was a common prefix at this time (cf. *ukiyo* patterns, Tr. I, 4, p. 26).

[18] *Gyōzui-bune:* 'bath-house boats' appear to have been fairly common by 1688, when they are mentioned in *Irozato Mitokoro-zetai* (1688), III. That these boats and the subsequently mentioned articles were all invented by the unnamed hero of this story is, of course, improbable. But Saikaku may be following a popular tradition.

[19] *Reigan-jima ni inkyo shite:* Reigan-*jima* is a district in the present Chūō-*ku*, Tōkyō-*to*, near Eitai bridge. It forms an island, bounded on three sides by canals, and by the Sumida river on the other. Until Meiji times it was a quiet residential quarter.

It would appear from this passage that the young man from Ise retires at the age of twenty-eight. Saikaku's adverse comments on *waka-inkyo* ('premature pensioners'—see Tr. IV, 1, p. 84) presumably do not apply to a man of such outstanding ability.

[20] *Sanmonjiya to ieru hito:* Sanmonjiya Tsunesada of Tōri-*chō*, an exceedingly thrifty merchant of the mid-seventeenth century, mentioned in *Kōken Roku*, III, is possibly the Sanmonjiya of Nakabashi (in Tōri-*chō*) whose career Saikaku here outlines. Saikaku's Sanmonjiya seems to be the reverse of cautious and thrifty, however.

[21] *Kaichū-kappa:* raincoats (*kappa*=Spanish 'capa') were usually of oiled paper, like umbrellas. 'Riding capes' (*ba-dōgu*) were made for travellers along the Tōkai-*dō* and similar highways, to protect both the rider and his baggage.

[22] *Shōshō-hi:* (here lit. 'orang-outang red', but elsewhere, in some cases, written with the characters for 'orang-outang skin') was a type of deep red imported woollen fabric (see *Sansai Zue*, XXVII, 'Rasha'). Saikaku here means the woollen cloth, but by coupling it with 'tiger skins' he humorously implies that the cloth is actually the skin of the beast. To the contemporary Japanese, orang-outangs were in the fabulous monster category. They had completely human faces covered by a mop of long hair, spoke like children, drank *sake*, and wore straw sandals (see *Sansai Zue*, XL, 'Shōshō', where there is also an illustration).

[23] *Ki-rasha* has the double significance of 'yellow woollen fabrics' and 'never out of stock' (*kirashi ya*, suggesting *kirasanu*).

[24] *Zengorō:* Daikokuya Zengorō, of Muromachi street, Kyōto, a leading *ryōgaeya* of Kanbun times (1661–73). (See *Kōken Roku*, II, 'Ryōgaeya Zengorō'.)

[25] *Nihyaku sanjū-go monme:* approximately six *ryō*.

[26] *Utai wa sanbyaku gojū-ban:* the present canon consists of about two hundred plays. The repertoire in the seventeenth century appears to have been much broader.

[27] *Go-futatsu:* a grading corresponding to the modern *go-dan* (fifth step).

[28] *Murasaki no koshi:* the right to wear purple *hakama* (overskirts) while playing *kemari* was awarded by various recognised specialists to those who had reached a high degree of skill in the game. For *kemari* see Com. I, 3, n. 22.

[29] *Kanagaki-gurai:* the *kanagaki* grade in miniature archery (written more usually with the characters for 'golden shell', and pronounced *kana-gai*) was the highest, awarded to those who averaged one hundred and fifty hits or more with two hundred arrows. For *yōkyū* (miniature archery) see Com. I, 3, n. 22.

[30] *Hon-te:* seven of the earliest collections of *samisen* pieces (*hon-te-gumi*), which represent the orthodox style of composition. They date from the early seventeenth century.

[31] *Yamamoto Kaku-dayū:* a Kyōto *jōruri* reciter, active in the last quarter of the seventeenth century.

[32] *Rikyū:* (d. 1591), also called *Sen-sōeki*. The founder of the Senke school of the tea ceremony.

[33] *Kagura, Gansai:* Kagura Shōzaemon and Gansai Yashichi, two well-known brothel entertainers of the Kyōto Shimabara quarter (see Com. I, 2, n. 24).

[34] *Makura-gaeshi:* a party game.

[35] *Inishie Dennai:* a juggler and manager of a theatre in Sakai-*chō*, Edo, in Enpō-Jōkyō times (1673–88), who started his career in Kyōto. His name was at first simply *Dennai*, but when Miyako Dennai opened a rival theatre in Sakai-*chō*, he changed it to *Inishie Dennai* (*inishie* = the original).

[36] *Renpai no tōryū:* the *Danrin haikai* style of Nishiyama Sōin and Saikaku himself.

[37] *Matsu-bayashi:* (lit. pine-music) annual New Year performances of Noh and dancing, taking place from the third to the fifteenth of the first moon. These performances were held alike at court, in military households, and among the ordinary people.

BOOK VI, 3 (pp. 137–139)

[1] *Senshū Sakai:* present Sakai-*shi*, Ōsaka-*fu*. Descriptions of Sakai and its people, similar to the one in this story, are to be found in Tr. IV, 5, pp. 98, 101. (See also Com. II, 3, n. 20.)

[2] *Kogatanaya tote Nagasaki-akindo:* a merchant called Kogatanaya Tarōzaemon appears in *Ito Ran Ki* (1719) as one of a number of Sakai dealers in imported silk who were active in 1685. There is possibly a connection with the Kogatanaya of Saikaku's story.

[3] *Shijū igo:* forty was assumed to be the beginning of old age (see Com. III, 1, n. 3).

[4] *Meibutsu no sho-dōgu:* the citizens of Sakai were noted for their interest in the tea ceremony. Rikyū, founder of the Senke school of tea, was a native of Sakai.

[5] *Kanei nenjū:* the Kanei period is 1624–44. The meaning here is presumably that these merchants were using only the money which their forebears had made prior to this time. Sakai's profits from foreign trade after Kanei 12 (1635) would be considerable since it was in that year that the *ito-wappu* ('silk licence) system was initiated, whereby the right to deal in raw silk imports, the most important of all commodities from overseas in early Tokugawa times, was limited to corporations of merchants in the five cities of Edo, Kyōto, Ōsaka, Nagasaki and Sakai (see *Nihon Shi Jiten*, 'Ito-wappu').

[6] *Jū-shi no yome-iri:* fourteen was a not unusual age for a girl to be married (cf. Chūsuke's daughter, Tr. III, 5, p. 77).

[7] *Hi-rinzu.*

[8] *Kachi-isha:* (lit. walking-doctor) a successful doctor would normally make his visits in a palanquin, as appears later in the story.

[9] *Gin hyaku-mai:* the weight of a hundred *chōgin* of silver would be about four *kanme*, three hundred *monme*, more than a tenth of Kogatanaya's fortune at that time (see App. 1, p. 235).

BOOK VI, 4 (pp. 140–143)

[1] *Shindai katamaru Yodo-gawa no urushi:* the moral of this story appears to be that men should work for their fortunes 'by orthodox methods' (not swindling or relying on luck), and that they should be constantly on guard against the pitfalls by which modern business is beset. The watchword is caution. As is frequently the case, however, the moral is difficult to disentangle from the other elements, and one receives the impression that its chief function is as a connecting link. The structure and continuity might be summarised as follows:

(i) Work unremittingly, like the Yodo water-wheel.
(ii) A Yodo merchant's fortuitous success.
(iii) Fortunes through luck are no more deserved than fortunes through swindling. A fortune should be made in the orthodox way by economy and honesty.
(iv) Surrounded as you are by confidence tricksters you must watch your money carefully. These are days of big profits, but, for the unwary, equally big losses.
(v) With this in mind, leave nothing to chance, lay the foundations firm, and avoid extravagant spending.
(vi) The merchant of Yodo is ruined by extravagant spending.

[2] *Hito no kasegi wa haya-kawa no mizu-guruma no gotoku...:* the opening phrases are largely a repetition of those in a previous story connected with Yodo, Tr. v, 2, p. 108. The water-wheel was a feature of Yodo castle.

[3] *Oi no nami tatsu Yodo: nami* (waves) is a pivot word, the metaphorical *oi no nami* (waves of old age, i.e. wrinkles) providing an opportunity for quick transition to the topic of *nami tatsu Yodo* (the river Yodo, where waves rise).

[4] *Yozaemon to ieru hito:* Yozaemon is possibly an authentic character. A certain *Yodo Yozaemon* is mentioned in *Setsuyō Kikan*, xx, under the entries for the year 1685. (See *Ōyabu*, p. 571.)

[5] *Ko-bashi:* Ko bridge spanned the Uji river at Yodo. (See Com. v, 2, n. 10.)

[6] *Awa no naruto:* the whirlpools formed in the narrow straits between Awaji and Shikoku islands, at the eastern entrance to the Seto inland sea, at certain stages of the tide.

[7] *Toba no kuruma-ushi:* the ox carts along the road from Fushimi to Toba are mentioned in Tr. III, 3, p. 67.

[8] *Urushi:* a bush widely cultivated at this time as the source of natural lacquer.

[9] *Kōya-san no gin wo mawashi:* for Kōya-*san* see Com. III, 4, n. 24. For borrowing money from temples see Tr. IV, 4, p. 96.

[10] *Eta-mura:* communities of *eta* outcasts in the big cities. Although socially beyond the pale, some of the *eta* were exceedingly rich. (For the locations of *eta* communities in the large cities, their various occupations, organisation, etc., see *Kinsei Fūzoku Shi*, I, 6.)

[11] *Koto hiku onna:* for a male party *samisen*-playing courtesans might be more usual, but this is a respectable party for the wife's relations. The players of the *koto* (for which see Com. I, 3, n. 9) were usually women.

[12] *Kuchi-kiri:* see Com. III, 1, n. 16.

[13] *San-bun han:* the value of a debtor's property at the time of its surrender was usually expected to amount to thirty to forty per cent of the total debts. For this and *bunsan* (bankruptcy) in general see Com. III, 4, n. 17.

[14] *Samusa . . . kaze . . . ame futte . . . kasa:* 'colds . . . draught . . . stormy weather . . . umbrella' are all related-words (*engo*), in *haikai* style.

[15] *Ame futte tsuchi katamaru:* 'Rain falls and the earth grows harder', i.e. an unexpected outcome—a proverb.

[16] *Sashikake-gasa . . . take-tsue . . . zukin:* umbrellas held over the head by an attendant, bamboo walking-sticks, and flat caps were all emblems of affluent retirement (see Tr. IV, 1, p. 84).

[17] *Mukashi Ōtsu nite . . . :* this passage is a fairly close repetition of that in Tr. III, 4, p. 73, where the topic of bankruptcies was discussed at length. The figure for the Ōtsu bankruptcy remains the same, but those for Kyōto and Ōsaka have been stepped up from 2500–3000 *kanme* to 3500–4000 *kanme*.

[18] *Aru chōja no kotoba ni, hoshiki mono wo kawazu oshiki mono wo ure to zo:* this appears to be the only direct quotation in the book from *Chōja Kyō*. It is to be found at the end of the section entitled *Fuku no kami jū-nin mi-ko* (The God of Wealth's Ten Sons), where it is possibly a continuation of the speech of the millionaire Izumiya (see App. 2, p. 243).

[19] *Mizu-guruma kyaku wo matsu yara, kuru-kuru:* Saikaku here plays upon a refrain which appears in many popular dancing songs of the time. Perhaps the first appearance is in the Kanei period (1624–44) publication *Kabuki no Sōshi: Yodo no kawa-se no mizu-guruma, tare wo matsu yara, kuru-kuru to* (The water-wheel in the Yodo river, whom is it waiting for? She will come, she will come—and round and round it goes). There is a play on the double sense of *kuru-kuru*, meaning 'round and round' and 'she will come, she will come'. Saikaku substitutes *kyaku* (guest) for *tare* (whom), thus suggesting the arrival of guests at the house. After *kyaku* the meaning of *matsu* also changes

slightly from 'wait for' to 'entertain'. (For other examples of the refrain in contemporary dancing songs see *Ōyabu*, p. 580.)

[20] *Fushimi:* present Fushimi-*ku*, Kyōto-*shi*, about four miles north-east of Yodo.

[21] *Hashimoto:* now a part of Yawata-*machi*, Kyōto-*fu*, two or three miles south-west of Yodo.

[22] *Kuzuwa:* present Kuzuwa-*mura*, a mile south of Hashimoto. Both Kuzuwa and Hashimoto were on the Kyō-*kaidō*, the road from Ōsaka to Kyōto.

[23] *Uji:* present Uji-*shi*, Kyōto-*fu*, celebrated for its high-grade tea. Five miles east of Yodo.

[24] *Matsu-no-o:* Matsu-no-o-*jinsha*, Matsu-no-o-*yama*, Ukyō-*ku*, Kyōto-*shi*, six miles north of Yodo. Its god was worshipped as the god of *sake*.

[25] *Iwa-shimizu Hachiman-gū:* a large *Shintō* shrine a few miles south of Yodo, in the present Yawata-*machi*, Kyōto-*fu*. The *ango* rites of this shrine were held annually for three days in the twelfth moon, from the thirteenth to the fifteenth days. The word *ango* is originally Buddhist, referring to a prolonged period of meditation and fasting in a Buddhist temple, and its use by a *Shintō* shrine is an example of the tendency of the times to mix the elements of Buddhism and *Shintō* together into one hybrid religion (*Shinbutsu-konkō*).

The leader (*tō*) of the *ango* rites was selected three years in advance from among the richer families of the district. His duties commenced on the first day of the twelfth moon. On the ninth he was obliged to entertain the local gentry in his house, usually providing performances of Noh or dancing. On the thirteenth he proceeded in ceremonial clothes to the shrine, where he remained in secluded prayer and fasting in the priests' quarters until the fifteenth.

[26] *Sono na wa odori-uta ni nokoreri:* in a song connected with the Yodo water-wheel, quoted in Enomoto Kikaku's *Ruikōji* (1707), I, 'Kita no mado', occurs the line, *Yozō ka mon ni tare wo matsu yara* (For whom is the water-wheel waiting, at Yozō's gate?). *Yozō ka mon* is possibly a hint at the name *Yozaemon*.

BOOK VI, 5 (pp. 143–146)

[1] *Oyoso shijū-go nen nari:* Saikaku perhaps selects the figure forty-five because that was his own age at the time of *Eitai-gura*'s composition.

[2] *Jū-shi monme go fun no toki:* the current price of one *koku* of rice was approximately forty *monme*. It is possible that Saikaku has in mind the prices of the period from 1608 to 1627 which were in the region of fifteen to sixteen *monme*. (See *Goi Kōshō*, 'Kome ikkoku jū-shichi-hachi monme no toki'.)

[3] *Odori-yukata...ushiro-obi:* the *yukata*, as its name suggests (an abbreviation of *yu-katabira*, 'light clothes for the bath'), was originally a garment

worn in the bath, in the days when Japanese were shy of appearing before each other in nakedness. From some time in the fifteenth century both men and women began to bathe in much scantier apparel, however, and later, when complete nakedness became the rule, the *yukata* was used principally as an informal dress to be donned after the evening bath (*Nihon Fukushoku Shiyō* (1949), p. 187). It also came to be used as a general garment for the hot weather, and, because of its lightness and comparative freedom, for dancing of a popular nature, such as that at *Bon*.

It seems that the *obi* (waistband) was generally tied in a bow or knot in front until Enpō times (1673–81), but that thereafter it became fashionable for the younger women to tie them behind (see *Ōyabu*, p. 223). The 'service girls' of the Abumiya broker's agency in Sakata (Tr. II, 5, p. 54) wore their *obi* bound at the back.

[4] *Saru-matsu:* a type of toy-pedlar of Enpō, Tenna and Jōkyō times (1673–88), selling monkeys on strings, straw wind-wheels, toy flutes, etc.

[5] *San monme go fun...roku monme:* I have given these figures in rough proportionate value to the fifty *zeni* mentioned earlier in the text, taking the exchange rate at 12 *monme* to 1000 *zeni*.

[6] *Kinin kōnin:* it is to be assumed from the context that Saikaku has in mind both the court and the military aristocracy, though whether *kinin* specifically refers to one, and *kōnin* to the other, is dubious. The word *kōke*, however, was sometimes used in the special sense of certain famous military families, and Saikaku's *kōnin* may possibly echo this sense.

[7] *Taishoku-kan Nai-daijin* was a title of Fujiwara Kamatari (614–69), the founder of the great noble family of Fujiwara.

[8] *Saru-mawashi.*

[9] *Sono kokoro yama no gotoku ni shite, bungen wa yoki tedai aru koto dai-ichi nari:* commentators, without exception, assume that *bungen wa* governs both these sentences, which should logically read *Bungen wa sono kokoro yama no gotoku....* It seems to the present translator, however, that Saikaku places *bungen wa* in the later position for a very good reason, and that the reason is connected with *Chōja Kyō.* Here, in the last story of his *Daifuku Shin Chōja Kyō* (the subtitle of *Eitai-gura*), he appears to have the acknowledged source of his inspiration far more in mind than in the stories occupying the middle portion of the book. The word *chōja* (millionaire) appears six times in a short space of the story, and the word *daifuku* three times. The sentence under discussion, I think, should be considered in relation to the preceding one, with which it has a *haikai* link: *daifuku wo negai, chōja to naru koto kanyō nari; sono kokoro yama no gotoku....* The related words are *daifuku*, *chōja*, and *yama*. The *yama* is the *chōja-yama* (millionaire mountain) of *Chōja Kyō* (see App. 2, p. 239), which all who aim to be millionaires must climb.

This in itself is reason enough for the late appearance of *bungen wa*, making way for a more forceful juxtaposition of *chōja* and *yama*. There are also difficulties in the last remark about clerks, however, which the commentators fail to elucidate. It seems a sad anticlimax to the rhetorical passage on money and *chōja*. Perhaps it is intended as a sly reminder that even the man with *chōja* qualities will not get far unless he is helped by able men of a humbler kind—a point which the more impassioned sections of the *chōja* creed were apt to overlook. In any case, I wonder whether *bungen* is not used here in apposition to *chōja*, in the sense of the definition given in the very first story of *Eitai-gura* (Tr. p. 16), but largely ignored thereafter.

[10] *Edo-zake: sake* manufactured in or near Ōsaka for sale in Edo. This is possibly a reference to the rich Kōnoike family of Ōsaka merchants, who started as brewers of *sake* for Edo, and later branched out into the shipping and money exchange businesses.

[11] *Akagane-yama...niwaka-bungen:* possibly Izumiya, the founder of the Sumitomo business house, which was the most important copper mining concern in Tokugawa Japan.

[12] *Yoshino-urushiya:* lacquer from the Yoshino region (in the present Nara-*ken*) was noted for its superior quality. In the Enpō era (1673–81) a group of merchants in Ōsaka were granted monopoly rights in the sale of Yoshino lacquer.

[13] *Kobaya:* speedy transport vessels running chiefly between Ōsaka and Edo. It seems that this particular type of ship first came into use in about 1660. Its cargoes were chiefly *sake*, but included a variety of other goods such as soy sauce, cotton cloth, ginned cotton, lacquer goods, and paper (see *Ōyabu*, p. 592).

[14] *Cha-ire hitotsu:* a canister of porcelain or lacquered wood used for high-grade teas. Itoya's purchase of this particular *cha-ire* is mentioned in *Kōken Roku*, I, 'Itoya Jūemon'. For Kameya, a noted collector of expensive curios, see *Ukiyo Monogatari*, I, 6.

[15] *Hachi-jū-hachi:* the auspicious nature of the number eighty-eight has already been noted (Com. I, 2, n. 6). From this list of ages it appears that the ideal age difference between a man and his wife was seven to eight years.

[16] *Tsukuri-dori dōzen:* exemption from the yearly tax on produce was sometimes granted to farmers as a reward for outstanding filial piety or other virtuous qualities (see *Ōyabu*, p. 596).

[17] *Masu-kaki:* bamboo sticks for levelling the surface of grain in the measuring boxes. (For their significance in connection with the age of eighty-eight see Com. I, 2, n. 6.)

[18] *Aru monogatari:* the *mono* of *monogatari* serves also to conclude the preceding sentence, *kingin...aru mono* (money...most certainly exists, i.e. in abundance).

[19] *Nippon Daifuku-chō ni shirushi:* here Saikaku alludes to the title and subtitle of his book. *Daifuku-chō* was an alternative name for the *dai-chō* or

principal account-book of a merchant house, and Saikaku had played upon this sense, upon *daifuku chōja* (a great millionaire), and upon *Chōja Kyō*, in his subtitle *Daifuku Shin Chōja Kyō*. The *Nippon* of the main title *Nippon Eitai-gura* is introduced at the same time, and is capped later in the sentence by *Eitai-gura*.

[20] *Osamaru toki tsu mi-kuni shizuka nari:* lit. 'the august country which has now been securely settled is peaceful'. This concluding phrase, a reference to the blessings of peace and security brought by the Tokugawa government, has no logical connection with the sentence which precedes it, but a purely verbal link is provided by the use of *osamaru* as a pivot, in the double sense of 'stored' and 'securely settled'.

GLOSSARY OF JAPANESE TERMS APPEARING IN THE COMMENTARY

A list of frequently occurring words left untranslated, together with their English approximations, is here appended. Where suffixes marked by an asterisk * are an essential component of district names they are not hyphenated in the Commentary, e.g. Higashiyama, Dōtonbori, Ōshima.

*-*bori*	canal
-*borigawa*	canal
-*chō*	block of houses
*-*dera*	temple (Buddhist)
-*dō*	highway
-*fu*	equivalent of -*ken* in the case of Tōkyō, Kyōto and Ōsaka
-*gashi*	river bank
-*gishi*	river bank
-*gū*	shrine (*Shintō*)
-*guchi*	place where highroad enters town
-*gun*	rural subdivision of -*ken*. 'District'
-*hime*	princess (F. title)
-*ji*	temple (Buddhist)
*-*jima*	island
-*jingū*	shrine (*Shintō*)
-*jinja*	shrine (*Shintō*)
-*jinsha*	shrine (*Shintō*)
-*jō*	castle
-*kaidō*	highway
kamigata	the region around the old capital of Kyōto (usually the provinces of Yamashiro, Yamato, Kawachi, Settsu, and Izumi, but sometimes including Ōmi, Tanba, and Harima). Sometimes rendered by the translator as 'the home provinces'
kansai	'west of the barriers': a vaguely defined term for the provinces stretching westwards, on the main island of Japan, from certain military barriers on the Tōkai-*dō* and Nakasen-*dō* routes. In Tokugawa times the most easterly of this group were the provinces of Owari and Mino
kantō	'east of the barrier': in Edo times a term indicating the provinces on the main island east of

	Hakone, a military barrier on the Tōkai-*dō* in Sagami province
-ken	largest territorial and administrative division. 'Prefecture'
-koji	narrow street
-kōri	= *-gun*
-ku	administrative division of *-shi*. 'Ward'
-machi	block of houses
-mine (*-ga-mine*, *-no-mine*)	mountain peak
-mura	subdivision of *-gun*. 'Village'
-naikai	inland sea
no daidō	broad highway
no sato	village; rural group of houses
no tsuji	cross-roads
-san	mountain or hill, when well-known or revered (alternative reading of *-yama*)
-seki (*-no-seki*)	military barrier at strategic point. Sometimes denoting the current existence of such a barrier, sometimes merely its existence in ancient times
-sekido	see *-seki*
-shi	urban subdivision of *-ken* where population reaches a certain figure
**-shima*	island
-ten	title appended to names of certain gods
-to	equivalent of *-shi*, applied only to the modern capital
-yama	mountain; hill
-za	theatre

Where exact English equivalents for Japanese words exist, they have sometimes been used, e.g.:

bridge	*-bashi*, *no hashi*, *ō-hashi*, etc.
castle	*-jō*
gate	*-mon*, *no mon*
hall	*-dō*
harbour	*-minato*, *no minato*
park	*no kōen*
plain	*-no*
province	*-kuni*
river	*-gawa*
road	*-ji*
street	*-dōri*, *-suji*
waterfall	*-taki*

APPENDICES

APPENDIX I

COINAGE

In Tokugawa Japan there were two great centres of urban civilisation, separated by some three hundred miles, and each of these employed its distinctive currency system. In Edo, the seat of the *shōgun*'s government, the currency was of gold. In Ōsaka and Kyōto, the business and industrial centres of Tokugawa Japan, the medium of exchange was chiefly silver. There was, moreover, a copper currency for the lowest denominations of the nation's coinage, and this was freely circulated throughout the whole of Japan. Tables are here appended, showing the weight and composition of the coins circulating during the period covered by *Eitai-gura* (Table A), a general description of the coins (Table B), and rates of exchange 1625–93 (Table C).

The names of the coins (using the terminology most frequently employed by Saikaku in *Eitai-gura*, and arranging each list in order of value) were as follows:

Gold	Silver	Copper
1. *Bankin*	4. *Chōgin*	6. *Zeni*
2. *Koban*	5. *Mame-ita*	
3. *Ichibu*		

TABLE A. WEIGHT AND COMPOSITION OF COINS[1]

	Coin	Weight (*monme*)	Weight (gm.)	Composition: Gold (*monme*)	Composition: Silver (*monme*)	Composition: Other metals (*monme*)	Composition: Copper (*monme*)
'Gold' currency (Edo)	1. *Bankin*	44	165·4	30	13	1	0
	2. *Koban*	4·8	18·04	4 approx.	0·7	0·1 approx.	0
	3. *Ichibu*	1·2	4·51	1 approx.	0·175	0·25 approx.	0
'Silver' currency (Kyōto, Ōsaka)	4. *Chōgin*	43 approx.	161·64 approx.	—	34 approx.	0	9 approx.
	5. *Mame-ita*	Variable	Variable	—	34 parts	0	9 parts
'Copper' currency (all Japan)	6. *Zeni*	1 approx.	3·76 approx.	—	—	1 (iron or brass)	*or* 1

[1] The information in this appendix is largely compiled from *Heibonsha Daijiten* (1935) and various commentaries on *Eitai-gura*.

TABLE B. DESCRIPTION OF COINS

Coin	General description	Approx. size (inches)	Shape	Stamps and inscriptions	Actual value[1]	Other names[2]
1. *Bankin*[3]	Largest gold coin	5·7 × 3·5	Rounded oblong, both surfaces flat	Pawlonia crests; *Jū-ryō—Gotō*	Variable:[4] 8–9 *ryō* in Saikaku's time	*Keichō Ōbankin* *Ōbankin* *Ōban* *Bankin*
2. *Koban*	Second largest gold coin—largest in everyday use	2·8 × 1·5	Oval, both surfaces flat. Finishing of surface varied according to mint	Fan-shaped pawlonia crests; *Ichi-ryō*	1 *ryō*	*Keichō Kobankin* *Kobankin*
3. *Ichibu*	Smallest gold coin	0·7 × 0·4	Rectangular, both surfaces flat and granular	Fan-shaped pawlonia crests	¼ *ryō*	*Keichō Ichibu Bankin* *Ichibu Bankin* *Ichibu-kin* *Tanzaku Ichibu* *Kotsubu-kin* *Ikkaku*
4. *Chōgin*	Largest silver coin	Variable: about 3·6 × 1·2	Oval, flat obverse, rounded face. Roughly finished	*Tsune-kore*	Varied according to (1) weight—hence in business transactions values were determined by weighing in the scales; (2) exchange rates	*Keichō Chōgin*
5. *Mame-ita*	Smallest silver coin	Variable but small	Variable, rounded	*Tsune-kore*	(Ditto)	*Keichō Mame-ita-gin* *Mame-ita-gin* *Komagane* *Kodama-gin* *Kodama*
6. *Zeni*[5]	Small copper coins (sometimes iron or brass)	1 in diameter	Round, square hole in centre	*Eiraku Tsūhō*, or *Kanei Tsūhō*	Variable	*Kanei Tsūhō Ichimon-sen* *Ichimon-sen* *Shinsen*

[1] See Table C.

[2] Each coin has its numeral classifier, and these must not be confused with the coin itself: e.g. *Ōbankin ichi-mai* (1 *Ōbankin*); *Kobankin ichi-ryō* (1 *Kobankin*); *Chōgin ichi-mai*; *Zeni ichi-mon.*

[3] The *Bankin* was not employed in day-to-day business transactions, but was reserved for ceremonial occasions, being presented to superiors, temples, etc. as a gift.

[4] The value of the *Bankin* was fixed by an edict of 1725 at 7·5 *ryō,* and many commentators arbitrarily apply this rate in Saikaku's texts. For a discussion of the actual contemporary value see *Goi Kōshō*, 'Bankin Ichi-mai'.

[5] Through the holes in the centre of *zeni* it was customary to thread a string, collecting the coins into groups of 'a hundred' or 'a thousand', called *hyaku-zashi* and *kan-zashi* respectively. Although these groups were in some localities genuinely composed of 100 or 1000 coins, the more usual practice was to call a string of 96 coins a *hyaku-zashi,* and one of 960 a *kan-zashi.* The first Japanese *zeni* were minted in 1636, replacing the old *Eiraku Tsūhō* coins which were imported from China and were an accepted currency in Japan up to that time. The new coins were differentiated from the old by the official term *Kanei Tsūhō* stamped on their face, or by the unofficial term *Shinsen.* The practice of putting only 96 coins on a *hyaku-zashi* arose from the fact that the exchange rate between the new coins and the old *Eiraku Tsūhō* was officially determined at 96 of the new to 100 of the old.

STANDARD UNITS OF WEIGHT

(*a*) For gold the standard unit of weight was 1 *ryō*[1] (4·76 *monme*, or 17·86 gm.).

1 *ryō* = 4 *bu* = 16 *shu*

(*b*) For silver the standard unit of weight was 1 *monme*[2] (3·76 gm.).

1 *monme* = 10 *fun* = 100 *rin*
1000 *monme* = 1 *kanme*

TABLE C. EXCHANGE RATES[3] 1625–93

Date	Silver: 1 *ryō* gold	Copper: 1 *ryō* gold	Silver: 1000 *zeni*	Sources
1624–43	62 *monme*	—	—	*Dai Nippon Kahei Shi*
1625	—	4000 *zeni*	—	*Tokugawa Jikki* (1849)
1645*	62·45 *monme*	—	12–13 *monme*	*Dai Nippon Kahei Shi*
1654	63·1 *monme*	—	—	*Dai Nippon Kahei Shi*
1655*	—	—	17 *monme*	*Dai Nippon Kahei Shi*
1658*	—	—	20 *monme*	*Dai Nippon Kahei Shi*
1661*	—	—	16·5 *monme*	*Dai Nippon Kahei Shi*
1668	—	—	14 *monme*	*Dai Nippon Kahei Shi*
1674	—	4000 *zeni*	—	*Bokumin Kinkan*
1681*	—	—	12 *monme*	*Dai Nippon Kahei Shi*
1684	60 *monme*	—	13–15 *monme*	*Dai Nippon Kahei Shi*
1693*	60 *monme*	—	12–13 *monme*	*Dai Nippon Kahei Shi*

* Ōsaka.

As can be seen, the unofficial fluctuations on the money market were considerable, and they offered many opportunities for astute speculation.

In 1694 the shogunate decreed that all the existing gold and silver coins should be withdrawn from circulation, and a new debased coinage was issued.

[1] The *ryō* was an ancient Chinese weight, varying considerably in each dynasty. In Japan the *ryō* varied according to the commodity being measured: e.g. 1 *ryō* of silver = 4·3 *monme*; 1 *ryō* of medical herbs = 4 *monme*. (*Wakan Sansai Zue*, xv.)

[2] A *monme* is properly the weight of a Chinese coin, the *Mon* (*Wakan Sansai Zue*, xv). One *monme* was approximately 3·76 grammes.

[3] The dates and figures in this table are taken from *Ōyabu*, p. 600.

APPENDIX 2

CHŌJA KYŌ

(*The Millionaires' Gospel*)[1]

LONG ago there were three *chōja* called Kamadaya, Nabaya, and Izumiya. A clever young boy lived in their neighbourhood, and he went to the home of the *chōja* Kamadaya and said: 'Such a fine store of treasure! Did your forefathers bequeath it to you? Although it is like dipping from a river and seeking to guess its source, or like pruning the leaves and forgetting to examine the roots, inadequate though my abilities are kindly direct me along the road.' The *chōja* said in reply: 'Truly, you have put your request in a clever way! Originally we have nothing. There is no such thing as a Miroku Buddha by birth. There is no such thing as a Shaka Buddha by birth. There are Buddhas of Full Enlightenment, of course, but there is no Buddha who had not to learn at first. Master and pupil are like needle and thread, or like the dew of the topmost branches falling to become the nourishment of the roots. Though you will emerge from darkness on to a dark road, and will be like a blind man, follow close to the sound of my voice. The fact that you have started to think on these matters at an even earlier age than I did means that you are naturally gifted to become a great *chōja*.' Speaking thus, he invited him into his guest room, and spoke to him of the past and the future.

'Now, there is a mountain called Mount Chōja. It is the height of twenty Mount Hiei's piled on top of one another, and in shape it is like a calabash. At its foot is a great river. This is as broad as one hundred Uji rivers side by side, and the speed of its current is like a waterfall. There are few people who cross this river and climb that mountain. To be a rich man, to make a fortune, is not possible without extraordinary effort.[2]

'However, even if you have not a single *rin*, if you are determined to become a *chōja*, it can be done. When I was young, I served apprentice for three years with a temple carpenter. Of the five *gō* of rice which I received each day for my meals, I ate only half, saving two-and-a-half *gō*. In one hundred and seventy days, I had four *to*, two *shō*, five *gō*. I lent this out to people, charging ten per cent interest, and from that time I took the whole five *gō* for my meals. In three years the four *to*, two *shō*, five *gō* of rice became

[1] The translation is based on the 1627 text as reproduced in *Saikaku Shinkō* (Noma Kōshin, 1948), app. III, occasionally following the readings of other texts quoted in the same work.

[2] The reading followed here is that given in a 1644 manuscript copy of *Chōja Kyō*: *Sore, kane wo mochi kane wo mōkuru wa tsune no sei ni arazu.* Both the 1627 and the 1628 texts read ...*tsune no sei nari*, which is difficult to understand.

one *koku*. After it had become one *koku*, I charged a rate of interest of thirty per cent, and in twenty years it became more than five hundred *koku*. Using the remainder for my various needs, I continued to draw interest on the five hundred *koku*. In time it grew to more than one thousand *koku*, and after this, multiplying itself three, four times, it flowed on like running water, or like the days and months, and not for a moment did it lie idle. One leads to Two, Two leads to Three. Dust piles up and grows into a mountain. In this way I became a *chōja* worth a hundred thousand *koku*. People nicknamed me "*Gebon Koji*"[1]—all that I set my heart on had been achieved. But even if an arrow misses the target it lodges in the butt; and, though you may fail in your aim of a thousand thousand, and strike only a hundred thousand, you must make the attempt. That, broadly speaking, is the way to get on in the world.'

Nabaya speaks:

'Even if your wife annoys you, it is wrong to dismiss her too hastily. The reason is that you must always regard housekeeping as of prime importance. By exercising economy you can save two *gō*, five *shaku* of rice from the morning meal, and two *gō*, five *shaku* from the evening meal. In one month, this rice will become one *to*, five *shō*. Lending it at ten per cent interest, it will mount in three years to more than forty-four *koku*, eight *to*, six *shō*. Lending this each year at thirty per cent, in twenty years it will reach five thousand *koku*.

'To expect to become rich in a moment is a sure foundation for poverty. Here is an example. When climbing a ladder, you climb step by step. If you think to go more quickly, and you take two steps at a time, you fall. Again, although plum trees mature rapidly, there are no large plum trees. With camphor trees, the growth is slow, but large trees are plentiful. You should plan with this in mind. The man who makes money by normal economies, saving one copper at a time, is the steady man whose present and future alike are assured.'

Izumiya speaks:

'Our credit from former lives is limited. Our appetites in this life are without end. If we spend our own store heedlessly, we covet our neighbour's. Because we covet, we enter upon a round of Desires. Though ten coppers are soon spent, one copper is difficult to acquire.

'Again, to be without pain is bad. It is good to endure with patience a certain amount of pain. If we enjoy too much pleasure, evil follows therefrom.

'If we know our proper station, and if we live always at a level one degree below that, sacrificing all else, a steady economy is assured. But even in

[1] The Buddhist paradise was in nine grades (*ku-hon*), and the lowest three were called the *ge-bon*. *Ge-bon Koji* means literally 'a lower-paradise Buddhist', but I have been unable to find any other example of the use of this phrase.

being thrifty, we should do it so that we do not incur others' dislike. It is like ringing a wooden barrel: if you bind it too tightly the staves are pressed out of position.

'All that men can do, for their part, is to exercise good judgement, to economise, and to put their means of livelihood before all else. For instance, if a man, though born in poverty, acquires a fortune of around one *kanme* in silver, that is due to his own resources; but if he acquires more, you should understand, it is due to his credit from a former life. However, if a man lives in idleness, even such credit will prove insufficient to preserve him from poverty.'

Principles to Cherish at All Times:

1. To use common sense.
2. To act with honesty.
3. To endure with patience.
4. To regard every man as a thief, every fire as a conflagration.
5. To abandon pride and listen to advice.
6. To know that remorse serves no purpose.
7. That conceit is anathema.
8. That small-talk leads nowhere.
9. That moderation is only half a virtue.
10. That playing bosom-friend to all is pointless. (However, one should seek close acquaintance with the great and the good. To behave like a hen—keeping no one distant, and allowing no one nigh—is the way of an adept in the art of life.)

Verses on Necessary Studies:

1. Writing, accountancy, judging at sight, medicine, etiquette, a knowledge of food and the way to prepare it—all these should be understood.
2. Games of *Go* and Backgammon too—an addict is an idler, but it is good to play now and again to entertain guests.
3. The thing you must study to a certain degree is housekeeping. Indeed, all else is secondary, a matter of personal taste.
4. If it will make you rich, you may study anything—the only course you must not take is that of a thief.

A Verse on Reliable People:

Men of talent, intelligence, resource, and accurate accountancy; men of unswerving purpose, virtue, and honesty.

Verses on Useless People and Things:

1. Illiterate, dull, unperceptive, lie-abed, venture-nothing invalids and idlers.

2. Self-opinionated, knowing-faced, interfering, smooth-tongued, conceited people.

3. Carnal lusts, hasty temper, heavy drinking, gambling, playing Lord Bountiful; laziness, self-pity, bickering, lies.

Cautionary Verses:

1. To lend without surety is simple-minded. Your unpopularity when you refuse to lend is nothing compared to that when you press for repayment.

2. To friends you may give freely—but never lend. When you ask for it back, friendship surely cools.

3. In everything trust only what you see. Hearsay is a contradictory witness.

4. Though your talents are exceptional, if you have know-all looks and are swollen with conceit, you will never succeed.

5. Since youth comes not twice, do not relax! Even for the old there is pleasure from money.

6. You make merry, perhaps, thinking this transient life a brief dream... but if death is delayed, in the interim lies beggary!

7. It is a habit of the poor to scoff at the rich. These are the know-all airs of those who know nothing.

8. Think not that good times will last for ever. If summer is warm, there follows the chill of winter!

9. No matter how you pray, good luck is not yours for the asking. Always rely on your own common sense.

10. If you must make love, compose no poems, send no letters. Watch every single *zeni*.

(If a man is without money, he is not to be reckoned as a human being. It is an ignominious condition. The meaning of this should be well and firmly grasped.)

In Verse it is Said:

1. Even in your waking moments at night, ponder your affairs for the morrow. Think not of profitless things.

2. If, saying 'later', you enter it not in your notebook at once, the loss comes not 'later' but now.

3. If you waste no time in profitless pursuits, that you will succeed is beyond question.

The God of Wealth's Ten Sons:

Takuwae Tarō Tanemochi	(Saving Tarō Have-capital)
Asaoki Jirō Munekiyo[1]	(Early-rising Jirō Brain-clear)

[1] *Munekiyo*, the reading of the 1628 text. The text of 1627 has *Munekiki*.

Sanyō Saburō Kanemasu	(Accountancy Saburō Cash-increase)
Uchii no Shirō Ieyoshi	(Stay-at-home Shirō House-in-order)
Gojō Gorō Naomasu	(All-the-virtues Gorō Honest-profits)
Eshaku Rokurō Tameyoshi	(Courtesy Rokurō Good-business)
Ariai Shichirō Muneyasu	(Make-do Shichirō Level-headed)
Shinshaku Hachirō Sueyoshi	(Considerate Hachirō Future-prosperity)
Monokorae Kurō Shigeyoshi	(Patience Kurō Great-prosperity)
Kokorodate Jūrō Suetaka	(Good-natured Jūrō Future-advancement)

Final words of enlightenment to the above ten: Stock necessities in superabundance; go short of unnecessary things. Gambling, wenching, and riotous living must stop. Sell what you begrudge, and refrain from buying what you fancy. Think of money as your master—do not treat it like a slave.

The God of Poverty's Ten Sons:

Date-shi no Tarō	(Tarō the Dandy)
Bugyōgi Jirō-tarō	(Jirō-tarō the Ill-mannered)
Monozuki no Saburō-jirō	(Saburō-jirō the Dilettante)
Hito-atsume no Shirō-zaburō	(Shirō-zaburō the Party-thrower)
Nyōbō-sari Gorō-shirō	(Gorō-shirō the Wife-divorcer)
Keizu-date Rokurō-tarō	(Rokurō-tarō the Pedigree-proud)
Ōhi-taki no Shichirō-jirō	(Shichirō-jirō the Fuel-waster)
Kenbutsu-gonomi Hachirō-zaburō	(Hachirō-zaburō the Idle-spectator)
Ajiwai-guchi Kurō-tarō	(Kurō-tarō the Sweet-tooth)
Atsugi-shi no Jūrō-shirō	(Jūrō-shirō the Heavily-clothed)

Final words of enlightenment to the above ten:[1]

1. You must be fond of lotteries.
2. You must make empty promises to everyone.
3. You must gamble for money.
4. You must not buy what you need—you must buy up stocks of useless things.
5. You must be at everyone's beck and call, and be praised by all.
6. You must interfere in everything.
7. You must let the housekeeping take care of itself.
8. You must trust to luck in everything.
9. You must arrange losses for yourself and profits for others.
10. You must long for fame and glory.

If you fail not to observe each of these articles, no blemish will mark the names you bear.

[1] *Migi jū-nin e matsugo no koto,* the reading of the 1628 text. The 1627 text has *migi jū-nin wo mainichi kurubeki koto,* which does not make sense.

The god of poverty once said to a man: 'Even among rich people there is poverty. Most of them have no experience of the feelings common to ordinary folk, nor do they know what relaxation is. Thinking that their lives will continue for a thousand or ten thousand years, they plunge deeper and deeper into miserly avarice, till they are derided by men as beasts. They eat boiled barley and rice-bran gruel for breakfast and dinner. They use their bed-sheets as kimono. Such things one may call the poverty of rich men. Again, even among poor people, there are things which one should call their wealth. They understand the Principle of Retribution, which governs our short span of fifty or sixty years. Moreover, they know the transience of things—that both youth and old age are on the borders of life and death, that last year is this year's "long ago"; and that breathing out is not always followed by breathing in. If they live in harmony with others, showing compassion and coveting no man's goods, though they live in poverty, we should call such people men of wealth. Again, in poverty there is much freedom from care:

> If a man has no valuables, he suffers no robbery.
> If a man has no house, he suffers no loss from fire.
> If a man has no money, he fears no market fluctuations.

Indeed, many are his advantages....' Thus, with plausible airs, spoke the god of poverty. But the man replied: 'That is like the chastity of an ugly woman, or the abstinence of a beggar.'

How true! For the rich there are pleasant excursions and none but joyous things. On every count money is desirable. Put gold in fire, and it suffers no damage. Put it in water, and it does not decay. It merely increases in brilliance. So ponder again and again the golden sayings of these three men —Kamadaya, Nabaya, and Izumiya—and do not idly spend a single *fun* or *rin*.

This is the heart of the Millionaires' Gospel.

The above text is published as in the manuscript.[1]
Kanei, Fourth Year (1627).

[1] Possibly *Chōja Kyō* circulated for some years in manuscript before its publication. Some at least of its material is known to date in conception from the previous century. In *Nobunaga Ki* (Kose Dōki, publ. *c.* 1615) the following entry appears under the year 1581:

Shibuya told them that nowadays, ever since the physician Dōsan had invented fanciful names for the God of Wealth's Ten Sons, children in Kyōto were for ever writing them on folding screens, on fans, or on their wads of handkerchief paper, and singing them in the streets. 'And what sort of names are they?' asked Lord Nobunga. 'Penny-wise Tarō Have-capital, Sleep-at-home Jirō House-in-order, Consideration Saburō Steady-future...', began Shibuya. But before he could get further with his recital Lord Nobunga's expression changed, he straightened his back in anger, and cried: 'Enough! Those may be Gods of Wealth for merchants and artisans, but for military families they are Gods of Poverty!'

APPENDIX 3

'SHIMAI SŌSHITSU NO YUIKUN JŪSHICHI-KA-JŌ' (1610)[1]

(*The Seventeen Injunctions of Shimai Sōshitsu*)

Article One

That throughout life you should be pure in heart and upright goes without saying. To your parents, to Sōi, to your brothers and to your relations, you should act with filial piety and love. Moreover, with your friends—and of course in your dealings with strangers—you should show respect for others, humility and courtesy. First, you must never speak a word of falsehood, nor —even if you are speaking reprovingly of another man—of things akin to falsehood.

Article Two

It is forbidden to worry about the after-life until you have reached the age of fifty. Such thoughts are for old men only, or for members of the Jōdo or Zen sects. For anyone else they are a waste of time. Above all, conversion to Christianity is forbidden—even though Dōyu or Sōi should use all means to press it upon you. The reason is this: a Christian sets his mind on the after-world at the age of ten, and from that early age he starts repeating religious catch-phrases, begging forgiveness for his sins. He spends his days and nights in prayer at church, neglecting his duties at home, and with a rosary draped about his neck, he takes open pride in his surprising behaviour. Christianity is the greatest of afflictions for a man whose concern is the management of a household. People who grasp the distinctions between this world and the next are rare beings, one in ten. Just as even the birds and beasts living in this world are concerned only with immediate worries, so human beings are in no different category. In this life, our first consideration should be not to forfeit the respect needed for this life. It is said that even the gods and Buddhas do not know about the next world. How much less can ordinary people know! Bear it well in mind that preoccupation with the next world is not permissible until you have reached the age of fifty.

Addendum: People die even at the age of two, three, ten or thirty. If they die before forty or fifty, the question of their future existence must be considered problematical. At these ages, they must be considered in the same

[1] The Japanese text is included in *Dai Nippon Shiryō* (1900–), XII, 22.

category as children who die aged two or three. Children of two or three cannot think about the next life.

Article Three

Dice, backgammon, and all gambling games, are forbidden throughout life. *Go*, chess, fencing, and recitations or dances from Noh plays are forbidden, at least until the age of forty. (However, after a man has reached fifty, artistic accomplishments, no matter of what sort, are no longer unbecoming.) Excursions to pine slopes, river-fishing expeditions, moon-viewing, flower-viewing, and all kinds of sightseeing are naturally forbidden. Even when visiting temples, take only one attendant. If you go largely for amusement, your prayers can be acceptable to neither gods nor Buddhas.

Article Four

No matter how trifling the matter, all luxuries are forbidden till forty. A general mode of thinking or living which is more expensive than one can afford, is even more reprehensible. In Trade, the making of money is the principle thing in which one should strive to be inferior to no one else. Even so, do not be over-tempted through envy of the profits made by others in China and in the Southern Lands. To invest too large a sum of capital in this trade, or—worst of all—to fit out a ship and send it to China and the South, are things to be regarded with abhorrence throughout your life. Invest a little capital at a time in several different ventures, taking Sōi's advice on these matters. In all other matters as well, you should live at a level only half as high as you can afford, or even lower. Even if people should advise you to the contrary, saying, 'To be too retiring is a bad thing. Come out into society a little more', you must not budge from your ways. As for artistic interests, eccentric tastes, the tea ceremony, elegance, stylish manners, ornamental swords and daggers, and smart clothes—in all these things, a little is sufficient: a conspicuous display is absolutely forbidden. Above all, of course, military implements are unnecessary. Even if you should be given an ornamental sword as a present, sell it, and turn it into money. Until the age of forty, cotton *kimono*, or clothes of an inconspicuous sort (naturally, also—on occasions—woven materials of rough or knotted silk, provided they are not too noticeable), are the most suitable. Repair the house frequently, mending the rope in walls and fences where it has rotted away. Building a new house is absolutely forbidden.

After reaching the age of fifty, you may act according to your own judgement. In all matters, since your powers will by then be fully developed, you may exercise your own discretion to the full. However, the great majority of people are fated to be poverty-stricken by the time they die. Even amongst those who have made their fortune by their own efforts and ingenuity, the ones who retain their wealth to their dying day are rare—not one in ten or twenty. How much more is a man who inherits his fortune from his father likely to lose everything in a trounce, and die leaving his descendants in poverty for the rest of their days! To bear this in mind should be your first concern.

Article Five

Until forty, you should not give entertainments, nor thoughtlessly accept invitations. Once or twice each year—if your parents, brothers or relatives ask you—you may visit your various relations. However, it is not permitted to visit them frequently. If you are invited merely for a night's gossip or recreation, even if it is your brothers who ask you, do not go.

Article Six

Do not covet other people's household valuables. If you are offered them, unless by relations, on no account accept. Do not give away your own. Carefully store the really valuable ones, and show them to no one.

Article Seven

For friends, throughout life you should choose good men of business; men who care for domestic matters; people who do not meddle; upright, reliable people; even-tempered and noble-natured people. With these you may enter deeply into friendship. Again, those whom you must not make your friends are: quarrelsome people; fault-finding people; mean-minded, double-tongued people; slanderous people; stylish people; heavy drinkers; liars; admirers of court manners; lovers of dancing, *samisen*, and song; prattlesome people, and pretentious people. You should not even sit in company with such as these.

Article Eight

Never make idle calls at houses where you have no business. Walking about in strange places is forbidden. Naturally, you may take presents of fish-food—not rarities, but things like abalone or sea-bream (selecting fresh ones)—to the lord of the castle; and naturally, you may also call on Inoue Suwo-dono, and Ogawa Kura-dono. Apart from these, you may pay the usual calls at New Year and Year's End. But generally you should remain at home.

With your own hands kindle the fire under the stove, for breakfast and dinner, damping the embers afterwards. Make sure that your servants burn no more fuel or firewood than is necessary. Going out behind the house, collect all the bits and pieces of rubbish: small lengths of rope should be cut up for mixing in cement, longer lengths should be spliced together; fragments of wood or broken bamboo, even as small as half an inch, should be stored, cleaned, and used as fuel for watch-fires; scraps of paper, even half an inch or less in length, should be gathered up and soaked to make new paper.

Use your ingenuity, just as I myself have done, and see to it that not the slightest needless expense is incurred.

Article Nine

As a principle, when buying things for the first time...go out and buy them for yourself. Buy at the cheapest rates, and make a careful note of the prices. Afterwards, no matter whom you send to do the shopping, you will know whether the articles he brings are too expensive or not. If you do this, you will not be cheated even by your servants....Housekeeping may be said to be a matter of firewood, charcoal and oil; but your first care should be the firewood. There are great differences in ways of burning it. Find out by practice how much is required for cooking the rice and soup for one day, and give that amount only to the kitchen-maids for cooking....With firewood and fuel in general, if it is green or rotten, it is useless. Always buy dried wood....In making *sake* and boiling bean-paste, try for yourself how much damping-charcoal is needed for so many bundles of firewood. Afterwards, get the others to burn the wood, and apply the damping-charcoal according to your calculations. No matter what his calling, if a man does not take these troubles upon himself, he can never run a household successfully.

Article Ten

In making *sake*, weigh out the rice yourself. If you delegate it to others, do not take your eyes off them for a moment. Never allow them to do anything out of your sight. You should understand that maids and men-servants are thieves without exception. Watch the people who are making the *sake* too. Construct a special place for leaving the rice in soak, and have locks fitted to the doors. Even cold boiled rice is stealable, and as long as you are awake you should keep an eye on it.

In taking sureties for loans, accept no trifling swords, daggers, or military equipment; no houses or children; no trifling tea implements; and, of course, no land.

As a principle, the employment of too many servants is forbidden. First, it is forbidden to have many maid-servants. When your wife goes out for a walk, there is absolutely no need for more than two female attendants and one male. As for your children, do not dress them in fine clothes; and when they go out, send only one servant to accompany them as a nurse. Providing them with attendants to hold sunshades, or giving them ornamental daggers is strictly forbidden. Make them small bamboo hats for their outings.

Article Eleven

...Scrape the bean-paste morning and night. After thoroughly straining it and making soup, add salt to the remaining dregs; collect odd scrapings, stalks, and discarded peel of radish, turnip, marrow, egg-plant, beans, onions, and so forth, and put them in with the bean-paste dregs. Give this to the serving-maids for breakfast and dinner as a side-dish....

Article Twelve

[is concerned with the proper methods of investing and loaning money. Advice is given not to loan money to *daimyō*, except—in certain cases—to Matsura, the lord of Hirado.]

Article Thirteen

When a man has capital, small though it may be, he must allow himself no relaxation in his attention to household problems or the running of his business, and must continue to make the earning of a living his principal concern. This is his lifelong duty. If, when one has capital, one begins to relax, to buy things one longs for, to behave in a wilful manner, to live in style, and to do all the things which one wishes to do, the money is soon spent. Full of repentance though a man may be when faced with this startling fact, he now has no means of making a livelihood, he has nothing even with which to be thrifty, and for the future there is only the prospect of begging in the streets....One must set to work from the moment one has capital; trade and domestic management are, as it were, the two wheels of the Cart of Success, and all your worries should be centred about them.

No matter how one has saved and filled one's purse, man must buy food and clothes. At such times, it is essential to take money out and spend it. Military lords and retainers draw money from their territories. With merchants, if they are not continually making profits, the money stored in their purses will soon be reduced to nothing. On the other hand, no matter how they replenish their purses with profits, if they spend wildly and unnecessarily it will be as though they are putting their money into a purse with a hole in the bottom.

Article Fourteen

Rise early in the morning. As soon as the day is over, retire to bed. To use lamp oil for idle purposes is wasteful. Going out after dark on matters not connected with business, and spending long hours in other people's houses, making no difference between day and night, is forbidden....

Article Fifteen

[outlines certain economies to be observed when travelling on business.]

Article Sixteen

[forbids any participation in quarrels, no matter what the provocation.]

Article Seventeen

Husband and wife should live in lifelong harmony. They should love each other, feeling a common concern for household and business problems, and strive together to be thrifty and unremitting in effort. If there should be a quarrel or coolness between them, no matter of what kind, they must not make too much of it. Household affairs are easily disrupted.

Again, after my death, immediately change the family name and assume that of *Kamiya.* It is my wish that the name *Shimai* should not outlive me. However, if you do not call yourself *Kamiya, Maeda* is not a bad alternative. I leave the choice to yourself.

Addendum: On no account must you become an invalid. No matter how you feel at the time, apply herbal poultices and drink medicine with regularity, five or six times in the year.

Keichō fifteenth year (1610), first moon,
fifteenth day.

To Kamiya Tokuzaemon-*dono.*

APPENDIX 4

LIST OF REFERENCES

(Japanese characters are inserted only when the names are not well known or when they cannot be readily deduced from the romanised form or found in reference works.)

Anthology of Japanese Literature, New York, 1955, Keene, Donald.

Arashi Mujō (嵐無常) *Monogatari*, 1691, (?) Ihara Saikaku.

Azuma Kagami, *c.* 1180–1266, author unknown.

Bokumin Kinkan (牧民金鑑), *c.* 1850, Araki Akimichi (荒木顯道).

Budō Denrai Ki (武道傳來記), 1687, Ihara Saikaku.

Buke Giri (武家義理) *Monogatari*, 1688, Ihara Saikaku.

Bukkyō Daijiten, 1917, Oda Tokunō.

Bunshō-zōshi (文正草子), 15th cent. (?), author unknown (*Nihon Bungaku Taikei*, XIX, *q.v.*).

Chikusai (竹齋), *c.* 1620, Karasumaru Mitsuhiro (烏丸光廣).

Chōja Kyō (長者教), 1627, author unknown.

Chōja Kyō Kō (考), Appendix II to *Saikaku Shinkō*, *q.v.*

Chōja On-etsu Kyo (音悅經) (*Taishō Shinshū Dai Zōkyō*, XIV, *q.v.*).

Chōja Shisei Kyō (子制經) (*Taishō Shinshū Dai Zōkyō*, XIV, *q.v.*).

Chōnin-bukuro (町人嚢), 1719, Nishikawa Joken (西川如見).

Chōnin Kōken Roku (考見錄), *c.* 1726–33, Mitsui Takafusa (三井高房).

Chōnin Shisō to Chōnin Kōken Roku, Tōkyō 1940, Mitsui Takaharu.

Dai Jinmei Jiten, Tōkyō 1953, publ. by *Heibonsha*.

Dai Nihon Dokushi Chizu, Tōkyō 1935, Yoshida Tōgo.

Dai Nippon Shiryō, Tōkyō 1900– , publ. by *Tōkyō Daigaku Shiryō Hensanjo*.

Danrin Toppyaku In (談林十百韻), 1675, Nishiyama Sōin (西山宗因).

Denpu (田夫) *Monogatari*, *c.* 1624–44, author unknown.

Eboshi-ori (烏帽子折), 15th cent. (?), author unknown (*Shin Gunsho Ruijū*, VIII, *q.v.*).

Edo Bungaku Jiten, Tōkyō 1940, Teruoka Yasutaka.

Edo Bungaku Kenkyū, Tōkyō 1933, Yamaguchi Gō.

Edo Zukan Kōmoku (圖鑑綱目), 1689, Ishikawa Ryūsen (石川流宣).

Enkin Shū (遠近集), 1666, Nishimura Chōai-shi (西村長愛子).

Futokoro-suzuri (懷硯), 1687, Ihara Saikaku.

Fuyu no Hi, 1684, Matsuo Bashō.

Gei Shikō (鯨史稿), *c.* 1840, Ōtsuka Seijun (大槻清準).

Genji Monogatari, *c.* 1001–20, Murasaki Shikibu.

Hachi no Ki (鉢木), *c.* 1380, Kanami.

Haikai Dokugin Ichinichi Senku (俳諧獨吟一日千句), 1675, Ihara Saikaku.
Haikai Ishi-guruma (石車), 1691, Ihara Saikaku.
Haikai Meisaku Shū, Tōkyō 1935, Ehara Taizō (*Hyōshaku Edo Bungaku Sōsho*, VII, *q.v.*).
Hakata Kojorō Nami-makura (博多小女郎波枕), 1718, Chikamatsu Monzaemon.
Hakurakuten (白樂天), *c.* 1400, Seami.
Han Fei-tzu, 3rd cent. B.C., Chinese legalist philosopher.
Heibonsha Daijiten, 26 vols., Tōkyō 1935, publ. by *Heibonsha.*
Heike Monogatari, *c.* 1219, author unknown.
Hinami Kiji (日次記事), 1676, Kurokawa Genitsu (黒川玄逸).
History of Japan, The, London 1727, Kaempfer, E. (transl. J. G. Scheuchzer).
History of Japanese Literature, London 1899, Aston, W. G.
Hitome Tamaboko (一目玉鉾), 1689, Ihara Saikaku.
Honchō Koji Inen Shū (本朝故事因緣集), 1689, author unknown.
Honchō Nijū Fukō (二十不孝), 1686, Ihara Saikaku.
Honchō Ōin Hiji (櫻陰比事), 1689, Ihara Saikaku.
Honchō Seji Danki (世事談綺), 1733, Kikuoka Koryō (菊岡沾涼).
Hyōshaku Edo Bungaku Sōsho, 11 vols., Tōkyō 1935–7, publ. by *Dai Nippon Yūben Kai Kōden Sha.*
Iguchi (爲愚痴) *Monogatari*, 1662, Soga Kyūji (曾我休自) (*Tokugawa Bungei Ruijū*, II, *q.v.*).
Ikutama Manku (生玉萬句), 1673, Ihara Saikaku.
Inga (因果) *Monogatari* (*Hiragana* version), *c.* 1660, author unknown.
Irozato Mitokoro-zetai (色里三所世帶), 1688, Ihara Saikaku.
Ise Monogatari, *c.* 905–50, author unknown.
Ito Ran Ki (絲亂記), 1719, Takaishi (高石).
Japanese Literature, London 1953, Keene, Donald.
Jikata Hanrei Roku (地方凡例錄), 1871, Ōishi Kyūkei (大石久敬).
Jinrin Kinmō Zui (人倫訓蒙圖彙), 1690, author unknown.
Kabuki no Sōshi (歌舞伎の草子), *c.* 1624–44, author unknown.
Kankatsu (寛闊) *Heike Monogatari*, 1710, publ. by *Hachimonjiya*, author unknown.
Kannin Ki (堪忍記), 1661, Asai Ryōi (淺井了意).
Kashō Ki (可笑記), 1642, Jorai Shi (如儡子).
Keisei Kintan Ki (傾城禁短氣), 1711, Ejima Kiseki (江嶋其磧).
Kenmon Dansō (見聞談叢), 1738, Itō Baiu (伊藤梅宇).
Kii Zoku Fudoki (紀伊續風土記), 1839, Niida Kōko (仁井田好古).
Kinsei Fūzoku Shi (志), *c.* 1837–53, Kitagawa Morisada (北川守貞).
Kinsei Shōnin Ishiki no Kenkyū, Tōkyō 1941, Miyamoto Matatsugu.
Kiyū Shōran (嬉遊笑覽), 1830, Kitamura Shinsetsu (喜多村信節).
Kobun Shinpō Goshū (古文眞寶後集), *c.* 1391–1500, compiler unknown.
Kōchū Nippon Eitai-gura, I, Tōkyō 1937, Shuzui Kenji.
Kokaji (小鍛治), *c.* 1363–1443, Seami.

Kokin Haikai Nyo-kasen (古今俳諧女歌仙), 1684, Ihara Saikaku.

Kokin Shū, 905, compiled Ki no Tsurayuki.

Kokka Manyō Ki (國花萬葉記), 1697, Kikumoto Gaho (菊本賀保).

Kokugo to Kokubungaku, periodical, publ. by *Shibundō*.

Kōshoku Gonin Onna (好色五人女), 1686, Ihara Saikaku.

Kōshoku Ichidai Onna (一代女), 1686, Ihara Saikaku.

Kōshoku Ichidai Otoko (男), 1682, Ihara Saikaku.

Kōshoku Kai-awase (具合), 1687, Yoshida Hanbei (吉田半兵衛).

Kōshoku Kinmō Zui (訓蒙圖彙), 1686, Yoshida Hanbei.

Kōshoku Seisui Ki (盛衰記), 1688, Ihara Saikaku.

Kōshoku Tabi Nikki (旅日記), 1687, Kataoka Shijo (片岡旨恕).

Kyō Habutae Oritome (京羽二重織留), 1689, Koshō-shi (弧松子).

Li Chi, Confucian classic.

Lun-yü, Confucian classic.

Mankin Sangyō-bukuro (萬金産業袋), 1732, Miyake Yarai (三宅也來).

Mayama Seika (眞山青果) *Zuihitsu Senshū*, 3 vols., Tōkyō posth. 1952.

Meikan Sanzesō Tenmon Sō (命鑑三世相天文鈔), 1667, Tensei (天生).

Monomi-guruma (物見車), 1690, Yanabuchi Houn (柳淵歩雲).

Nagasaki Miyage (長崎土產), 1680, author unknown.

Naniwa Monogatari, 1655, author unknown.

Naniwa Suzume (雀), 1679, author unknown.

Nanshoku (男色) *Ōkagami*, 1687, Ihara Saikaku.

Nara-zarashi Kokin Rigen Shū (奈良曝古今俚諺集), 1748, Mieda Chiribito (三枝散人).

Narihira Kawachi-gayoi (業平河内通), 1694(?), Tominaga Heibei (富永平兵衛).

Nihon Bungaku Taikei, 25 vols., Tōkyō 1925–7, Ishikawa Sakutarō *et al.*

Nihon Fukushoku Shiyō, Kyōtō 1949, Ema Tsutomu.

Nihon Meicho Zenshū, 31 vols., Tōkyō 1926–9, publ. by *Nihon Meicho Zenshū Kankō Kai.*

Nihon Shi Jiten, Kyōtō 1954, publ. by *Kyōto Daigaku Bungaku-bu.*

Nijū-shi Kō (二十四孝), *c.* 1596–1614, trans. unknown (*Nihon Bungaku Taikei*, XIX, *q.v.*).

Nippon Eitai-gura (日本永代藏), 1688, Ihara Saikaku (井原西鶴).

Nippon Eitai-gura Hyōshaku, Tōkyō 1930, Satō Tsurukichi (佐藤鶴吉).

Nippon Eitai-gura Kōgi (*Mayama Seika Zuihitsu Senshū*, II, *q.v.*).

Nippon Eitai-gura Shinkō, Tōkyō 1937, Ōyabu Torasuke (大藪虎亮).

Nippon Shin (新) *Eitai-gura*, 1713, Hōjō Dansui (北條團水).

Nobunga Ki (信長記), *c.* 1615, Kose Dōki (小瀬道喜).

Ogura Hyakunin Isshu, *c.* 1200, Fujiwara Teika.

Ōita-shi Shi, Ōita 1937, Itō Masao.

Okashi-otoko (をかし男), 1662, author unknown.

Ōsaka Dokugin Shū (獨吟集), 1675, *Danrin-ha* (談林派).

Ōyakazu Sen Happyaku In (大矢數千八百韻), 1678, Gesshō-ken Kishi (月松軒紀子).

Pamela, 1740, Richardson, Samuel.

Retsudentai Shōsetsu Shi, Tōkyō 1929, Mizutani Futō.

Risshin Daifuku-chō (立身大福帳), 1703, Yuiraku-ken (唯樂軒).

Rōjin Zatsuwa (老人雜話), 1710, Emura Sōgu (江村宗具).

Ruikōji (類柑子), 1707, Enomoto Kikaku (榎本其角).

Sabishiki-za no Nagusame (寂しき座の慰め), 1676, author unknown.

Saga (嵯峨) *Monogatari*, *c.* 1460 (?), author unknown.

Saikaku Goi Kōshō (語彙考證) (*Mayama Seika Zuihitsu Senshū*, II, *q.v.*).

Saikaku Haikai Ōkukazu (大句數), 1677, Ihara Saikaku.

Saikaku Higan-zakura (彼岸櫻), *posth.* 1694 (Edo edition of *Saikaku Okimiyage*, *q.v.*), Ihara Saikaku.

Saikaku Kenkyū Nōto, Tōkyō 1953, Teruoka Yasutaka.

Saikaku Meido Monogatari, 1697, author unknown.

Saikaku Meisaku Shū, Tōkyō 1935, Fujii Otoo (藤井乙男) (*Hyōshaku Edo Bungaku Sōsho*, I, *q.v.*).

Saikaku Meisaku Shū, Tōkyō 1929, Yamaguchi Gō (山口剛) (*Nihon Meicho Zenshū*, II, *q.v.*).

Saikaku Nagori no Tomo (名殘の友), posth. 1699, Ihara Saikaku.

Saikaku Nenpu Kōshō, Tōkyō 1952, Noma Kōshin (野間光辰).

Saikaku no Haireki (俳歴), Tōkyō 1933, Ehara Taizō (穎原退藏).

Saikaku Okimiyage (置土產), posth. 1693, Ihara Saikaku.

Saikaku Oritome (織留), posth. 1694, Ihara Saikaku.

Saikaku Ōyakazu (大矢數), 1681, Ihara Saikaku.

Saikaku Shinkō (新攷), Kyōto 1948, Noma Kōshin.

Saikaku Shokoku-banashi (諸國ばなし), 1685, Ihara Saikaku.

Saikaku to Edo Chiri (*Mayama Seika Zuihitsu Senshū*, II, *q.v.*).

Saikaku to Koten Bungaku, Shimazu Hisamoto (島津久基) (*Kokugo to Kokubungaku*, 1939–40, *q.v.*).

Saikaku Zoku Tsurezure (俗つれづれ), posth. 1695, Ihara Saikaku.

Saiyū Ki (西遊記), 1795, Tachibana Nankei (橘南谿).

Seidan (政談), *c.* 1720, Ogyū Sorai (荻生徂徠).

Seken Munesanyō (世間胸算用), 1692, Ihara Saikaku.

Seken Tedai Katagi (手代氣質), 1730, Ejima Kiseki.

Sendai Ōyakazu (仙臺大矢數), 1679, Ōyodo Sanzenpū (大淀三千風).

Setsuyō Kikan (攝陽奇觀), *c.* 1833, Hamamatsu Utakuni (濱松歌國).

Shakkyō (石橋), *c.* 1400, Motomasa (元雅).

Shikidō (色道) *Ōkagami*, 1678, Hatakeyama Kizan (畠山箕山).

Shimabara Yamato-Goyomi (島原大和暦), 1683, author unknown.

Shimai Sōshitsu no Yuikun Jūshichi-ka-jō (島井宗室の遺訓十七ケ條), 1610, Shimai Sōshitsu (*Dai Nippon Shiryō*, XII, 22, *q.v.*).

Shin Gunsho Ruijū, 10 vols., Tōkyō 1906–8, publ. by *Kokusho Kankō Kai*.

Shin Kashō Ki (新可笑記), 1688, Ihara Saikaku.
Shinsen Zōho Kyō Ō-ezu (京大繪圖), 1686, Hayashi Yoshinaga (林吉永).
Shinsen Zōho Ōsaka Ō-ezu, 1687, Hayashi Yoshinaga.
Shison Daikoku-bashira (子孫大黑柱), 1709, Getsujin-dō (月尋堂).
Shoen (諸艷) *Ōkagami*, 1684, Ihara Saikaku.
Shōgatsu-zoroi (正月揃), 1688, Hakugan Koji (白眼居士).
Shuin-sen Bōeki Shi, Ōsaka 1921, Kawashima Genjirō.
Shumadai (須摩提) *Chōja Kyō* (*Taishō Shinshū Dai Zōkyō*, XIV, *q.v.*).
Shunei (春榮), *c.* 1400, Seami.
Sōjiku Yuisho (宗竺遺書), 1720, Mitsui Hachirōemon (三井八郎右衛門).
Sōshi Hen (喪志編), 1745, Kajitori Uohiko (楫取魚彥).
Ssu-shu, Four Confucian classics.
Sujaku Shinobu-zuri (朱雀信夫摺), 1687, author unknown.
Sujaku Tōmegane (遠目鏡), 1681, author unknown.
Taihei Ki, *c.* 1370, Kojima Hōshi (?).
Taishō Shinshū Dai Zōkyo, 100 vols., Tōkyō 1924–32, publ. by *Taishō Issai Kyō Kankō Kai*.
Tako Shinkei Kakun (多胡辰敬家訓), 15th cent., Tako Shinkei.
Tedai Sode Soroban (手代袖算盤), 1713, Hachimonji Jishō (八文字自笑).
Teihon (定本) *Saikaku Zenshū*, 9 vols., Tōkyō 1949–55, Ehara Taizō, Teruoka Yasutaka, Noma Kōshin.
Tōkai-dō Meisho Ki (東海道名所記), *c.* 1658–61, Asai Ryōi.
Tokugawa Bungei Ruijū, 12 vols., Tōkyō 1914–15, publ. by *Kokusho Kankō Kai*.
Tokugawa Jidai Kinrei Kō, 62 vols., 1894–5, compiled by Min. of Justice.
Tokugawa Jikki (實紀), 1849, Narishima Motonao (成島司直).
Tokugawa Shoki no Kaigai Bōeki-ka, Ōsaka 1916, Kawashima Genjirō.
Tōru (融), *c.* 1400, Seami.
Tsurezure-gusa, c. 1330, Yoshida Kenkō.
Tsūzoku Keizai Bunko, 12 vols., Tōkyō 1916–17, publ. by *Nippon Keizai Sōsho Kankō Kai*.
Ukiyo Monogatari, *c.* 1661, Asai Ryōi.
Usuyuki (薄雪) *Monogatari*, 1632, author unknown.
Waga Koromo (我衣), 1825, Eibi-an Nanchiku (曳尾庵南竹).
Wakan Sansai Zue (和漢三才圖繪), 1715, Terajima Ryōan (寺島良安).
Wakun Shiori (和訓栞), 1883 (revised ed. 1898), Tanigawa Kotosuga (谷川士清).
Wankyū Isse (椀久一世) *no Monogatari*, 1685, Ihara Saikaku.
Wankyū Nise (二世) *no Monogatari*, 1691, Ihara Saikaku.
Yodare-kake (よだれかけ), 1665, Baijō-ken (楳條軒).
Yorozu no Fumi-hōgu (萬の文反古), posth. 1696, Ihara Saikaku.
Yoshiwara Kagami (吉原鑑), 1661, author unknown.
Zenkai Yōshi (全堺詳志), 1757, author unknown.
Zoku-Goshūi Shū, *c.* 1325, Fujiwara Tamefuji and Fujiwara Tamesada.
Zoku Shoshū-meguri (續諸州めぐり), *c.* 1685, author unknown.

INDEX

NOTES

1. The index is chiefly to the introduction, translation and commentary, but a few references to appendices have also been included.

2. References are given in the following order: introduction, translation, commentary (in italics), appendices (e.g. xx; 46; *205=3*; Ap. 2, pp. 240–1).

3. Where a reference is to be found both in the translation and in the note to that passage in the commentary, the translation reference is accompanied by a note number, and no separate reference is given to the commentary (e.g. 35=1 signifies translation p. 35, and commentary II, 1, note 1).

4. Proper names appearing in the translation, and the more important of those in the commentary, are listed individually in the main index, and they may also be found, together with related entries, under certain general headings. The ten principal headings, under which all entries have been classified, are as follows:

Arts	*Nippon Eitai-gura*
Brothel Quarters	Religion
Chōja Kyō	Saikaku
Cities and Towns	Society, Divisions
Manners and Customs	Trade

TRADE AND CRAFTS (*cont.*)
nawaya (rope twisting), 143
o-kashi-dokoro (confectionery), 105=5
o-miyage-uri (souvenir dealing), 89
ori-mono (textile trade); *see* COTTON; MATERIALS FOR DRESS; SILK TRADE
ryōgae (banking, etc.); *see* *RYŌGAE*
ryōshi (fishing), 15; 52=20; 55=14; 110; *207=5*; *213=14, 16*
sakanaya (fishmongery), 47=17; 92; 111=15, 17; *208=7*
sake trade, q.v.
sarashi (bleached cloth, wholesale), 30=7, 8
saru-mawashi (monkey-training), 144=8
sashimono-saiku (joinery), 24; 77
setomono-mise (crockery shop), 132
shichiya (pawnbroking), 68=11; 69=12; 96; 113; 131; 137
shioya (salt manufacture, peddling), 66=17; 120
shiroganeya (silversmiths), 92
shitatemonoya (tailoring), 26
shoki (scribes), 89
shokumotsu no shōbai (grocery), 131
shomotsu (book dealing), 131
shōyu (soy sauce peddling), 39
shōyu, su (soy sauce and vinegar peddling), 120
somemonoya (dyeing), 26=5; 81=5; 83=16–19
shuza (red ink manufacture), 101=18
take-saiku (bamboo weaving), 77; *196=20*
teppōya (fire-arms manufacture), 101=19
toiya (broking); see *TOIYA*
toriya (poultry dealing), *208=7*
tsukuri-bana (paper flower manufacture), 24
tsuzura (wicker basket manufacture), 68=9
urushiya (lacquer, wholesale), 92; 144=12
wataya (cotton dealing), 49=25; 83; 92=30; *210=13*; *see also* COTTON TRADE
yaoya (greengrocery), 62=10; *172=17*
zaimoku (timber), 62=11–14; *205=2*
TSURUGA, 93–6; 129–32
communications, 93=2; *166=2*
comparison with Kyōto, 93
market, 93=2
tabi-shibai (travelling theatres), 93
tea-brokers, 96; *205=2*
tolls, 93=2

Tsushima, *200=7*
Tsuyama, *218=3, 4*
Twenty-four Filial Sons, 67=6

Ueda-*jima*, 14=14
Uji, 142=23; *212=12*
Uji Kadayū, 47; *172=21*
Uji river, *188=1*; *190=8*; *191=17*; *222=10*; *225=5*
ukiyo-zōshi; *see* LITERATURE
Uojima, 52=20
Ushi-tenjin-*jinsha*, 49=26
Usuyuki Monogatari, 114=22

Wake river, 123=2
Wakoku *tayū*, 118=29
weighing implements, *see* TRADE
Wên, king, 129=1
whaling industry, 50=6

Yamada, 90=13; 133=11
Yamamoto Kaku-*dayū*, 136=31
Yamaoka Genrin, xxviii=1
Yamashiro province, 110=6
Yamato province, 23=17; 46=16; 115; 117; *214=12*; *215=13*
Yamatoya no Jinbei, 47; *172=21*
Yamazakiya, 110=7
Yasaka-*jinsha*, *182=7*
Yatsuhashi Kengyō, 47; *172=21*
YODO, 67–8; 110–11; 140–3
castle, *212=1*; *225=2*
kawa-bune (river boats), xxxiv=1; 70=17; 93=3
koi-buna (carp and gibel), 111=14
proverb, 111=13
ushi (oxen), 67=8; 111=13; 140=7
~*-guruma* (water wheel), xxxvii; 108=1; 111=13; 140=2; 142=19; *227=26*
~river, 22=12; 110=10; 140; 142; *154=1*; *156=8, 10*; *192=4*; *215=13*
Yōmei Tennō, *184=6*
Yonomiya-*jinsha*, 40=6
Yonosuke, xli
Yorozuya, 123=5
Yorozuya Sanya, 63=6; 63–6
Yoshida Hanbei, xxi–iii; 4
Yoshino, 115=2; 144=12
Yoshiwara; *see* Shin-Yoshiwara
Yozaemon, 140=4; 143=26

za (monopoly corporation), 101=18
zaibatsu, *161=17*
Zaimoku-*chō*, 62=12

MAPS

NOTE. The aim of the maps is first to give a clear impression of the main features of Japan and its three large cities as they were in Saikaku's age, and secondly to indicate the position of localities mentioned in the present work. Place-names judged unnecessary for this limited purpose have accordingly been omitted.

Sources:

ŌSAKA, based on photographic copy in *Kokushi Jiten*, II of *Shinsen Zōho Ōsaka Ō-ezu* (1687).

EDO, based on photographic copy in *Kokushi Jiten*, I of the map in *Edo Zukan Kōmoku* (1689).

JAPAN, collated from various maps of Tokugawa Japan in *Dai Nihon Dokushi Chizu* (1935).

KYŌTO, based on photographic copy in *Kokushi Jiten*, III of *Shinsen Zōho Kyō Ō-ezu* (1686).

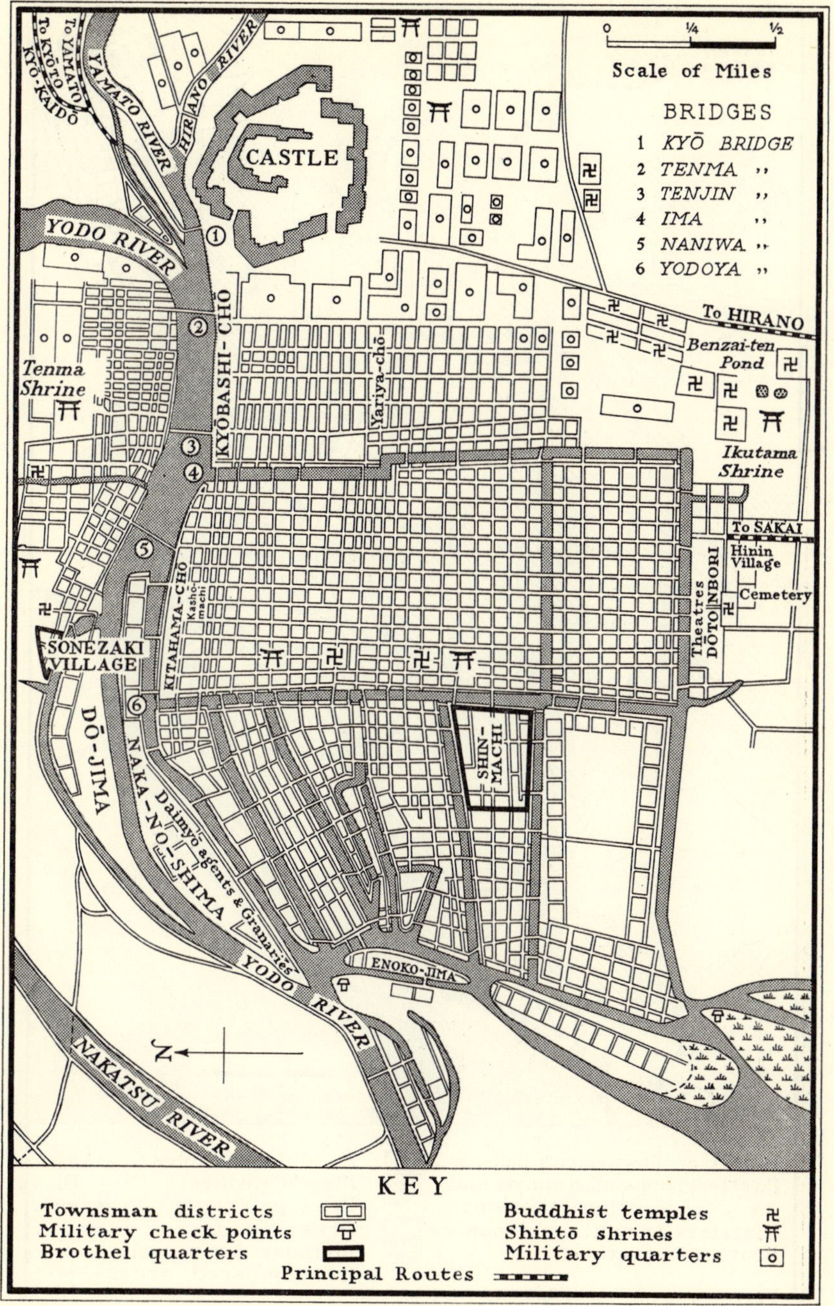

Map 1. Ōsaka (based on a map of 1687).

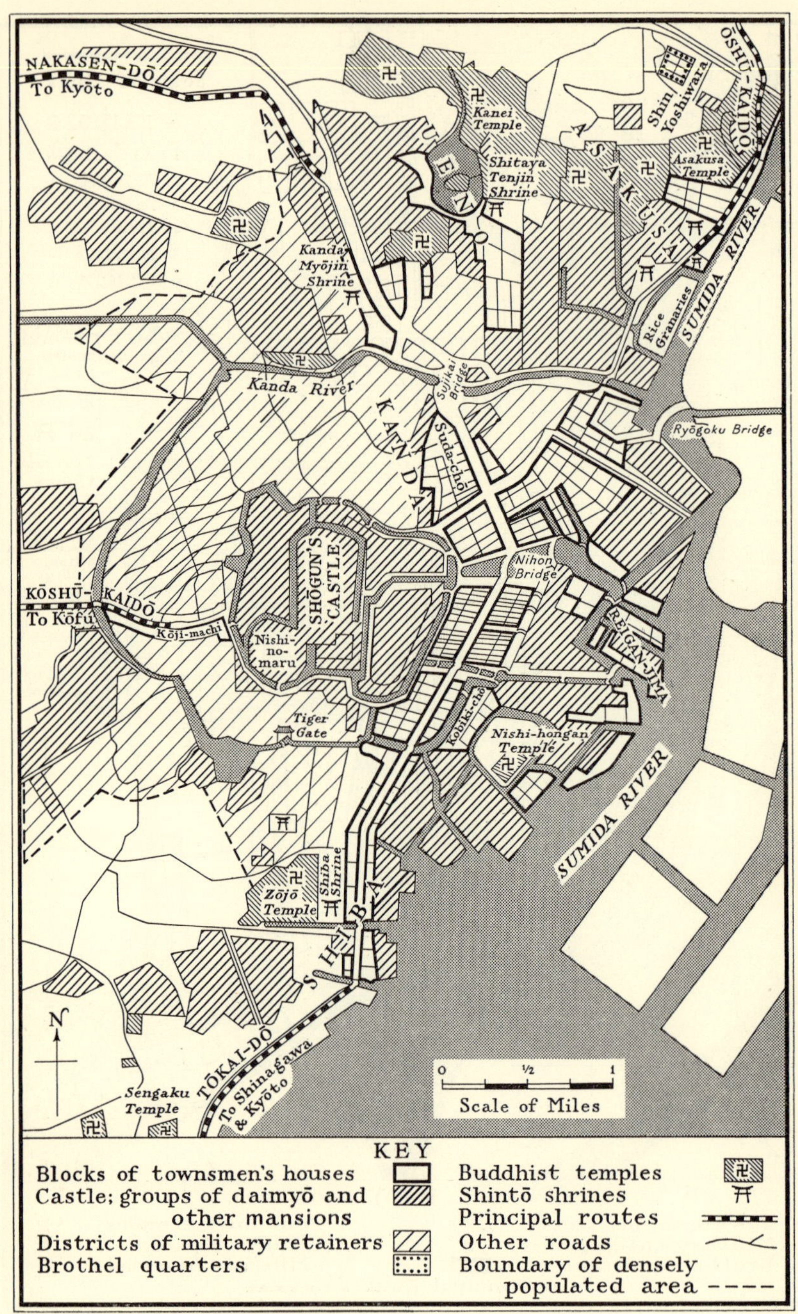
NAKASEN-DŌ
To Kyōto
Kanei Temple
UENO
Shitaya Tenjin Shrine
ASAKUSA
Shin Yoshiwara
ŌSHŪ-KAIDŌ
Asakusa Temple
Kanda Myōjin Shrine
Rice Granaries
SUMIDA RIVER
Sujikai Bridge
Kanda River
KANDA
Ryōgoku Bridge
Suda-chō
SHŌGUN'S CASTLE
Nihon Bridge
KŌSHŪ-KAIDŌ
To Kōfu
Kōji-machi
Nishi-no-maru
REIGAN-JIMA
Tiger Gate
Kobiki-chō
Nishi-hongan Temple
SUMIDA RIVER
Shiba Shrine
Zōjō Temple
SHIBA
TŌKAI-DŌ
To Shinagawa & Kyōto
Sengaku Temple
N
0
½
1
Scale of Miles
KEY
Blocks of townsmen's houses
Castle; groups of daimyō and other mansions
Districts of military retainers
Brothel quarters
Buddhist temples
Shintō shrines
Principal routes
Other roads
Boundary of densely populated area

Map 2 (*a*). Edo (based on a map of 1689).

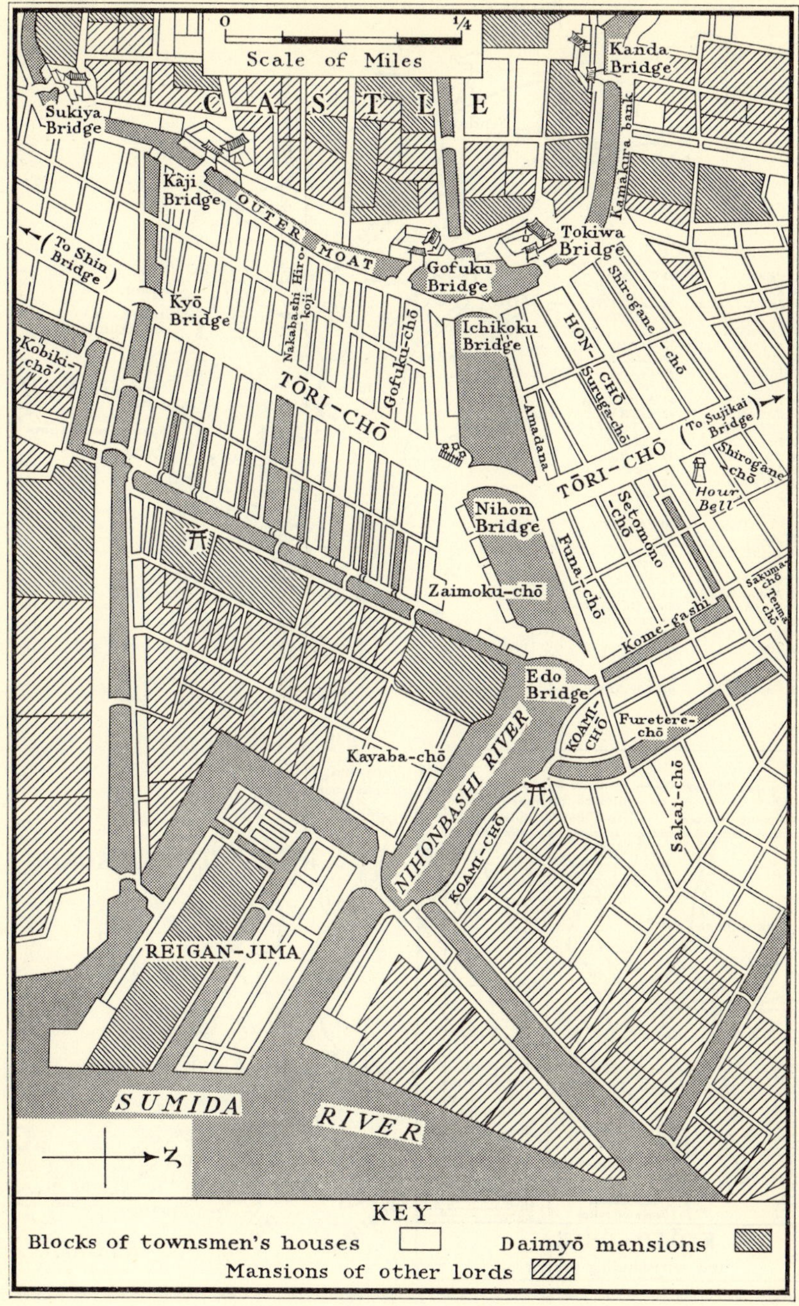
0
1/4
Scale of Miles
CASTLE
Kanda Bridge
Sukiya Bridge
Kamakura bank
Kāji Bridge
OUTER MOAT
Tokiwa Bridge
(To Shin Bridge)
Gofuku Bridge
Kyō Bridge
Nakabashi Hiro-koji
Gofuku-chō
Ichikoku Bridge
Shirogane-chō
HON-CHŌ
Suruga-chō
Kobiki-chō
TŌRI-CHŌ
Amadana
(To Sujikai Bridge)
TŌRI-CHŌ
Shirogane-chō
Hour Bell
Nihon Bridge
Setomono-chō
Funa-chō
Zaimoku-chō
Sakuma-chō
Temma-chō
Kome-gashi
Edo Bridge
KOAMI-CHŌ
Furetere-chō
Kayaba-chō
NIHONBASHI RIVER
Sakai-chō
KOAMI-CHŌ
REIGAN-JIMA
SUMIDA
RIVER
N
KEY
Blocks of townsmen's houses
Daimyō mansions
Mansions of other lords

Map 2 (*b*). Edo business quarter (1689).

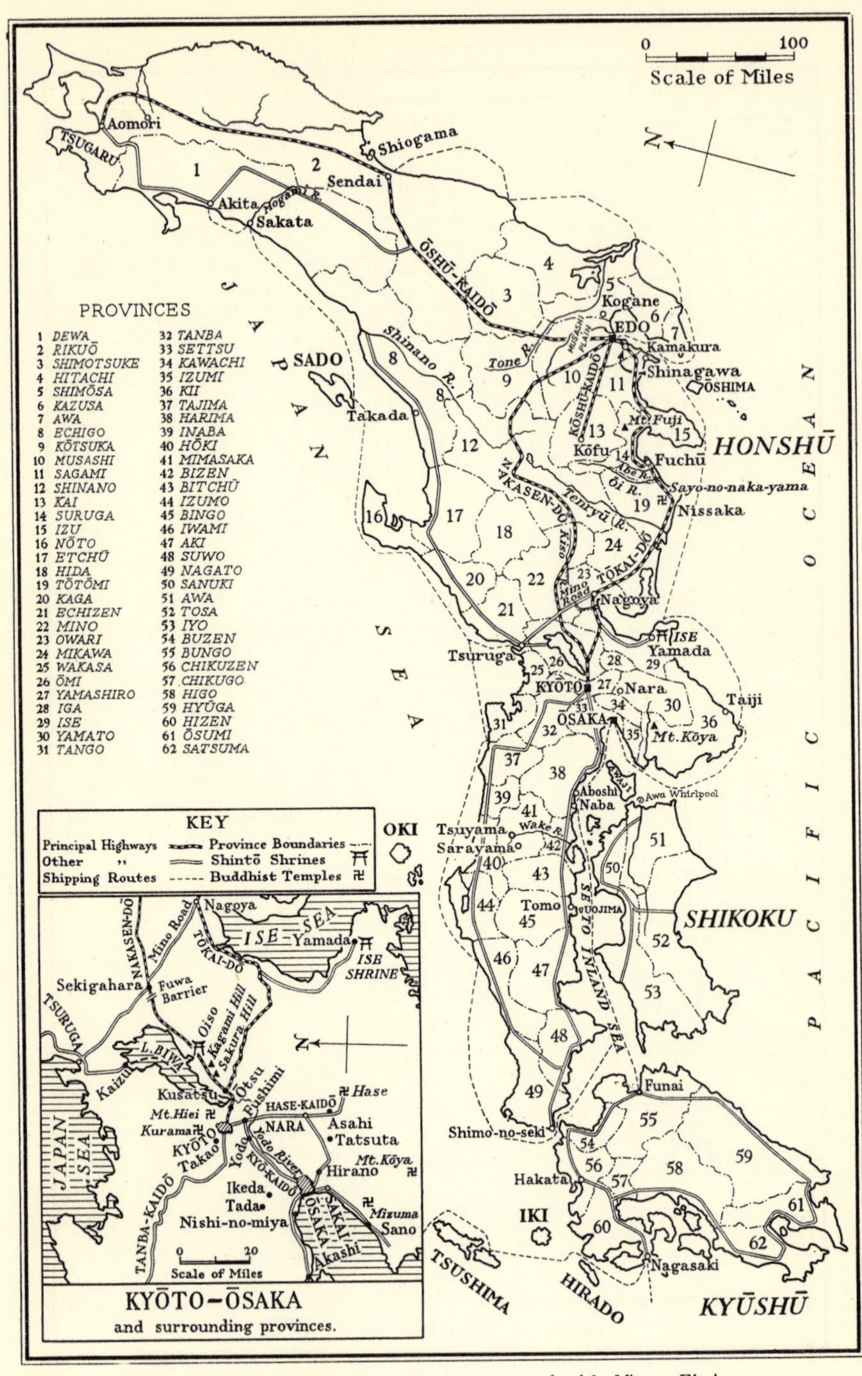

Map 3. Japan, showing place-names connected with *Nippon Eitai-gura*. (Provinces and communications in the Tokugawa period.)

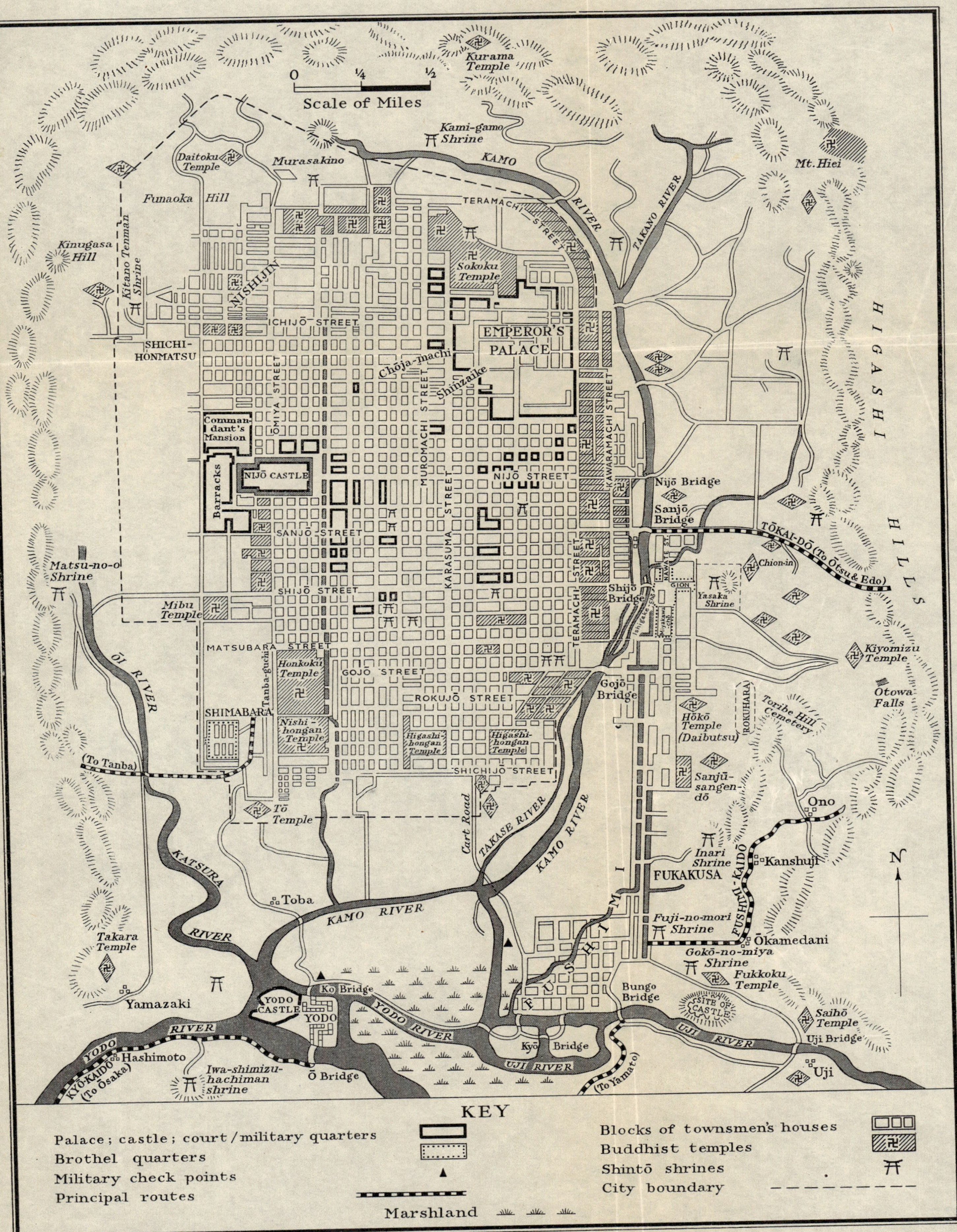

Map 4. Kyōto and environs (based on a map of 1686).